W0079082

Starting Points for ICT Regulation

Deconstructing Prevalent Policy One-Liners

Series Editors

Aernout H.J. Schmidt, *Editor-in-Chief*
Center for eLaw@Leiden, Leiden University

Philip E. van Tongeren, *Publishing Editor*
T·M·C·ASSER PRESS, The Hague

For other titles in the Series see p. 293

INFORMATION TECHNOLOGY & LAW SERIES ⑨

STARTING POINTS FOR ICT REGULATION

Deconstructing Pevalent Policy One-Liners

edited by

Bert-Jaap Koops, Miriam Lips,
Corien Prins and Maurice Schellekens

T·M·C·ASSER PRESS

The Hague

The *Information Technology & Law Series* is published
for ITeR by T·M·C·ASSER PRESS
P.O. Box 16163, 2500 BD The Hague, The Netherlands
<www.asserpress.nl>

T·M·C·ASSER PRESS English language books are distributed exclusively by:

Cambridge University Press, The Edinburgh Building, Shaftesbury Road,
Cambridge CB2 2RU, UK,
or
for customers in the USA, Canada and Mexico:
Cambridge University Press, 100 Brook Hill Drive, West Nyack, NY 10994-2133, USA

<www.cambridge.org>

The *Information Technology & Law Series* is an initiative of ITeR, the National Programme for Information Technology and Law, which is a research programme set up by the Dutch government and the Netherlands Organisation for Scientific Research (NWO) in The Hague. Since 1995 ITeR has published all of its research results in its own book series. In 2002 ITeR launched the present internationally orientated and English language *Information Technology & Law Series*. This series deals with the implications of information technology for legal systems and institutions. It is not restricted to publishing ITeR's research results. Hence, authors are invited and encouraged to submit their manuscripts for inclusion. Manuscripts and related correspondence can be sent to the Series' Editorial Office, which will also gladly provide more information concerning editorial standards and procedures.

Editorial Office
NWO / ITeR
P.O. Box 93461
2509 AL The Hague, The Netherlands
Tel. +31(0)70-3440950; Fax +31(0)70-3832841
E-mail: <iter@nwo.nl>
Web site: <www.nwo.nl/iter>

Single copies or Standing Order
The books in the *Information Technology & Law Series* can either be purchased as single copies or through a standing order. For ordering information see the information on top of this page or visit the publisher's web site at <www.asserpress.nl/cata/itlaw7/fra.htm>.

ISBN 10: 90-6704-216-1
ISBN 13: 978-90-6704-216-1
ISSN 1570-2782

All rights reserved.
© 2006, ITeR, The Hague, and the authors

No part of the material protected by this copyright notice may be reproduced or utilized in any form or by any means, electronic or mechanical, including photocopying, recording, or by any information storage and retrieval system, without written permission from the copyright owner.

Cover and lay-out: Oasis Productions, Nieuwerkerk a/d IJssel, The Netherlands
Printing and binding: Koninklijke Wöhrmann BV, Zutphen, The Netherlands

PREFACE

The intellectual development and writing of this volume has been a true co-production not only for the editors and authors of the various chapters and comments in this book, but for the many other national and international colleagues as well. First and foremost, it is the result of a close collaboration of researchers working at the Tilburg Institute of Law, Technology, and Society (TILT). This book is the outcome of their work and thinking developed under the fundamental research programme of the Institute, and can therefore be considered as a true departmental or TILT production. The editors and authors would like to thank all of their TILT colleagues for their valuable practical support[1] and also warmly thank their international colleagues Herbert Burkert, Yves Poullet and Dan Burk for their co-operation and their contributions to this volume.

At an early stage in the development of the book, in Autumn 2002, we organised a workshop sponsored by the Netherlands Organisation for Scientific Research's IT and Law Research Programme and chaired by Professor Ignace Snellen. During this workshop we shared our first thoughts on potential principles of e-regulation with a substantial number of national and international colleagues, both from academia and e-regulatory 'practice'. Our colleagues persuaded us to think about the phrases we encounter in regulatory practice, such as 'regulation should be technology neutral', as 'starting points' of ICT regulation. Their valuable insights heavily influenced the further elaboration of this book. We are therefore very grateful to the chairman, participants and sponsor of this workshop, and cordially thank them all for their important contributions.

Tilburg, 2005

On behalf of TILT:

Bert-Jaap KOOPS
Miriam LIPS
Corien PRINS
Maurice SCHELLEKENS
Simone VAN DER HOF
Sjaak NOUWT
Kees STUURMAN

---

[1] Our special gratitude goes to Ineke Sijtsma for her valuable correction activities, Vivian Carter for her support in editing this volume, and Marije van der Marel who helped us with the consistency checking of this volume.

SUMMARY OF CONTENTS

TABLE OF CONTENTS

ABBREVIATIONS

ABA	Australian Broadcasting Authority
ADR	Alternative Dispute Resolution
AEA	American Electronics Association
ANSI	American National Standards Institute
APEC	Asia-Pacific Economic Cooperation
ASEAN	Association of South East African Nations
B2B	Business-to-Business
B2C	Business-to-Consumers
BEUC	Bureau Européen des Consommateurs
BIAC	Business and Industry Advisory Committee
BMI	Bundesministerium des Innern
Cal. L. Rev.	California Law Review
CAs	Certification Authorities
CDA	Communications Decency Act
CEN	Comité Européen de Normalisation
CENELEC	Comité Européen de Normalisation Electrotechnique
CFR	Code of Federal Regulations
CIPA	Children's Internet Protection Act
CIS	Center for Internet Security
CIS	Commonwealth of Independent States
CNIL	Commission Nationale de l'Informatique et des Libertés
DPA	Data Protection Authority
DNS	Domain Name System
DRM	Digital Rights Management
DTI	Department of Trade and Industry
ECHR	European Convention for the Protection of Human Rights and Fundamental Freedoms
ECtHR	European Court for the Protection of Human Rights
ECOSOC	Economic and Social Council of the UN
EEJ	European Extra Judicial
EJIL	European Journal of International Law
EPIC	Electronic Privacy Information Center
ERC	Evolution and Reform Committee
ESCAP	Economic and Social Commission for Asia and the Pacific
ETSI	European Telecommunications Standards Institute
FAO	Food and Agriculture Organisation
FCC	Federal Communications Commission
FTC	Federal Trade Commission
GAC	Governmental Advisory Committee
GATT	General Agreement on Tariffs and Trade

GBDe   Global Business Dialogue on Electronic Commerce
GMPCS   Global Mobile Personal Communications by Satellite
GUID   Globally Unique Identifier

IAB   Internet Architecture Board
IANA   Internet Assigned Numbers Authority
ICANN   Internet Corporation for Assigned Names and Numbers
ICC   International Criminal Court
ICH   Internet Content Host
ICRA   Internet Content Rating Association
ICT   Information and Communication Technology
IEC   International Engineering Consortium
IETF   Internet Engineering Task Force
IESG   Internet Engineering Steering Group
ILIS   Internationalisation and Law in the Information Society
ILM   International Legal Materials
IMSN   International Marketing Supervision Network
INCORE   Internet Content Rating for Europe
INHOPE   Internet Hotline Providers in Europe
IP   Intellectual Property
IPR   Intellectual Property Rights
IPSE   Initiative for Privacy Standardization in Europe
IRC   Internet Relay Chat
IRTF   Internet Research Task Force
ISFE   Interactive Software Federation of Europe
ISO   International Standardization Organization
ISOC   Internet Society
ISP   Internet Service Provider
ISSS   Information Society Standardization System
ITU   International Telecommunication Union
IWF   Internet Watch Foundation

JAVI   Juridische Aspecten Van Internet

LEH   Law on the Electronic Highway

METI   Japanese Ministry of Economy, Trade, and Industry
MITI   Japanese Ministry of International Trade and Industry
MoU   Memorandum of Understanding
MPEG   Moving Picture Experts Group

NAI   Network Advertising Initiative
NEAC   National Electronic Authentication Council
NII   National Information Infrastructure
NJB   Nederlands Juristenblad
NJW   Neue Juristische Wochenschrift
NLIP   Dutch Foundation for Internet Providers
NOIE   National Office for the Information Economy
NTD   Notice and Take Down
NTIA   National Telecommunications and Information Agency

OAS   Organization of American States
OASIS   Organization for the Advancement of Structured Information Standards
ODR   On-line Dispute Resolution
OECD   Organization for Economic Co-operation and Development

OFCOM	Office of Communications
OFLC	Office of Film and Literature Classification
OJ	Official Journal of the European Communities
OPA	On-line Privacy Alliance
PbEG	Publicatieblad van de Europese Gemeenschappen
PEGI	Pan European Games Information
PET	Privacy Enhancing Technology
PKI	Public Key Infrastructure
POTS	Plain Old Telephone System
Profeco	Mexican Federal Consumer Protection Agency
P3P	Platform for Privacy Preferences
RabelsZ	Rables Zeitschrift für ausländisches und internationals Privatrecht
RIPE NCC	Réseaux IP Européens Network Coordination Centre
SECE	Secure Electronic Commerce Environment
SET	Secure Electronic Transaction
Stb.	Staatsblad
Stcrt.	Staatscourant
TLD	Top Level Domains
TRIPs	Trade Related aspects of Intellectual Property Rights
UCITA	Uniform Computer Information Transactions Act
UDRP	Uniform Dispute Resolution Polict
UDRP	Uniform Domain Name Dispute Resolution Policy
UETA	Uniform Electronic Transactions Act
UIFN	Universal International Free Phone Numbers
UN	United Nations
UNHCR	United Nations High Commissioner for Refugees
UNCITRAL	United Nations Commission on International Trade Law
UNECE	United Nations Economic Commission for Europe
UNICE	Union des Industries de la Communauté Européenne
UNESCO	United Nations Educational, Scientific and Cultural Organisation
UNDP	United Nations Development Programme
U. PA. J. Int'l Econ. L.	University of Pennsylvania Journal of International Economic Law
U. PA. L. Rev.	University of Pennsylvania Law Review
USC	United States Code
UWB	Ultra-Wide-Band
VAT	Value Added Tax
W3C	World Wide Web Consortium
WCT	WIPO Copyright Treaty
WDA	Western District Appeal
WIPO	World Intellectual Property Organization
WMRM	Windows Media Rights Manager
WPPT	WIPO Performances and Phonograms Treaty
WSIS	World Summit on the Information Society
WTO	World Trade Organization
WTPF	World Telecommunication Policy Forum
WWW	World Wide Web
3G	Third Generation

Chapter 1
INTRODUCTION

Miriam Lips

1.1 Introduction: The Complexity of Designing Regulation for 'On-Line' Activities

What does 'on-line' mean nowadays? When do we actually enter this new environment and leave the 'off-line' world? In what cases then is the on-line environment different, separate, or even unique compared to the off-line world? And in what cases do we need to regulate it, and how? These have become important but complex questions to law makers, policy makers, regulators, and politicians dealing with the design of regulatory frameworks to address societal changes related to fast-moving technological developments.

As an example, in the Spring of 2002, the European Parliament adopted a new directive for privacy in the telecommunications sector, allowing national governments possibility to store traffic data related for various on-line movements of citizens.[1] Obviously, police organizations, the judiciary, and intelligence agencies like to have access to these (historical) traffic data for purposes of combating crime. Traffic data consist of address information and route information arising from telecommunication activities. This needs to be separated from the contents of these activities. This is important because of the higher legal protection of communication contents in many European countries. For instance, police organizations can get access to telephone numbers called and to information on the length of a phone call, but it usually is not easy for them to get permission to tap communication activities.

Telecommunication activities can be conducted by means of a fast increasing number of communication systems, provided, for instance, through fixed telephony, mobile telephony, the Internet, or digital broadcasting. Besides, depending on the technology used, it is no longer possible to always make a clear distinction between communication contents, address information, and route information. E-mail head-

---

[1] Directive 2002/58/EC of the European Parliament and of the Council of 12 July 2002 concerning the processing of personal data and the protection of privacy in the electronic communications sector (Directive on privacy and electronic communications), OJ 2002, L 201, pp. 37-47.

B-J. Koops, et al. (Eds), Starting Points for ICT Regulation
© 2006, ITeR, The Hague, and the authors

ers for example can be acknowledged as address information and route information but also contain the subject of an e-mail-message, which is often a summary of its contents. URLs appear to be address information but often contain well chosen words to easily find the communication contents on the Internet. The use of a mobile phone creates location data and also reveals the geographic position of the user.

In many European countries, obligations to store traffic data of various on-line activities for a certain period of time have now been implemented in national legislation. In this way, several governments have claimed more powers for themselves to store and monitor different kinds of traffic data. In Spain, for instance, data on visitors of web sites are not only obliged to be stored but the Spanish government also has the power to take the initiative to close down web sites.[2]

This example clearly shows the complexity of designing and implementing regulations to be able to deal with the emerging on-line environment and related societal processes. Since the mid-1990s, various technological developments centered around Information and Communication Technologies (ICTs) have been adopted by society, and are currently contributing to a rapidly expanding on-line environment where all kinds of social activities are taking place. Several authors even claim that these technological developments represent a technological revolution transforming the material basis of society and, with that, the economic and socio-cultural landscape of human life.[3]

1.2   THE MUTUAL INFLUENCE OF TECHNOLOGICAL, SOCIETAL, AND REGULATORY DEVELOPMENTS

What the final outcomes will be of the broad societal take-up of the Internet and ICTs in general is still unknown. Fact is that people and organizations are making more and more use of the newly available technological possibilities, leading to various developments in on-line activities. Castells[4] indicates that during the last two decades, the application of new network technology such as the Internet has gone through three different stages. These stages successively, are the automation of tasks, experiments with applications, and the reconfiguration of applications. In the first two stages technological innovation was caused by 'learning-by-using', in the last stage by means of 'learning-by-doing' through which finally new networks and types of applications were developed. Castells observes a feedback loop between the introduction of new ICT, its use and the development towards new areas. He therefore perceives new ICTs not simply as instruments, but as processes that have to be developed.

---

[2] Bits of Freedom, 'Verkeersgegevens', available at <http://www.bof.nl/verkeersgegevens.html>.
[3] E.g., Castells 1996; Hall 1998; Mitchell 2000.
[4] Castells 1996, p. 32.

Hall describes the current situation of transition as a result of technological developments as follows: 'We already know in essence what is happening to us, but we do not know exactly where it will lead.'[5] According to Hall, history shows that new technological developments often have had unexpected outcomes in society. In the 19th century, for instance, people were conscious of the fact that the train would change the country's spatial order. However, nobody anticipated that the train would enable people to commute from and to the suburbs of cities, which, in the end, strongly influenced the spatial organization of cities. Besides, general expectations of the coming of the motorcar were the changing of life at the farm. However, nobody envisioned the origination of a new type of suburb (Los Angeles) within a decade.

In general, so far the emerging on-line environment has confronted governments all over the world with new regulatory questions. Various activities undertaken in the new on-line environment are forcing governments to deal with the question of whether and, if so, to what extent, existing laws and rules in their countries are enforceable. In addition, in many countries and in international organizations, the question of whether existing national laws and rules *should* be applicable to this developing on-line environment is being debated as well: for various reasons, governments are faced with the possibility that the developing global on-line environment may be treated as a new or different kind of 'territory', which may need its own, perhaps international regulatory measures or even regime.

Consequently, although it is still highly unclear where these ICT developments will lead us, the developing on-line environment is challenging governments all over the world to fundamentally rethink their existing legal frameworks and to figure out a regulatory approach towards the range of activities that are happening there. Although governments are aware of the turbulence in current technological developments[6] and of the resulting complexity of adjusting the existing legal framework to be able to deal with on-line events, they feel the urgent need to create a legitimization for their actions. Technological developments can be steered so that, for instance, fundamental values and norms can continue to be guaranteed. Their position provides governments with the opportunity to actively support ICT developments and, thus to, stimulate the further development of the e-society (e.g., e-commerce, e-government, e-learning, e-health) in their countries.

On the other hand, governments are also aware of the fact that national laws and rules may impede ICT developments or may lead towards unforeseen, undesirable social outcomes. A scenario in this respect would be that national governments are more or less 'ignored' by the emerging on-line world, as activities which used to be easily controllable by governments because of their authority over a specific geographical area (e.g., imposing taxes), can take place in the on-line world out of their sight or under another jurisdiction, or even under no jurisdiction at all.

---

[5] Hall 1998, p. 943.

[6] See for instance the Dutch Ministry of Justice 1998; 2000a.

Put differently, in accordance with the observations of Castells presented earlier, governments are in a position to play an important part in the feedback loop between the introduction of new ICTs in society, their use, and their development towards new areas. Therefore, to be able to effectively influence the ongoing ICT process, governments try to get involved as early as possible in the 'design' process of the new on-line world, looking for the most optimal regulatory approach with their current knowledge of ICT developments.

1.3   NEW REGULATORY QUESTIONS, DILEMMAS, AND OPTIONS IN A NETWORKED SOCIETY

1.3.1   Traditional regulatory frameworks, technical characteristics and societal transformations

In the 1990s, the German Federal Government found itself confronted with a completely new and difficult situation. Adolf Hitler's book '*Mein Kampf*', which is forbidden in Germany, appeared to be easily downloadable for German citizens from web sites in the USA. As the USA has a much stronger constitutional provision that protects freedom of speech (i.e., the First Amendment), these web sites could not be forbidden in accordance with US law. In this case, ICT developments forced the German Federal Government to rethink its regulatory regime: regulatory instruments that were used to prevent certain activities in the off-line world turned out to be unsuitable in the new on-line environment. To be able to effectively deal with this problematic situation, the German government had to look for alternative regulatory solutions.

Another example of confronting ICT developments interfering with existing regulatory practices can be found in the case of Napster. With the coming of the Internet, combined with developments in data storing and streaming technologies, new possibilities for music delivery over the global network became available, of which the free sharing and exchange of stored music, allowed by pioneer Napster and peer-to-peer technologies offered by other companies (e.g., Gnutella, Freenet), became widely popular. With this new possibility to evade copyright legislation and related fees through direct peer-to-peer interaction via a global network, this development is causing major problems to the music recording industry. In trying to cope with this new phenomenon, music recording companies are simultaneously going to court to protect their intellectual property rights, looking for ways to develop security technologies (e.g., electronic watermarks), and attempting to invent new business models. Besides, a remarkable fact is that about one half of Americans do not consider the free downloading of music over the Internet as stealing.[7] In 2001, a US court ordered Napster to block access to copyrighted materials. Later in that year,

---

[7] Castells 2001, p. 196.

Napster was ordered to close down. By paying songwriters and artists about USD 36 million for infringed intellectual property rights in the past and the loss of royalties, Napster intended to re-open as a commercial service. In 2002, having provided capital injections to Napster on several occasions already, the German media conglomerate Bertelsmann bought the Napster company to save it from bankruptcy.

Both examples point at the complexity of the confrontation between (emerging) on-line activities, on the one hand, and traditional regulatory frameworks and approaches, on the other. This complexity originates in at least four important technical characteristics of currently used ICT networks, the Internet in particular, which are changing the organization of information exchange and communication in innovative ways.[8] A first important technical characteristic is the open architecture of current ICT networks. In principle, this technical feature offers the opportunity for each individual who has access to the necessary equipment, to connect to the Internet. Secondly, current ICT networks do not have a center in which data flows come together, but can be characterized as being decentralized or 'center-less'. This particular characteristic leads to a situation in which information exchange cannot be prevented. Not only access points but also available knowledge is distributed over the global network, which makes it possible to collect information and to communicate regardless of distance, time, or location. A third important characteristic of current ICT networks is the ability of many-to-many communication. With that, the Internet is not only a network of networks in a technical sense, but its added value particularly results from the fact that it is a network of users who are able to share and exchange information in an interactive way. Finally, the multi-media character of current ICT networks offers new opportunities to create, present, and exchange data. As a result of digitalization, different communication means like text, images, sound, and voice, can be integrated into one product or service, which can be exchanged via the network.

Together, these technical characteristics support three major social transformations in the networked society:[9]

–   *Virtualization*: digitalization of various information and communication services makes space and time increasingly relative, as stored data are no longer tied to a specific physical storage device and can also be easily exchanged through the network. An on-line global environment emerges without a material basis. Digitally available information in the network is inexhaustible in the sense that it can be shared and copied without any losses to either the 'owner-provider' or the receiver. Besides, virtualization offers the opportunity towards simulation of physical representations (e.g., virtual child pornography) and the creation of new realities.

---

[8]   Lips and Frissen, 2000.
[9]   Frissen 1996, 1998.

– *Deterritorialization*: the open architecture of the emerging on-line environment leads to a situation in which information exchange is no longer tied to a
   specific place, space, or time. Acts and their effects are disconnected in an
   on-line world. In addition, the scale and scope of information exchange and
   communication can be both large and small. Each individual can be a global
   player. As a result, information exchange and communication can take place
   more or less independently of territorially based authorities.

– *Horizontalization*: as a result of the diffusion and sophistication of ICT networks, significant changes in organization structures and functioning are
   taking place. ICT developments bring about network-type organizational
   configurations, as they for instance, facilitate the splitting up of organizations, the creation of independent agencies, and horizontal communication
   between separate organization units inside and outside a specific organization. As a result, in many countries around the world, the traditionally uniform and hierarchical bureaucratic organization is changing. Not only at an
   organizational, but also at an individual level can we observe a growing significance of non-hierarchical, more horizontal relationships. Individual autonomy is increased through access to an enormous number of information
   sources. Well-informed citizens are, for instance, able to discuss with their
   own doctors about the treatment of diseases, can easily compare products and
   prices between companies all over the world, or can directly approach political administrators with individual complaints or special needs. ICT developments also facilitate dis-intermediarization of traditional institutions in
   information and communication relationships. Peer-to-peer relationships in
   which music files are exchanged without a music recording company involved, or passengers buying flight tickets directly from an airline corporation instead of a travel agency are some examples in this respect.

Together, these ICT developments and related social transformations are bringing
about new regulatory questions and dilemmas such as indicated above. For instance,
who is accountable for an on-line service? What is 'copyright' in an open environment with infinite duplication opportunities? Where do we need to pay tax for an
on-line service? How can local norms and values be protected in an international
open environment? Can a digital identity legally be treated equally to its physical
counterpart? And which organization(s) would have the authority to combat
cybercrime? Such emerging regulatory questions and dilemmas cause tensions with
regard to existent regulatory frameworks, in particular to traditional regulatory institutions like laws, judiciaries, and other territorially based authoritative organizations (e.g., national governments).

1.3.2 **Alternative regulatory options**

Current ICT developments may not only lead to confrontations with existing regulatory frameworks, but may also themselves offer alternative options for regulation. The design of the technological architecture, through which information exchange and communication takes place, will have a certain impact on social practices in on-line interaction. Put differently, the choice for a specific code (e.g., hardware, software) in an ICT application regulates on-line activities in a specific way.[10] Timely awareness of regulation by the technology, or 'code as Code' as Lessig himself expresses, may offer a window of opportunity to influence the design of these regulations. With regard to the ongoing development of the Internet, Lessig even warns that, under the influence of commercial interests, the window of opportunity to influence the design of these technological regulations narrows every day.[11]

However, activities in the on-line environment are not only regulated by the technological architecture or by traditional regulatory frameworks such as laws and rules, but also by social norms, for instance, through moderation of on-line activities, and by the market. In the first years of the public Internet, for example, the flat rate charged for local telephone services (and, thus, Internet traffic) in the USA, turned out to be an important factor to stimulate and develop on-line activities. Consequently, to be able to understand the regulation of a particular kind of activity in the on-line environment, not one regulatory instrument but the interaction among the different modalities available of regulation should ideally be focused upon.[12] Besides, as traditional regulatory instruments like legislation in many cases of on-line developments turned out not to be easily applicable, these other modalities of regulation available have drawn the attention of policy makers as possible alternative regulatory solutions, also in combination ways (e.g., self-regulation, co-regulation).

1.4 DEVELOPMENTS TOWARDS REGULATORY STARTING POINTS

To be able to deal with the pressing regulatory questions resulting from activities in the on-line world, policy and law makers all over the world started to develop lines of action for regulation purposes since the mid-1990s. In the course of time, we may observe that governments and international organizations have developed certain regulatory 'starting points' to be able to more consistently and effectively deal with emerging activities in the on-line environment. In many cases, these regulatory starting points are used by policy and law makers as a frame of reference for legislative issues to guarantee fundamental norms and values on the one hand and

---

[10] Lessig 1999.
[11] Ibid.
[12] Ibid.

to stimulate (or: to not prevent) the further development of the e-society, on the other hand. In the Netherlands and the UK, for instance, national policy makers created a list with starting points to be taken into account in policy and law making dealing with or related to on-line activities. In 2000, the Dutch Ministry of Justice presented the following 'rules of thumb' to be used as measures for the Dutch government in policy and law making activities in a fast changing technical and social environment.[13] These rules of thumb could contribute to consistency in Dutch policy and legislation regarding the information society, especially at an international level where many regulatory issues in this respect are being raised:

- The 'on-line' protection level needs to be equivalent to the protection level 'off-line';
- What applies off-line is indicative for government decisions on what should apply on-line;
- Co-regulation and self-regulation at an international level should be aimed for;
- Alternative dispute resolution should be promoted;
- Technology independency of rules is point of departure;
- Harmonization of rules is point of departure;
- The principle of 'country of origin' is point of departure;
- From the perspective of law enforcement, rules should be established that provide the possibility to catch up with 'offenders' on the Internet;
- Rules on the exercise of jurisdiction should avoid overlap in the execution of powers by different national governments.

In 2001, the UK central government published a set of so-called 'e-Policy Principles' to ensure that new policy proposals (including regulation and legislation) would not hinder e-commerce and would work effectively on-line. Developed for policy makers across the UK government, the following eight e-Policy Principles were established to function as an analytic tool to determine the impact that local, national, and international policy decisions and legislative proposals might have on e-commerce developments. After their publication in December 2001, these e-Principles were to be formally reviewed every two years as concerned their relevance and topicality:[14]

- Always establish the policy consequences for e-commerce.
- Avoid undue burdens on e-commerce.
- Consider self and co-regulatory options.
- Consult fully on e-commerce implications.

---

[13] The Dutch Ministry of Justice 2000b, pp. 20-21.
[14] See <http://www.e-envoy.gov.uk/oee/OeE.nsf/sections/about-epolicy-modernmarkets-pressreleases/$file/Principles_of_ePolicy_making.doc.>.

- Regulation should be technology neutral in its effects.
- Check that your proposals are enforceable in an electronic age.
- Take account of the global market place – the EU and international angle.
- Consider the implications for e-government.

In comparing these two lists of regulatory starting points we can observe several similarities between the approaches of the two national governments. Also many other national governments around the world as well as international organizations appear to use comparable or even similar starting points in policy-making and law-making activities regarding the emerging on-line environment. In various policy documents around the globe, we may come across the same kind of regulatory adages, such as 'what holds off-line, should also hold on-line', 'regulation should be technology neutral in its effects', and 'self-regulation should be the starting point' (see chapter 2 for an overview). The development of such regulatory starting points at an international level seems to be easy to explain: the world-wide open character of current ICT developments and the resulting international nature of regulatory problems (e.g., the case of the German Federal Government mentioned above) will force policy and law makers to become aware of the limited room to manoeuvre for national or even supranational governments, and to look for opportunities to harmonize different national regulatory approaches at an international or even global level. Another explanation may be a diplomatic one in the sense that national governments may try to convince other countries to make use of a specific regulatory approach to deal with the developing on-line environment. The 1997 policy memorandum of the US federal government '*A framework for Global Electronic Commerce*' may be perceived as an example of the latter explanation.

However, with their publications of 'rules of thumb' for policy and legislation regarding the information society and 'e-Policy Principles', respectively, the Dutch and UK government have triggered some interesting and highly important questions, particularly at this moment of time. What regulatory starting points are being developed and used by policy and law makers in various countries and international organizations around the world to approach the emerging on-line environment? Are these manifesting regulatory starting points generally and internationally applicable to on-line activities, and to what extent will they stand firm through time? Put differently, might these regulatory starting points be acknowledged as more than occasional 'rules of thumb' and become regulatory *principles* for the on-line world? Would it be possible at this stage of development of the on-line environment, this moment of time in the 'design process' of the Internet, for instance, to establish general regulatory principles which policy makers all over the world can use to effectively deal with the regulatory questions they are confronted with? As Castells, for instance, reminds us: 'The wonderful thing about technology is that people end up doing with it something different from what was originally intended.'[15]

---

[15] Castells 2001, p. 195.

1.5 EXPLORING REGULATORY STARTING POINTS: METHODOLOGICAL JUSTIFICATION AND CONTENTS OF THE BOOK

To be able to answer these questions, we need to have a closer look at regulatory starting points as they are being developed and used in several countries and international organizations around the world. To do so, we first would need to know not only in which countries and international organizations we come across similar regulatory starting points, but also in what policy areas: where are comparable regulatory starting points applied, how are they applied, and under what circumstances? The second question then is what these regulatory starting points actually mean: how can these regulatory starting points be further analysed and explained? Finally, we would need to assess the value of these regulatory starting points for international policy making in the field of ICT regulation: are, and if so, to what extent, these regulatory starting points generally and internationally applicable to on-line activities and, with that, to be acknowledged as ICT regulatory principles? If not: are there maybe other alternatives which could be acknowledged as guiding regulatory principles, and if so, for what reasons?

In this book, these questions will be further explored, including the question of whether it is possible to arrive at general ICT regulatory principles to be able to deal with current and future ICT developments from a global regulatory and legislative perspective. To do so, we will first of all explore in *chapter 2* which regulatory starting points can be identified as potential regulatory principles. Therefore, an inventory has been made of regulatory starting points that have been used by policy makers in various countries and international organizations around the world since the mid-1990s when the Internet became public and activities in the on-line environment rapidly increased. Which similar regulatory starting points are used in the various countries and organizations for a longer period of time? An analysis of policy documents published by national governments and international organizations will serve as input for this inventory. The selection of these governments and international organizations was based on criteria like international policy impact regarding ICT-related regulatory questions, authority regarding the regulatory approach of ICT-related policy issues, and regional spreading. With this inventory we are aware of a potential bias in this book towards North American, European, Asian, and Pacific policy perspectives. Unfortunately, we did not have good access to particularly South American and African policy perspectives towards ICT regulation.

Secondly, in *chapters 3* to *7* of this book, we will have a closer look at each of the identified regulatory starting points. Where exactly does the regulatory starting point concerned come from: where can it be found, how is it applied, and what does it actually mean? Which cases are illustrative for the way the regulatory starting point works in practice? And how can the existing regulatory starting point be assessed in terms of its validity to be used and, possibly, to be acknowledged as an ICT regulatory principle?

Finally, the third part of this book, *chapters 8* and *9*, focus on the analyses of the regulatory starting points, both individually and in coherence. Are these regulatory starting points or even principles for policy makers and law makers around the world meaningful to work with? If so: in what sense? Also, would it be possible to define a coherent general approach to *e-regulation* from the analyses of the different regulatory starting points?

Chapter 2
INVENTORY OF GENERAL ICT REGULATORY STARTING POINTS

Miriam Lips

2.1 INTRODUCTION

In the last decade, especially since the broad societal introduction of the Internet in the mid-1990s, national governments and international organizations were confronted with a developing international on-line space, leading to various regulatory questions. On the one hand, these organizations were confronted with the general question of whether and, to what extent existing laws and rules are applicable to activities in this new on-line environment. On the other hand, they are faced with the possibility that, for various reasons, the developing on-line environment can be treated as a new or different kind of 'territory' and therefore may need its own regulatory regime. In addition, these organizations had the option whether to play an active role in stimulating ICT developments in their countries and, with that, in promoting further development of the on-line world and its underlying ICT infrastructure.

Part of this underlying ICT infrastructure, namely, the telecommunications sector, has traditionally been regulated by national governments. Moreover, national governments in Europe and Asia have always had a strong influence on at least substantial parts of the communications sector, such as public broadcasting. Another part of this ICT infrastructure, the IT sector, has largely been unregulated so far. As a result of technological convergence however, ICT developments like the Internet have entered the domain of regulators, bringing about the question of whether these developments may be treated as 'like' technologies and therefore may be put under the existing regulatory regime. At the same time, in European and Asian countries, for instance, liberalization of the telecommunications sector has caused a restructuring of traditional regulatory frameworks in this area, as a result of which policy and law makers may take new ICT developments into account as well.

As ICT developments and related social transformations are bringing about new regulatory questions and dilemmas, which cause tensions with regard to existent regulatory frameworks, we may expect that national governments, supranational governments and international organizations all over the world, like the UK central government and the Dutch Ministry of Justice (see chapter 1), have developed lines

B-J. Koops, et al. (Eds), Starting Points for ICT Regulation
© *2006, ITeR, The Hague, and the authors*

of action or regulatory starting points to be able to deal with this confronting emerging ICT environment. The question is then to what extent these ICT regulatory starting points are unique for certain countries or organizations, or may be acknowledged as (more) universal regulatory principles, maybe even at a global level. Moreover, it may be interesting to see to what extent ICT regulatory starting points have been developed through time.

Therefore this chapter will explore which ICT regulatory starting points are prominent, or can be recognized more implicitly, in ICT policy and law making of national governments and international organizations in the last decade. Next, it will be examined whether, or to what extent, any similarities in these regulatory starting points can be detected. With the knowledge that it would be too extensive for the purpose of this exploratory chapter to substantially conduct this study for every country and international organization, only those ICT regulatory starting points have been explored of national governments and international organizations which are internationally renowned for their influence on ICT policy and regulation.

As ICT policy and regulation in many countries and organizations are applicable to more and more 'e-Domains' like e-commerce, e-government, e-health, and e-learning, and are related to an increasing number of regulatory themes and issues, such as privacy, security, access to information, spam, procurement, etc., the selection of relevant policy and legislative documents has taken place on the basis of the presence of some line of action or regulatory starting point. It may be observed that in many countries and regions the development of regulatory starting points at first instance in particular has been taken place for the domain of e-commerce. As explained earlier, in some cases, these regulatory starting points are explicitly presented in policy documents, such as documents presenting policy visions on regulation of the information society. In other cases, however, regulatory starting points are more implicit and therefore need to be derived from policy and law making activities. In the last mentioned situation, policy documents, after some time, can become of such importance in ICT policy and regulation, that their determining role towards specific lines of regulatory action is obvious. Compared to the first mentioned type of documents, these documents more often can be located within specific ICT domains, or focused on certain regulatory themes or issues.

In the tour along governments and international organizations around the world, it will be tried to detect both types of documents as much as possible, with a primary attention for the first type of documents and an additional focus on the second. Since the Internet as we know it today originated from the US Defence and University sectors respectively, we will start our inventory of ICT regulatory starting points in the USA in section 2.2. In section 2.3 we will continue our inventory tour in Europe with an exploration of ICT policy and regulation at the European government level. Section 2.4 will look into ICT regulatory and policy developments in countries within the Asian and Pacific regions, and explore potential ICT regulatory starting points in these specific areas. ICT regulatory starting points of several influential international organizations like the OECD, ITU, and the G8, but also those developed in preparing the World Summit on the Information Society (WSIS) will be further explored in section 2.5. Finally, in section 2.6, some first observations regarding worldwide similarities in ICT regulatory lines of action, potentially leading to the acknowledgment of ICT regulatory principles, will be presented.

2.2 US ICT Regulatory Starting Points

On 15 September 1993, the Clinton-Gore Administration launched the US National Information Infrastructure (NII) initiative and, with that, officially introduced the 'electronic highway' to the American public. Launched at a time of accelerating change in communications, computing, and publishing, this initiative recognized the need to address technological convergence not just between adjacent industries such as telephone services and cable television, but as a broader phenomenon generating unpredictable externalities and blurring boundaries among many different industries.[1] Two important policy developments for the US Federal Government came together with the NII initiative: on the one hand, long-evolving efforts to increase competition in facilities-based telecommunications; and, on the other, a history of strategic federal investment in advanced computing and networking that gave rise to the Internet.[2] In the accompanying policy document Agenda for Action, the following nine principles and goals for government action to further develop the NII initiative were presented: to promote private sector investment; to extend the 'universal service' concept to ensure that information resources are available to all at affordable prices; to promote technological innovation and new applications; to promote seamless, interactive, user-driven operation; to ensure information security and network reliability; to improve management of the radio frequency spectrum; to protect intellectual property rights; to co-ordinate with other levels of government and with other bodies; and, to provide access to government information and improve government procurement.[3]

Already in the early days of Internet developments, however, the US Federal Government shifted its major policy focus from the general development of the NII to 'global electronic commerce'.[4] With its 1997 policy memorandum the Clinton-Gore administration indicated to be in favor of a non-regulatory, market-oriented approach to the development of the Internet and e-commerce, with minimal government involvement to enforce a predictable, consistent and simple legal environment. The regulatory starting points of the US Federal Government were to encourage

---

[1] Kahin 1997, p. 152.
[2] Ibid.
[3] US Federal Government 1993.
[4] US Federal Government's Policy Memorandum, *A Framework for Global Electronic Commerce*, 1997, <http://www.technology.gov/digeconomy/framewrk.htm>.

industry self-regulation wherever appropriate, to implement a legal environment based on a decentralized, contractual model of law rather than one based on top-down regulation, and to refrain from imposing new, unnecessary and/or technology-specific regulations on Internet activities. The US Federal Government also recognized that the Internet had gradually become a global medium and therefore decided to initiate a development towards privatization and self-regulation of the technical management of the Internet. As an answer to this latter decision, the international Internet Corporation for Assigned Names and Numbers[5] (ICANN) was founded by a large coalition of companies and technological, scientific, and user organizations. In addition, the US Federal Department of Commerce and ICANN established a Memorandum of Understanding (MoU) in which it was decided to organize a test period for handing over the management of Internet Domain Names from the US Federal Government to ICANN.[6] As this contract between the US Federal Department of Commerce and ICANN is regularly renewed, the US Federal Government has kept a strong regulatory influence on ICANN's activities through time.

In 1999, under the US Government Working Group on Electronic Commerce, the Clinton-Gore Administration created an Electronic Commerce Advisory Group to identify legal barriers to further growth of e-commerce. Three central regulatory starting points were determined for the activities of the Advisory Group, namely, technological neutrality, to minimize legal and regulatory barriers to e-commerce, and to take into account cross-border transactions that are likely to occur electronically.[7] Additionally, public interest protection for on-line transactions had to be equivalent to that provided for off-line transactions. In July 2000, with the adoption of the Electronic Signatures in Global and National Commerce Act, the equivalent protection of on-line consumers was legally guaranteed, providing business with a predictable, technologically neutral legal environment. The US Federal Government, however, also expressed its awareness of the fact that this regulatory starting point might imply different regulatory measures for the on-line world in comparison with existing off-line rules and regulations.

During these years, a stronger tendency of the US Federal Government towards 'co-regulation' besides industry self-regulation became clear. Essentially, the reason behind the general claim for a government with a more interventionist role was that the Internet is too important *not* to regulate.[8] In several new policy areas, such as on-line gambling and databases, government legal intervention was proposed to protect certain general interests. Besides, the US Federal Government was increasingly called upon to take a more steering role in order to safeguard a uniform and consistent, long-term policy approach.[9]

---

[5] Ibid.
[6] <http://www.icann.org/general/icann-mou-25nov98.htm>.
[7] White House 1999.
[8] Litan 2001, p. 12.
[9] Koops, et al., 2000, p. 112.

This development towards more legal intervention by the US government with regard to ICT developments became particularly clear in the field of content regulation. Probably one of the best examples in this respect was the controversial Communications Decency Act (CDA) of 1996. With this Act, the US Congress wanted to deal with the increased utilization of telecommunications facilities to transmit obscene and violent content, prohibiting the transmission of obscene images and words with the intention to annoy, abuse, threaten, or harass another person, as well as the transmission of offensive communication to persons under the age of 18. To put these provisions into practice, the CDA required special technical devices to scramble or block prohibited content. With this law, the US Congress adopted a speech code for the first time in US history, and mandated technology to enforce it.[10] In 1997, however, the US Supreme Court partly invalidated the CDA on the grounds of incompatibility with the First Amendment of the US Constitution. Acknowledging the Internet as a medium with unique characteristics, the federal judges in this lawsuit decided to grant the Internet full First Amendment protection. After this part invalidation of the CDA by the Supreme Court, various Bills have been proposed to protect minors against harmful information on the Internet. As a result, the so-called Child Online Protection Act (47 USC § 231) was enacted in October 1998, seeking to reduce access by minors to material that is harmful to minors on the Internet. Also, the Act established a temporary 19-member Commission that studied methods and technologies to help reduce access by minors to harmful material on the World Wide Web (WWW) to minors. Besides, limiting to the collection of information from children on-line, the Children's Internet Protection Act (CIPA) was enacted.[11] This Act directed the US Federal Trade Commission (FTC) to promulgate rules that prohibited unfair and deceptive acts and practices in connection with the collection and use of personal information from and about children on the Internet. Pursuant to the CIPA, the US Federal Government agency NTIA regularly conducted research to examine whether technology protection measures available at that time would adequately address the needs of educational institutions in protecting children's safety on the Internet; how to foster development of measures that meet such needs; and the development and effectiveness of local Internet safety policies in operation at that time.

Another US Act came into effect in 2000, which disclosed some US Federal Government's lines of action regarding ICT regulation. In October 2000, the US Electronic Signatures in Global and National Commerce Act (the 'E-SIGN Act') went into effect with the aim to facilitate the use of electronic records and signatures in national and foreign commerce activities by ensuring legal validity and enforceability of electronic signatures, contracts, and records.[12] US Congress in-

---

[10] Wilsey & Bauer 1996.

[11] April 2000.

[12] See <http://www.ntia.doc.gov/ntiahome/frnotices/2002/esign/report2003/toc.htm>. Nine exceptions to the ESIGN Act were defined, involving contracts and records governed by the following documents: 1) wills, codicils, and testamentary trusts; 2) laws governing domestic law matters; 3) state

tended this Act to have a positive impact on the continued growth of e-commerce and consumer confidence. Careful to preserve the underlying consumer protection laws governing consumer rights to receive certain information in writing, US Congress imposed special requirements on businesses that wanted to use electronic records or signatures in consumer transactions. For instance, section 101(c)(1) of the E-SIGN Act provides that information required by law to be in writing can be made available electronically to a consumer only if he or she affirmatively consents to receive the information electronically and the business clearly and conspicuously discloses specified information to the consumer before obtaining his or her consent (the 'E-SIGN Act'). In section 105(b) of the E-SIGN Act, US Congress directed the US Department of Commerce and the FTC to do research on the impact of the consumer consent provision specified in section 101(c)(1) of the Act. More specifically, US Congress asked to report on the benefits and burdens that the provision imposed on e-commerce by both consumers and businesses. The research results in general indicate that, although not enough time had passed since the law took effect, benefits of this provision outweigh burdens. Benefits to consumers were particularly perceived in 1) ensuring access to documents and promoting awareness; 2) providing a bright line to identify legitimate businesses; and 3) helping to prevent deception and fraud.[13] To businesses the following benefits and burdens concerning e-commerce were identified: 1) the provision of legal certainty and protection in on-line business transactions; 2) the technological neutrality of the provision which provides businesses the flexibility to design ICT applications that fit their unique needs; 3) the loss of potential customers because of the extra steps consumers have to take to agree to receive electronic versions of written documents, particularly for transactions that begin in a face-to-face setting; and 4) existing laws which would be sufficient as anti-fraud and unfair trade statutes require businesses to make disclosures to consumers and therefore could address any of the on-line problems that may arise.[14]

The attacks of 11 September 2001, had a major impact on US policy making in general and led to new issues and priorities for ICT regulation in the USA as well. On October 29, 2001 for instance, the Patriot Act (P.L. 107-56) was enacted, leading to an enhancement of law enforcement investigating tools for US federal agencies. As a result of the Patriot Act, US federal agencies were allowed to intercept wire, oral and electronic communications relating to terrorism and computer fraud. The 9/11-events also demonstrated to the US government the increased importance

---

Uniform Commercial Code, except Sections 1-107 and 1-206, Arts. 2 and 2A; 4) court orders or notices; 5) utility cancellation notices; 6) default, foreclosure, or eviction notices; 7) health or life insurance benefit cancellation notices; 8) product recall notices; and 9) hazardous, toxic, or dangerous materials notices.

[13] FTC and Department of Commerce, *Electronic Signatures in Global and National Commerce Act. The Consumer Consent Provision in Section 101(c)(1)(C)(ii)*, June 2001, available at <http://www.ftc.gov/os/2001/06/esign7.htm#III.%20Summary%20of%20Public%20Comments%20And%20Workshop>.

[14] Ibid.

and societal acceptance of wireless communication, when passengers on the ill-fated planes made invaluable phone calls to loved ones and others and also when representatives of public safety agencies, through a variety of wireless technologies, communicated with each other at the crash sites.[15] At the same time, the downturn of the US e-commerce sector continued.

As a consequence, the Bush administration decided, in 2002, to pursue deregulatory and pro-competitive policies to help the e-commerce industry overcome existing regulatory obstacles and to return to long-term, sustainable growth. To this end, it presented policy aims to make more efficient use of the radio frequency spectrum, to promote the continued growth of wireless services through the elimination of unnecessary or outdated regulations, and to encourage the growth and vitality of telecommunications firms offered by developing regulatory policies that encouraged investment.[16] The Bush administration started to promote policies to remove barriers to the deployment of new ICT services, including broadband, third generation (3G) wireless services, Ultra-Wide-Band (UWB) technologies, and digital television.

2.3   EUROPEAN STARTING POINTS FOR ICT REGULATION

One of the first important reports in the EU on new ICT infrastructures and their implications for society was presented at the Corfu European Council meeting in June 1994 by the chairman of the High Level Expert Group that prepared this report, European Commission vice-president Bangemann. In the report, entitled 'Europe and the Global Information Society. Recommendations to the European Council'[17] (also known as 'the Bangemann Report'), the High Level Expert Group emphasized the urgency of EU actions to ensure competitiveness for European enterprises in the international information services markets. For instance, to support new dynamic sectors of the economy, the High Level Expert Group perceived the need of fostering an entrepreneurial mentality within the EU. Financing the emerging ICT infrastructures was acknowledged to be mainly the responsibility of the private sector. Besides, a common regulatory approach had to be developed by the EU and its Member States to bring about a competitive European information services market. The High Level Expert Group, for instance, indicated the need to speed up the process of liberalization with regard to national telecommunication markets while consolidating the important policy principle of universal service. EU legislative measures regarding standardization issues, intellectual property rights, privacy, and security of data transmission, were also perceived to be needed. On the

---

[15] US Department of Commerce National Telecommunications and Information Administration's Annual Year Report 2002, available at <http://www.ntia.doc.gov/ntiahome/annualrpt/2002/cy2002annualreport.htm>.

[16] Ibid.

[17] See <http://europa.eu.int/ISPO/docs/basics/docs/bangemann.pdf>.

basis of the recommendations in this report, the High Level Expert Group proposed an Action Plan of concrete initiatives based on partnerships between the private and public sectors to carry Europe forward into the information society.

At the European level during the last decade, a strong preference could be perceived in the last ten years to let the private sector have the lead in further developing the European information society, with a restricted but clear and predictable role for both national, European, and international legislation to protect certain general interests. In July 1997, at the EU Ministerial Conference in Bonn entitled 'Global Information Networks: Realising the Potential', national ministers of 29 European countries agreed upon a number of key principles to pave the way for further stimulating the use of global information networks in Europe. Besides the further development of national policy and action plans towards the use of international information networks, the national ministers agreed upon strengthening their co-operation at the European and international levels. Several ICT regulatory starting points have been made explicit in the recommendations presented in, what has become known as the Bonn Ministerial Declaration:[18]

–   'Ministers stress the role which the private sector can play in protecting the interests of consumers and in promoting and respecting ethical standards, through properly functioning systems of self-regulation in compliance with and supported by the legal system' (*Recommendation 19*).

–   'Ministers agree that any regulatory framework for e-commerce should be clear and predictable, pro-competitive, strike the right balance between the freedom of expression and the protection of private and public interests, in particular the protection of minors, and ensure consumer protection' (*Recommendation 21*).

–   'Ministers stress that the general legal frameworks should be applied on-line as they are off-line. In view of the speed at which new technologies are developing, they will strive to frame regulations which are technology-neutral, whilst bearing in mind the need to avoid unnecessary regulation (*Recommendation 22*).

–   'Ministers agree to work together towards global principles on the free flow of information whilst protecting the fundamental right to privacy and personal and business data, building on the work undertaken by the EU, the Council of Europe, the OECD, and the UN' (*Recommendation 46*) and

–   'Ministers advise that full use be made of multilateral forums to strengthen international co-operation, while ensuring that their activities are properly co-

----

[18] See <http://europa.eu.int/ISPO/policy/isf/documents/declarations/Bonn-Ministerial-Declaration.htm>.

ordinated ... in order to identify and dismantle existing obstacles to the use of e-commerce, to prevent the establishment of new barriers, and to establish a clear and predictable legal framework at national and, where appropriate, European and global levels' (*Recommendation 59*).

In line with Recommendation 19 of the Bonn Ministerial Declaration but also more in general in the EU, an important ICT regulatory line of action turns out to be self-regulation. This ICT regulatory starting point can be found in for instance the field of suppressing the offer of harmful – not illegal – content. As a result of the European Commission's 1996 Green Paper on Illegal and Harmful Content on the Internet, the subsequent European Action Plan provided for the development of alternatives to legislation and regulations, such as rating and filtering techniques. Related to these technical measures, international co-operation and the development of international compatible (technological) security measures were considered to be important lines of regulatory action in the EU. An important third line of activities was focused on increasing public awareness (particularly the knowledge of Internet users), due to the general difficulty of enforcing of off-line rules in an on-line environment (e.g., the difficulty to determine who is responsible or liable for harmful content in a context of hyperlinked and dynamic web sites).

However, opposed to the EU approach towards illegal and harmful content on the Internet, the Council of Europe's Convention on Cybercrime, approved in 2001, pointed at the importance acknowledged by the international community to have rules in an electronic environment to avoid a legal vacuum. Therefore, the aim of the Cybercrime Convention was to harmonize substantive criminal law for a number of offences.[19] However, experiences with the Cybercrime Convention show that harmonizing legislation in the field of content-related offences on the Internet need not to be viable as a result of diverging national legislative characteristics. Here, the main problem is that the necessity of harmonization for enforcement in the on-line world also leads to the necessity of harmonization in the physical, off-line world. An exception to this seems to be the field of child pornography. Here, at least in the proposed penalization for activities in the on-line world, the off-line situation is more or less followed.[20]

With regard to jurisdiction and responsibility for law enforcement within a certain territory, the European Commission usually employs the country of origin principle, i.e., legislation of the country in which the supplier is physically located applies. This country of origin principle, for instance, can be found in the European Directives on electronic commerce and electronic signatures. Moreover, the European Directive on electronic commerce combines this country of origin principle with an identification obligation for the supplier of the information, namely its physi-

---

[19] See <http://www.coe.int/T/E/Legal_affairs/Legal_co-operation/Combating_economic_crime/Cybercrime/_Summary.asp#TopOfPage>.
[20] Dutch Ministry of Justice 2000, p. 51.

cal location. Besides, the European Directive on distant selling of financial services requires suppliers to inform consumers about the applicable law and the competent court if the agreement does not relate these to the consumers' place of residence in a national state where the Directive applies. This Directive also encourages Member States to create out-of-court dispute resolution bodies for cross-border consumer disputes. At the Lisbon Summit in March 2000, the European bodies were called upon to generally consider how to promote consumer confidence in e-commerce, in particular, by means of Alternative Dispute Resolution (ADR) systems.[21]

Other results of the Lisbon Summit were the endorsement of the e-Europe Initiative as part of the Lisbon Strategy to modernize the European economy. The aim of the e-Europe Initiative was to accelerate Europe's transition to a knowledge based economy and to realize the potential benefits of higher growth, more jobs, and better access for all citizens to the new services of the information society.[22] To be able to do so, the first e-European Action Plan 2000-2002 had three aims: a cheaper, faster, more secure Internet, investment in people and skills, and greater use of the Internet.[23] Consequently, in July 2000, the European Commission adopted a package of legislative proposals designed to strengthen competition in the converging electronic communications markets in the EU. These legislative proposals came down to liberalizing the 'last mile' of telecommunications markets by unbundling access to the local loop, leading to cheaper and faster Internet access over local copper-wire networks; introducing flexible mechanisms in European legislation, such as the already mentioned ADR solutions, to allow it to evolve with future technology and market changes and to roll back regulation when markets become competitive; creating a level playing field across the EU by facilitating market entry through simplified rules and ensuring harmonised application through strong co-ordination mechanisms at the European level; adapting regulation to increasing competition by limiting most of market power-based regulation to dominant operators, as defined in EC competition law; maintaining the universal service obligations in order to avoid exclusion from the information society; and ensuring the protection of the individual's right to privacy on the Internet.[24]

As a follow-up to the first e-Europe Action Plan, the e-Europe Action Plan 2003-2005 was endorsed by the European Council in Seville in 2002. With the aim to stimulate secure services, applications and content based on a widely available broadband infrastructure, this e-Europe 2005 Action Plan focuses on a limited number of areas for government action, namely, the modernization of public services to make them more productive, accessible, and equitable, the further promotion of a favorable environment for e-business, and a secure broadband and multi-platform infor-

---

[21] Lisbon European Council, Presidency Conclusions, 23 and 24 March 2000, SN 100/00.

[22] European Commission's Information Society Directorate-General, *Towards an Information Society for all*, September 2003, p. 15.

[23] Ibid.

[24] European Commission, Press Release IP/00/749, 12 July 2000, Brussels. See <http://europa.eu.int/ISPO/infosoc/telecompolicy/press/ip00-749en.htm>.

mation infrastructure.[25] Moreover, a new regulatory framework for electronic communication services was adopted at the European level and applies from July 2003. With the aims to encourage competition and innovation in the electronic communications markets, to improve the functioning of the internal market, and to guarantee basic user interests that would not be guaranteed by market forces alone, major features of the new legal framework are presented as follows:[26]

- it covers all communications networks used to deliver e-Communications services, not just traditional telecommunications networks. This technological neutrality meets the requirements of the Internet-driven convergence between telecommunications, information systems, and the media;
- it provides for regulation to be rolled back, by ensuring that regulatory obligations on market players are lifted as soon as markets become competitive;
- it drastically cuts unnecessary red tape which obstructs entry to national markets by replacing individual licenses by general authorizations to provide services.

The new EU regulatory framework for electronic communication services consists of the following measures:[27]

- a *Framework Directive* setting out the main harmonizing principles, objectives and procedures for an EU regulatory policy regarding the provision of electronic communication services and networks;
- an *Access and Interconnection Directive* stipulating procedures and principles for imposing pro-competitive obligations regarding access to and interconnection of networks;
- an *Authorization Directive* introducing a system of general authorizations instead of individual licenses;
- a *Universal Service Directive* requiring a minimum level of availability and affordability of basic electronic communications services and guaranteeing a set of basic rights for users and consumers of electronic communications services;
- a *Directive on privacy and electronic communications* setting out rules for the protection of privacy and of personal data processed in relation to communication over public communication networks;
- a *Radio Spectrum Decision* establishing principles and procedures for the development and implementation of an internal and external EU radio spectrum policy applicable to all sectors using radio spectrum, including the communications sector;

---

[25] See *supra* n. 22, at p. 11.
[26] See *supra* n. 22, at p. 23.
[27] See *supra* n. 22, at p. 25.

- a European Commission *Competition Directive* consolidating the legal measures based on Article 86 of the EU Treaty that have underpinned the liberalization of the telecommunications sector over the years.

In addition to these basic regulatory instruments, the European Commission has
adopted additional measures that will play an important role in the functioning of
the new framework:[28]

- Commission guidelines on market analysis and the assessment of significant
  market power, setting out a common methodology and principles for the national regulatory authorities charged with these tasks;
- a Commission recommendation on relevant product and service markets
  within the electronic communications sector susceptible to prior regulation.

In several other European Directives at present, such as those on Electronic Signatures, Distant Selling, and e-Commerce, the general regulatory line of action can be
found that similar 'on-line' and 'off-line' activities should be governed by the same
regulatory norms. However, aiming at promoting the European internal market, the
European Commission has chosen for a slightly different solution for the 'off-line'
situation in the European Directive on electronic commerce, by imposing less far-
reaching liabilities on the Internet provider than on comparable professional groups
in the 'off-line' world. With regard to copyright issues, the European Commission
has also chosen to propose specific, viz. technology-dependent legislation for the
Internet (private copying).

In the field of European private law more specifically, a gradual change in the
approach to ICT regulation may be observed. From a regulatory preference for self-
regulation by means of, for instance, Codes of Conduct, a dominant tendency has
emerged to protect general interests of legal certainty and confidence through specific regulatory measures. This development is reflected in the European Directives
on electronic commerce, electronic signatures, and on Copyright Harmonization.
As an example, the latter Directive proposes a stricter regulatory regime than the
international WIPO Internet treaties, perceiving technical security measures as important options (see also section 2.5).

2.4   ASIAN AND PACIFIC ICT REGULATORY STARTING POINTS

2.4.1   **Singapore**

In 1992, earlier than the first major ICT policy strategy of the US Federal Government, Singapore presented its IT2000 Master Plan to develop into an 'Intelligent

---

[28] Ibid.

Island'. Starting as a broad vision with hardly any details, this Master Plan identified several strategic objectives with the creation of a nation-wide ICT infrastructure, such as the development into a global hub, boosting the Singaporean economy, enhancing the learning potential of individuals, linking communities locally and globally, and improving the quality of life of Singaporeans.[29] In 1996, the Singapore national government implemented a nation-wide multimedia high-capacity network infrastructure to which all Singaporeans were connected ('Singapore ONE initiative').

In Singapore, however, an open network approach towards this new ICT infrastructure was not an obvious choice. The general promotion of a communitarian ideology by Singaporean political leaders who, unlike western politicians, prescribe the restriction of individual freedom of expression in the public domain and exercise control over freedom of the press,[30] led both to a delay in widespread Internet take up and a continuing tight control on information distribution through the new ICT infrastructure. Only just at the end of 1994, the Singapore national government decided to make the Internet more broadly accessible than to the R&D community only and started to stimulate Internet penetration into businesses and households. To this end, a clear policy decision of the Singaporean Minister of Information and the Arts was needed. Although the increasing difficulty of controlling information distribution through an open network such as the Internet, a substantial number of content categories[31] have been indicated by the Singapore national government to which Internet Service Providers have to block access for Singaporean citizens. In addition, cross-border Internet traffic has to be directed through a limited number of proxy servers, where content is filtered.[32] Currently, Singapore employs a three-step approach towards Internet content regulation: first, it has a class license scheme providing minimum standards to safeguard values and promote growth of Internet service provision; second, it encourages industry self-regulation; and third, it has an active public education program towards Internet use to promote parental supervision. At the moment, personal communications, such as email or Internet Relay Chat (IRC), personal web sites and corporate Internet use by employees or for business transactions within Singapore, are not regulated.[33]

To develop e-commerce services and basic legal and technical infrastructures to support secure and reliable e-commerce, the Singapore national government introduced the e-Commerce Hotbed Program in 1996 and the e-Commerce Master Plan in 1998. With the e-Commerce Master Plan, the Singapore national government aimed to develop Singapore as an international e-commerce hub, trying to create an e-commerce services sector and to harmonize cross-border e-Commerce laws and

---

[29] Wong 1997, pp. 33-34.
[30] Ibid., p. 26.
[31] I.e., general security and national defence, racial and religious harmony, public morals, and certain other content.
[32] Koops, et al., 2000, p. 164.
[33] 'E-Commerce, Legal and Policy environment', at <http://www.ec.gov.sg/policy.html>.

policies.[34] The Singapore government took the view that increased e-commerce service provision requires transparent, market-favorable regulation together with legislation in specific areas, acknowledging the fact that the legal, regulatory, and business environments required to support the emerging digital economy significantly differ from those environments needed for traditional enterprises. Consequently, the Singapore national government perceived it as its task to adapt national and international policies to the new digital economy and to ensure that present legislation did not impede the development of new and innovative products and services, nor the growth of new or existing markets.

Besides, it perceived the necessity for new regulations to be flexible enough to cater for technological changes and new global policy. In addition, the government wanted to stimulate industry self-regulation in those areas where industry practices were aligned with international practices.[35]

Since 1998, several legislative measures have been taken by the Singapore national government to support secure and reliable e-commerce. In July 1998, for instance, the Electronic Transaction Act was enacted to provide a uniformity of rules, regulations, and standards regarding the authentication and integrity of electronic records in Singapore. Generally, under Singaporean Law, electronic records and digital signatures enjoy the same status as traditional records and signatures by virtue of the principle of non-discrimination.[36] From an international perspective, the Singapore Electronic Transaction Act closely follows the UNCITRAL Model Law on E-Commerce (see also section 2.5.3). Next, in order to strike a balance between the protection of rights for copyright owners and increased public access to intellectual property, Singapore has ensured that its intellectual and copyright laws are harmonized with underlying principles in global intellectual property rights laws.[37]

Other legislative measures taken by the Singapore national government were the amendment of the Singapore Evidence Act to allow the use of electronic records as evidence in courts and the adoption of the Computer Misuse Act, which deals with new potential abuses of computer systems (for example: denial or interruption of computer services and unauthorized disclosure of access codes) in defining a class of critical computer systems and providing them with greater protection. In the legislative areas of income tax and goods and services tax, the same laws which exist in the off-line world apply to the on-line world. Whether or not a company needs to pay income tax in Singapore on its business activities conducted on the Internet depends on the broad principle of a so-called operations test, implying that any Internet-based operation based in Singapore which is deemed to be generating revenue, is liable to pay income tax.[38]

---

[34] Ibid.
[35] Ibid.
[36] Nicoll 1999, p. 128.
[37] See *supra* n. 33.
[38] Ibid.

In 1999, after having largely implemented the IT2000 Master Plan, the Singapore national government presented its successor, the InfoComm 21 Master Plan, with the aim to develop Singapore into a leading ICT hub in Asia. Measures to establish this leading position were, for instance, the liberalization of Singapore's telecommunications market from April 2000, helping Singaporeans to go on-line, developing ICT manpower and talent, building Singapore's ICT industry, and gearing Singapore up to be leading in e-government.[39]

The most influential and far-reaching regulatory document regarding the ICT policy in Singapore, by far has been the Code of Practice for Competition in the Provision of Telecommunications Services, also called the Competition Code. This Code was drafted as the blueprint for government regulation of the competitive telecommunications industry in Singapore.[40] It introduced asymmetrical regulation and a range of consumer-protection provisions, and laid the foundation for interconnection policies. The text of the Code was prepared with major involvement of outside consultants from the USA, which provided legal and other expertise deemed to be lacking in Singapore.[41] The Code is designed to embody several regulatory principles:[42]

- The principle of asymmetrical regulation: where competition exists in the market only a light regulatory hand needs to be applied, which should allow market forces to dictate operator behavior. As competition increases, the Singapore government is supposed to increasingly step away from dominant-carrier regulation, concentrating on enforcement of consumer protection rules and encouraging the industry to police itself through mutually agreed private sector codes of practice;
- The principle of technology neutrality: operators of networks are subject to the same rules and obligations regardless of what platform these operators use. Under the Singapore Telecommunications Act the concept of 'telecommunications service' is very broadly defined and includes Internet or other media services;
- The principle of fostering short-term market entry and long-term investment.

In general, the observation can be made that the Singapore national government has invested very heavily in the idea of technological convergence, both as a global industry trend and as a concept to organize its regulatory and promotional activities.

---

[39] Lips 2001, p. 82.
[40] ITU, *Effective regulation case study: Singapore*, 2001, p. 32.
[41] Ibid.
[42] See *supra* n. 40, at p. 25.

2.4.2 **Japan**

In 1993, several Japanese ministries, leading industrial companies, corporate think tanks, and academia started to debate plans for a nation-wide digital communications network.[43] At that time, the debate reverted to old intellectual concepts of a Japanese information-based society,[44] traditional top-down policies favoring producers over consumers, and established bureaucratic procedures. More radical policy changes were far away until recently, although the Japanese continued to pay close attention to ICT regulatory and policy developments in the USA, taking the view that Japan lagged behind in both technological and policy developments. Another important motivation for the Japanese to closely watch international ICT regulatory and policy developments was that technological developments could be used to increase productivity and, with that, support the recovery of the Japanese economy.

In 1998, a shift of attitude in national ICT policy making could be recognized, leading to active, more radical policy changes with regard to ICT developments in Japan. Particularly in the field of e-commerce the Japanese government perceived various opportunities to quickly improve technical, economical, and social developments. For instance in March 1998, sponsored by the Japanese Ministry of Justice, a special Study Group published the Report on the Legal System of Electronic Commerce. Divided into two subcommittees, the Study Group discussed the foundation of systems necessary to realise secure e-commerce and electronic applications, on the one hand, and issues concerning the need for new and/or amended of substantive law, on the other.[45] Major motives for this Study Group were the exchange of digital data through open computer networks, the perceived indispensability of promoting e-commerce to establish legal systems for certifying the identity of a generator of data and the integrity of data, and issues concerning the legal effects of electronic signatures, which in Japan are functionally equivalent to handwritten signatures or seals.[46] The Recommendations of the Study Group were to establish electronic authentication systems utilizing information registered in the Japanese Commercial Registration System, to establish electronic notarization systems based on the existing Japanese notarization system, and to design legislation on electronic signatures in order to establish the same effects as hand-written signatures.[47] To this end, the Study Group took the view that the private and public sectors should co-operate with one another and rapidly carry out the establishment of systems and legislation. Besides, the Japanese should take discussions by private

---

[43] West, et al., 1997.

[44] I.e., a transformation of the Japanese economy from traditional heavy industries to 'knowledge-intensive' ones as, for instance, expressed in the 1994 Japanese Ministry of Post and Telecommunications' policy document Reforms toward the intellectually creative society of the 21st century.

[45] Report on the Legal System of Electronic Commerce, 1998, at <http://www.moj.go.jp/EN-GLISH/CIAB/ciab-17.html>.

[46] An important means in Japan to certify the existence and representation power of a company in commercial activities.

[47] See *supra* n. 45.

companies on international standards concerning e-commerce and formed into consideration, as well as discussions in this field held within the framework of international organizations and conferences, such as UNCITRAL and the OECD (see also section 2.5). In May 1998, the Japanese and US Federal Government issued a joint statement on e-commerce, signalling agreement between the Japanese and US governments on policy directions for basic principles and individual issues in e-commerce.

In November 1998, the Advanced Information and Telecommunication Society Promotion Headquarters of the Japanese government presented revised basic guidelines to facilitate further efforts towards establishing an advanced information and telecommunication society, made possible by the digital revolution. This need for revision was perceived to come from several unforeseen developments leading to rapidly expanding networks in Japanese society, such as the global increase in the use of the Internet and e-mail, the spread of portable remote information terminals such as mobile phones, and the emergence of global mobile radio communication systems.[48] In addition, a strong growth in e-commerce and rapid progress towards e-government had not been taken into account in the previous Japanese basic guidelines. To achieve an ideal advanced information and telecommunication society the Japanese government indicated three main action principles.[49] First, following the USA where, in the eyes of the Japanese government, free competition was enabling rapid responses to current challenges, the private sector should take the lead in establishing an advanced information and telecommunication society. Secondly, the government should create a regulatory environment favourable to the private sector's initiative. Therefore, the government must restrict its regulatory measures to the necessary minimum, refrain from unnecessary regulations, and avoid creating an atmosphere of uncertainty. Guidelines on government involvement should be implemented on a sector-by-sector basis, following thorough discussions. Thirdly, given the progressing globalization of the economy and society, the Japanese government must work together with international organizations and other national governments in the field of international harmonization and international standards wherever possible, demonstrating initiative in establishing international consensus.

According to the Japanese government, the role of the private sector in building an advanced information and telecommunication society by means of setting rules or developing guidelines and model agreements for e-commerce and creating ICT standards would only increase in importance. The idea behind this point of view was that rules developed in the marketplace could be quickly and effectively substituted for institutions traditionally established by the Japanese government.[50] However, the government would also have an important role in building an advanced

---

[48] Advanced Information and Telecommunications Society Promotion Headquarters, Basic Guidelines on the Promotion of an Advanced Information and Telecommunications Society, 9 November 1998, at <http://www.kantei.go.jp/foreign/990209guideline-aits.html>, p. 3.

[49] See *supra* n. 48, at p. 6.

[50] Ibid., p. 7.

information and telecommunication society in Japan, more specifically in implementing countermeasures against unlawful acts such as crimes committed using a network, and in rectifying disparities among regions or between individuals due to advanced age or disability.[51] For instance, the Japanese government announced the establishment of an open, seamless ICT infrastructure, giving full consideration to implementation of lower fees, prevention of geographical imbalances, alleviation of vulnerability to disaster, and evolution of trends in foreign countries.[52] In the opinion of the Japanese government, striving to deploy a nationwide fiber-optic network by 2005, the private sector should, in principle, take the initiative under conditions of fair and effective competition. Besides, the Japanese government indicated it wanted to study the legal aspects of new fields, such as e-commerce transactions, creation and use of on-line content, electronic payments, and electronic money. More specifically, the government needed to undertake the responsibility of establishing fair regulations for the governance of electronic money and payments, a system of user protection, requirements for validating the issuer of electronic money, and measures of how to respond in the event that when the issuer of electronic money becomes insolvent.[53]

To be able to further promote e-commerce in Japan, the development in the private sector of electronic authentication technologies and guidelines for self-regulation was believed to need stimulating by the Japanese government. Besides, to further promote international e-commerce, the Japanese government was expected to negotiate with foreign governments to keep regulations introduced in other countries to a minimum and to prevent discrimination against the authentication methods of other countries. In addition, in the opinion of the Japanese government, electronic signatures should at least have the same legal status as their off-line counterparts in Japan, i.e., hand written signatures and seals. As each business sector had a different way of using, method of collecting, and content of personal data, the private sector was pointed towards formulating guidelines and setting up specific registration, labelling, and marking data systems. However, government regulations needed to be considered concerning entities dealing with highly confidential information, such as personal credit or medical data. In addition, businesses would be encouraged to disclose the way in which they protected personal data to their customers. All together, Japan's privacy protection policy needed to be in line with international discussions in this area, such as the OECD Guidelines governing the Protection of Privacy and Transborder Flows of Personal Data.

In order to promote global e-commerce, the Japanese government perceived it of importance to establish a taxation structure consistent with international tax laws, in order to avoid dual taxation or tax leakage. Therefore, the Japanese government needed to contribute to the OECD activities in this field. Besides, as no customs duties are imposed in Japan on content transmitted electronically, the government

---

[51] Ibid., p. 3.
[52] Ibid., p. 20.
[53] Ibid., p. 11.

needed to actively participate in the WTO or in other international forums and, at the same time, to consider the imposition of customs duties, for instance, on software transmitted over the Internet (as compared to the customs duties imposed on imported software recorded on physical storage devices).

With regard to illegal content transmitted over ICT networks, the Japanese government applied the off-line should be on-line regulatory adage, by placing these illegal activities under the current Japanese obscenity and libel laws. Problems regarding propaganda and advertising transmitted through ICT networks would also be handled within the existing legal framework. In addition, on-line content which was legal but harmful to young Internet users, needed to be controlled, in the opinion of the Japanese government. Therefore, new laws would be needed to regulate adult-oriented businesses offering sexual content over the Internet.[54] Besides, to generally ensure the safety and security of ICT networks, the establishment of appropriate laws needed to be made to prevent intrusions and indicate and arrest offenders. The Japanese government also announced to generally promote technologies (e.g., content-filtering systems, systems for screening advertisements and processing complaints, development of counter-technologies to prevent criminal activities, development of technologies related to prevention of unauthorized use, promotion of computer anti-virus measures, development and diffusion of encryption technologies, development of rights-protection technologies), education, and self-regulation by the private sector for the benefit of protecting ICT users.[55] In addition, to promote countermeasures against high-tech crimes over global ICT networks, the Japanese government announced active participation in debates on the nature of co-operation in international criminal investigations and co-operation between legislative organizations and to promote dialogue between industries and governments regarding high-tech crime prevention measures.[56]

In August 2000, the IT Strategy Council, an advisory body to the Japanese Prime Minister on ICT policy, called for the creation of a national ICT strategy which would cause Japan to overtake the USA in IT in five years.[57] To create the regulatory framework for the implementation of this effort, the Japanese Diet passed the 'Basic Law on the Formation of an Advanced Information and Telecommunications Network Society' (also called IT Basic Law) to promote the use of ICT in Japan (among other things, in the domains of e-commerce and e-government). In conformance with the basic guidelines of the Japanese government as mentioned earlier, basic points of view presented in the IT Basic Law[58] were (1) the promotion of the economic structural reform (facilitation of e-commerce, creation of new busi-

---

[54] Ibid., p. 9.

[55] For example: the Japanese Trust Mark System. Jointly promoted by the Japan Direct Marketing Association and the Japan Chamber of Commerce from the viewpoint of consumer protection, a mark is granted to service providers who have met certain requirements as being trustworthy towards consumers.

[56] Idem, p. 27. See also *supra* n. 48, at p. 27.

[57] Mitchell, at <http://www.coudert.com/practice/japanIT.htm>.

[58] Cabinet Secretariat, 2000, at <http://www.kantei.go.jp/foreign/it/it_basiclaw/summary.html>.

nesses); (2) the realization of vital, individualized local communities (creation of local employment opportunities, expansion of diverse interchanges); (3) appropriate role-sharing between the public and private sectors in which the private sector takes the lead in principle, and the government creates favourable conditions, for example, by promoting, fair competition; (4) the correction of gaps in opportunities and skills for use of ICT (measures against the digital divide); and (5) the solution of new problems in areas of employment, etc. At the time of the adoption of the IT Basic Law, the Japanese Fair Trade Commission also took action to further promote e-commerce. In October 2000, it announced the introduction of an e-commerce monitoring system consisting of about 350 watchdogs from the private sector to take action on false advertising on the Internet.

Having taken effect in January 2001, the IT Basic Law would be reviewed within three years after entering into force. Besides, in accordance with the Law, an Action Plan with concrete goals and timetables had to be designed including policies to guide government action in the use of IT in connection with (1) the establishment of an advanced ICT infrastructure, (2) the promotion of education and learning, (3) reform of regulations and facilitation of e-commerce, (4) the promotion of e-government, and (5) measures to promote public safety and trust.[59]

Another outcome of this Law was the creation of a new IT Strategy Headquarters in the office of the Japanese Prime Minister (i.e., the Cabinet), leading to a situation in which one central authority within the Japanese government was given the responsibility for the design and implementation of ICT policy. Consequently, the Advanced Information and Telecommunication Society Promotion Headquarters was dissolved. At the start of its activities, the IT Strategy Headquarters concluded that, compared with other countries (for example, the USA and the European countries), the main cause for Japan's delay in the popularization of the Internet had been institutional problems, such as high telecommunications fees stemming from a monopoly of the local telecommunications market and regulations hindering fair and free competition.[60]

In January 2001, in order to quickly implement the necessary institutional reforms and measures, the IT Strategy Headquarters presented its national 'e-Japan Strategy' which identified goals and priority policy areas to establish the intended national ultra high-speed network infrastructure, to facilitate e-commerce aggressively by 2002 through constructing the appropriate regulatory framework by means of reviewing regulations hindering e-commerce, clarifying the interpretation of existing rules, and introducing new rules for liabilities of Internet Service Providers, such as for electronic contracts and information goods contracts, and to ensure security and reliability over advanced ICT-infrastructures. Moreover, market rules were defined as a result of which every Japanese citizen could safely conduct

---

[59] Mitchell, A.M., *Japan's New Information Technology Basic Law*, Information Memorandum, 6 December 2000, Coudert Brothers, New York, at <http://www.coudert.com/practice/japanIT.htm>.

[60] IT Strategy Headquarters, 22 January 2001, at <http://www.kantei.go.jp/foreign/it/network/0122summary.html>.

activities via the national ICT infrastructure (among others the development of various alternative means of dispute resolution). Also, by 2003, e-government was realized which would handle electronic information in the same manner as paper-based information.

In order to promote the establishment of an advanced national ICT infrastructure, the IT Strategy Headquarters indicated the ruling of conditions for fair competition as another priority policy area. It proved to be necessary to create regulatory frameworks under which local telecommunications facilities are effectively utilized as a shared infrastructure for providing Internet-related services, with the basic regulatory principles of maximizing consumer benefits and of promoting fair competition. The Japanese government also announced the reform of its administrative attitude, from prior regulations-oriented to ex-post-facto check approach according to transparent rules. To this end, the Japanese government formulated conditions for fair competition in the telecommunications market, such as the introduction of asymmetrical regulations, the introduction of incentive-based competition promotion measures toward the NTT Group (i.e., the incumbent Japanese telecommunications corporation), the establishment of a Telecommunications Business Dispute Settlement Commission (among other things acting to mediate of disputes on interconnection), and the strengthening of functions of the Japanese Fair Trade Commission.[61]

In the field of ensuring security and liability on ICT infrastructures, the IT Strategy Headquarters decides, among other things, standardize cryptographic technology, review and revise criminal legislation, establish a collaboration system between the public and private sectors to protect vital ICT infrastructures against cyber terrorism, and to develop prevention and detection techniques for illegal access and cyber terrorism and establish information security certificates in international cooperation.

As of April 2001, the Law Concerning Electronic Signatures and Certification Services became effective in Japan. With this Law, the genuine establishment presuming the authenticity of electromagnetic records created in order to represent information, was provided for. Besides, the Japanese Ministry of International Trade and Industry (MITI) promoted the use of an Electronic Commerce security protocol called SECE (Secure Electronic Commerce Environment), which was developed by Japanese companies[62] and complied with another security protocol developed by private sector companies, known as SET (Secure Electronic Transaction). Japanese banks were involved in a large-scale experimental use of SECE with the aim to run their Internet banking system on this new protocol.

In June 2003, the Japanese Ministry of Economy, Trade, and Industry (METI) published Interpretative Guidelines on e-Commerce to serve as a guide to the specific interpretation of Japanese laws and therefore to help in the establishment of

---

[61] See *supra* n. 60, at pp. 4-5.
[62] I.e., Hitachi, Fujitsu, and NEC.

new rules.[63] Several actual problems concerning varying on-line activities were explored to the extent to which they could be dealt with under existing Japanese law. In cases where Japanese law did not offer legal solutions, proposals for new rulings were suggested. On-line activities and situations discussed in this document were among others the conclusion of contracts on-line (e.g., the problem of spoofing), the development of new transactions (e.g., Internet auctions), consumer protection (e.g., implications of web advertising), information property trading, and intellectual property (e.g., use of peer-to-peer file exchange).

2.4.3 **Australia**

In 1997, the Australian Prime Minister emphasized the importance of ICT developments for his country in a policy entitled statement Investing for Growth. For the development and co-ordination of advice to the Australian Federal Government on information economy issues a new executive agency within the Department of Communications, IT and the Arts, the so-called National Office for the Information Economy (NOIE), had been given direct responsibility. The Australian Federal Government further underlined the importance of its leadership role in adopting new ICTs in the 1999 policy statement A Strategic Framework for the Information Economy. In this statement, ten national priority areas were identified to make Australia a leading player in the global information economy:[64]

1. maximise opportunities for all Australians to benefit from the information economy;
2. deliver the education and skills Australians need to participate in the information economy;
3. advance the growth of a world class infrastructure for the information economy;
4. increase significantly the use of e-commerce by Australian business and B2B electronic transactions, assuming the policy principle that the growth of e-commerce will be led by the private sector;
5. develop a legal and regulatory framework to facilitate e-commerce, particularly in building the confidence of businesses and consumers that on-line information and transactions are authentic, private, secure, and legally sound;
6. promote the integrity and growth of Australian content and culture in the information economy;
7. develop the Australian information industries;
8. unlock the potential of the health sector;
9. influence the emerging international rules and conventions for e-commerce: this objective is to ensure that the international policy and regulatory envi-

---

[63] METI 2003, p. 2.
[64] NOIE 2000.

ronment for e-commerce reflects Australian national priorities, business and user needs;

10. implement a world class model for delivery of all appropriate government services on-line.

Later on, an eleventh priority area to stimulate Regional Information Economies in Australia was added to this Strategic Framework.

To make progress with strategic priority 4, i.e., to significantly increase the use of e-commerce, the Australian Federal Government acknowledged the establishment of a clear and consistent legal and regulatory framework for e-commerce which provides legal certainty while facilitating self-regulation and technology neutrality (also strategic priority 5), to be a major activity. One of the main elements of the legal framework for e-commerce is the Electronic Transaction Act, effective since July 2003, which enables the acceptance of on-line communications as traditional forms of communication for most purposes. Besides, since June 2000, on-line activities have to comply with the Australian Privacy Act 1988. Additionally in April 2000, the Australian Federal Government introduced the Privacy Amendment (Private Sector) Bill 2000 in parliament, to support and strengthen self-regulatory privacy protection in the private sector. Another legal measure introduced by the Australian Federal Government was the Copyright Amendment (Digital Agenda) Bill 1999, which aimed to promote both the creation of Australian cultural content in the digital environment and reasonable access for all Australian citizens to this material. Among other things, this Bill transposed existing present exceptions for copyright material users including cultural and educational institutions to the digital environment. In addition, in 1999, the Copyright Amendment (Moral Rights) Bill was introduced, aiming to provide additional protection to creators in the digital environment.

The Australian Federal Government also introduced several regulatory measures to try and stimulate the use of e-commerce. In 1999, for instance, the National Electronic Authentication Council (NEAC) was established to enhance business and consumer confidence in e-commerce through overseeing the development of a national framework for electronic authentication of on-line communications. NEAC's tasks include: stimulating interoperability between different systems, developing relevant technical standards, and providing information and advice to government, businesses, and consumers. In order to provide for adequate consumer protection in e-commerce, the Australian Federal Treasury developed a Best Practice Model Code of Conduct to provide guidance to businesses on standards and practices should be adopted in the area of B2C e-commerce. Together with NOIE, the Australian Federal Treasury published several fact sheets for consumers shopping on-line. In addition, Australian industry associations are producing codes of conduct for their members and introducing initiatives such as seals of approval. To assist with management of offensive material, NOIE has established a special community advisory body called NetAlert.

From an international perspective, the Australian Federal Government made joint statements on e-commerce with the governments of Japan (1999), Korea (1999), China (1999), and Canada (2000), setting out common approaches and areas of cooperation in the promotion of e-commerce. Australia led an Asia-Pacific Economic Cooperation (APEC) task force on international charging arrangements for Internet services, with broad involvement of the US and Asian governments and industry.

2.5   ICT REGULATORY STARTING POINTS OF INTERNATIONAL ORGANIZATIONS

2.5.1   Organization for Economic Co-operation and Development (OECD)

In the last decade, the OECD has given increased priority to activities relevant to ICT developments and their impact on the world's economies. More specifically, OECD discussions on ICT policy directions and research publications have been provided in the fields of telecommunications (including analysis of trends and impacts in the communications sector, interconnection issues, mobile issues, and spectrum allocation), the information economy (including analysis of trends and impacts in e-commerce and the IT sector in general), information security and privacy (including maintenance of OECD guidelines on privacy protection, cryptography, and information security), and consumer policy (including model codes of conduct for e-commerce and consumer protection). In the past, several OECD Ministerial Conferences have had an important impact on the development of ICT regulatory starting points, both internationally and in national contexts.

One of these influential conferences was the OECD Ministerial Conference in Ottawa in October 1998. Here it was generally decided that the main aspect of the role of government towards the developing international electronic environment should be the establishment of trust. To reach this goal, acknowledged as an important instrument, the OECD Ministerial Conference decided that legislation should primarily serve to facilitate the developing electronic environment and that the legislator should make every effort to take a reserved approach. In cases where legislation was perceived to be not suitable or even not feasible, self-regulation was acknowledged to be an important regulatory means to support the development of the international electronic environment.

The Ottawa Conference of OECD Ministers also summoned member countries to apply as the regulatory line of action technology neutrality in the field of electronic authentication, through amending media-specific requirements in legislation. It called on member countries to take into account possibilities to harmonize national legal frameworks at an international level and to further stimulate the developing international electronic environment. Among other things, Member States were called upon to give favourable consideration to the UNCITRAL Model Law on e-Commerce (see section 2.5.3) and adopt a non-discriminatory attitude to foreign authentication.

At the 1999 OECD Ministerial Conference in Paris a shift in regulatory approach became apparent, referred to as 'co-regulation' or the 'integrated approach'. According to this new approach, legislation and self-regulation were no longer perceived as a dichotomy (i.e., government at a distance) but were acknowledged to be complements of each other (i.e., the government involved): the conclusion was that the regulatory environment should be a balance between self-regulation by industry and regulation by government and international bodies, developed co-operatively by government, business and the public.[65] In practice, this implies that government legislation provides a basic legal infrastructure in which social parties may apply, for instance, codes of conduct. According to the OECD, this approach has the advantage of speed and flexibility, providing room to innovation and competition, and also enables specific rules for specific sectors.

In the last few years, also influenced by the events on 11 September 2001, two important policy themes to the OECD have been building trust in on-line environments and the security of information systems and networks. For instance, at an international conference in The Hague in December 2000, on-line Alternative Dispute Resolution mechanisms (ADR) for disputes arising from privacy and consumer protection issues in Business-to-Consumer (B2C) on-line interactions were presented and discussed as an important alternative means to improve trust for global e-commerce. On 25 July 2002, the OECD Council adopted guidelines for the security of information systems and networks with the aims to raise awareness about the risks to information systems and networks and to promote the development of a culture of security, i.e., a focus on security in the development of information systems and networks and the adoption of new ways of thinking and behaving when using and interacting within information systems and networks.[66]

2.5.2 G7/G8

In February 1995, Ministers of the Group of Seven (G7) and Members of the European Commission met in Brussels at a Ministerial Conference on the Information Society. At this G7 Summit, a shared vision of human enrichment as a result of progress in ICT was formulated. Consequently, the smooth and effective transition towards a Global Information Society was considered as one of the most important tasks in the last decade of the 20th century, with the commitment of the G7 partners to play a leading role in its development. In order to realize their common vision of the Global Information Society the G7 partners agreed upon international collaboration on the basis of the following eight core principles: 1) promoting dynamic

---

[65] OECD 1999, p. 11.
[66] OECD 2002, p. 8.

competition; 2) encouraging private investment; 3) defining an adaptable regulatory framework; 4) providing open access to networks; while 5) ensuring universal provision of and access to services; 6) promoting equality of opportunity to the citizen; 7) promoting diversity of content, including cultural and linguistic diversity; and 8) recognizing the necessity of worldwide co-operation with particular attention to less developed countries.

The appropriate regulatory framework envisaged at the G7 Summit was a framework designed to allow choice, high quality services, and affordable prices. Open access to networks for service and information suppliers and the mutual enrichment of the citizen through the promotion of diversity, including cultural and linguistic diversity, as well as the free expression of ideas, were perceived to be essential for the creation of the Global Information Society.[67] In the light of technological convergence, market liberalization and encouragement of new entrants, and growing global competition, competition rules needed to be interpreted and applied. In addition, competition authorities were not allowed to avoid the emergence of global players and risks of anti-competitive behaviour. In particular, risks of abuse of market dominance needed to be prevented in productive forms of co-operation. Therefore, the G7 partners were committed to ensuring citizens' access through universal service in the respective markets; opening up markets to allow the development of global systems; pursuing the interconnectivity of networks and the interoperability of services; providing open access to networks for service and information suppliers; implementing fair and effective licensing and frequency allocation; allowing for productive forms of co-operation while shielding against anti-competitive behavior; protecting privacy and personal data; increasing information security; and to protect creativity and content provision.

In July 2000, the Group of Eight (G8[68]) presented the Okinawa Charter on the Global Information Society at their Kyushu-Okinawa Summit. In this Charter, the G8 acknowledged a leading role for the private sector in the development of ICT networks in the information society. Governments would be responsible for creating a predictable, transparent and non-discriminatory policy and regulatory environment to allow for the information society.[69] Moreover, the G8 considered it of importance to avoid undue regulatory interventions that would hinder productive private sector initiatives in creating an ICT friendly environment, and also to ensure that ICT-related rules and practices would be responsive to revolutionary changes in economic transactions, while taking into account the principles of effective public-private sector partnership, transparency, and technological neutrality. The following ICT policy principles and approaches were agreed by the G8:[70]

---

[67] G7 1995.
[68] I.e., the G7 now also including Russia.
[69] Okinawa Charter 2000, Art. 7.
[70] Ibid.

- To continue to promote competition in open markets for the provision of ICT products and services, including non-discriminatory and cost-oriented inter-connection for basic telecommunications;
- The protection of intellectual property rights for ICT related technology is considered to be vital to promoting ICT related innovations, competition and diffusion of new technology;
- To facilitate cross-border e-commerce by promoting further liberalization and improvement in networks and related services and procedures in the context of a strong World Trade Organization (WTO) framework, continued work on e-commerce in the WTO and other international flora, and application of ex-isting WTO trade disciplines to e-commerce;
- Consistent approaches to taxation of e-commerce based on the conventional principles, including neutrality, equity and simplicity, and other key elements agreed in the work of the OECD;
- To continue the practice of not imposing customs duties on electronic trans-missions, pending the review at the next WTO Ministerial Conference;
- To promote market-driven standards including, for example, interoperable technical standards;
- To promote consumer trust in the electronic marketplace consistent with OECD guidelines and provide equivalent consumer protection in the on-line world as in the off-line world, including through effective self-regulatory ini-tiatives such as on-line codes of conduct, trustmarks and other reliability programmes, and explore options to alleviate the difficulties faced by con-sumers in cross-border disputes, including use of Alternative Dispute Resolu-tion (ADR) mechanisms;
- Developing effective and meaningful privacy protection for consumers, as well as protection of privacy in processing personal data, while safeguarding the free flow of information;
- Further development and effective functioning of electronic authentication, electronic signature, cryptography, and other means to ensure security and certainty of transactions.

Moreover in the opinion of the G8, international efforts to develop a global infor-mation society needed to be accompanied by co-ordinated action to foster a crime-free and secure cyberspace. Effective measures, such as set out in the OECD Guidelines for Security of Information Systems, needed to be put in place to fight cyber crime. The dialogue with industry, building on the success of the G8 Paris Conference on the Government/Industry Dialogue on Safety and Confidence in Cyberspace should be further promoted. Since security issues such as hacking and viruses also require effective policy responses, the G8 planned to continue to en-gage industry and other stakeholders to protect critical information infrastructures.[71]

---

[71] See *supra* n. 69, Art. 8.

2.5.3   United Nations Commission on International Trade Law (UNCITRAL)

The drafting of a model law on e-Commerce in the context of UNCITRAL has mainly been directed at international uniformity through removing improper legal obstacles in the market. This includes promoting the predictability of the law and increasing its practical applicability. The UNCITRAL approach tries to reach a regulatory touch that is as light as possible with plenty of room for self-regulation. The aim of the model law is to set down a minimum package of conditions that Member States involved must meet if electronic signatures are to be legally valid. It is left to Member States to decide what is right by national law if these conditions are violated. Additionally, the regulatory line of action that the same regulatory norms should apply to on-line activities as to off-line activities can be found here, in the sense that, wherever the applicable law sufficiently and clearly suggests a correct solution, no specific rules are made.[72]

2.5.4   World Intellectual Property Organization (WIPO)

The WIPO Copyright Treaty 1996 (WCT) and WIPO Performances and Phonograms Treaty 1996 (WPPT) take the regulatory approach that no distinction should be made between on-line and off-line situations, and that use of self-regulation should be made wherever possible. Both treaties establish basic standards of protection of copyright and related rights in the on-line environment, such as the Internet. Enforcement of copyright law is, to a large extent, trusted by using technology. According to the WIPO treaties, in aiming to prevent unauthorized access to and use of creative works, Member States may take suitable legal measures if technical security measures are abused.

In its recently adopted medium-term plan for WIPO program activities, WIPO has indicated that its main objective continues to be maintenance and further development of the respect for intellectual property throughout the world through co-operation with and among WIPO Member States and all other stakeholders.[73] This is to be achieved by creating an enhanced understanding of the contribution of Intellectual Property (IP) to human life through economic, social, and cultural development, and, in particular, by assisting developing countries in their capacity building for greater access to, and use of, the IP system. Consequently, WIPO has set the following strategic goals for the coming four-year period:[74]

- promotion of an IP culture;
- development of balanced international IP laws which are considered to be responsive to emerging needs, effective in encouraging innovation and

---

[72] Dutch Ministry of Justice 2000, p. 59.
[73] See <http://www.wipo.int/about-wipo/en/dgo/pub487.htm#introduction>.
[74] Idem.

creation, and sufficiently flexible to accommodate national policy objectives;

- provision of consistent and customised assistance to Member States in developing national or regional IP systems, including legal infrastructure, institutional framework, and human resources;
- enhancement of global protection systems to make them more easily accessible and affordable to all stakeholders, in particular; and
- further streamlining of the management and administrative processes within WIPO.

2.5.5 World Trade Organization (WTO)

Established in 1995 to deal with the rules of trade between nations and consisting of about 148 member countries, the World Trade Organization (WTO) is the global international organization for international trade. As a result, the topic of e-commerce in many respects has become important to the WTO over the past years. In May 1998, the Declaration on global e-commerce adopted by the Second (Geneva) Ministerial Conference urged the WTO General Council to establish a comprehensive work program to examine all trade-related issues arising from global e-commerce. At this Ministerial Conference the decision was taken not to impose customs duties on electronic transactions. However, this decision expired at the 1999 Seattle Ministerial Meeting, but has been continued under the Doha Declaration established in 2001. The Doha Declaration states that WTO members will continue this practice until the 5th Ministerial Conference in September 2003.

2.5.6 International Telecommunication Union (ITU)

Founded some 135 years ago and consisting of about 189 members, the International Telecommunication Union is an international, intergovernmental organization within the United Nations system, where governments and the private sector co-ordinate global telecommunications networks and services. The activities of the three Sectors of the Union (Radiocommunication (ITU-R), Telecommunication Standardization (ITU-T), and Telecommunication Development (ITU-D)) cover all aspects of telecommunications, from setting global standards that facilitate interoperability and interconnectivity of equipment and systems to adopting operational procedures for wireless services and designing program to improve the telecommunication infrastructure in the developing world.[75] All ITU Recommendations are non-binding, voluntary agreements. In the last decade, developments such as the liberalization and deregulation of the telecommunication sectors in many countries, technological and economic convergence, and changes in the way telecommunication services are delivered, have caused changes in the Union's client base, with traditional ITU members looking at ITU to provide new services placing greater emphasis on policy development and regulatory guidance.

---

[75] See <http://www.itu.int/aboutitu/overview/role-work.html>.

In 1996, ITU initiated the World Telecommunication Policy Forum (WTPF), an informal international gathering convened on an *ad hoc* basis to harmonize telecommunication policies on issues beyond the domain of any single country. The first World Telecommunication Policy Forum on Global Mobile Personal Communications by Satellite (GMPCS) systems took place in Geneva. A result of this meeting has been the first international standard for Universal International Free Phone Numbers (UIFN). In 1997, ITU adopted the First Memorandum of Understanding to restructure the Internet. In 1999, it became the founding member of the Protocol Supporting Organisation of the Internet Corporation for Assigned Names and Numbers (ICANN PSO).

In December 1996, ITU organized its Sixth Regulatory Colloquium on Regulatory Implications of Telecommunications Convergence, focusing on convergence in telecommunications services, multimedia distribution, and multimedia content, and on the evolution of the Internet. In light of these developments of convergence a central question for the experts was how regulation should change. According to the Colloquium participants, regulation needed to be transformed to support market solutions if necessary corrected by means of regulatory intervention to achieve legitimate public objectives. A trend was observed that institutions and policies relating to telecommunications that are determined at the international and global level, were beginning to supersede national policies and regulatory practices. However, national governments were acknowledged to continue to have a central regulatory role in some specific areas, namely, in the management of the radio spectrum (to assure equitable allocation of frequencies among competing services and to limit interference), promotion of minimal technical standards if needed to ensure universal compatibility of systems, and, for many countries, the promotion of national social objectives for information content.[76]

In 2002, the ITU held its quadrennial treaty review conference, the Plenipotentiary Conference. During this Conference, a series of Internet-related policy proposals was discussed, focusing on the management of Internet domain names and addresses, Internet security, and multilingual domain names. In the policy negotiation efforts, the US delegation turned out to be successful in ensuring that the international legal definition of basic telecommunications was not expanded to include the Internet, government control over commercially negotiated Internet charging arrangements was not imposed, and a shift in Internet domain name and management responsibility from ICANN to the ITU did not take place.

2.5.7 Preparations of the World Summit on the Information Society (WSIS)

The acknowledged combined development of a global digital revolution caused by emerging ICT as well as an emerging global digital divide between those people

---

[76] Lips, Frissen and Prins 1998, p. 154.

benefiting from this revolution and those who have remained unhooked so far, brought the ITU, to hold a World Summit on the Information Society (WSIS) and place it on the agenda of the United Nations. In December 2001, UN General Assembly Resolution 56/183 endorsed the holding of this Summit in two phases, the first from 10 to 12 December 2003 in Geneva, and the second from 16 to 18 November 2005 in Tunis.[77] The objective of the Geneva Summit would be to lay the foundations for the Summit with a Declaration of Principles and a Plan of Action. The Tunis Summit would monitor and evaluate progress on the Action Plan and devise an Agenda that would target goals for achievement by 2015.[78] The UN General Assembly invited ITU to assume the leading managerial role in the Executive Secretariat of the Summit. It further recommended that preparations for the Summit would take place through an open-ended intergovernmental Preparatory Committee, or 'PrepCom', that would define the agenda of the Summit, decide on the modalities of the participation of other stakeholders, and finalize both the draft Declaration of Principles and the draft Plan of Action.[79]

Based on an exploratory research exercise of important declarations of principles and reports on ICT and the information society published in the last decade, Sarrocco[80] concludes an enabling regulatory environment, a favourable investment climate, and co-operation and funding of the international community to be fundamental elements for the overall development of the information society. She points out that, although it is difficult to define an 'adequate enabling regulatory environment', given that each country has different needs and a different level of development, some basic requirements for the development of the information society can be indicated, including:[81]

- an appropriate policy adapted to the new demands of the information society, and transparent and non-discriminatory regulation, to favor investment in telecommunication technology, mobilization of new resources, and participation of private enterprises in ICT development;
- co-operation, at international, regional, and national levels, co-ordination of efforts, exchange of information, transfer of technology and knowledge and sharing of experiences and best practices.

Sarrocco indicates that all the declarations examined have recognized the necessity of policy and regulatory reform, which could imply market liberalization, the introduction of private investment and the creation of independent regulators.[82] Moreover, a reform could entail a reorganization of the old regulatory framework in

---

[77] <http://www.itu.int/wsis/basic/about.html>.
[78] <http://www.itu.int/wsis/basic/un-summits.html>.
[79] <http://www.itu.int/wsis/basic/background.html>.
[80] Sarrocco 2002.
[81] See *supra* n. 80, at p. 10.
[82] Ibid.

order to better deal with new ICT regulatory issues and problems. Various declarations around the world indicate the need for more flexible regulation, which should be adaptable to the rapid development of new ICTs and to growing private sector involvement (e.g., the ECOSOC Ministerial Declaration 2000, Art. 11; the ESCAP Round Table 2002;[83] the Buenos Aires Declaration 1994; the Valletta Declaration 1998; Okinawa Charter, 2000).[84] This would not only imply the lifting of existing regulatory obstacles, but also the existence of a stable and transparent ICT regulatory environment. However, as a 'one-size-fits-all' solution is not deemed to be possible according to the Okinawa Charter, it would be critically important for developing countries in particular to adopt coherent national regulatory strategies.[85]

At the WSIS PrepCom 2 Meeting in Geneva in February 2003, one of the presenters during the Enabling Environment Roundtable meeting, Kuner, pointed to the development of the legal infrastructure of the information society being at a critical juncture. He perceived a paradox of traditional governmental ICT regulation to have reached its limits, on the one hand. At the same time the need to spread the benefits of the information society more broadly. Kuner observed that, since the mid-1990s, the world had had several years of experience in establishing a legal and regulatory framework for the information society through the following means:[86]

- international treaties;
- international harmonization efforts;
- regional legal instruments;
- national laws;
- self-regulatory instruments, codes of conduct, etc.

In his opinion, the only way forward would be co-operation between the various actors who create and use the information society, namely, governments, businesses, and users and in doing so, keeping in mind the lessons that have learned so far. Kuner noted the following important lessons:[87]

- *Lesson 1*: Attempting to create markets through regulation for products or services that no one wants is not very effective (e.g., European regulatory framework for Third Generation (3G) mobile telephone networks; various directives, national laws, model laws, etc., dealing with Public Key Infrastructure (PKI) for electronic signatures;

- *Lesson 2*: A new regulatory initiative should be based on an actual need rather than purely on theoretical considerations. Consequently, the problems

---

[83] (ESCAP), 2000 New Delhi Paragraph I-1(1)d and II-5.
[84] See *supra* n. 80, at p. 10.
[85] See *supra* n. 69, Art. 14.
[86] Kuner 2003.
[87] Idem.

that have been encountered in practice and the solution that a regulatory initiative would offer should be identified, and those who actually use the technology at issue should be consulted. Moreover, regulators should avoid creating parallel legal structures for on-line and off-line situations wherever possible. Kuner observed that existing legal instruments can often deal with many of the issues that arise in the electronic environment as well (e.g., electronic contracting).

- *Lesson 3*: Co-ordination of governmental and regulatory initiatives is critical. Kuner indicated that nearly every regulatory issue is presently worked on by some international body, as well as at the national level. Consequently there is a need for co-ordination of and co-operation between such initiatives, in order to avoid duplication and conflicts.

- *Lesson 4*: A better connection should be made between the scope of regulation and the possibility of enforcing it. Kuner observed the trend of an increasing number of international jurisdictional disputes in the on-line world. In his opinion, too few national or regional legislators take into account the fact that they may have an effect beyond national borders.

In preparation of the WSIS, another exploratory effort was undertaken by the UN Economic Commission for Europe, the UNDP for Europe, and the CIS. They constructed a joint vision on the ten main directions for developing the information society, both in the sense of developing a knowledge-based sustainable economy and bridging the digital divide. Based on a collection and integration of principles established by several internationally prominent policy exercises of the recent past,[88] these UN organizations defined the following ten core, Fundamental Principles of the Information Society to provide an agreed framework for identifying the critical factors and dimensions of policy performance for information societies around the world:[89]

- Principle 1: Public rights to information;
- Principle 2: Legal, regulatory and policy environment;
- Principle 3: Access: development of infrastructure;
- Principle 4: Networked learning, education and training;
- Principle 5: Affordability and other users' issues;

---

[88] In particular: the Okinawa Charter 2000; the 9 action points of the G8 Genoa Plan of Action; the e-Europe 2005 Action Plan of the EU and the e-Europe+Plan for the candidate countries; the OECD Guidelines on e-commerce, on security of information systems, etc.; the 10 fundamental principles on e-commerce of the ICC, BIAC, etc.; the 'Knowledge-Based Economy Indicators' of the Centre for International Development at Harvard University; the Digital Opportunity Report by UNDP, Markle Foundation, and Accenture.

[89] The 10 Fundamental Principles of the Information Society, available at <http://www.un-az.org/undp/Doc/10fpEN.doc>.

- Principle 6: e-Government: more effectiveness and accountability;
- Principle 7: e-Business: more competitiveness and better jobs;
- Principle 8: e-Society: support of local communities;
- Principle 9: National e-Strategies;
- Principle 10: The international dimension of the information society; the role of e-policy dialogue at the regional level.

Principle 2, the legal, regulatory, and policy environment of the information society, was perceived to be essential to provide access, consolidate ICT infrastructures, promote ICT applications, and ensure data protection. According to the UN organizations,[90] it would be important for the ICT regulatory framework to recognize the role of the private sector and therefore to promote entrepreneurship and enterprise development. The conviction was that over-regulation should be avoided and users should be protected with regard to privacy and security. Choice, individual empowerment, self-regulation and industry-led solutions should be favored under the ICT regulatory framework, and freedom of the press and the media should be guaranteed. Moreover, it was indicated that interoperability should be facilitated within an international voluntary and consensus-based environment for standard setting.[91]

With Principle 10 of the Fundamental Principles of the Information Society, the authoring UN organizations acknowledged ICT developments to be important for international integration at a global, regional, and sub-regional level, but at the same time requiring support and guidance from the international community in relation to the promotion of ICT standards and norms, the transfer of know-how and technical assistance, and the exchange of experience and identification of best practice.[92] In order to mainstream information society developments, a systematic approach to national policies had to be promoted, bringing together different policy domains in a consistent ICT regulatory framework. E-strategies therefore needed the highest level of national political commitment and needed to be tailor-made to the specific requirements of each country. Consequently, Principle 9 on national e-Strategies indicates that governments all over the world should commit themselves to developing comprehensive information society strategies.[93] In the eyes of the authors, weaker countries should be supported in the development of such e-Strategies. The regional dimension would be most appropriate to promote the exchange of experience on national e-Strategies, identify best practice, monitor performance, and engage in peer dialogue and reviews.

---

[90] Ibid.
[91] Idem.
[92] Idem.
[93] Idem.

2.6 General ICT Regulatory Starting Points: Some First Observations

Looking at regulatory lines of action in various countries and international organizations, several similarities may be detected. In the last decade a general development could be observed in ICT regulatory approaches towards the uptake of technological developments in society. The first policy views on ICT developments (e.g., US Federal Government, Singapore, Japan), for instance, show the preference for a largely unregulated ICT environment, with the private sector determining (market) regulation. By that time, in most countries around the world, more traditional sectors of the emerging ICT environment, such as the telecommunications sector and the broadcasting sector, were still largely regulated by national governments. In order to further promote and develop new ICT developments, many national governments and international organizations decided to develop a coherent ICT policy strategy to create a competitive, transparent environment for newly emerging on-line activities. As it was often unclear whether these on-line activities should be treated as a unique technology or 'like technology' (which, in the latter case, often become subject to government regulation), national governments and international governments initially took a reserved position to be able to learn about the characteristics of 'on-line' activities, particularly also compared to similarly appearing 'off-line' practices.

A few years later, when the Internet had become more embedded in daily societal life, a general trend could be observed that the newly emerging on-line environment was acknowledged by many governments and international organizations to be 'too important not to regulate': certain fundamental societal norms and values are considered of such importance that they need to be protected in the on-line environment as well. With this shift in regulatory thinking about the developing on-line environment a general shift in ICT regulatory approach can be recognized towards 'co-regulation', or a balance between market regulation, (industry) self-regulation and regulation by governments and international bodies. Depending on the substance of the ICT regulatory issue of concern, but also on the feasibility of law enforcement regarding a particular ICT regulatory issue, protection was offered by 'soft' regulatory means, such as self-regulation, or by 'hard' regulatory measures embedded in legislation.

In thinking about and deciding upon ICT regulatory measures to take, the following similar ICT regulatory lines of action or, what may be called 'ICT regulatory starting points' can be recognized in the ICT policy and regulatory approaches of various national governments and international organizations.

– *Regulation should be technology neutral*: to be found in, e.g., the US framework for global e-Commerce, the US Electronic Signatures in Global and National Commerce Act, Recommendation 22 of the 1997 EU Ministerial Conference in Bonn, Singaporean ICT-regulation, strategic priority No. 5 of the Australian Federal Government, the conclusion of the OECD Ministerial Conference in Ottawa in the field of electronic authentication.

- *What holds off-line, should also hold on-line*: to be found in, e.g., the US Electronic Signatures in Global and National Commerce Act, Recommendation 22 of the 1997 EU Ministerial Conference in Bonn, electronic notarization systems in Japan, Japanese legislation on electronic signatures, illegal content transmission over ICT networks under the current Japanese obscenity and libel laws, the Electronic Transaction Act in Singapore, the Singapore Evidence Act, the Australian Electronic Transaction Act, compliance of on-line activities to the Australian Privacy Act and the Copyright Amendment Bill, UNCITRAL, the G8 Okinawa Charter, the WIPO treaties.

- *Self-regulation should be the starting point*: to be found in, e.g., the US framework for global electronic commerce, Recommendation 19 of the 1997 EU Ministerial Conference in Bonn, European private law: Codes of conduct, the e-commerce monitoring system of 350 watchdogs from the private sector in Japan, the European Commissions Green Paper on Illegal and Harmful Content on the Internet, OECD Ministerial Conference in Ottawa, UNCITRAL, G8 Okinawa Charter, WIPO treaties.

- *ICT-related regulation should be accomplished at an international level*: to be found in, e.g., Recommendation 46 of the 1997 EU Ministerial Conference in Bonn (Recommendation 59 of the same EU Ministerial Conference puts this regulatory point of departure into perspective), the Council of Europe's Convention on Cybercrime, the EU regulatory framework for electronic communications services, the action principles of the Japanese government, the efforts of the Singapore government towards harmonization of cross-border e-commerce laws and policies and harmonization of intellectual and copyright laws, OECD Ministerial Conference in Ottawa, the WTPF on Global Mobile Personal Communications by Satellite systems, UNCITRAL.

However, we may observe several developments in the same policy and regulatory documents presented above that would put these general ICT regulatory starting points into perspective by means of specifying them, challenging them or, in some cases, even changing them:

- With regard to the regulatory starting point that '*regulation should be technology neutral*', some developments in the opposite direction may be observed, namely, technology-specific regulation to be able to better deal with the new ICT environment. An example can be found in Singapore in the technology-specific legislation adopted with the aim to offer greater protection to potential abuses of computer systems (the Computer Misuse Act).

- Regarding the potential ICT-regulatory adage '*What holds off-line should also hold on-line*', the US Electronic Signatures in Global and National Commerce Act expressed the awareness that this regulatory starting point might imply different, instead of similar regulatory measures for the on-line world in comparison with existing off-line regulations. In addition, the European Commission's Green Paper on Illegal and Harmful Content on the Internet even indicated the general difficulty of the enforcement of off-line rules in an on-line environment. In the European Directive on electronic commerce, a slightly different solution to the on-line situation has actually been chosen in imposing less far-reaching liabilities on the Internet provider than on comparable professional groups in the off-line world. Also with regard to copyright issues, the European Commission has chosen to propose specific, i.e., technology-dependent legislation for the Internet. In Japan, too, the desire to have more control over on-line content, which, in fact is legal but perceived to be harmful to the youth, has led to new legislation to regulate sexual content on the Internet. Another international organization that has treated electronic transactions differently compared to 'physical transactions' is the WTO, by means of not imposing customs duties.

- So far, the general ICT regulatory line of action of '*Self-regulation as the starting point*' seems to have known two major adaptations in several countries. First, this general ICT regulatory starting point may have become more subtle in the sense that various forms of self-regulation can be indicated at present (for instance, codes of conduct, watchdogs from the private sector, technological means, ratings, filters, parental supervision, seals of approval, fact sheets, ADR). Second, a shift in regulatory approach towards this adage may be acknowledged to the effect that it is no longer being perceived as a starting point for regulation, but as an additional regulatory means to legislation (for instance, in Singapore, Australia) or even as a complementary regulatory means (OECD Ministerial Conference in Paris).

- With regard to the ICT regulatory starting point '*ICT related regulation should be accomplished at an international level*', not only international or even global harmonization efforts can be recognized in the policy documents described above, but also, at a less ambitious level, different forms of international co-operation. Examples in this respect are bilateral joint statements of national governments to develop common approaches and co-operate in the promotion of e-commerce (e.g., Australia with Japan, Korea, China, and Canada) and co-operation efforts at an international regional level towards the further development of e-commerce activities (for instance, the Asia-Pacific Economic Cooperation). Besides, by means of introducing a Country of Origin principle (i.e., the physical location of the supplier determining who has jurisdiction and responsibility for law enforcement), national legislation can in fact be made applicable in an international regulatory context (see, for example, the EU Directives on electronic commerce and electronic signatures, the action principles of the Japanese government). Moreover, experiences with the Council of Europe's Convention on Cybercrime even show that an international harmonization of legislation concerning activities in the on-line world may not be viable due to national legislative characteristics. The policy issue of child pornography however turns out to be an exception in this respect.

The ICT policy documents presented above therefore shed some doubts on the extent to which these similar ICT regulatory starting points may be treated as general principles for ICT regulation. To learn more about the pros and cons of treating these ICT regulatory lines of actions as such, a closer look will be taken at each of the ICT regulatory starting points set out above in the next chapters of this volume.

Chapter 3
WHAT HOLDS OFF-LINE, ALSO HOLDS ON-LINE?

Maurice Schellekens

3.1 INTRODUCTION

The starting point that is the title and subject of this chapter is sometimes used as a guideline for dealing with regulatory problems which the emergence of ICT presents to society. In this chapter, I will try to delineate what meanings can be attached to the starting point, where it comes from, how it applies, and in what cases it applies. Based on these analyses, I will turn to the question of whether the starting point is useful.

3.2 WHERE DOES IT COME FROM?

In the beginning, the Internet was the exclusive domain of academics and especially academics in the exact sciences. It was their spot where they could imagine themselves far away from regulators, policy makers and other interfering nitwits. They did not need these persons and were perfectly able to take care of their own affairs. The Netiquette that was formulated by cybernauts was more than enough. The 1990s saw the rise of commercial Internet providers. The Internet became known and available to other users. It also became more commercial. The broad public was not just interested in the peaceful potential of the Internet. The perceived and actual risks of the Internet became much more apparent. These (perceived) risks lay at the basis of claims of policy makers and lawyers pertaining to the regulation of the Internet.

From the very beginning, the Internet users were very opposed to the interference by the outsiders (policy makers and lawyers) with the Internet. They proclaimed that the law was not applicable to the Internet. They saw no advantage in applying the law to the Internet. In their view, such application could only lead to trouble. A number of events possibly confirmed the fear of the Internet users.

The American legislator was the originator of one such events, when it announced the Communications Decency Act (CDA). According to this Act, 'indecency' on the Net would be banned. The concept of indecency was not well thought through

B-J. Koops, et al. (Eds), Starting Points for ICT Regulation
© 2006, ITeR, The Hague, and the authors

and it was clear that the freedom of speech would be further curtailed on the Internet than the existing legislation did with respect to utterances in the off-line world. This Act, which stemmed from a conservative senator, exuded an atmosphere of the 'Internet as a danger for the existing moral order.' The provision concerned was declared unconstitutional by the Supreme Court a few years later (see also chapter 2 of this Volume). It is striking that the opponents of the Act appealed to treatment equal to the off-line situation, where indecent utterances were not unlawful.

The dealings of the Scientology Church also inspired some with the thought that the law had better not be applied to the Internet. In the 1990s, the Scientology Church regularly availed itself of legal means for suppressing (Internet) speech that was not to its liking. The idea that laws could be an obstacle to bringing to light the true facts about the Scientology Church was simply not understood, and caused considerable turmoil amongst cybernauts.

Last but not least, also the Internet Service Providers – almost all Internet users right from the early beginnings and mostly technicians – came under legal fire. Courts handed down decisions that held ISPs liable for the utterances of their subscribers. The most well-known is probably *Stratton Oakmont* v. *Prodigy* in which provider Prodigy was held responsible for making available a news message that was libelous against a broker firm. The older case of *Playboy* v. *Frena* was also considered to be little positive towards ISPs: the court held that the operator of a bulletin board directly infringed the copyrights of Playboy. Furthermore, voices from outsiders were heard to the effect that the decisions were too kind for ISPs and that severe duties of care should be imposed on ISPs with respect to the information offerings of their subscribers.

The examples mentioned above show the extent of separation from the traditional off-line world. In 1996, John Perry Barlow proclaimed 'A Declaration of Independence of Cyberspace.'[1] In this declaration, the Internet is described as a space that is beyond the powers of governments. The following quotation is from the first and fifth section:

'Governments of the Industrial World, you weary giants of flesh and steel, I come from Cyberspace, the new home of Mind. On behalf of the future, I ask you of the past to leave us alone. You are not welcome among us. You have no sovereignty where we gather.

…

You claim there are problems among us that you need to solve. You use this claim as an excuse to invade our precincts. Many of these problems don't exist. Where there are real conflicts, where there are wrongs, we will identify them and address them by our means. We are forming our own Social Contract. This governance will arise according to the conditions of our world, not yours. Our world is different.'

---

[1] <http://www.eff.org/~barlow/Declaration-Final.html>, accessed in September 2004.

The credibility of this viewpoint was increased by the influential article by Johnson and Post 'Law and borders. The rise of law in cyberspace', published in the Stanford Law Review. They concluded:

> 'Global electronic communications have created new spaces in which distinct rule sets will evolve. We can reconcile the new law created in this space with current territorially based legal systems by treating it as a distinct doctrine, applicable to a clearly demarcated sphere, created primarily by legitimate, self-regulatory processes, and entitled to appropriate deference but also subject to limitations when it oversteps its appropriate sphere.'[2]

All in all, this 'turning away' from the established order presents a somewhat one-sided view of a reality that had its shady aspects. Internet users do for example not need much encouragement to make unauthorized use of copyrighted materials, such as software, music, and certain graphic depictions. As a consequence of views stating that the law is not applicable to the Internet, Internet users may feel justified not to bother about law and copyright at all. In view of such civil disobedience, an answer of the governments was to be expected. The governments devised the starting point that is the focus of attention in this chapter: what holds off-line, also holds on-line. It had to be stated once and for all that the Internet is part and parcel of society, in which legal rules must be adhered to.[3] The Netiquette was simply not sufficient: its 'rules' were susceptible to multiple interpretations and its means of enforcement were too limited. Libel in a news group can be just as detrimental as libel committed by traditional media. Swindle committed by means of an Internet shop makes its victim lose money just as a traditional swindle would. Child pornography on the Internet is the result of child abuse, which is as serious as abuse for other purposes.

What holds off-line, also holds on-line is therefore a bold statement that must counterweigh claims for separatism of the pioneers of the Internet that saw their relative independence melt away by the desire to regulate. The starting point therefore has its roots in a period in which relations between the Internet community and the legislator were characterized by polarization and ignorance of the interests and concerns of the parties involved.

If the starting point is placed in a somewhat more favorable perspective, a certain concession to the Internet community can also be observed. Legislators will not try to subject the Internet to more severe norms than are applicable in the off-line sphere. Not less, but also not more than in the off-line sphere! A certain tendency towards reconciliation can therefore be observed.

By now, the relations between the two groups is somewhat normalized. The sharp edges of the opposite views have worn off and the desire to stubbornly hold a

---

[2] Johnson & Post 1996, pp. 1399-1400.

[3] See, for example, Kamerstukken II [Parliamentary Papers], 1997/98, 25880, no. 1-2, p. 106 (Dutch policy document entitled: 'Legislation for the Electronic Highways'). This development was echoed in the literature. Perhaps the most prominent article was Goldsmith 1998.

resolute viewpoint has nearly disappeared. In this respect, the starting point has therefore lost its function, but that does not say anything about its validity.

In the second half of the 1990s, the starting point appeared in the following policy documents. In Bonn in 1997, the EU ministers issued a joint declaration about global information networks. They addressed the issue of the starting point as follows: 'Ministers stress that the general legal frameworks should be applied on-line as they are off-line. In view of the speed at which new technologies are developing, they will strive to frame regulations which are technology-neutral, whilst bearing in mind the need to avoid unnecessary regulation.'

In a Memorandum entitled 'Legislation on the Electronic Highway' (1998), the Dutch government stated that the same norms have to be applied on-line as are applied off-line. Two years later (in 2000) the government watered the starting point considerably down. The Dutch Minister of Justice stated: 'I am of the opinion that in international consultations, the Netherlands must be receptive to a differentiation of the starting point that the same holds off-line and on-line. The level of protection however must be equivalent off-line and on-line. It remains a starting point that the Internet is not a domain where other values and norms hold than in the physical society.'[4]

In the G8 Okinawa Charter on the Global Information Society, the following declaration can be found:

> 'Promote consumer trust in the electronic marketplace consistent with OECD guidelines and provide equivalent consumer protection in the on-line world as in the offline world, including through effective self-regulatory initiatives such as on-line codes of conduct, trustmarks and other reliability programs, and explore options to alleviate the difficulties faced by consumers in cross-border disputes, including use of alternative dispute resolution mechanisms.'[5]

The UK government does not seem to distinguish between the starting point of technology-neutrality and the 'off-line = on-line' starting point, as is apparent from one of its UK e-principles:

> 'Regulation should be technology neutral in its effects. The effects of the offline and on-line regulatory environments, including the criminal and civil law, should be as similar as possible. There may be occasions when different treatment is necessary to realize an equivalent result.'[6]

The US-Government does not embrace the starting point, as is exemplified by the following phrase from the 1997 US Framework for global electronic commerce:

---

[4] Unofficial translation of Kamerstukken II, 1999/2000, 25880, no. 10, p. 13.

[5] Okinawa Charter on Global Information Society, 2000, <http://www.dotforce.org/reports/itl.html>.

[6] <http://www.e-envoy.gov.uk/publications/guidelines/eprinciples/>.

'Electronic commerce faces significant challenges where it intersects with existing regulatory schemes. We should not assume, for example, that the regulatory frameworks established over the past sixty years for telecommunications, radio and television fit the Internet. Regulation should be imposed only as a necessary means to achieve an important goal on which there is a broad consensus. Existing laws and regulations that may hinder electronic commerce should be reviewed and revised or eliminated to reflect the needs of the new electronic age. [7]

3.3   WHAT DOES IT MEAN?

3.3.1   On-line and off-line

In the starting point this chapter is dedicated to, the focus is on the distinction between off-line and on-line. Some reflection on the topic soon shows that it is far from easy to indicate how the two concepts can be demarcated. The question can be viewed from two, not necessarily disjunctive, perspectives: the data transport perspective and the communication perspective. From the data transport perspective, the following issues are relevant. In the first place, how does data transport take place, by moving the material support on which the data are affixed or by sending the data over a wired or wireless network? In this chapter, the meaning of on-line is restricted to the latter. This means that postal networks fall into the 'off-line' category.

Having established that an on-line network concerns 'carrierless' transport, the second step is to distinguish between digital and analogous data transport. It must be remarked, however, that analogous data transport is increasingly being replaced by digital data transport. The digital/analogous dichotomy is losing significance. Often data transport consists of a consecutive chain of analogous and digital transport of the 'same' data, making it difficult to label it either as analogous or as digital. Therefore, this distinction will be ignored for the purpose of this book. The most important traditional example of analogous data transport, the telephone network, is slowly but surely being digitalized. The telephone network therefore falls in the 'on-line' category.

If networks are regarded from a communication or application perspective, the following criterion becomes relevant: interactivity. For the purpose of this book, non-interactive services are considered to be off-line. This distinction between interactive and non-interactive network services places traditional radio and television in the off-line environment. Surfing on the Internet is considered to be on-line: a web surfer determines in his own time and place to visit certain sites.

---

[7] White House 1997.

3.3.2 **What holds off-line, also holds on-line**

The starting point that sounded so simple appears to hold several meanings. The following four can be distinguished:

- The starting point as a statement: the Internet is not beyond the law. In principle, the law is applicable in on-line situations.
- The starting point as a method: in finding the law for an on-line situation, it is always necessary to first try and find an off-line rule that can potentially serve as a template for the law in on-line situations.
- The starting point as a substantive guideline: as such, the starting point has two elements: (1) if off-line and on-line cases are equivalent, they must be dealt with similarly and (2) if they are not equivalent they must be dealt with differently to the extent of their inequivalence.
- The starting point as a policy statement: for meeting extra-legal policy objectives, a familiar legal context must be created for the on-line environment. The starting point expresses this necessity, but it does not say anything about how this objective is to be reached. The law is a black-box, and its output needs to meet certain requirements.

The starting point as a statement
The starting point as a statement has lost its function. Nobody seriously contends that the law is not applicable to on-line situations.

The starting point as a method
One method of finding the law that is applicable in on-line situations is going back to existing law, that is applicable to off-line situations. With the help of the usual methods for finding the law, such as *interpretatio per analogem* and *interpretatio a contrario*, can be determined, whether an existing rule can be used in the on-line situation(s) and, if so, what rule that is. This of course also means that the process of finding the law can result in finding that no existing rule offers a suitable template for the on-line situation(s). It must be noted that this result is only reached *after* the suitability of existing rules has been tested.

The starting point as a substantive guideline (I)
As a substantive guideline, the starting point tells us that an off-line rule offers the best starting point for governing on-line situations. This may mean that an existing (off-line) rule must be used on-line. What off-line rule that is or how it is to be applied the starting point does not say.

The starting point as a substantive guideline (II)
The starting point could also mean that the result or level of protection to which application of an off-line rule gives rise must be recreated for the on-line situation(s).

This may be done by applying the same rule to on-line situations that would be applied in the equivalent off-line situation, but not necessarily. It may also be that an altogether other rule is needed to recreate the 'same' result for the on-line situations. In the latter case, it could be said that the on-line and off-line situations are inequivalent and that they must be treated differently to the extent of their inequivalence. It is of course difficult – if not impossible – to say *in abstracto* how another rule can be formulated that nonetheless gives rise to an equivalent result.

The starting point as a policy statement
In this view, the starting point links up with the idea that comparable functionalities must be dealt with under comparable legal conditions. How this ideal situation, viz. that laws do not stand in the way, or at least not more than is the case off-line, is to be reached is left open. In particular, the starting point does not say that existing off-line rules are the means to reach the desirable result. The law is a black-box and its output must meet certain requirements. It is for lawyers to figure out how the requirements can be met. In this view of the starting point, the law is seen, for example as an obstacle to the realization of a policy. For instance, the law is the reason that it is impossible to contract on-line or that certain investigations by the authorities are forbidden. The starting point then functions as a motivation for taking away the legal obstacles.

In this chapter, the emphasis will be on the second and third meanings of the starting point. The validity of the starting point in its first meaning (the law is applicable to the Internet) is so self-evident that it is not or hardly contested. The fourth meaning is less interesting because it bypasses the difficult part: what is a comparable legal context?

The second and third meanings of the starting point are much more legal in nature. The application of the starting point is motivated as follows:

- The application of the starting point enhances the system of law and, in its wake, the clarity of the law. If phrased negatively, it could be said that the creation of separate divisions in the law (a part that deals with off-line cases and a part that is applicable to on-line cases) would create additional sources of disputes. As we have seen before, it is far from easy to find an unambiguously criterion for the division the two spheres. It is therefore not recommendable to make an unnecessary division a subject of legal dispute. In this respect, it is worthwhile to mention Art. 12 Dutch directives for the legislator that explicitly names reduction of sources of dispute as one of the directives that rule makers must adhere to.[8] This reason for application of the starting

---

[8] It reads (my translation): 'A regulation is designed in such a way that it provokes as little dispute as is possible. To reach this goal, the following measures can be taken:
a. The number of decision situations to which the regulation gives rise, must be reduced to the absolute minimum;

point appears to be mainly relevant if the starting point is to be applied at the level of rules of law. To put things in perspective, the following can be said. The aim to keep the law as simple as possible and to subsume new cases as much as is possible under existing rules is a commendable undertaking. However, it cannot be denied that simplicity and accessibility of regulations are often viewed as side issues. It is rather the dynamism of the problem to be regulated that, to a much higher degree, is determinative for the decision to opt for legislation and for the form this legislation eventually takes.

- The application of the starting point makes that the law is 'neutral' with respect to the on-line and the off-line spheres. Neither the one nor the other is favored by the law, this neutrality may not always be accomplished by applying the same rules to both situations. Here, application at the level of the results of regulation may be needed. The idea of neutrality can be inspired by ideas about the role of law in society. One idea may be that it is not up to lawyers to decide or unduly influence what technology is to be used. The idea of neutrality may also be inspired by the idea that there should not be undue interference between the spheres as a side effect to application of the objective law. The off-line sphere may undergo influence from the way in which the law deals with the on-line sphere. For instance, a weak copyright in the on-line sphere may affect positions in the off-line sphere. Freely available music on the Internet may very well exert a negative influence on the sale of music CDs. By the same token, the thinking about the off-line sphere can influence the way we think about on-line relations. The American Communications Decency Act (CDA) forbade 'indecent' utterances on the Internet, while such utterances were simply allowed in the off-line sphere. The inequality in the way the law deals with the two spheres has always been a strong argument supporting the unacceptability of the provision. The starting point may help prevent or alleviate negative interferences that are thought to be undesirable. Here again, things must be put into perspective. Although neutrality is in general a desirable aim, there can be policy reasons to diverge from it. The EU Directive on electronic commerce, for example regulates the liability of providers of services of the information society that has no equivalent in the off-line sphere with respect to traditional information intermediaries. The thought behind this regulation is that the information society is going to bring economic advantages and that the liability of Internet Service Providers could delay this development. Here, it is clear that the idea of economic stimulation (which is deemed relevant on-line, but not or less so off-line) has been the reason for the divergence from the starting point.

---

b. If administrative fines are made possible, binding tariffs are being determined;
c. The nature and the extent of allowances, provisions, and other benefits must be described as accurately as is possible in generally applicable legal rules or in well-publicized policy rules.'

- By going back to old law, authority can be bestowed upon the law as it is applied to or proposed for the on-line sphere. The law as it is applied to the on-line sphere is often newly 'found' law. It is customary in legal argumentation to base the acceptability of a proposed application of the law, a proposed adaptation of the law or newly found law on the argument that it already lies within existing law, that it is, in a manner of speaking, handed down by existing law. In this context, it is useful to point out the relevance of precedent in the law and to methods of legal reasoning such as reasoning by analogy or reasoning *a contrario*. They illustrate the meaning lawyers attach to old law in accepting new law. In particular with respect to the legislator, Article 6 section 1 Dutch directives for the legislator can be referred to: new statutory regulation is only brought in after the necessity to do so has been established. In other words, old law is all right, new law has to be legitimated. Application of the starting point increases the acceptability of the law that is to be applied to the on-line sphere. The law for the off-line sphere can already build upon a high degree of acceptation. The starting point is that the law for the on-line sphere must, as much as is possible, build on law that has proven its worth already. To put the above in perspective, the following can be stated. Building on old law can endow new law with authority, but building on existing law is not always feasible for this purpose. This is especially the case if the application of old law gives rise to unjust results in the on-line sphere. In that case, it may be better to opt for a new regulation that does give rise to equitable results. 'Equity' may bestow new law with authority as well.[9] Building on existing law is therefore not an exclusive means to that end.

3.4   HOW DOES IT APPLY?

The starting point has hitherto been described in a rather abstract way. In order to create a feel for the practical application of the starting point, hereinafter two cases are elaborated. The first case concerns the liability of ISPs and the second case concerns private use of works protected by copyright.

Liability of ISPs for libelous utterances of their subscribers

Is an ISP responsible for the content its subscribers place on the Internet? I will analyze the problem with respect to liability of the ISP for libelous utterances of his

---

[9] The following issue could be of interest as well. If it is accepted that the starting point is mainly directed at the legislator, this restriction is even more relevant. Because of their respective constitutional roles, the legislature rather than the courts are in a position to create law that hardly fits in with existing law or not at all. Innovation of the law is more the domain of the legislator; a court is responsible for evolution of the law.

subscribers. There are two ways to approach this question. The first method is to try and draw an analogy with a traditional information intermediary. The second approach is to try and build up a liability standard from general rules about liability.

The most predominant way is to model the liability of the ISP on the liability of traditional information intermediaries. This approach was strongly fuelled by two early cases in American case law: *Cubby* v. *CompuServe* (1991) and *Stratton Oakmont* v. *Prodigy* (1994). In these cases providers of electronic information services were tackled about libelous utterances that certain others had placed on their servers and which had therefore become accessible to their subscribers. In both cases, the analogy with traditional publishers and distributors was made. This approach is briefly substantiated in the *Cubby* case:

'CompuServe's CIS product is in essence an electronic, for-profit library that carries a vast number of publications and collects usage and membership fees from its subscribers in return for access to the publications. '

In both cases, the courts reiterate what the applicable standards of liability are when dealing with publishers and distributors. The following excerpt is drawn from the *Cubby* case:

'Ordinarily, "one who repeats or otherwise republishes defamatory matter is subject to liability as if he had originally published it." Cianci v. New Times Publishing Co., 639 F.2d 54, 61 (2d Cir.1980) (Friendly, J.) (quoting Restatement (Second) of Torts s 578 (1977)). With respect to entities such as news vendors, book stores, and libraries, however, "New York courts have long held that vendors and distributors of defamatory publications are not liable if they neither know nor have reason to know of the defamation." Lerman v. Chuckleberry Publishing, Inc., 521 F.Supp. 228, 235 (S.D.N.Y. 1981); accord Macaluso v. Mondadori Publishing Co., 527 F.Supp. 1017, 1019 (E.D. N.Y.1981).
The requirement that a distributor must have knowledge of the contents of a publication before liability can be imposed for distributing that publication is deeply rooted in the First Amendment, made applicable to the states through the Fourteenth Amendment.'

Once, it is clear what law applies off-line, the question is dealt with from which of the two models – the publisher or the distributor model – an analogy can be drawn to the modern day intermediaries (CompuServe and Prodigy). The criterion to be used for deciding what analogy is suitable is primarily the exercise of editorial control by the information intermediary. In the *Prodigy* case, this was formulated as follows:

'However, a newspaper, for example, is more than a passive receptacle or conduit for news, comment and advertising. [Miami Herald Publishing Co. v Tornillo, 418 US 241, 258.] The choice material to go into a newspaper and the decisions made as to the content of the paper constitute the exercise of editorial control and judgment (Id.), and with this editorial control comes increased liability. (See Cubby, *supra*) In short, the critical issue to be determined by this Court is whether the foregoing evidence establishes a prima facie case that PRODIGY exercised sufficient editorial control over its computer bulletin boards to render it a publisher with the same responsibilities of a newspaper.'

The next step is of course the application of the criterion and the analogy to the cases at hand. CompuServe had outsourced every involvement with the content to a company called DFA. The result the court came to was the following:

'While CompuServe may decline to carry a given publication altogether, in reality, once it does decide to carry a publication, it will have little or no editorial control over that publication's contents. This is especially so when CompuServe carries the publication as part of a forum that is managed by a company unrelated to CompuServe.
With respect to the Rumorville publication, the undisputed facts are that DFA uploads the text of Rumorville into CompuServe's data banks and makes it available to approved CIS subscribers instantaneously. CompuServe has no more editorial control over such a publication than does a public library, book store, or newsstand, and it would be no more feasible for CompuServe to examine every publication it carries for potentially defamatory statements than it would be for any other distributor to do so.'

In the *Prodigy* case, the same technique of comparing the modern day information intermediary to a traditional one was used. Prodigy even referred to the *Cubby* decision. However Prodigy's policy with respect to the information on its servers was somewhat different:

'The key distinction between CompuServe and PRODIGY is twofold. First, PRODIGY held itself out to the public and its members as controlling the content of its computer bulletin boards. Second, PRODIGY implemented this control through its automatic software screening program, and the Guidelines which Board Leaders are required to enforce. By actively utilizing technology and the man power to delete notes from its computer bulletin boards on the basis of offensiveness and "bad taste", for example, PRODIGY is clearly making decisions as to content (see, Miami Herald Publishing Co. v. Tornillo, *supra*), and such decisions constitute editorial control. That such control is not complete and enforced both as early as the notes arrive and as late as a complaint is made, does not minimize or eviscerate the simple fact that PRODIGY has uniquely arrogated to itself the role of determining what is proper for its members to post and read on its bulletin boards. Based on the forgoing, this Court is compelled to conclude that for the purposes of plaintiffs' claims in this action, PRODIGY is a publisher rather than a distributor.'

The line of reasoning that an ISP who does not exercise (editorial) control over the content is only liable if he actually knows of the libelous or otherwise unlawful content has become the predominant way of dealing with ISP liability. The very idea to draw analogies between traditional information intermediaries and their electronic counterparts is apparently considered so natural and self-evident that little effort is made to substantiate it. I want to show that it is not necessarily the self-evident, 'only' way.

In literature, a second approach has been described.[10] This approach starts off from the general open texture rule about due care in the Netherlands: one must not act against 'a rule of unwritten law pertaining to proper social conduct' (Art. 6:162 Dutch Civil Code).[11] The duty thus described may mean that in certain circumstances measures must be taken to prevent damage from occurring. In determining what measures befit, four factors can be distinguished: (1) the severity of the damage, (2) the probability of the damage occurring if the measures are not taken, (3) the nature and usefulness of the act that caused the damage and (4) the troublesomeness of the measures that are to be taken. From this general norm, the following rule can arguably be construed: to prevent damage an ISP must do what he can reasonably do. The rule that is thus devised has not the 'all-or-nothing' character that the liability rules of the first approach have. After all, an ISP can easily perform more checks than no checks at all. At the same time, the approach does not force the ISP to perform exhaustive checks if this exceeds the resources it can reasonably allocate to checks. This does, however, highlight the difficulty of this approach. How can the extent of the ISP's duties of care be delineated? At this point, the elaboration of the approach is lacking. There is a need to formulate precisely what checks may be expected from the ISP, those formulations must be generally accepted and the ISP must be able to show (make verifiable) that it has fulfilled its duties of care. In the absence of such elaboration, it is difficult for ISPs to follow the second approach. In view of the predominance of the first approach, an ISP would take a great risk in following the second approach. In performing some checks, an ISP takes responsibility for the contents if viewed from the perspective of the first approach. At the same time, its checks are not exhaustive, so there is a risk that some 'wrongs' remain undiscovered. If someone claims that the ISP is liable for such a wrong, the ISP is defenseless in terms of the first approach: it has taken responsibility for 'the' contents and therefore falls in the publisher model of liability.

The second approach however is not completely dead and buried. Traces from this approach can be found in the recitals preceding the Directive on electronic commerce:

'(47) Member States are prevented from imposing a monitoring obligation on service providers only with respect to obligations of a general nature; this does not concern monitoring obligations in a specific case and, in particular, does not affect orders by national authorities in accordance with national legislation.

(48) This Directive does not affect the possibility for Member States of requiring service providers, who host information provided by recipients of their service, to apply

---

[10] Kaspersen 1996, p. 11.
[11] Haanappel 1990.

duties of care, which can reasonably be expected from them and which are specified by national law, in order to detect and prevent certain types of illegal activities.'

So hope is not given up that one day a more differentiated body of duties of care of ISPs is brought about.

The first approach is a clear application of the starting point: what holds for traditional intermediaries also holds for ISPs. One drawback of this approach is the tacit assumption that an ISP is just another information intermediary. At the same time, the low threshold of access to the Internet and the diminishing intervention of intermediaries could give rise to the thought that an ISP is actually quite another type of animal. However, the approach leaves little room to accommodate such differentiation.

The second approach is perhaps not an application of the starting point. Starting from the most general formulation of liability, the open texture formulation of Article 6:162 Dutch Civil Code, liability can be molded much more to fit the specific characteristics of ISPs. However, such a tailor-made solution is not readily available. Given the highly complex situation and ISPs that understandably are wary to accept responsibility for contents in view of the predominance of the first approach, this approach is in arrears compared to the first approach. The arguments for stating that there is a relevant difference between ISPs and traditional intermediaries do not seem to be strong enough to discard the first approach. This example of the liability of ISPs therefore shows that a problem of whether or not to opt for application of the starting point has a dynamism of its own. I think here above all of the complexity and difficulty to define duties of care from nothing. This constitutes a problem that becomes all too apparent if the starting point is not applied. To some extent, it could be said that the application of the starting point is an admission of weakness. More positively formulated, you could say that non-application of the starting point entails the risk of a legal vacuum.

Exemption for private use in copyright
In most copyright laws, the copyright holder possesses the exclusive right to reproduce his work. Everybody who wants to reproduce the work must, in principle, obtain the consent of the right holder. In most European states, however, copyright law has an exemption for private use. A copy for strictly private use may be made, even without the consent of the right holder. With the advent of the Internet, the following question became relevant: should this exemption be retained for on-line situations? This is a question about which much controversy exists. You could say that, on-line, the balance of power has shifted towards the consumer of copyrighted works. Works circulate freely on the Internet and can be viewed, read, and downloaded by anyone. The difference between primary exploitation (making money for the copyright holder) and secondary uses (which can be left unattended) is slowly fading in on-line situations.

Those in favor of abolishing the exemption for on-line situations contend that the exemption was a compromise for want of a better solution in off-line situations. Private copying cannot be licensed, neither can it be enforced. The market fails and the law 'surrenders' to the reality of the market by allowing what cannot be enforced anyhow: private copying. This solution is acceptable from the – not uncontested – perspective that private copying is '*de minimis*' in off-line situations. It is held not to prejudice the normal exploitation of a work or the justified interests of the right holders. In short, the advocates of 'abolition' state that there are only pragmatic reasons for the exemption. Because there are 'only' pragmatic reasons for the exemption, it can easily be abolished for on-line situations. Even more so, on-line, the prejudice to right holders has become much more realistic. On-line private copying is no longer *de minimis*; so the exemption cannot be maintained. An example of this approach can be seen in the Database Directive.[12] With respect to copyright protection of databases, the directive instructs Member States to restrict exemptions for reproduction for private purposes to non-electronic databases (Art. 6 section 2):

> '2. Member States shall have the option of providing for limitations on the rights set out in Article 5 in the following cases:
> (a) in the case of reproduction for private purposes of a non-electronic database;'

On the other hand, those in favor of retention of the exemption for on-line situations see a much more principled role for the exemption. Enforcement of a copyright in case of private copying would mean interference with the private life of the consumer of the work, which is of course undesirable. Furthermore, the exemption serves the free flow of information, because an unimpaired application of copyright law may very well have a rigidifying effect on the handling of information. The legislators making the exemption have thus balanced *in abstracto* the interests of the copyright holder against the principles of respect for the private life and the information freedoms. They have apparently found that, within the confines of the exemption, the latter must be given priority. The issue of protecting the principles mentioned is of course still valid in on-line situations, so the exemption has to be maintained. For a possible prejudice to right holders, a solution can be found in the form of a levy on blank carriers or in technical protection measures. An example of this approach can be seen in the Copyright Harmonization Directive (Art. 5 section 2).[13]

---

[12] Directive 96/9/EC of the European Parliament and of the Council of 11 March 1996 on the legal protection of databases, OJ 1996, L 077 , pp. 20-28.

[13] Directive 2001/29/EC of the European Parliament and of the Council of 22 May 2001 on the harmonization of certain aspects of copyright and related rights in the information society, OJ 2000, L 167, pp. 10-19.

'Member States may provide for exceptions or limitations to the reproduction right provided for in Article 2 in the following cases:

[...]

(b) in respect of reproductions on any medium made by a natural person for private use and for ends that are neither directly nor indirectly commercial, on condition that the right holders receive fair compensation which takes account of the application or non-application of technological measures referred to in Article 6 to the work or subject-matter concerned.'

The example of private copying shows that diverging views about a rule and its ratio have an enormous impact on the view of whether off-line and on-line situations are equivalent. The diverging views can even lead to fragmented legislation.

The example also clearly shows the difference between the starting point as a method and the starting point as a guideline in substantive issues. The abolitionists and the retentionists come to diverging results, but the method they use is similar. If you want to know what law holds on-line you first go the law for off-line situations and try to figure out whether the on-line situation is equivalent or inequivalent in view of the particular rule. It seems that the starting point as a method has almost universal validity.

3.5   WHEN SHOULD IT APPLY?

In dealing with the question of when the starting point should apply the second and third meanings of the starting point must be distinguished.

The starting point as a method
Using the starting point as a method has advantages and disadvantages. The starting point as a method seems to be very much in the nature of the legal profession. Law develops in an evolutionary way, not in a revolutionary way. New situations need to be carefully assessed. Existing law can shed light to the way in which interests, values, and principles interrelate. Since the law has to function amongst people, they have to be won over for a new legal solution. An assessment of the existing law can then give important arguments for arguing that the existing solution is or is not appropriate for the on-line situation.

The point could be raised whether the tendency to go back to existing law does not slow down the innovation of the law. In going back to the law as it exists, new solutions do not get a fair chance. Innovation of the law in the form of rethinking a problem from a blank sheet of paper may take place insufficiently or not at all.

The starting point as a substantial guideline
The phrasing of 'What holds off-line also holds on-line' hides one important aspect. There are many rules that hold off-line and the starting point does not say what off-line rule should be applied (directly or analogously) in an on-line situation. In other

words, under what conditions is an on-line situation in relevant legal respects equivalent to the off-line situation in which an envisaged rule applies. Is for example an e-mail message comparable to a letter (which is protected under Art. 13 Dutch Constitution and Art. 10 ECHR) for the purposes of the telecommunications secret or is it comparable to a post card (which is not protected)?

The question of equivalence between off-line and on-line situations is thus relevant for the purpose of determining the 'reusability' of existing rules in on-line situations. In other words, for the starting point to be workable, there must be clarity about the determination of what rule is, directly or analogously, applicable to an on-line situation. This problem is akin to the traditional problem of a court in determining whether a rule can be applied analogously to a situation to which it is not directly applicable. Perhaps the fact that the question of applicability is raised by the off-line and on-line dichotomy is only one special case amongst all cases in which a court may be confronted with the problem of analogous application. Knowledge of how courts deal with analogous application is therefore relevant for our problem as well. The central question is whether for the purposes of the rule, the on-line situation is equivalent to the off-line situation addressed in the rule. This begs the question in what respect the off-line and on-line situations have to be equivalent. In other words, what is the criterion for determining the equivalence of the off-line and on-line situation? It is of course the rule, its interpretation, and its rationale that provide the criterion. In order to distil the criterion from the rule, a number of methods for its interpretation can be used:

- In the first place, one can resort to linguistic arguments: does the meaning of the words used allow that the new situation is subsumed under the rule? Is for example an electronic signature a signature?
- Secondly, systematic arguments may be brought forward, such as the comparable range of application, the comparable field of law, or the comparable underlying legal principles.
- Finally, teleological arguments can be put forward: are comparable goals to be met.[14]

If situations are equivalent, the rule written with off-line situations in mind is still valid for on-line cases. If one sees a rule as the outcome of a balancing of values, interests, and principles by the legislator, it could be said that the balance is still valid in case of equivalence. Given the validity of the balancing, it is not said that the rule can be applied without a problem. Perhaps the rule is formulated in a technology-dependent way or perhaps other 'details' make the rule ineffective, unenforceable, or unusable in the on-line situation. This may mean that the rule has to be reformulated or that additional rulemaking is required. In such cases, the underlying norm is usable, but the concrete specification of the norm in the form of the rule has to be adapted.

---

[14] Kloosterhuis 2002, p. 144 and pp. 171-172.

In case of application by a court, it is relevant whether a rule that lends itself for analogous application (the balancing is also valid for the on-line situation) can be applied analogously. In criminal law, for example, the legality principle blocks analogous application of criminal provisions. Some examples may further clarify this.

Example: cases equivalent, rule effective
In the US, a distributor of information, such as a bookshop, is as a rule not liable for defamation occurring in the information it distributes, unless it has exercised editorial control. Can this rule of distributor liability be applied to ISPs? It can be argued that the case of the ISP and that of the distributor are equivalent, since neither of them exercise editorial control, i.e., the criterion for equivalence. A court can furthermore easily apply the rule on distributor liability to ISPs, given the predominant position of courts in the formation of the law in common law countries, such as the US.

Example: cases equivalent, rule ineffective but salvageable
For an agreement of hire-purchase to be valid in Dutch law, the form requirement of a signed writing must be fulfilled (Art. 7A:1576i Dutch Civil Code). The case of the on-line hire-purchase agreement is equivalent to the off-line situation: the criterion for equivalence is the need to protect the weaker party. This need also exists on-line. However, the rule is ineffective because it is formulated in a technology-dependent way: a handwritten signature is impossible on-line and whether an electronic document qualifies as a writing is uncertain. However, the rule can be salvaged: additional rules could state under what conditions an electronic signature and an electronic document must be considered equivalent to a handwritten signature or to a writing respectively. In the Netherlands, an Act stating under what conditions an electronic signature qualifies as a signature has received royal assent in 2003.[15] An Act about functional equivalence with respect to writings received royal assent a year later.[16]

---

[15] Wet van 8 mei 2003 tot aanpassing van Boek 3 en Boek 6 van het Burgerlijk Wetboek, de Telecommunicatiewet en de Wet op de economische delicten inzake elektronische handtekeningen ter uitvoering van richtlijn nr. 1999/93/EG van het Europees Parlement en de Raad van de Europese Unie van 13 december 1999 betreffende een gemeenschappelijk kader voor elektronische handtekeningen (PbEG L 13) (Wet elektronische handtekeningen), Stb. 2003, 199, i.e., the Dutch Electronic Signature Act.

[16] Wet van 13 mei 2004 tot aanpassing van het Burgerlijk Wetboek, het Wetboek van Burgerlijke Rechtsvordering, het Wetboek van Strafrecht en de Wet op de economische delicten ter uitvoering van Richtlijn nr. 2000/31/EG van het Europees Parlement en de Raad van de Europese Unie van 8 juni 2000 betreffende bepaalde juridische aspecten van de diensten van de informatiemaatschappij, met name de elektronische handel, in de interne markt (PbEG L 178) (Aanpassingswet richtlijn inzake elektronische handel), Stb. 2004, 210, i.e., the Dutch Act implementing the EU Directive on Electronic Commerce.

Example: cases equivalent, rule ineffective but repairable
Off-line, the privacy of correspondence is protected in the Dutch Constitution (Art. 13). Must the privacy of e-mail correspondence also be protected? The on-line case is equivalent: users of e-mail are vulnerable in the same way as off-line correspondents and need legal protection. However the existing rule is ineffective: Article 13 Dutch Constitution is formulated in a technology-dependent way. The rule can be repaired: reformulation of the rule can solve the problem.

Example: cases equivalent, rule ineffective but supplementable
Article 350 Dutch Penal Code criminalizes the intentional and unlawful destruction of physical property. This raises the question of whether the destruction of data is also a criminal offense. The answer is affirmative: the cases are equivalent, because considerations with respect to availability and integrity have equal validity with respect to physical property and data. However, the existing rule is ineffective: the criminal law requirement of legality blocks analogous application of criminal provisions on destruction of physical property to data. Supplementing the existing rule about destruction of physical property with a new rule on destruction of data (Art. 350a Dutch Penal Code) solved the problem.

Example: cases equivalent, rule ineffective but supplementable
Child pornography is a criminal offense on-line as it is off-line. However, on-line, the global character of the Internet complicates the enforcement of the law. Enforcement has come to depend on mutual assistance between law enforcement agencies in different countries. Requests for assistance, extradition, transfer of proceedings, and transfer of the execution of criminal judgments depend on the requirement of double criminality. In this respect, the fact that virtual child pornography (not involving 'real' children or the abuse of 'real' children) is not a criminal offense in some countries can become a stumbling block for mutual assistance. In the Netherlands, virtual child pornography has been criminalized.[17] A peculiarity in this case however is that off-line virtual child pornography is now also a criminal offense. In the opinion of the legislator, the off-line and on-line cases are equivalent after all.

Example: difficulty in determining equivalence
It is not always easy to determine whether two situations are equivalent or not. The law regulates relations between persons. Every person has his own position and interests, worthy of legal protection. A rule is, in one way or another, the outcome of a balancing of the interests involved. A rule has, for example, the rationale to protect one interest and in doing so, it takes account of other, flanking interests. The

---

[17] Wet van 13 juli 2002 tot wijziging van het Wetboek van Strafrecht, het Wetboek van Strafvordering en de Gemeentewet (partiële wijziging zedelijkheidswetgeving), Stb. 2002, 388, i.e., a Dutch Act amending the Penal Code and a few other acts.

relation between the interests or the way in which a balance can be found between conflicting interests on-line may be quite different off-line. It is not always easy to determine whether an on-line situation is equivalent to an off-line situation as regards the application of a rule. The Communications Decency Act can illustrate this point. This Act introduced a rule making indecent utterances on the Internet illegal. This rule was devised from the perspective of protection of minors against information that was deemed harmful for them. Creating the same level of protection on the Internet required perhaps a stricter rule than was applicable off-line. The Internet is arguably more easily accessible than the traditional media, it is not bound to a certain place for consultation and there does not exist a 'late evening' because the Internet is global. The actual risk of an infringement of the protected interests is therefore larger. A rule that affords an equal level of protection from the perspective of protection of minors may be unacceptable from the perspective of a flanking interest, such as the freedom of information. What perspective must be determinative?

Example: cases inequivalent
Theft of physical property is a criminal offense. Is the theft of data also a criminal offense?

The answer is negative because the cases are inequivalent: information freedoms are not at stake off-line. On-line they are, and criminalizing theft of data is a far from neutral measure from the perspective of the information freedoms. The balancing of interests, values, and principles therefore cannot be considered to be valid for the on-line situation. The basic norm, underlying the rule, cannot be applied *in digitalibus*.

Example: cases inequivalent
Off-line, opt-out protection is provided against unsolicited commercial communications. Should there also be opt-out protection against unsolicited e-mail? Both off- and on-line, the receiver must be protected against unsolicited commercial communications. However, on-line, the cost of spam has shifted from the sender to the receiver, thus weakening the position of the receiver. The opt-out rule no longer offers adequate protection to receivers and the cause lies at the heart of the rule, so the opt-out rule cannot be 'repaired'. Another rule is required, necessitated by a renewed balancing of the interests of senders (autonomy in conducting business activities) and the interests of receivers (being spared from annoyance and cost, the right not to be disturbed).

If the cases are not equivalent and no existing rule can be used in an on-line situation, a complicated situation arises. Two approaches are imaginable. In the first place, it is possible to state that the starting point does not concern this situation. Only if the norm underlying the rule is reusable in the on-line situation can the starting point function. If the norm is unusable, the starting point no longer applies.

This does not mean that there is no problem, it just means that the starting point is not of any help.

In the second place, a more differentiated approach could be taken. Such an approach does take into account what the reason is for the inequivalence of the cases. Two possibilities must be distinguished. In the first place, it is possible that not only the off-line norm cannot be used on-line, but that the reason for non-applicability also implies that the (rationale of the) off-line norm need not be realized in the on-line situation. In this case, it is generally enough to conclude that the off-line rule cannot be applied and that no new rule needs to be put in its place, at least, from the perspective of the off-line norm. An example can make this clear. Consider again the case of theft of data. Can the rule about theft of physical property be applied to 'theft of data'? The answer is negative. The reason is that copyright law already protects the economic interests in data, so the provision about theft need not be used for taking care of the economic interests of the data 'owner'. Even more so, it is undesirable that the theft provision is applied to data, because it does not take account of the fact that data constitute information and that the free flow of information is involved. Copyright law does take those considerations into account and can therefore be seen as an exhaustive regulation of the economic interests in data. Given this reason for the non-equivalence between theft of physical property and the theft of data, it suffices not to apply the theft provision to the theft of data. No additional rule needs to be created for realizing the rationale of the theft provision on-line.

The second possibility concerns the following. The off-line rule cannot be applied on-line, because the balancing of the interests, values, and principles involved and underlying the norm, cannot be considered to be valid on-line. However, the rationale of the off-line norm can still be considered to be valid for on-line situations. In such cases, it may not suffice not to apply the off-line rule, but a new rule may have to be formulated that can realize the rationale for the on-line situations.

Again an example can illustrate this point: consider the opt-out protection against unsolicited commercial mail. Opt-out is the prevalent form of protection off-line. Opt-out represents the balance that has been found between the interests of senders (autonomy in conducting business activities, low burden) and the interests of receivers (being spared from annoyance and cost, and realization of the right to be let alone) in the off-line context. However, the technology of sending on-line is completely different from the off-line technology in a relevant respect: on-line the cost of unsolicited mail has shifted from the sender to the receiver; after all, sending e-mail is very cheap. Downloading spam and having to separating wanted messages from unwanted ones, on the other hand, is expensive and annoying and costs a lot of time. It can thus be said that the position of the receiver has weakened and that the opt-out protection of the receiver has become inadequate on-line. For the on-line situation, opt-out no longer represents a valid balance between the interests of senders and receivers. The off-line and on-line situations are therefore not equivalent. It follows that saying that opt-out must not be applied on-line does not suffice. After all, doing away with opt-out protection would even further weaken the position of the receiver, who would then have no protection at all. It is clear that the reason for stating that the on-line and off-line cases are inequivalent implies that a new rule has to be devised for improving the protection of the receiver.

This brings us to the next problem area. If it is clear that the rationale of an off-line rule is still valid on-line and that it can only be realized by a new rule, how should the content of this rule be determined? More specifically, to what extent must the rationale (originating off-line) be determinative for the resulting rule? After all, the latter aspect is the translation of the starting point for this type of problem.

In this problem area, at least two sub-problems can be discerned. In the first place, what must be done to materialize the rationale on-line. In the opt-out example, it could be asked whether an equivalent level of protection of on-line receivers is reached by opt-in, or is a total ban on electronic commercial communications necessary? What are different, but nonetheless equivalent, levels of cost and annoyance for the receiver? How can the equivalence of the effects of the application of rules be determined? Is a lawyer 'equipped' to make such comparisons? Discussion is possible on this type of question; perhaps experts from other disciplines than the legal field are needed to shed light on certain aspects. In general, however, I think this question is resolvable.

However, the second sub-problem may be much harder to resolve: How far can you go in realizing the purpose? After all, it may appear that the 'cost' of realizing the rationale is much higher on-line. The word 'cost' can here be taken in a wide sense: cost is the strain on other interests, values, and principles involved in the type of case that is to be regulated. How much can the collateral cost of realizing the rationale be pushed up? Consider again the case of commercial communications. Suppose opt-in protection of on-line receivers is adopted.[18] It can then very well be argued that the senders are worse off on-line than off-line. On-line, they have to obtain the consent of the receivers, therefore making life hard for them. The fact that e-mail is cheaper than snail-mail may not be a real compensation. If a total ban on electronic commercial mail would be introduced the collateral cost would be even higher. The autonomy to conduct business as the sender sees fit would be enormously diminished. Here, an important drawback of the starting point becomes visible. Resolving this second sub-problem is a difficult problem, but the starting point does not provide clues as to how this question should be resolved. Perhaps this point can even be taken a bit further: the starting point should say nothing about this question, because it is not clear that the situation off-line always contains 'valuable information' for resolving this question on-line.

---

[18] Compare Directive 2002/58/EC of the European Parliament and of the Council of 12 July 2002 concerning the processing of personal data and the protection of privacy in the electronic communications sector (Directive on privacy and electronic communications), OJ L 201, 31/07/2002. In this directive, the European Commission opts for a so-called soft opt-in regime.

As a conclusion, the starting point as a substantive guideline tends to converge to the starting point as a method. General 'substantive' indications for when the starting point is to be applied are difficult, if not impossible, to conceive. Often, the only thing that can be done is finding an argument for application of an off-line rule or an off-line result to an on-line situation.

In policy documents, only few indications can be found about the scope of application of the starting point. The Dutch ILIS Memorandum addresses this issue explicitly. The Dutch government distinguishes four situations in which a need to divert from the starting point may exist.

- There are sometimes phenomena on the Internet that are truly new. I can agree with this 'exception', but the main question remains what a 'truly' new phenomenon is? The memorandum does not say anything about that and therefore runs the risk of being considered a *petitio principii*.
- The lack of trust in electronic judicial matters may require a specific legal framework, while equivalent issues in the physical world can be left for courts to decide. On the one hand, this position can be argued against. Increasing legal certainty by laying the law down in statutory rules is not a reason to make a statutory rule that diverts from what would have held if no statutory rule had been enacted. Increasing legal certainty and the starting point are not necessarily antipodes. On the other hand, it may be true that codifying the law can never be completely neutral. Codifying the law is changing the law.
- Harmonization of legislation can diminish on-line law enforcement problems, also in domains where comparable problems of law enforcement – emanating from differences in national legislations – do not exist off-line. The example of the criminalization of virtual child pornography is a case in point. Above, we saw however that what holds off-line has been assimilated to what holds on line.
- The desirability of specific forms of alternative dispute resolution in the electronic environment may entail the need for a specific legal framework.

3.6   How Can It Be Applied?

The starting point can applied in several ways. In the first place, it can be used by applying existing rules. The rules may have to be made technology-independent beforehand. In the second place, the starting point can be applied by designing new rules for on-line situations, in such a way that an equivalent 'result' is reached, when applied. Finally, it is possible to design new rules that are applicable to both off-line and on-line situations. The emergence of an on-line problem requires redesigning the rules for the equivalent off-line situation. A striking example is the new Dutch Intelligence and Security Services Act.[19] The government observed that un-

---

[19] Kamerstukken II, 1997/98, 25877, nrs. 1-2 (Wet Inlichtingen- en veiligheidsdiensten).

der the 'old' Act, the security services had the authority to inspect e-mail, while they did not have the authority to inspect traditional mail. In the new Bill, the government rectified the anomaly by introducing the authority to inspect traditional mail as well.[20]

A final point that has to be addressed is the question to whom the starting point is addressed. Apart from the cybernauts to whom it had to be made clear that they were not in a fifth dimension in which there is no place for the law, the starting point is primarily meant for the legislator. In analyzing the meaning of the starting point for the legislator, it can be helpful to structure its meaning along the lines of a number of layers. When a legislator is confronted with a problem in on-line situations, it first has to investigate whether an existing legal norm can be applied. If that is possible, it need not take any further action or it must, in a legal-technical sense, update the norm. The starting point is then of course applied on the level of the legal rules. If an existing norm cannot do the trick, the legislator will have to devise a new legal norm. The legislator will now have to investigate how the law in general deals with the interests concerned and to what arguments weight has been accorded. It must now follow the lead of the existing law in order to formulate a new legal rule that is as much as is possible in line with existing law. In this case, the emphasis is rather on the interests worthy of legal protection, and the arguments and considerations that are involved in the regulation of the matter in hand.

Application of the starting point by a court is also possible within certain boundaries. Of course, a court will have to apply a rule that is tailored to on-line situations if the occasion arises, irrespective of any other rule that may give another substantive norm for a comparable off-line situation.

If a court is asked to render a decision in a case that has arisen in an on-line setting, while no rule is available that is directly applicable, a real problem of law finding has emerged. In such cases, the court will have to interpret existing law or have to construct new law based on existing law. This could be considered to be an application of the starting point. However, this is nothing new. The court only takes the existing law as a starting point.

What is the meaning of the starting point for self-regulation? The question presupposes that self-regulation is a uniform concept. There are many forms of self-regulation. It may for example serve the purpose of a further concretization of norms of conduct. Sometimes self-regulation is preferred over state-legislation, because the parties concerned have more knowledge about and insight in the subject-matter that is to be regulated. Application of the starting point in such cases is less evident. Self-regulation gains authority especially, because of it being nicely embedded in the 'on-line' practice of the parties concerned. Regulation is then neatly tailored to the particularities of that practice. Fitting in with what holds in some off-line practices need not be the most compelling guideline.

---

[20] See also Koops 2002.

3.7   WHAT SHOULD IT MEAN?

The starting point as a method
Whether existing regulation can be used to solve problems that present themselves
on-line requires a thorough analysis and much discussion. It is impossible to bypass
this analysis and discussion by simply appealing to the starting point. So how should
new ICT-developments be dealt with? In the short run, they may lead to legal uncertainty. A discussion is most likely to be started about the best legal approach
towards challenging technical developments. The starting point must then function
as an invitation to engage in such a discussion. Apart from an invitation, the starting
point is also a means to structure the discussion. Proponents of the starting point
can defend the adequacy of the existing legal framework. Perhaps even more, important is that other participants in the discussion oppose against the starting point.
They have to come up with innovative legal approaches. In that way, they will
counterbalance the preponderance of the legal professionals towards traditional
solutions. Unconventional ideas have a better chance in an open discussion.

The starting point as a substantive guideline
If one thing has become clear in this chapter, it is that the starting point is not
universally valid. Careful analysis of individual situations has shown that the starting point can be applied in some situations and not in others. Does this mean that
nothing general can be said about the application of the starting point and that it can
never be more than an invitation to engage in a meticulous analysis of the situation
concerned? Or is it possible to indicate some 'bigger lines' along which the application of the starting point can be explicated? In order to discover a possible further-
reaching applicability of the starting point, two approaches are possible. In the first
place it is possible to try and determine general factual circumstances in which the
starting point must be applied and circumstances in which it is better not applied.
The Dutch government indicated a number of circumstances in which the starting
point should not be applied. However, this only gives a very partial image of the
scope of application of the starting point, especially, since it is formulated negatively: circumstances in which the starting point may not be used. An overall idea
of the circumstances in which the starting point is to be applied is therefore not
given. In the second place, it is possible to explore the starting point in more depth
and try and find out what its rationale is, what deeper values are to be protected by
the application of the starting point. Legislators can weigh a value against other
values and interests when reflecting on the regulation of on-line situations. A starting point itself cannot be weighed, but the values it stands for can. If the starting
point is read against the background of the value(s) it stands for, its meaning becomes more specific and easier to apply. The value may shed light to how the starting point is to be applied. If the reason to apply the starting point is to bestow new
law (building on existing legal practices) with authority or if the reason is to introduce distinctions between legislation for off-line and on-line situations only if such

is absolutely necessary, the starting point is much more a drafting guideline for the legislator. In such a case, the starting point does not imply that the values and interests involved indicate that the same should hold on-line and off-line. If the reason to apply the starting point is to avoid discrimination between off-line and on-line situations, it becomes an instrument to reach technology neutrality. If the reason to apply the starting point is to afford a similar level of protection on-line as is the case off-line, the starting point has a much more limited scope of application. It only regards situations in which legislation seeks to protect a weaker party.

Policy documents discussing the starting point have hitherto paid little attention to the rationale of the starting point. The rationale of the starting point has therefore remained far from clear. This rather makes it a means to an unknown end. It is this lack of purpose that makes that the importance of the starting point is put into perspective. It even raises doubts on its very legitimacy. The way forward with the starting point is to open up the discussion about its rationale. Given a rationale, it will be easier to handle the fact that it is not universally valid, because the rationale will shed light to the relative value of the starting point in a discussion. The question is however whether the starting point has not already been abandoned by too many policy makers for such an exercise to be worthwhile.

Chapter 4
SHOULD ICT REGULATION BE TECHNOLOGY-NEUTRAL?

Bert-Jaap Koops

> 'Attempts to be technology-neutral should be interrogated,
> lest in our blindness we reduce democratic protections
> and oversight under the deterministic veil of progress.'
> (Ian Hosein & Alberto Escudero Pascual)

4.1   INTRODUCTION

This chapter analyses the starting point that ICT regulation should be technology-neutral. It starts with an overview – far from exhaustive – of e-policies that mention this as a starting point. Then I will analyze the various components of the starting point and its potential meanings, in order to better define what is meant by the starting point. After a description of three illustrative cases that show how the starting point works in practice, I will try and give a set of criteria to elaborate the starting point; these criteria can be used to assess whether and to what extent the starting point can be put into practice in concrete cases. Subsequently, I will indicate how the starting point could be effected in such cases. I will end with an assessment to what extent the starting point is a useful one, and I will redefine it in the light of the analysis given to formulate the starting point in its most useful form.

4.2   WHERE DOES IT COME FROM?

The starting point that ICT regulation should be technology-neutral features in many policy documents and legislative instruments throughout the world.

It is mentioned in the two general policy documents on ICT regulation that have been formulated by the Dutch and UK governments. The Dutch policy memorandum Legislation for the Electronic Highways of 1998 formulates it as follows:[1]

> 'Technology-independent legislation is to be preferred. This usually establishes an
> equality between the 'off-line world' and the 'on-line world'. Also, technology-inde-

---

[1] LEH Memorandum 1998, p. 12. All translations in this chapter are mine.

B-J. Koops, et al. (Eds), Starting Points for ICT Regulation
© *2006, ITeR, The Hague, and the authors*

pendent legislation can better withstand technological turbulence. However, sometimes technology-dependency will be called for instead. For instance, the need for legal certainty could be a reason for technology-dependent legislation.'

The follow-up memorandum on internationalization formulates it somewhat differently: 'A starting point is that rules are technology-neutral. In formulating technology-independent rules, however, it should be considered whether these guarantee
sufficient legal security.'[2] Whereas the Dutch statements emphasize the formulation of the rules, the UK e-Principles stress the effects of regulation:[3]

'Regulation should be technology neutral in its effects. The effects of the off-line and
on-line regulatory environments, including the criminal and civil law, should be as
similar as possible. There may be occasions when different treatment is necessary to
realise an equivalent result.'

Besides these general e-policy documents, the starting point is mentioned in numerous other e-policy documents. For example, in the European Union, the 1997
Bonn Ministerial Conference declared: 'Ministers stress that the general legal frameworks should be applied on-line as they are off-line. In view of the speed at which
new technologies are developing, they will strive to frame regulations which are
technology-neutral, whilst bearing in mind the need to avoid unnecessary regulation',[4] and the 2001 Green Paper on Consumer Protection mentions 'a comprehensive, technology-neutral, EU framework directive to harmonize national fairness
rules for business-consumer commercial practices.'[5] The G8 Okinawa Charter on
Global Information Society stated: 'We should ensure that IT-related rules and practices are responsive to revolutionary changes in economic transactions, while taking into account the principles of effective public-private sector partnership,
transparency and technological neutrality.'[6] And the World Summit on the Information Society (WSIS) declared a principle that the 'rule of law, accompanied by a
supportive, transparent, pro-competitive, technologically neutral and predictable
policy and regulatory framework reflecting national realities, is essential for building a people-centred Information Society.'[7]

The US Framework for Global Electronic Commerce of 1997 mentions under
principle 2 (Governments should avoid undue restrictions on electronic commerce):
'government attempts to regulate are likely to be outmoded by the time they are

---

[2] ILIS Memorandum 2000, p. 20.
[3] <http://e-government.cabinetoffice.gov.uk/assetRoot/04/00/60/79/04006079.pdf>.
[4] Recommendation 22 of the 1997 Bonn Ministerial Conference, *Ministerial Declaration*, <http:
//europa.eu.int/ISPO/bonn/Min_declaration/i_finalen.html>.
[5] *Green Paper on European Union Consumer Protection*, 2 October 2001, COM(2001) 531final.
[6] Okinawa Charter on Global Information Society, 2000, <http://www.dotforce.org/reports/
it1.html>.
[7] World Summit on the Information Society, *Declaration of Principles*, 12 December 2003, available at <http://www.itu.int/wsis/>.

finally enacted, especially to the extent such regulations are technology-specific.'[8] The Australian government has chosen as one of its strategic priorities to '[i]ncrease significantly the use of electronic commerce by Australian business'; a consequent key priority for action is to '[e]stablish a clear and consistent legal and regulatory framework which provides legal certainty while facilitating self-regulation and technology neutrality.'[9]

Apart from such explicit statements, many legislative instruments apply the starting point implicitly, for example, in the field of electronic signature regulation (see section 4.4.1).

It should be noted that there are also many ICT documents and laws that do *not* mention the starting point, and that many regulations and laws are quite technology-specific.

4.3   What Does It Mean?

4.3.1   'ICT'

ICT stands for Information and Communication Technology, that is, technologies that store, transmit, and/or process information and communication. Although the term can be read literally to include all kinds of information-processing technologies, such as printing presses, xerox machines, and abacuses, the term is generally used to indicate 'modern' or 'high' technology, in particular electronic data-processing technologies. Thus, ICT focuses on computers, telecommunications, and computer and telecommunication networks. The term is sometimes used as a virtual synonym for the Internet, but that is too restricted an interpretation. Even so, it is open to debate whether older forms of telecommunication should fall within the scope of 'ICT', in particular the Plain Old Telephone System (POTS) and telegraphy. In my view, there is no particular reason why we should exclude fixed telephony or even telegraphy from the scope of 'ICT' – they are, after all, communication technologies.

Incidentally, it is ironic that if, instead of 'ICT regulation', we speak of 'e-regulation' or 'e-principles', a technology-specific element is introduced. Whereas 'ICT' refers to information and communication technologies, that is, to technologies defined by their use (communication) or area (information), 'electronic' and 'e' refer to a specific technological means. As such, e-regulation is, in terminology at least, narrower than ICT regulation.

A telling example of the difference can be seen in the Dutch Computer Crime Act [*Wet computercriminaliteit*] of 1993, in which a definition of a computer was

---

[8] Clinton & Gore 1997, p. 4.
[9] NOIE 2000.

formulated. The original bill did not give a definition in the bill itself, but only a broad definition in the explanatory memorandum: a computer was described as 'any construction that has been technically designed for the storage, processing, or transfer of data.' The text continues: 'With the current state of the art in technology, it concerns the handling of data with electro-technical or optical means. In the near future, it may perhaps also cover biotechnological developments.'[10] However, at a later stage, parliament proposed to insert a definition in the bill itself: a computer was then defined as 'a construction designed to store and process data by electronic means.' The explanation of 'electronic' reads: 'The restriction to 'electronic' was suggested by the wish to exclude merely mechanically functioning information systems from the scope of the definition.'[11] The minister noted that this was a more technology-specific definition, since 'the explanation spoke of the biochip. It does not seem a difficulty that this now falls outside the scope. It [the biochip] is still so far in the future that it does not have to be taken into account in the definitions now.'[12] Now, some ten years later, bio computers and quantum computers still seem a long way off, so it appears that the legislator was right in this respect.

However, the need for a starting point for *ICT* regulation could be questioned in this respect. After all, similar problems are encountered in other areas of regulation. For instance, traffic law is generally based on a distinction between pedestrians, cyclists, and drivers of (motor) vehicles. The rights and duties of road users are closely related to the category they belong to. With the emergence of inline skates and the quickly growing popularity of people who travel on inline skates on the road, the legislator faces the problem of whether someone on inline skates is a pedestrian or a cyclist, or falls in a separate category altogether. It seems that in many countries, skeeler users are often treated as pedestrians in traffic law, but with the increasing numbers of inline skaters on the road and the speed with which they normally travel, this is an unsatisfactory solution. Therefore, traffic law should be updated to incorporate this new category of road users.[13] This example shows that even traffic law contains technology-specific elements. It could be argued that the idea that regulation should be technology-neutral is not specific to ICT regulation, but applies to regulation in general.

Therefore, the starting point is somewhat hypocritical: through its focus on ICT regulation, the starting point is itself technology-specific. This is not to say that the starting point may not be useful, though. Particularly in the area of ICT, with its high rate of development and its impact on many sectors of society, a specific starting point may be valuable that warns legislatures not to focus too much on specific developments.

---

[10] Kamerstukken II [Parliamentary Documents] 1989-1990, 21 551, no. 3, p. 6.
[11] Kamerstukken II 1991-1992, 21 551, no. 26.
[12] Handelingen II, 24 June 1992, 93-5868.
[13] See Remmelink 2000.

4.3.2 'Regulation'

Regulation roughly means controlling human or societal behavior by rules or restrictions. It can have many different forms: government regulation (laws and decrees), co-regulation, self-regulation and market regulation, or social regulation, etc.

Most of the documents that defend this starting point (see section 4.2) focus on *regulation* as the subject of the starting point; this is also called a 'regulatory framework'. A number of them refer to *rules* that should be technology-neutral, and some mention only *legislation*. Since the broad range of regulation also covers quite specific instruments dealing with specific technologies, for example, standardization and ministerial decrees outlining technical requirements, the starting point seems more appropriate for the higher-level forms of regulation.

The particular focus on regulation, rules, or legislation is related to the purpose that the starting point is put to (see section 4.3.5). In general, there are perhaps two different ideas that emerge from the difference in wording. One idea stresses that regulation in its broad meaning should be technology-neutral; this idea seems more related to a focus on the *effect* of regulation. The other idea emphasizes that legislation or legal rules should be technology-neutral; this is related to a focus on the *formulation* or *wording* of regulation.

4.3.3 'Technology'

The 'technology' part of 'technology-neutral' seems fairly straightforward. In the field of ICT regulation, it will usually refer to information and communication technologies. The emphasis, at least, will usually be that ICT regulation should not focus on specific forms of ICT.

However, this is not as logical as it might seem. On the contrary, from the point of view of the on-line/off-line starting point, it is stressed that ICT technologies should be regulated in the same way or to the same effect as pre-ICT technologies – although this depends on the meaning given to off-line/on-line (see chapter 3).

ICTs perform certain functions that, in some cases, non-ICTs can also execute. For instance, Dutch law penalizes eavesdropping with a 'technical device' [*technisch hulpmiddel*], and the corresponding investigatory power allows the police to eavesdrop with a 'technical device'. The explanatory memoranda seem to suggest that the term 'technical' relates more or less to ICT: they mention, for example, 'technical equipment' [*technische apparatuur*];[14] this suggests that eavesdropping by means of a champagne glass against the wall is not covered by this legislation. It is not obvious that there should be a difference between ICT and non-ICT in this respect, although there are arguments in favor of a distinction. For example, you cannot record a conversation with a champagne glass, but you can with ICT.

---

[14] Kamerstukken II 1996-1997, 25 443, no. 3, p. 3.

It is therefore open to debate what exactly 'technology' in 'technology-neutral' denotes. Does it mean technology in a very broad sense, that is, all forms of 'tech', including traditional technologies? Or rather technology in a restricted sense, such as 'hi-tech' or data-processing technologies, and computers?

An interesting question is why there should be a specific rule on *technology* neutrality. What is specific to technology that the law should not specifically refer to it? There are numerous other categories that the law should not specifically target: for instance, Western countries generally do not like gender-specific or age-specific laws, and they usually abhor race-specific laws. In fact, the starting point seems a specification of a general principle that regulation should not unduly discriminate, regardless of the object of discrimination.

Interestingly, non-discrimination regulation may also in effect lead to technology-specific provisions. The US Workforce Investment Act of 1998 provides that disabled people should have equal access to information as non-disabled people. As a result, 'the U.S. government specified the design and structure of thousands of Web sites by regulating their code' in great technical detail. 'A text equivalent for every non-text element shall be provided (e.g., via "alt", "longdesc", or in element content)', and '[w]eb pages shall be designed so that all information conveyed with color is also available without color, for example from context or markup.' Moreover, '[r]edundant text links shall be provided for each active region of a server-side image map.'[15]

4.3.4 'Neutral'

Most formulations of the starting point use the word 'neutral'. The first Dutch memorandum, however, mentions 'technology-independent' legislation; the second Dutch memorandum mentions both 'technology-neutral' and 'technology-independent' (see section 4.2). Perhaps there has been a shift from 'technology independence' to 'technology neutrality' in the thinking about ICT regulation. It is a significant difference, since technology independence seems a more far-reaching requirement than technology neutrality. Technology-independent regulation ought to abstract completely away from technology, whereas technology-neutral regulation might be closely related to or intertwined with technology, as long as it does not favor one specific technology over another. Thus, the choice of the term 'independent' or 'neutral' influences the meaning of the starting point.

The opposites should also be taken into account. Technology-independent regulation is opposed to technology-dependent regulation, but what is the opposite of technology-neutral regulation? The most likely candidate is 'technology-specific' regulation, as mentioned, for example, in the US Framework for Global Electronic

---

[15] Geist 2003, p. 349, quoting 36 CFR § 1994, 22 (2003) at (a), (c), and (e).

Commerce.[16] But depending on what exactly is meant by the starting point, the opposite might also be 'technology-favoring' or 'technology-stimulating', 'technology-driven' or 'technology-triggered' regulation. Hence, it is important to discuss the purpose of the starting point itself in order to know just what 'neutral' means.

4.3.5 'ICT regulation should be technology-neutral'

The statement that ICT regulation should be technology-neutral is used in policy documents and regulatory instruments in order to stress something. What is stressed, however, may not always be the same point. As a starting point for ICT regulation, the statement can be used in somewhat different ways. In this section, I will give several potential meanings of the starting point. These meanings are closely interrelated, of course, but they stress different points. There are roughly three potential uses of the starting point, having to do with the purpose of regulation, with avoiding certain side effects of regulation, and with general principles for the technique of law-making.

A. Purpose of regulation

A1. Regulating functions and effects, not means
Regulation is intended to achieve certain effects in society. In general, regulation aims at regulating people's behavior. It does not regulate the behavior of machines, except to the extent that machine behavior influences people's behavior. Moreover, behavior as such is not the point of regulation, it is rather the effect of behavior on society or on other people that is the focus of regulation. For instance, throwing a vase on the ground is unregulated if it is your own vase, but it is regulated if it is someone else's vase or a vase that belongs to a nation's cultural heritage, or if you happen to throw the vase at someone else's head. In other words, regulation generally is focused on the effects of actions, not on the actions or the means of the actions themselves.

This general focus of regulation represents one meaning of the starting point that ICT regulation should be technology-neutral. Regulation should not regulate the technology itself, but only the effects of technology use. This is particularly stressed in the UK wording of the starting point: 'Regulation should be technology neutral in its effects.' The functions of technologies can also be regulated, since these functions generally define the uses to which the technology can be put and hence the effects that can be achieved.

Of particular importance is exactly what effects must be regulated. For instance, in the case of regulating unsolicited commercial communications (also known as spam), an obvious aim may be to protect people from being bothered by messages

---

[16] See also Stuyt 1999.

they did not request nor wished to receive. But the extent of bother can vary for different technologies: telephone 'spamming' is physically distracting because it makes a noise, and facsimile 'spamming' is intrusive because it requires paper and machine time and thus costs money, whereas e-mail spamming does not distract physically nor does it cost as much as a fax. For that reason, legislatures have enacted different laws for commercial communications through different communications media, apparently considering that the effects of the technologies differ.[17]

This sense of the starting point of regulating effects is especially relevant to 'protective' or to 'fundamental' regulation. One major function of law is to protect fundamental rights and values in society, and for this purpose, regulation is not concerned with *how* this is achieved, but only *that* it is achieved.[18] For the other major function of law, to order society and to ensure that it runs smoothly, the starting point is less relevant: ordering things will often require regulating specifically how things are to be done.

So, if the starting point is used in this sense, it is usually applied in areas like criminal law and constitutional law, which particularly focus on legal protection. For instance, the Dutch legislator applied it in this sense in the Computer Crime Act: 'Generally, in the wording of the law, we have tried to abstract as much as possible away from the current state of the art in technology and instead to connect to the societal *function* of the new technical possibilities'[19] (BJK: my italics).

In areas of the law that focus more on ordering things, such as large areas of civil and administrative law, the starting point is not usually applied in this sense. It is either not applied at all, because technology-specific regulation is most suited to achieve the required order, or it has a different meaning.

This is of course not to say that it is never used in civil or administrative law, since also in those areas, protective regulation is may be necessary. Many regulations of electronic signatures, for example, in which the functional approach has gained particularly wide acclaim over the years, clearly use the starting point in the functional sense, in order to safeguard the values of, for example, protecting weak parties or enhancing legal certainty (see section 4.4.1).

---

[17] See 47 USC § 227, protecting consumers from unsolicited fax messages but not from unsolicited e-mail messages, *Aronson* v. *Bright-Teeth Now LLC*, Pa. Super. Ct., No. 1179 WDA 2002, 5/8/03. See also Art. 12 of Directive 97/66/EC of 15 December 1997 (privacy in the telecommunications sector, now replaced by Directive 2002/58/EC), that created an opt-in regime for automated calling machines and and faxes, and an opt-out regime for all other means of direct marketing.

[18] Note, however, that there may be indirect ways in which means influence results. Legal protection is often based on the possibilities that technology offers to achieve the protection. For instance, in the early nineteenth century, it was not feasible to require the presence of an investigating judge in every search, since, in certain districts, it took several days for the judge to reach a place by horse. The resulting law – a search may be conducted without a judge being present – is seemingly 'technology'-neutral but is effectively dependent on travel technology, and the provision may continue to exist long after it has become possible for judges to be on the spot in an hour.

[19] Kamerstukken II 1989-1990, 21 551, no. 3, p. 4.

A2. What holds off-line should also hold on-line

The starting point that ICT regulation should be technology-neutral is closely related to the starting point that what holds off-line should also hold on-line. In a sense, it is the means to achieve the goal of the other starting point: if regulation is technology-neutral, then it will establish equivalence between the off-line and on-line worlds. The close relationship is mirrored in several documents that assert the starting point of technology neutrality. For instance, both the UK e-principles and the Bonn Ministerial Conference declaration see technology neutrality as a means to achieve the goal of off-line and on-line equivalence (see section 4.2).

This meaning is similar to the first meaning of the starting point (A1): if the effects of a technology are regulated rather than the technology itself, the regulation will usually establish functional equivalence between 'off-line' and 'on-line' technologies. It does not always work the other way around: in order to achieve functional equivalence between 'off-line' and 'on-line', it may be necessary to adapt the on-line regulation to specific technologies. As the UK e-principle says: 'There may be occasions when different treatment is necessary to realise an equivalent result.'[20] An example would be the regulation of Digital Rights Management (DRM) systems (see section 4.4.3). This is a technology-specific or technology-driven regulation, which aims to create the same copyright-law effect in the on-line era as it had in the off-line era. Whether it achieves that aim is another matter; the power balance is now arguably tipped deeper towards copyright holders than it has ever done before.

Thus, different treatment of off-line and on-line technologies may result in technology-specific regulation, but this is done to achieve the stated goal of the regulation: similar societal effects of 'off-line regulation' and 'on-line regulation'. Thus, when the starting point of technology neutrality is used in this sense, it is secondary to the off-line/on-line starting point.

B. Consequences of regulation

The starting point may also be used in a less substantive way. Rather than being related to the immediate purpose of the regulation, it can also be understood as a requirement to consider the potential consequences of the regulation. In this sense, the starting point is mainly a negative requirement: to avoid undesirable consequences of regulation.

B1. Regulation should not discriminate against certain technologies

As noted in section 4.3.3, the starting point might be regarded as a specification of a general principle that regulation should not unduly discriminate. Regulation ought to be value-neutral with respect to technology: it should not favor some specific technologies over other specific technologies. Technology-specific regulation is

---

[20] <http://e-government.cabinetoffice.gov.uk/assetRoot/04/00/60/79/04006079.pdf>.

acceptable only if there is a significant difference between technologies. What counts as significant will probably be related to meaning A1: technologies differ only inasmuch as their effects or functions differ in a legally relevant way. Therefore, regulation may target specific kinds of technologies if the effects or functions of these technologies significantly differ from those of other technologies. Within one type of technology, however, the regulation should not discriminate.

For example, in the area of electronic signatures, various countries have enacted legislation targeting a specific kind of technology: digital signatures (see section 4.3.1).

Another example of this use of the starting point is the Australian government's telecommunications policy: 'An effective infrastructure strategy must be based on the right mix of market freedoms, an appropriate regulatory environment including adequate pricing arrangements, and targeted government assistance. It must be technology-neutral, that is, it must not discriminate between different forms of technology used in infrastructure and service provision.'[21]

B2. Regulation should not hinder the development of ICT
A related meaning of the starting point is that regulation should not hinder the development of ICT as such. This is similar to meaning B1 in that it stresses the value neutrality of regulation with respect to technology, but it is a more general statement. It does not stress the non-discrimination principle, but it focuses on the potential negative effect that regulation may have on the development of ICT in general or of specific areas of ICT. Pamela Samuelson mentions this as one reason for technology-neutral laws: 'such a law may unwittingly tilt the market so as to benefit certain developers to the detriment of competitors who offer a different solution, as well as the public who might have preferred that other technology if given a chance.'[22] In this sense, it is closely related to the starting point that self-regulation is to be preferred, since that is a better instrument to foster the development of ICT (see chapter 5 of this Volume).

An example of this use of the starting point is Article 14 of the Directive on privacy and electronic communications, that reads:

> 'In implementing the provisions of this Directive, Member States shall ensure, subject to paragraphs 2 and 3, that no mandatory requirements for specific technical features are imposed on terminal or other electronic communication equipment which could impede the placing of equipment on the market and the free circulation of such equipment in and between Member States.'

Paragraph 2 states that if provisions of the Directive can only be implemented by requiring specific technical features, Member States must notify the Commission. Consideration 46 of the Directive explains that the background of this article is the

---

[21] NOIE 1998.
[22] Samuelson 2000.

technology neutrality of the general Directive on the protection on personal data.[23]

The desire not to hamper the Internet may also have been a reason for the UK government to propose to restrict content-regulating parts of the Communications Bill to traditional broadcasting media, i.e., television and radio, and not to apply them to the Internet: '[F]or reasons of policy and pragmatism, [the Government] has stated that it does not intend that content delivered via the Internet should be subject to such a regime.' This creates problems now that media increasingly converge: '[I]dentical content will be subject to regulation when it is broadcast, but not when it is webcast.'[24] Thus, the desire to have technology neutrality in the sense of not hampering certain technologies may result in technology-specific regulation, which particularly counters the meaning of the starting point in the sense of regulation effects, not means (A1).

Another example is the regulation of electronic signatures (see section 4.4.1), where, in the US, it was argued that 'technology-neutrality fosters innovation, whereas regulating specific technologies inhibits the marketplace from continuing to develop more effective technologies than current e-sign technology.'[25] However, some people feel the reverse in this case, arguing that the recognition of a specific technology by the legislature 'could have served to boost the security industry forward, creating and standardizing the most secure and viable technology that exists.'[26] Therefore, it may be open for debate to what extent technology-neutral or rather technology-specific regulation is best suited to stimulate, or not to obstruct, the development of technology in a specific case.

C. Legislative technique

The starting point that ICT regulation should be technology-neutral may also be regarded as an elaboration of traditional, general principles for law making. In this sense, it deals not with regulation in general but with legislation. Moreover, contrary to the first two meanings, it focuses more on the formulation of rules than on the content or consequences of rules.

C1. The law should be sustainable
A general principle of law making is that the law should be sustainable. In Lon Fuller's tale of principles for legislation, monarch Rex, who is trying hard to make law for his citizens, is exasperated that, when finally he manages to publish an acceptable code of laws, events have overtaken the substance of the code.

'Accordingly as soon as the new code became legally effective, it was subjected to a daily stream of amendments. Again popular discontent mounted; an anonymous pam-

---

[23] Directive 2002/58/EC, OJ L 201/37.
[24] Lee 2003, p. 19.
[25] Koger 2001, pp. 507-508.
[26] Ibid., p. 513.

phlet appeared on the streets carrying scurrilous cartoons of the king and a leading article with the title: "A law that changes every day is worse than no law at all".[27]

It is obvious that nowadays, technology develops more quickly than laws. Therefore, one of the most logical requirements of ICT regulation is that ICT laws should be sustainable enough to cope with technological development over a sufficiently long period of time. If a law is too technology-specific, it is not likely to cover future technological developments, and it will therefore have to be adapted sooner rather than later.[28] There are numerous examples of ICT laws that had to be adapted relatively soon because they were insufficiently resistant to technological changes.[29] For instance, the Dutch Data Registries Act [*Wet persoonsregistraties*] of 1988 was soon outdated because it only covered *registries* of data but not the processing of data as such, and therefore was not fit to deal with network technology. The EC telecommunication framework of 1998[30] was written largely with the telephone infrastructure in mind and covered the development of electronic communications insufficiently, hence the new e-communications framework of 2003.[31] In such cases, one might have wished the legislature to have been slightly more visionary.

On the other hand, eminently sustainable laws may also contain the risk that over the years, the interpretation of the law will diverge for different technologies and hence will lead to unintended technology specificity. As Burk and Lemley have shown, the application of patent law in the United States differs significantly for software, where relatively few but broad patents are issued, and biotechnology, which receives many but narrow patents. 'As a practical matter, it appears that while patent law is technology-neutral in theory, it is technology-specific in application.'[32] This need not be a problem, since it is perhaps desirable to distinguish between areas of technology, but it should be borne in mind that sustainability of a law carries the risk of backfiring if the law abstracts too much away from technology.

Another and more important risk with sustainability is that, in order to create sustainability, laws are formulated that are so technology-neutral that they become meaningless (see also section 4.3.2). As the Earl of Northesk has commented on the UK 2000 Regulation of Investigatory Powers Act:

---

[27] Fuller 1969, p. 37.

[28] Cf., 'proponents of E-SIGN argued that legislation should remain neutral enough to accept any technology that the market could develop in the near future' (Koger 2001, p. 507). See section 4.4.1 on E-SIGN.

[29] In fact, this is nothing new. After the Dutch government had proposed a bill in February 1903 on 'driving on roads with motor vehicles', they noted, when discussing the bill in parliament in March 1904, that 'a new vehicle is concerned, that is still in the stage of fast development indeed. Since the bill was submitted, significant further developments can again be observed that have stimulated further research and adaptation' of the bill. Kamerstukken II 1903/04, 14, no. 1, p. 1.

[30] See <http://europa.eu.int/information_society/topics/telecoms/regulatory/98_regpack/index_en.htm>.

[31] See <http://europa.eu.int/information_society/topics/telecoms/regulatory/new_rf/index_en.htm>.

[32] Burk & Lemley 2002, p. 1156.

'One of the many difficulties I have with the Bill is that, in its strident efforts to be technology neutral, it often conveys the impression that either it is ignorant of the way in which current technology operates, or pretends that there is no technology at all.'[33]

Indeed, there is a paradoxical element in creating laws to regulate technology and at the same time arguing that laws should not need to be adapted when future technologies emerge.[34]

The sustainability requirement may also need to be qualified in yet another respect. Our perspective of the sustainability of laws is influenced greatly by the past, and law-making processes are still largely the same as they were in the pre-ICT era. But time is a relative matter. The rate of change in current society is much higher than it used to be, and it might therefore be necessary to adapt our requirements of sustainability accordingly. In the industrial era, there may have been a requirement that laws should be sustainable for a period of, say, twenty or thirty years, but such a period seems much too long in the ICT era. An illustration may be found in the laws that, over the years, have dealt with telecommunications. In the Netherlands, the first law was the Telegraph Act [*Telegraafwet*] of 1852. In 1903, this was replaced by the Telegraph & Telephone Act 1904 [*Telegraaf- en telefoonwet 1904*]. Although this act was adapted regularly, its framework lasted until 1988, when it was replaced by the Telecommunications Facilities Act [*Wet op de telecommunicatievoorzieningen*]. This Act, however, lasted only ten years, being replaced by the Telecommunications Act [*Telecommunicatiewet*] of 1998. And six years later, in 2004, the new European e-Communications framework caused the Telecommunications Act to be substantially changed, although not replaced. It seems pointless these days to require telecommunications laws to last for decades, and the same holds for many other ICT laws.

In other words, the starting point that regulation should be technology-neutral can be interpreted as a specification of the traditional law-making principle that legislation should be sustainable, but the extent of the sustainability called for may be considered less in terms of years than can be required for non-technological areas of law.

C2. Regulation should be subsidiary and proportionate
Legislators can choose between various instruments of law-making: constitutional laws, acts of parliament, and decrees. Besides, other regulatory instruments can also be considered, such as stimulating self-regulation or facilitating standardization processes. A general principle for regulation is that the most appropriate instrument must be chosen that can achieve the purpose of the regulation: the instrument

---

[33] Quoted in Hosein & Escudero Pascual 2002, p. 1.

[34] '[O]ne can not have the mandate of updating laws for new technologies then in the same breath argue against updating for the next new technology and thus require technology-neutral policy' (Hosein & Escudero Pascual 2002, p. 2).

should be subsidiary, i.e., a 'heavier' instrument should be avoided when a 'lighter' instrument will do the trick, and it should be proportionate to its goal.

The starting point that regulation should be technology-neutral might also be seen as a variant of this legislative requirement: laws, and particularly acts of parliament, are 'heavy' instruments, generally requiring long and cumbersome procedures, and they are therefore not suited to technology-specific aims, given the rapid developments in technology. Thus, it can be taken together with the previous requirement to hold that (formal) laws should, in principle, be sufficiently sustainable by abstracting away from specific technologies, whereas lighter regulatory instruments can be more technology-specific. Or, conversely, an appropriate regulatory instrument may be chosen depending on the extent to which specific technologies should be regulated.

C3. The law should be transparent

Another traditional requirement of legislation is that it be transparent: it should be known and understandable to those who have to comply with it. The starting point is rarely used in this sense. One example may be the Dutch 2001 Bill on requesting traffic data for criminal-investigation purposes, in which the government did not want to enumerate in the law itself the kinds of data that would be covered by 'traffic data': one reason for this was that 'including this in the text of the Act rather than in the governmental decree leads to a regulation that is difficult to read.'[35]

Thus, the starting point that regulation should be technology-neutral may be viewed as a means to achieve the goal of transparency. The more detailed the legislation, the less transparent it may be and, particularly with technology, it will be the case that the more technology is put into the law or into its formulation, the less understandable it will be to ordinary citizens. If the addressees of the law, however, are more technology-knowledgeable, the regulation can – and perhaps should – be more technology-specific.

In this respect, it is important to note that the requirement of transparency also works the other way around. If laws are very technology-neutral, in the sense that they abstract away from technology to a great extent, they may become less transparent, since it may be unclear whether specific technologies fall within their scope. An example is the constitutional protection of the secrecy of communications (see section 4.3.2).

From the perspective of transparency, therefore, the starting point ought rather to be that regulation should be as much technology-neutral as is compatible with sufficient legal certainty.

---

[35] Kamerstukken II 2001-2002, 28 059, no. 5, p. 17.

4.4   HOW DOES IT APPLY?

After the outline of the potential uses of the starting point, and before moving on to an analysis of the conditions and approaches of using the starting point, it is good to take a more in-depth look at how the starting point works in practice. In this section, I will describe three illustrative cases of regulation that give a good indication of the problems and the pros and cons that the starting point gives rise to in practice. I have chosen one example each from the fields of civil law, constitutional law, and criminal law. Apart from the illustrative character, this will also yield inspiration for the criteria and approaches that follow.

4.4.1   Electronic signatures

Electronic authentication can be achieved in many ways, for instance, with biometrics, for example, a face or iris scan, or a dynamic pen, digital signatures, which are based on public-key cryptography, PIN codes, and pass phrases. The technologies function in different ways, and they usually have characteristics that differ from those of paper-based, handwritten signatures. Legislators therefore have to deal with the question of whether electronic signatures should be legally recognized.

Since the first electronic-authentication statute was passed, the Utah Digital Signature Act of 1995, a host of laws has been passed in this field – self-regulation is definitely not a starting point here.[36] Within this plethora of laws and regulations, three major approaches can be discerned, as indicated by Aalberts and Van der Hof.[37]

First, there is the minimalist or functionalist approach, which is presented as a technology-neutral one. In this approach, electronic authentication is regulated by providing legal recognition to any electronic signature scheme that meets certain general criteria that indicate its capability of providing authentication. The uniforming US laws on electronic signatures (UCITA, E-SIGN Act) are prime examples of this functional approach to ICT regulation. The US E-SIGN Act of 2000[38] provides a very general provision on authentication: '(…) with respect to any transaction in or affecting interstate or foreign commerce – (1) a signature (…) relating to such transaction may not be denied legal effect, validity, or enforceability solely because it is in electronic form' (section 101(a)). Likewise, Article 7 paragraph 1 of the 1996 UNCITRAL Model Law on Electronic Commerce[39] is a broad provision on signatures:

---

[36] See Van der Hof 2005 for an overview.

[37] Aalberts & Van der Hof 2000.

[38] Electronic Signatures in Global And National Commerce Act, S. 761, available at <http://thomas.loc.gov>.

[39] UNCITRAL Model Law on Electronic Commerce, 1996, <http://www.uncitral.org/english/texts/electcom/ml-ec.htm>. The draft convention on electronic contracting that the UNCITRAL is working

'Where the law requires a signature of a person, that requirement is met in relation to a data message if: (a) a method is used to identify that person and to indicate that person's approval of the information contained in the data message; and (b) that method is as reliable as was appropriate for the purpose for which the data message was generated or communicated, in the light of all the circumstances, including any relevant agreement.'

This minimalist approach is a prime example of technology-neutral regulation in the sense of regulating functions, not means (A1), and thus providing equivalence between 'off-line' and 'on-line' signatures (A2).

Second, there is a more technology-specific approach, which may be called the digital-signature approach. Most of the early laws in the field targeted a specific kind of technology: digital signatures, that is, signature systems based on public-key cryptography. This technology specificity was triggered by the notion that digital signatures were more reliable than other signature schemes, such as biometric authentication schemes; they were the only technology considered reliable enough to be treated on a par with hand-written signatures. There are several varieties of regulation: the German law of 1997[40] focused on standardization, the Utah law[41] on legal recognition, and the Netherlands aimed at self-regulation in a project called TTP.nl[42] to formulate criteria for a technical infrastructure. The technology-specificity is illustrated, for example, by the definition of a digital signature in section 102(10) of the Utah Digital Signature Act:

'"Digital signature" is a sequence of bits which a person intending to sign creates in relation to a clearly delimited message by running the message through a one-way function, then encrypting the resulting message digest using an asymmetrical cryptosystem and the person's private key.'

Obviously, technology neutrality did not play a primary part in the regulations of this type. Even so, there is some technology neutrality even in these laws: they target digital-signature schemes in general, but they do not differentiate between various forms of digital-signature schemes, for example, schemes based on the Diffie-Hellman algorithm, on the RSA algorithm, or on elliptic-curve algorithms, let alone between various digital-signature products. Technology neutrality is a matter of degree here: one type of technology is singled out for regulation, which is technol-

---

on has a similar provision in Art. 9, see Document A/CN.9/WG.IV/WP.108, 18 December 2003, <http://www.uncitral.org/english/workinggroups/wg_ec/wp108-e.pdf>.

[40] Signaturgesetz [Digital Signature Act], Art. 3 of the Informations- und Kommunikationsdienste-Gesetz of 1997 [Information and Communication Services Act], <http://www.iid.de/rahmen/iukdgebt.html#a3>.

[41] Utah Digital Signature Act, Utah Code §§ 46-3-101 to 46-3-104, <http://www.jmls.edu/cyber/statutes/udsa-1.html>.

[42] Kamerstukken II 1998/99, 26 581, no. 1; Kamerstukken II 2002/03, 26 581, no. 2; see also <http://www.ecp.nl/dossieritem.php?dossier_id=7#ttpnl>.

ogy-specific; at the same time, within this type, technologies are not discriminated against, which is technology-neutral.

Both approaches have advantages. The primary advantage of the first, function-alist, approach is that it is sustainable. It leaves much room for interpretation and for future developments: the market and the courts will see how it works in prac-tice. The primary drawback, however, is that it provides little guidance: how do we know when an electronic signature 'is as reliable as was appropriate for the pur-pose' (UNCITRAL Model Law), and how do we know when electronic signatures will be denied legal effect for *other* reasons than their being in electronic form (E-SIGN Act)? The laws provide little legal certainty, and thus do not really satisfacto-rily answer the question of legal recognition.[43]

The second, digital-signature approach does exactly the opposite. By describing in detail a specific technology or a specific type of technology, it provides much legal certainty, but it is not very sustainable. If new technologies arise that may be considered reliable enough besides digital signatures, the law must be changed. In fact, the technology-specific laws *have* been adapted (Utah) or replaced (Germany) after a few years, although this was caused as much by federal and EU develop-ments, which chose a different legislative approach, as by technical changes.

Interestingly enough, there is a third approach, one that combines the functionalist and the digital-signature approach. The European 1999 Directive on electronic sig-natures provides legal acceptability of electronic signatures in general in a non-discrimination clause as well as positive legal recognition of 'advanced electronic signatures', i.e., signatures that meet extra criteria. Most of these criteria use for-mulations that focus on the function of signatures. For instance, an advanced elec-tronic signature is defined as a signature that meets the following requirements: '(a) it is uniquely linked to the signatory; (b) it is capable of identifying the signatory; (c) it is created using means that the signatory can maintain under his sole control; and (d) it is linked to the data to which it relates in such a manner that any subse-quent change of the data is detectable.' The functional approach is also stressed in consideration 8: 'Rapid technological development and the global character of the Internet necessitate an approach which is open to various technologies and services *capable of* authenticating data electronically'.[44] My italics show that the Directive is only concerned with the function of authentication technologies, not with spe-cific technologies. However, there are many quite specific requirements for ad-

---

[43] 'E-SIGN takes away the predictability and stability of traditional contract law and gives rise to uncertainty and litigation. (...) This uncertainty could create evidentiary presumption problems for judges and juries to solve. (...) E-SIGN places the burden of determining the sufficiency of security used to create an electronic contract on state agency workers. The U.S. legislature passed the transac-tion costs of creating parameters on to state governments, and also passed up the opportunity to create a uniform law. This leaves fifty states to promulgate their own, possibly unique, method of determining the sufficiency of a technology's security' (Koger 2001, pp. 508-509 and 511).

[44] Directive 1999/93/EC of 13 December 1999, OJ 2000, L 13/12.

vanced e-signatures listed in Annexes, and, on the whole, the requirements are closely related to the technology of digital signatures. Hence, it can safely be said that the Directive contains both a minimalist, non-discriminatory, technology-neutral approach and a functionally defined but technology-specific approach. The same holds for the UNCITRAL Model Law on Electronic Signatures of 2001.[45]

The advantage of this mixed approach is that it seems to combine the best of both worlds. It is sustainable, in that its non-discrimination clause is open to future developments in technology, and also because its technology-triggered criteria for advanced signatures are functionally formulated. At the same time, it provides legal certainty for those wanting to use e-signatures that are legally recognized on a par with handwritten signatures, by giving technology-specific rules for a certain type of e-signatures.

4.4.2   The constitutional right to secrecy of communications

In many countries, protection of the secrecy of (tele)communications is considered an important issue. Since governments have often traditionally operated monopolies on *tele*-communications (in the sense of distance communications) infrastructures, for example, the mail system and the telegraph infrastructure, and they also have a law-enforcement interest in prying into people's communications, it may be especially important to protect the secrecy of communications in the constitution.

In the Netherlands, the constitutional right to secrecy of communications has prompted a debate and a legislative process that is intricately related to technology neutrality. The current formulation of the right, dating largely from 1988, is quite technology-specific: 'The privacy of letters [*briefgeheim*] shall not be violated, except (…). The privacy of the telephone and telegraph [*telefoon- en telegraafgeheim*] shall not be violated, except (…)' (Art. 13 Dutch Constitution). The question arose whether e-mail was protected by the Constitution, because, not being a letter, a telephone message or a telegram, it was questionable whether it was covered by the current constitutional right. The government therefore proposed a bill to change the formulation into a technology-neutral right: 'The right to confidential communications is inviolable, except (…).'[46] The Lower House, however, was afraid that the wording was too vague – and rightly so, since the minister gave two radically different interpretations within a span of six months. The formulation was therefore changed to: 'The privacy of letters, of the telephone and telegraph, and of similar communication technologies [*het geheim van daarmee vergelijkbare communicatietechnieken*] shall not be violated, except (…).'[47] The Upper House was not happy with the text nor with the procedure leading to its formulation, and the Cabinet decided to withdraw the bill and to install a committee to investigate constitutional

---

[45] UNCITRAL Model Law on Electronic Signatures, with Guide to Enactment, 2001, <http://www.uncitral.org/english/texts/electcom/ml-elecsig-e.pdf>.

[46] Kamerstukken II 1996/97, 25 443, nos. 1-3.

[47] Kamerstukken I 1997/98, 25 443, no. 232.

rights in the digital era, with the specific requirement of drafting technology-neutral texts. The committee thereupon proposed the formulation: 'Everyone shall have the right to communicate confidentially', which the Cabinet agreed with.[48]

The proponents of this and similar technology-neutral formulations stress the need for sustainability: changes to constitutional law require a long and cumbersome process, so the text must be sustainable for many years. Technology-specific formulations that refer to means of communication are undesirable in view of the rapid technological changes. The opponents, however, consider the formulation too vague: it is not clear what means of communication are protected by it, and it may even occur that traditional means of communication that have been constitutionally protected since time immemorial, like letters, may suddenly cease to be protected if a government thinks it convenient to declare them no longer a 'confidential' means of communication.[49] The debate is still going on in the Netherlands; a new bill to change the Constitution in this respect has not yet been proposed.

It is interesting to see how other countries deal with this issue. This may depend on the status, structure, and function of the constitution within the legal framework of a country.[50] In Germany and Belgium, the wording of the secrecy of communications in the constitution is similar to that of the Netherlands: the German texts speaks of 'the privacy of letters as well as the secrecy of post and telecommunication' [*Briefgeheimnis sowie das Post- und Fernmeldegeheimnis*], Art. 10 German Constitution), the Belgian one only of 'the confidentiality of letters' [*briefgeheim*], Art. 29 Belgian Constitution). The German term 'telecommunications' is a broad one that may be interpreted as covering new forms of telecommunications, such as e-mail, so that there does not seem to be a need to change the text. The Belgian text is quite technology-specific, but the scope of the constitutional protection has been expanded, not by changing the Constitution, but by passing laws that extended the constitutional protection to the telephone and telegraph in 1930 and to modern means of communications in 1997.[51] The Swedish Constitution has a residual category: 'mail or other confidential correspondence, and (...) other confidential communications' (Ch. 2, Art. 6). Thus, the constitutions with a specific right to secrecy of communications, in contrast to the Dutch one, do not seem outdated as a result of new communication technologies, and they have accomplished this in different ways.

For constitutions that do not contain a specific right to secrecy of communications, the case is different. As part of the right to privacy, it may be interpreted as falling under the right to be protected 'against unreasonable search or seizure' (Art. 8 Canadian Charter; compare the US Fourth Amendment). In these countries, the question of whether new forms of technology are constitutionally protected will of

---

[48] Commissie GDT 2000; Kamerstukken II 2000-2001, 27 460, no. 1, p. 22.

[49] See Blok 2002, pp. 50-51.

[50] See Koekkoek, et al., 1999, who have analysed, among other things, the technology neutrality of constitutional rights in six other countries.

[51] Ibid.

course arise, but it is a question similar to numerous others that have come up over the years. The system of having a single briefly worded right in the constitution allows for much interpretation by the courts. Therefore, the technology neutrality of the wording of the right is less important: the courts tend to interpret the right functionally and in light of current developments, even though the formulation is technology-specific: 'seizure' is literally a particularly 'physical' action that cannot by its nature apply to intangible things, such as computer data or communications.

It appears that the issue of technology neutrality in the constitution with respect to the secrecy of communications is playing a much more prominent part in the Netherlands than in other countries. This may partly be caused by a happier wording, intentional or not, of the law in other countries. Another major, and probably more significant, reason is that, in the Netherlands, it is particularly important for the *legislator* to interpret the Constitution, and thus to be precise and clear in the wording of the Constitution, since constitutional review by the courts is prohibited in the Netherlands (Art. 120 Dutch Constitution). In the other countries, constitutional review is possible, so the courts have more leeway in interpreting the text of the Constitution.

4.4.3 Misuse of devices

Usually, criminal law penalizes acts that are considered directly harmful – theft, manslaughter, fraud. Acts that are not harmful in themselves but that may contribute to harmful actions are normally allowed to the extent that they do not constitute the harmful act itself. Sometimes, however, it is considered necessary to penalize contributory or preparatory acts as well, but this is artificial and only acceptable if penalizing the end results as such is not enforceable or if the danger of the act is so great that it should be prevented at all costs.

In the area of ICT law, the most common penalizations concern crimes directed against computers and data, for example, computer sabotage, and data alteration, and crimes committed by means of computer systems, both traditional crimes such as fraud, and new ones such as hacking. The development or use of computer or software devices as such is not an issue, as long as the use does not constitute a crime in itself.[52] However, recently, a new target of penalization has emerged, 'misuse of devices', where 'misuse' denotes a use that is contributory or preparatory to a crime rather than a use that is harmful in itself. Article 6 of the Cybercrime Convention of the Council of Europe[53] provides specifically for misuse of devices:

---

[52] See, for example, Recommendation R (89) 9 of the OECD for a list of acts that are considered punishable.

[53] Convention on Cybercrime, Budapest, 23 November 2001, <http://conventions.coe.int/Treaty/en/Treaties/Html/185.htm>.

'1. Each Party shall adopt such legislative and other measures as may be necessary to establish as criminal offences under its domestic law, when committed intentionally and without right:

a. the production, sale, procurement for use, import, distribution or otherwise making available of:

    i. a device, including a computer program, designed or adapted primarily for the purpose of committing any of the offences established in accordance with Article 2-5;

    ii. a computer password, access code, or similar data by which the whole or any part of a computer system is capable of being accessed with intent that it be used for the purpose of committing any of the offences established in Articles 2-5; and

b. the possession of an item referred to in paragraphs (a)(1) or (2) above, with intent that it be used for the purpose of committing any of the offences established in Articles 2-5 (…).'

A similar development has occurred in the field of copyright law, which recently has started to prohibit acts preparatory to the circumvention of Digital Rights Management (DRM) systems. DRM systems are technologies that protect the interest of copyright holders by making it technically impossible to copy a copyrighted work.[54] Although the legal protection called for need not necessarily be constituted by criminal law – it may also be provided by tort law –, the provisions target unlawfulness and are thus comparable to the Cybercrime Convention's criminalization of misuse of devices. Traditionally, the law has not been concerned with such protection schemes, but the advent of new technologies has threatened to shift the power balance between copyright owners and users to make users more powerful: they can cheaply and without limit make perfect copies, which formerly they could not do. Thus, the law reacts by shifting the power balance back towards copyright holders: it prohibits the circumvention of DRM systems.

For instance, Article 6, paragraphs 2 and 3, of the Copyright Harmonization Directive[55] provides:

'2. Member States shall provide adequate legal protection against the manufacture, import, distribution, sale, rental, advertisement for sale or rental, or possession for commercial purposes of devices, products or components or the provision of services which: (a) are promoted, advertised or marketed for the purpose of circumvention of, or (b) have only a limited commercially significant purpose or use other than to circumvent, or (c) are primarily designed, produced, adapted or performed for the purpose of enabling or facilitating the circumvention of, any effective technological measures.

3. For the purposes of this Directive, the expression 'technological measures' means any technology, device or component that, in the normal course of its operation, is de-

---

[54] This is an extension of earlier provisions on preparatory acts relating to software-protection circumvention, see Directive 1991/250/EEC.

[55] Directive 2001/29/EC of 22 May 2001 on the harmonization of certain aspects of copyright and related rights in the information society, OJ 22.6.2001, L 167/10.

signed to prevent or restrict acts, in respect of works or other subject-matter, which are not authorised by the rightholder of any copyright or any right related to copyright as provided for by law or the *sui generis* right provided for in Chapter III of Directive 96/9/EC.Technological measures shall be deemed 'effective' where the use of a protected work or other subject-matter is controlled by the rightholders through application of an access control or protection process, such as encryption, scrambling or other transformation of the work or other subject-matter or a copy control mechanism, which achieves the protection objective.'

Earlier, in the US, the Digital Millennium Copyright Act inserted similar clauses into the US Code.[56] The European provision is much more specific than the original provision of the WIPO Copyright Treaty that inspired it. Article 11 of that Treaty reads:

'Contracting Parties shall provide adequate legal protection and effective legal remedies against the circumvention of effective technological measures that are used by authors in connection with the exercise of their rights under this Treaty or the Berne Convention and that restrict acts, in respect of their works, which are not authorized by the authors concerned or permitted by law.'

Contrary to the examples of digital signatures and the secrecy of communications, technology neutrality has not featured in the debate over misuse of devices. This is interesting, since the provisions are technology-specific, at least in the sense that they target technology itself much more than is usually the case with criminal law or tort law. After all, it concerns not a harmful act, but the manufacture, import, distribution, sale, rental, advertisement, making available, or possession of – in short, almost anything you can do with – technologies that *can be* used in a certain harmful way, regardless of whether they *are* actually used in such a way. Although the formulation is functional and the provisions may, in that respect, be called technology-neutral (A1), the thrust of the law is to govern technology development and use, which may be discriminatory. For instance, a technology that can almost only be applied for the circumvention of DRM will be restrained by the law, whereas a similar technology that happens to also facilitate another application that has a commercial value will be less hampered by it. Moreover, it will definitely hinder the development of technology; hence, it is not technology-neutral in the sense of B1 and B2.

4.5   WHEN SHOULD IT APPLY?

In what situations should the starting point apply? Can criteria be defined to judge whether and to what extent the starting point should apply to cases where ICT regulation is called for?

---

[56] Section 1201 Chapter 17 USC, <http://www.copyright.gov/title17/92chap12.html>.

The first Dutch memorandum on ICT regulation is instructive in this respect: it already listed a number of criteria.

'Technology-independent rules are not suitable:
- as a definition of the scope of a regulation;
- when persons holding legal rights, in view of complex technology, have a need for understanding the technology;
- when technology-independent rules would insufficiently provide legal subjects with insight into the character of their rights and duties;
- [when] the conditions are being established under which the government may infringe upon those rights.

The preference for technology-independent regulation may lead to refrain from including substantive norms in specific, technical legislation. To explain this: for instance, all privacy rules are included in a general privacy statute and not in various technology-based, sector-specific laws.'[57]

From this and from the description given of what the starting point means and how it works, or does not work, in practice, several criteria can be distilled that seem relevant to the applicability of the starting point.

Criteria related to the purpose of regulation

1. What is the goal of the regulation?
Is the goal to provide equivalence between regulations in the off-line and the on-line worlds? In that case, the aim of regulation is technology neutrality (meaning A2). However, the means need not necessarily be technology-neutral. The example of misuse of devices and DRM systems shows that, in order to achieve equivalence, governments implement technology-specific rules that regulate a technology itself, potentially at variance with meaning C1, and that they do not target its effects, contrary to meaning A1. They may also discriminate certain technologies and are likely to hinder the development of technology itself, at variance with meanings B1 and B2. Thus, if the aim is to establish on-line and off-line equivalence, in some cases, one meaning may override most other meanings of the starting point, and indeed, the starting point is more or less identical with the starting point that what holds off-line should also hold on-line. In other cases, it need not be necessary to create technology-specific rules to establish the equivalence called for, and then the other meanings of the starting point may be relevant.

On the other hand, if the goal of the regulation is *not* to establish off-line and on-line equivalence, which may sometimes be the case, the starting point of technology neutrality seems rather pointless in the sense of meaning A. In that case, the purpose of the regulation is rather to establish technology-specific regulation, so meanings B and C come into view.

---

[57] LEH Memorandum 1998, p. 14.

An important related distinction with respect to the goal of regulation is whether the regulation at issue is aimed at safeguarding fundamental norms and values (protective regulation) or at making things run effectively and efficiently (ordering regulation). With protective regulation, the starting point will mainly be relevant in the sense of meaning A: it intends to provide the same level of protection as there is or used to be with non-ICT. With ordering regulations, however, the goal is usually not to achieve equivalence between off-line and on-line issues (meaning A2), although the regulations may try to regulate the functions and effects of technology rather than technology itself (meaning A1). Here, however, meanings B and C will usually be more relevant. To make society function well, regulation should avoid side effects of unduly hindering the development of technology (meaning B2), and with ordering regulation, non-discrimination will generally also be an important starting point (meaning B1). Moreover, particularly with ordering regulation, choosing the right level of regulation, also with a view to the sustainability and transparency of the regulation, will be relevant (meanings C).

2.   Is it desirable to control technology?
Related to the first criterion, the question is important to what extent it is desirable to leave technology itself alone or, rather, to control and steer technology. In certain cases, it may be necessary to target technology and its development or use itself; compare, again, the example of misuse of devices. In such cases, technology neutrality in the sense of meaning B is patently not the starting point, but technology neutrality in the sense of meaning A will be relevant (see the first criterion). In other cases, the idea that technology development should be left alone will be maintained, and in those cases, meaning B will be more relevant.

3.   What level of legal certainty is required?
A primary requirement of regulation in general is to provide sufficient legal certainty. However, the level of legal certainty may vary greatly, depending on numerous factors, such as the level and scope of regulation and its subject-matter. In order to know what degree and what kind of technology neutrality is acceptable in the light of the requirement of legal certainty, it should be closely assessed just what level of legal certainty is called for.

In any case, the requirement of legal certainty may at least call for a certain level of technology specificity. Particularly with legislation, the requirement of sustainability (C1), on the one hand, and subsidiarity, proportionality, and transparency (C2 and C3), on the other, are contradictory to a certain extent. That is, legislation that is too much focused on sustainability and hence abstracts very much away from technology will result in vague laws that provide little legal certainty. As the example of traffic data in criminal investigation shows, 'technology-neutral policy is often to the advantage of the policy-setters as new powers are granted through ambiguity rather than clear debate and due process'; i.e., the power of gathering traffic data is unrelated to specific technologies and therefore allows a much larger infringement of privacy than used to be possible with plain old tele-phony.[58] On the other hand, laws that focus too much on transparency by explicat-ing technologies risk being inflexible and restricted, so that they provide little legal certainty with respect to related but somewhat different technologies. Thus, a pre-carious balance has to be struck when defining the level of legal certainty called for: laws should be sufficiently sustainable in order to provide certainty, but they should also make clear what technologies they cover, and why, in order to provide adequate legal certainty.

4. How urgent is the need for regulation?

If there is an urgent need for regulation, for instance, because there is much need for legal certainty with respect to an emerging new technology such as digital signa-tures, it may be necessary to implement technology-specific regulation. If new tech-nologies threaten to disturb precarious balances in legal protection, regulation may need to discriminate between technologies and try and hinder the development of particularly threatening technologies, contrary to meanings B, but confirming mean-ing A2. For the sake of providing legal certainty promptly, it may also be acceptable to implement less sustainable regulations, for example, to give a legal status to digital signatures, at variance with meaning C1.

If, on the other hand, there is a less pressing need for regulation, it will probably be possible to create higher-level regulations that abstract away from particular technologies and that are formulated in a more sustainable way (meanings A1, B, and C1).

In short, the purpose of the regulation is relevant to assessing to what extent the starting point can or should apply, and, especially, to filling in the precise meaning and thrust of the starting point.

Criteria related to the context of regulation

5. How much technological turbulence is there?

The kind and degree of technology neutrality that are called for are closely related to the nature of the technology that is the object of regulation. If it concerns tech-nology that is very turbulent, that is, technology which is developing rapidly with substantial innovations, new functions, and big advances in scale occurring every one or two years, the need for technology neutrality of regulation is different from that with technology that is developing at a much slower rate.

The turbulence of technology is largely related to the abstraction level at which it is defined. ICT is a rather abstract term for a broad area of technology, and as

---

[58] Hosein & Escudero Pascual 2002, p. 8. 'The policy language developed under POTS and sus-tained through "technology-neutral" policy intentions now gives law enforcement agencies access to highly sensitive data; but only under the protections afforded to the more benign POTS procedures.'

such, the field of ICT is relatively stable, that is, radical changes in ICT do not occur every two or three years, but rather every decade or so, such as the emerging of the World Wide Web (WWW), and mobile telecommunications. A narrower area like telecommunications technology is still defined at a fairly high level of abstraction, where developments are more rapid but still foreseeable for a fair amount of time. It is only when focusing on lower-level instances of technology, such as mobile communications and computer processors, that there is indeed reason to speak of 'technological turbulence'.

The criterion of technological turbulence, then, is related to technology neutrality in the meaning of sustainability of regulation and choosing the right level of regulation (C1 and C2). With turbulent technologies, lower-level forms of regulation should generally be chosen, as these can be adapted more quickly than formal legislation; with more stable technologies, higher-level regulation is quite acceptable. Or to put it the other way around: formal legislation should focus on technologies defined on a high abstraction level, and lower forms of regulation can focus on more concrete technologies.

6.   What are the side effects on technology?
Assuming that no need is felt to control specific technologies or their development, an important criterion for judging whether the starting point of technology neutrality should apply is to what extent the regulation may have an effect on the technology. Here, meaning B is particularly relevant: if the nature of the regulation at stake is such that it may have an effect on certain technologies, unwarranted discrimination and undue obstacles for the technology market should be avoided. If, on the other hand, the regulation has no such potential consequences, the starting point in the sense of meaning B can be ignored.

7.   What is the scope for interpretation?
Apart from the technical context, the legal context is also important. A prime issue is the extent to which legislation leaves room for interpretation. If the legal system and the area of the law allow for much interpretation in legal practice, by legal subjects and by courts alike, the regulation may have a more general, and thus more technology-neutral, character. If, on the other hand, the legislation is to be applied quite strictly, there is a greater need for precise and clear regulations, potentially necessitating a more technology-specific formulation of rules.

8.   How is the regulation to be enforced?
A related legal criterion is the issue of enforcement and supervision. If the aim of regulation is to achieve certain effects in society, the regulation should be enforceable. It may be the case that certain types of regulation are less suitable to be enforced in practice, and this may be a reason to create technology-specific regulations. For instance, hacking and spreading viruses are often difficult to trace and may give few clues for evidence in court; therefore, the outlawing of hacking or virus tools

(see section 4.4.3) is an easier way to effectively combat hacking and viruses, since it is easier to prove that someone possessed a hacker tool than that he actually committed hacking. Thus, if regulating effects or results creates laws that are difficult to enforce, it may be necessary to resort to regulating means instead, contrary to A1 and B2, but achieving more effective regulation.

Another issue related to enforcement is that the enforcement of the traditional, 'off-line' laws may become increasingly difficult through technological innovations. Copyright law is a prime example of this, as the advent of digital copying, Internet transfer, and peer-to-peer networks seem to make copyright law a joke in certain areas. Thus, rightholders will look at technology rather than the law to protect their interests and use 'code as law' (see chapter 7 of this Volume). Now, as the example of DRM legislation shows (see section 4.4.3), the law may reinforce the protection already contained in the technology by outlawing the circumvention of this protective technology. In this way, the enforcement of protective law may be reinforced by creating technology-specific laws that aim to stimulate the development of enforcement-enhancing technologies.

Criteria related to the means of regulation

9.   What level of regulation is required?
The level of regulation influences the degree of technology neutrality that is acceptable or required: constitutional regulation will be formulated in an abstract, technology-neutral, and sustainable way (meanings A1, B, C1), low-level regulation such as ministerial decrees can be quite concrete and technology-specific.

Therefore, having ascertained the aim of regulation, a level of regulation must be chosen that is required for this aim. The subsidiarity principle generally calls for the lowest level of regulation that is apt to fulfill its purpose. Certain topics call for regulation at the level of the constitution, but other topics can well do with sector-specific decrees. The kind of technology neutrality that is desirable or not will also influence the choice of the level of regulation: if the aim is to govern particular technologies, being technology-specific in the sense of meaning B, low-level forms of regulation should generally be chosen. If the aim is to establish equivalent levels of protection in the on-line and off-line worlds, this may require high-level, abstract regulation, i.e., technology neutrality in the sense of meaning A, but it may also require technology-specific regulation (see the first criterion).

10.   What degree of sustainability is called for?
Related to the level of regulation is the degree of sustainability aimed for. High-level regulation must be more sustainable than low-level regulation. This implies that if regulation is required that is not very sustainable, for instance, because there is an urgent need to provide legal certainty with respect to specific technologies, this should generally not be accomplished by high-level regulation. Also, if a high degree of sustainability is not required, perhaps because interim legislation is needed

pending the outcome of negotiations on an international treaty, this can be achieved by lower-level regulation with a fair amount of technology-specificity.

4.6   HOW CAN IT BE APPLIED?

If the criteria indicate that a certain kind and degree of technology neutrality are called for, ways must be found to achieve this. The examples given of how the starting point works in practice suggest several strategies or approaches of achieving technology neutrality.

1.   Differentiate in levels of regulation
An obvious way of dealing with technology neutrality is to create high-level forms of regulation in an abstract, technology-neutral way in the sense of A1, B, and C1, if this is compatible with the purpose of the regulation. If this should create insufficient legal certainty, one can fill in the higher-level regulation with lower-level forms of regulation. For example, the constitutional protection of the secrecy of communications can be formulated in a technology-neutral way, for example, 'the privacy of communications shall not be violated', while the Criminal Code and Code of Criminal Procedure go into more detail as to what kinds of communication technologies are protected, for example, direct speech, telecommunications, and snail mail. Special laws and implementing decrees could then differentiate between different forms of telecommunications, for example, voice telephony, telegraphy, and email. A related example is the requirement of 'tappability': since the mid-1990s, many countries have required their telecommunications infrastructures to be technically interceptable. In Dutch law, this requirement is laid down in a general, technology-neutral way in the Telecommunications Act, with a decree [*Besluit*] outlining the main functional requirements of interception, which are elaborated in more technical detail in a ministerial regulation [*Regeling*].

Another way of achieving the same result is shown by the Belgian Constitution: although its formulation of the secrecy of communications is restricted to letters, a comparable protection level for other forms of communication has been established not at the constitutional level but at a lower level of legislation, thus effectively reaching the same result as a technology-neutral provision in the Constitution might have done.

2.   Use open-ended formulations
A more specific approach to achieving technology neutrality while at the same time guaranteeing sufficient legal certainty is to create technology-specific regulations that include open-ended provisions. Again, the secrecy of communications provides a good example: the constitution may protect 'mail or other confidential correspondence and other confidential communications', comparable to the Swedish Constitution. Likewise, to provide legal recognition for electronic signatures, it might be provided that 'recognized as valid legal evidence are digital signatures

and other electronic signatures that are sufficiently reliable in view of the all relevant circumstances.'

3. Use a mixed approach

More general than the technique of using open-ended formulations is combining technology-neutral with technology-specific regulations. The mixed approach in e-signature regulation is a case in point: the law establishes a general, technology-neutral regime that does not discriminate between technologies and that is sustainable, while at the same time creating a regime for specific technologies in order to create legal certainty for these technologies.

4. Allow for functional, teleological interpretation

Another way to deal with technology neutrality is to allow laws to be interpreted in a functionalist or teleological way. After all, laws are meant for a certain purpose, and the precise look and feel of legal provisions are less important than their rationale. As the Dutch Minister of Justice formulated it when the Computer Crime Act was discussed: 'Naturally a legislator can and may not exclude that there will be situations it did not foresee. (...) It is a general principle of interpreting the law that, within the usual interpretation limits, a court may understand the text of the legislator better than the legislator managed to intend when it was drafted.'[59]

Within a system of functional interpretation of laws, technology neutrality becomes a minor issue: practice can deal with laws that seem technology-specific by interpreting them in a functional way. This will not be a good approach in all cases, since it may provide too little legal certainty. Moreover, this approach may not always yield satisfactory results: it is not a matter of course that laws can always be interpreted in a functional way with respect to new technologies, simply because the cases may be incomparable, in the same way as it is not always possible to apply the starting point that what holds off-line should also hold on-line (see chapter 3 section 3.4). Moreover, interpreting in a functional way is not always easy to do in a consistent way, as the example of diverging patenting of software and biotechnology (see section 4.3.5 at C1) shows: in both cases, the function of patent law is to stimulate invention and to enhance publication of inventions, but the application of the law has quite different results.[60]

With these caveats, the possibility of functional interpretation may often be a good way of circumventing the problem of technology neutrality. For example, the Dutch constitutional problem with respect to the secrecy of communications would be less acute if constitutional review by the courts were allowed. If that was the case, it would matter less if the formulation were very technology-neutral, and thus vague, or quite technology-specific, and thus perhaps outdated.[61]

---

[59] Handelingen II 24 June 1992, 93-5869.

[60] Burk & Lemley 2002.

[61] For this reason, the Dutch advisory committee on constitutional rights in the digital era advised to allow constitutional review by the courts. See Commissie GDT 2000, p. 219.

5.   Establish frameworks of substantive principles

Perhaps in addition to the previous approach, rather than put all effort into creating specific regulations for specific problems, a legal framework may also be established that outlines the main substantive principles that are at stake. Such a framework would, for instance, indicate the fundamental rights and values that are at stake and the rationale that underlies areas of regulation. By nature, such a framework would be technology-neutral in all meanings. It would subsequently facilitate both the regulation process in concrete problem areas, since it gives direction to the regulation makers, and the practice of interpreting existing, technology-specific laws, since it helps in interpreting them in a functional, teleological way.[62] The Dutch memoranda could be regarded as efforts in this direction, but their framework cannot be put to much use in practice. After all, the scope of these memoranda is too broad, since they cover the whole field of ICT regulation and, as a result, are likely to contain too sweeping statements.

Of course, creating such frameworks is easier said than done, and it may be objected that most countries already have such a framework in the form of the Constitution. However, a framework of substantive principles should not be as all-encompassing as a constitution, nor as difficult to create. For more specific areas of ICT regulation, such as the area of criminal procedure and ICT or the area of business-to-consumer e-commerce, a framework could be drafted that outlines the major norms and values at stake, whereby the constitution and legal theory can provide good sources of inspiration. Also, procedures could be indicated that ought to be followed if the substantive norms provide insufficient guidance.

6.   Evaluation and sunset clauses

If, for one reason or another, technology-specific legislation is urgently called for, it may help to build in a clause that forces the legislature to evaluate the legislation after a certain period,[63] such as four years. This gives legal certainty for the short term and allows legal practice to move on, while at the same time ensuring that the overall development of law is not muddied by large amounts of *ad hoc* legislation. After a certain time, it may appear that the general rules and traditional law do cover the new technology after all, so that the technology-specific law can be abolished. Or, if it turns out that the new law has an added value, it can be brought more in line with the overall framework after some experience has been gained in the application of the law.

A somewhat more radical option is to include a sunset clause in the law, which provides that, as a default, the law will expire after a certain period, unless it will be extended. This offers the opportunity of providing legal certainty for this period, at

---

[62] Michael Geist characterises the Canadian e-commerce and e-evidence approach as being technology-neutral, i.e., 'statutory tests or guidelines that do not depend upon a specific development or state of technology, but rather are based on core principles that can be adapted to changing technologies' (Geist 2001, pp. 14-15).

[63] Stuyt 1999, p. 19.

the end of which it may be clearer where the technology is heading or whether the technology-specific rules have an added value over and above the general rules.

4.7   WHAT SHOULD IT MEAN?

The starting point that ICT regulation should be technology-neutral turns out to be a sweeping statement that can be put to many uses. From the perspective of the goal of regulation, the statement stresses that, in principle, the effects of ICT should be regulated, but not technology itself; it may thus serve as a means to achieve equivalence between off-line and on-line regulation. From the perspective of technology development, the statement stresses that, in principle, regulation should not have a negative effect on the development of technology and should not unduly discriminate between technologies. From the perspective of legislative technique, the starting point stresses that legislation should abstract away from concrete technologies to the extent that it is sufficiently sustainable and at the same provides sufficient legal certainty.

Is it useful to maintain such a starting point and if so, what should it mean? The goal-related meanings seem less relevant to me: that regulation should, as a rule, target effects and not means is an overarching characteristic of the law, which does not need particular emphasis in ICT regulation; as a means to achieve off-line/on-line equivalence, the starting point is subsidiary to the starting point that what holds off-line should also hold on-line. The second perspective basically comes down to another potential starting point: regulation should not target the development of technology. This might be treated as a starting point in itself; technology neutrality does not appear to have much added value there as a starting-point in its own right, since it is merely a means to achieve the goal of not targeting technology.

Therefore, the most fruitful perspective seems to be the legislative point of view. Here, it may be of some use. This is not because it is a stunning new insight: it is a long-standing principle of law-making that the law should be sustainable. But it may be useful to stress that, in ICT regulation, particular attention must be given to the sustainability of laws that target technology, because there is a greater risk than usual that changes in the subject matter may soon make the law obsolete. The other side of the matter is that sustainability is not all: legal certainty also imposes requirements on the clarity and precision of the law. Hence, laws cannot become too abstract.

The starting point that regulation should be technology-neutral can be seen as reflecting this trade-off. Legislation should abstract away from concrete technologies to the extent that it is sufficiently sustainable and at the same provides sufficient legal certainty. Depending on a number of criteria, such as the goal of the regulation at issue, the nature and turbulence of the technology at stake, the urgency of providing legal certainty, and the scope for interpreting the regulation, there are several ways to deal with this trade-off. Through multi-level legislation, open-ended

formulations, and a mixed approach of abstract and concrete rules that are periodi-
cally evaluated, adequate legal certainty with respect to current technologies may
be ensured, while at the same time sufficient scope is given for future technological
developments. Further safeguards for sustainability can be established by leaving
ample scope for interpreting the law in a functional way and providing clear guidance as to the aims and rationale of the regulation. And although these approaches
are particularly relevant for legislation, they can be equally valuable for other forms
of regulation, including self-regulation.

Chapter 5
SHOULD SELF-REGULATION BE THE STARTING POINT?

Bert-Jaap Koops, Miriam Lips, Sjaak Nouwt, Corien Prins and Maurice Schellekens

5.1 INTRODUCTION

In this chapter the concept of self-regulation will be discussed as the starting point in regulating ICT-related behavior. In his book *Self-Regulation in the Media Sector and European Community Law*, Jorg Ukrow defines self-regulation as follows: 'A regulatory activity carried out by specific organizational units in order to avoid or eliminate incorrect behavior within their internal structures, or within the structures from which they operate.'[1] We will take this definition as the working definition for our analysis of the starting point of self-regulation.

In its most extensive form, self-regulation implies that private actors themselves implement the applicable norms and rules and, ideally, monitor compliance and enforce the rules in case of non-compliance. Self-regulation is therefore often used as an argument in proposing a system that is different from formal regulation by national governments or international regulatory bodies.

However, many different forms of the concept emerged in the highly diverse areas in which self-regulatory initiatives have been implemented, varying from norms applicable to the environment, the media, and advertising, to diverse professional standards, such as those applied in the medical profession. As will be shown in this chapter, several of these forms play a role in the area of ICT as well. Some do not exclude government regulation, but are based on co-operation between official bodies and private actors. Forms are also available in which the general framework of norms has been established by means of legislation, but further details have been elaborated by the relevant sectors through, for example, codes of conduct.

Self-regulation is often embraced as a highly attractive alternative to regulation by means of laws and other legislative acts. Proponents of self-regulation complain, for example, about the lack of flexibility of legislation and are skeptical about the feasibility of efficient and adequate ICT regulation by means of legislation. However, various imperfections and adverse consequences for the Internet are at-

---

[1] Ukrow 1999, p. 12.

B-J. Koops, et al. (Eds), Starting Points for ICT Regulation
© *2006, ITeR, The Hague, and the authors*

tached to self-regulation and there is certainly reason to question the adequacy and effect of self-regulation in certain circumstances. For example, in their enthusiasm for self-regulation, proponents often seem to overlook the difficulties that arise in relation to the enforcement of self-regulatory initiatives. Furthermore, who may advocate a leading role for self-regulation and for what reasons? In ICT regulation, what strengths and weaknesses of self-regulation can be noted? Can criteria for ICT-related self-regulation be developed? These and many other questions are often ignored in the discussions on the role of self-regulation in the area of ICT.

The aim of this chapter is to show the complexity of the starting-point of self-regulation. In doing so, we will set the general stage for the discussion in the first part of this chapter. This analysis will start with a glance at the policy documents that make reference to self-regulation (section 5.2). Subsequently, we will analyze the meaning and types of self-regulation and its relationship with government regulation (section 5.3). In this section, the pros and cons of self-regulation will be addressed and several examples of self-regulatory initiatives to illustrate how they work in practice. In the second part of this chapter, we will present a more critical analysis of the concept of self-regulation. In section 5.4, criteria will be developed to decide when self-regulation should or should not be considered. To meet these criteria, various instruments will be available. We will focus in particular on the interaction between government and private action with respect to self-regulatory initiatives (section 5.5). We will finish by trying to define how and to what extent self-regulation should indeed be a starting point for ICT regulation (section 5.6).

5.2   WHERE DOES IT COME FROM?

In this section, we will pay attention to opinions about self-regulatory issues that can be found in policy documents. We will distinguish between opinions in policy documents at an international level, from international organizations and, at national levels in several countries. At the international level, many legal ICT-related questions have been addressed, for example, in the areas of network interconnection, intellectual property rights, information security, and privacy and personal data, and policy documents about such issues often voice support for self-regulation as a starting point (section 5.2.1). At a national level, we will focus on Australia, the Netherlands, the UK, and the US, as examples of countries that have called for self-regulation in various domains (section 5.2.2).

5.2.1   International initiatives

5.2.1.1   *European Union*

At the European Ministerial Conference, jointly organized by Germany and the European Commission, which took place in Bonn on 6-8 July 1997, the participating ministers drafted a declaration with starting points to identify barriers to the use of Global Information Networks, with possible solutions, and a call for an open dialogue on further options for European and international co-operation.[2] In Recommendation 19, the Ministers declared that self-regulation can be a useful instrument to regulate behavior in a Global Information Network: 'Ministers stress the role which the private sector can play in protecting the interests of consumers and in promoting and respecting ethical standards, through properly-functioning systems of self-regulation in compliance with and supported by the legal system.'

On 25 January 1999, the European Parliament and the Council adopted a multi-annual Community action plan, following-up on a European Commission's Green Paper of 23 October 1996, on promoting safer use of the Internet by combating illegal and harmful content on global networks.[3] In Article 3, the decision promoted industry self-regulation and content monitoring schemes, for example, dealing with content such as child pornography or content which incites hatred on grounds of race, sex, religion, nationality, or ethnic origin. Furthermore, industry was encouraged to provide filtering tools and rating systems, which would allow parents or teachers to select content appropriate for children in their care while allowing adults to decide what legal content they wish to access, and which take account of linguistic and cultural diversity.

In 2001, in a white paper called *European Governance*,[4] the European Commission focused on the way in which the Union uses the powers given by its citizens. The Commission is of the opinion that reform should start, so that the citizens see changes well before further modification of the EU Treaties. The White Paper proposed changes in the policy-making process to get more people and organizations involved in shaping and delivering EU policy. It promoted greater openness, accountability, and responsibility for all those involved, to show citizens how the Member States, by acting together with the EU, can to tackle their concerns more effectively.

The Commission proposed changes for 'better policies, regulation and delivery'. In this context, the Commission declared that it would promote greater use of different policy tools: regulations, framework directives, and co-regulatory mechanisms.

One of the factors that, according to the Commission, can improve the quality, effectiveness and simplicity of regulatory acts, is a framework of co-regulation. The use of co-regulation can be an effective way of achieving EU objectives: 'Co-regulation implies that a framework of overall objectives, basic rights, enforcement

---

[2] European Commission, *Ministerial Declaration*, Ministerial Conference, Bonn, 6-8 July 1997, <http://europa.eu.int/ISPO/bonn/Min_declaration/i_finalen.html> (last visited 10 February 2005).
[3] Decision No. 276/1999/EC of the European Parliament and of the Council of 25 January 1999, adopting a multi-annual Community action plan on promoting safer use of the Internet by combating illegal and harmful content on global networks. OJ, 6.2.1999, L 33/1.
[4] European Commission, *European Governance. A White Paper*, Brussels, 25.7.2001, COM (2001) 428 final, <http://europa.eu.int/eur-lex/en/com/cnc/2001/com2001_0428en01.pdf>.

and appeal mechanisms, and conditions for monitoring compliance is set in the legislation.'[5]

Co-regulation should combine binding legislative and regulatory action with actions taken by the actors most concerned, drawing on their practical expertise. Involving the stakeholders most affected creates a wider ownership of the policies, and this should result in better compliance, even where the detailed rules are non-binding. The Commission points at the internal market, where co-regulation has already been used (the 'New Approach' directives), and at the environment sector (reducing car emissions). The exact way in which legal and non-legal instruments are combined and the actor who launches the initiative (the Commission or stake-holders) will vary from sector to sector.

Furthermore, in the context of the EU's contribution to global governance, the Commission was convinced that, for example, the development of co-regulatory solutions to deal with aspects of the new economy could be tested at a global level. The Commission believed that, as in the EU, these approaches should complement successful elements of international public law, most notably the World Trade Organization and the International Court of Justice.[6]

On 28 May 2002, the European Commission presented a Communication entitled 'e-Europe 2005: An Information Society for All'. This Communication was an action plan presented in view of the Sevilla European Council on 21-22 June 2002. In this action plan, the European Commission stressed the initiative to promote self-regulation in the information society. The Commission stated that, since the publication of the e-Commerce Communication in 1997,[7] it had developed a comprehensive policy in this field. Among the achievements were a series of directives[8] aimed at establishing an Internal Market for information society services, as well as a number of non-legislative initiatives aimed at promoting self-regulation, notably in the field of 'e-Confidence' and On-line Dispute Resolution (ODR),[9] and the launch of the 'Go Digital' initiative to help small and medium-sized enterprises to improve e-Business use.

5.2.1.2   OECD

On 16-17 February 1998, the Organization for Economic Co-operation and Development (OECD) organized a workshop, with the support of the Business and In-

---

[5] Ibid.

[6] Idem, p. 27.

[7] A European Initiative in Electronic Commerce, COM (1997) 157 final of 16.4.1997.

[8] Directive 2000/31/EC on electronic commerce, Directive 1999/93/EC on a Community framework for electronic signatures, Directive 2001/29/EC on the harmonization of certain aspects of copyright and related rights in the Information Society, Directive 97/7/EC on the protection of consumers in respect of distance contracts.

[9] The Commission has established an alternative dispute settlement network, the EEJ net, in order to utilize and promote dispute resolution mechanisms for resolving cross-border consumer-business disputes throughout the EU.

dustry Advisory Committee (BIAC), which brought together representatives of governments, the private sector, user and consumer communities, and data protection authorities. They considered issues linked to the protection of privacy and transborder flows of personal data in the developing global networked society and examined how the OECD Privacy Guidelines may be implemented in the context of global networks. The OECD tried to find mechanisms and technological tools that could provide an effective bridge between the policies for protection of personal data offered by the legislators in the European Union and the policies of other Member countries aimed at encouraging the private sector to provide meaningful protection for personal data on global networks by effective self-regulation. The workshop sessions addressed the following issues:

- identifying and balancing the needs of the private sector and those of users and consumers and formulating efficient strategies for 'educating for privacy';
- developing privacy-enhancing technologies;
- implementing enforcement mechanisms developed in the private sector for privacy codes of conduct and standards;
- adopting model contractual solutions for transborder data flows.

At the end of the workshop, the chair, Michelle d'Auray (Electronic Commerce Task Force, Industry Canada), highlighted the need to survey the instruments available for data protection, including law, self-regulation, contracts, and technology, in order to assess their practical application in a networked environment and their ability to meet the objectives of the OECD Privacy Guidelines, for example, effectiveness, enforceability, redress, and coverage across jurisdictions.

On 7-9 October 1998, the OECD Ministers present at the Ottawa Conference 'A Borderless World: Realizing the Potential of Global Electronic Commerce' issued a declaration on behalf of the governments of the OECD Member Countries, including the European Communities.[10] The Ministers:

'will take the necessary steps, within the framework of their respective laws and practices, to ensure that the OECD Privacy Guidelines are effectively implemented in relation to global networks, and in particular:
1. encourage the adoption of privacy policies, whether implemented by legal, self-regulatory, administrative or technological means;
2. encourage the on-line notification of privacy policies to users;
3. ensure that effective enforcement mechanisms are available both to address non-compliance with privacy principles and policies and to ensure access to redress;
4. promote user education and awareness about on-line privacy issues and the means at their disposal for protecting privacy on global networks;

---

[10] OECD, Ministerial Declaration on the Protection of Privacy on Global Networks, DSTI/ICCP/REG(98)10/FINAL. On the Internet: <http://www.oecd.org/dataoecd/39/13/1840065.pdf>.

5. encourage the use of privacy-enhancing technologies; and
6. encourage the use of contractual solutions and the development of model contractual solutions for on-line transborder data flows.'

The Ministers invited relevant international organizations to take the Declaration into consideration as they develop or revise international conventions, guidelines, codes of practice, model contractual clauses, technologies and interoperable platforms for protection of privacy on global networks. Industry and business were invited to take account of the objectives of this Declaration and to work with governments to further the objectives by implementing programs for the protection of privacy on global networks.

In general, all work that the OECD has done in the area of privacy[11] suggests that it considers the most effective privacy protection on-line likely to be delivered through a mix of regulatory and self-regulatory approaches, blending legal, technical, and educational solutions that suit the legal, cultural, and societal context in which it operates. According to the OECD, statutory systems can be more effective while using the wide range of self-regulatory measures to implement and enforce law on-line. On the other hand, self-regulation will also be more effective when it is backed-up with appropriate legislation and effective government enforcement. Enforceability is crucial because it may not be assumed that there will be compliance with either system.

5.2.1.3   *UN/ITU*

On 10-12 December 2003, the International Telecommunication Union (ITU) in Geneva organized the first phase of the World Summit on the Information Society (WSIS). This world summit was endorsed by the General Assembly of the United Nations.[12] The ITU is the UN agency that holds the leading role in the organization of WSIS. The summit addressed a broad range of themes concerning the information society, and a Declaration of Principles and a Plan of Action were adopted. The second meeting will be held at Tunis in November 2005.

In the Declaration of Principles, key principles for building an inclusive information society were outlined,[13] one of these being an enabling environment. In this context, the Declaration of Principles states that:

'The rule of law, accompanied by a supportive, transparent, pro-competitive, technologically neutral and predictable policy and regulatory framework reflecting national realities, is essential for building a people-centered Information Society. Governments

---

[11] See also the OECD report *Privacy On-line: Policy and Practical Guidance*, 21 January 2003, <http://www.olis.oecd.org/olis/2002doc.nsf/LinkTo/dsti-iccp-reg(2002)3-final>.

[12] Resolution 56/183 (21 December 2001).

[13] World Summit on the Information Society, *Declaration of Principles*, Document WSIS-03/GENEVA/DOC/0004 (12 December 2003), available at <http://www.itu.int/wsis/documents/>.

should intervene, as appropriate, to correct market failures, to maintain fair competition, to attract investment, to enhance the development of the ICT infrastructure and applications, to maximize economic and social benefits, and to serve national priorities.'

Furthermore, within the context of the key principle to create an enabling environment, the Declaration of Principles pays attention to governance issues and also leaves room for self-regulation:

'The management of the Internet encompasses both technical and public policy issues and should involve all stakeholders and relevant intergovernmental and international organizations. In this respect it is recognized that:
a) Policy authority for Internet-related public policy issues is the sovereign right of States. They have rights and responsibilities for international Internet-related public policy issues;
b) The private sector has had and should continue to have an important role in the development of the Internet, both in the technical and economic fields;
c) Civil society has also played an important role on Internet matters, especially at community level, and should continue to play such a role;
d) Intergovernmental organizations have had and should continue to have a facilitating role in the coordination of Internet-related public policy issues;
e) International organizations have also had and should continue to have an important role in the development of Internet-related technical standards and relevant policies.'

Thus, it appears that governance is a joint effort of public and private parties. 'Governments, as well as private sector, civil society and the United Nations and other international organizations have an important role and responsibility in the development of the Information Society and, as appropriate, in decision-making processes.' There should be 'a mechanism for the full and active participation of governments, the private sector and civil society from both developing and developed countries, involving relevant intergovernmental and international organizations and forums, to investigate and make proposals for action, as appropriate, on the governance of Internet by 2005.'[14]

5.2.2 National initiatives

5.2.2.1 *Australia*

In August 2000, the Australian Taskforce on Industry Self-Regulation published their policy document *Industry Self-Regulation in Consumer Markets*.[15] The Taskforce was established in August 1999 by the then Minister for Financial Ser-

---

[14] Ibid.
[15] Available on the Internet: <http://www.selfregulation.gov.au/publications/TaskForceOnIndustry Self-Regulation/FinalReport/contents.asp>.

vices and Regulation, Joe Hockey. It reported to the Government in August 2000 following two rounds of consultation with business and consumer representatives all around Australia. The report outlines the nature and extent of self-regulation in Australia and sets out good-practice principles for self-regulatory schemes.

On 13 December 2000, the Minister for Financial Services and Regulation announced the publication of a guideline for businesses, consumers, and government advisers. This guideline, which is currently being drafted, is intended to provide practical advice on self-regulation and to be a gateway to other resources on self-regulation.[16]

In its report, the Taskforce describes how self-regulatory schemes can promote good practices and target specific problems within industries. These schemes can force lower compliance costs on business, and offer quick, low-cost dispute resolution procedures. They can also avoid the often overly prescriptive nature of regulation and allow industry the flexibility to provide greater choice for consumers and to be more responsive to changing consumer expectations.

The Taskforce gave two general recommendations. First, it encouraged the government to provide industries with further practical guidelines, based on the principles in their report, for the development and review of self-regulatory schemes. Second, it recommends the government to update its guidelines for policy makers on how to assess the range of options for addressing a particular market failure or social policy objective. By doing so, the Taskforce findings can be incorporated in the industry environment and market circumstances that are most likely to lead to effective self-regulation.

In its report, the Taskforce concluded, furthermore, that there is no one model for self-regulation. Nevertheless, it identified the following common characteristics, called principles:

- The appropriate form of self-regulation will depend on what is to be achieved – that is the way in which it is necessary to significantly improve market outcomes for consumers. This can vary within and between industries.
- The form of self-regulation adopted by industry should be one that effectively solves the identified problem and minimizes costs for industry.
- The type of dispute resolution scheme, if required, should depend on the nature of the complaints and type of self-regulatory model.
- A scheme is only as effective as its broader coverage of industry participants, so it should aim for comprehensive membership.

5.2.2.2   *The Netherlands*

At a national level, in the Netherlands, the importance of self-regulation has been stressed several times. In the 1998 policy document *Legislation for the Electronic*

---

[16] *Industry Self-Regulation – A how to guide*, <http://www.selfregulation.gov.au/ind_self_reg.asp>.

Highways,[17] some preference was voiced for self-regulation. According to the Dutch Guidelines for regulation [*Aanwijzingen voor de regelgeving*],[18] government legislation is only allowed when action by the central government is necessary, and when self-regulation is expected to yield insufficient results. Dematerialization, internationalization, and technological turbulence make this criterion even more important within the electronic environment. Within such a technically complex and international environment, social organizations sometimes have more expertise and knowledge of sector-specific problems and of the feasibility and adequacy of possible solutions than the government. Besides, self-regulation is not restricted to the territorial borders of a country.[19]

The Dutch government stresses that, in self-imposed standards, adequate attention should be paid to different interests, especially those of vulnerable parties. Also, the enforcement of the standards should be trustworthy. It is the government's duty to ascertain compliance with these conditions. However, the scope of self-regulation is restricted: self-regulation is not suitable for regulating the fundamental principles of the constitutional state. In that case, government itself needs to regulate.[20]

In the policy document *Internationalization and Law in the Information Society* (2000), the Dutch government formulated the following: 'The aim is to develop co-regulation and to stimulate self-regulation at an international level.' The Dutch government gave high priority to the development of co-regulation and to the stimulation of international self-regulation for the on-line environment.[21]

5.2.2.3 United Kingdom

In December 2001, the British government published a policy document entitled *E-Policy Principles*.[22] Like many others, the British government wants to make its country one of the world's leading knowledge economies. To that end it wants to provide an effective 'light-touch' regulatory regime for the UK to engage in e-commerce and use the Internet safely and securely. The policy framework aims to ensure consumer confidence and trust in e-commerce and the use of the Internet. The e-policy principles are addressed to all policy makers working on proposals that may affect the Internet and e-commerce (see also chapter 1 of this Volume). They are designed to make policy makers aware of the impact that local, national, European and other international policy decisions and legislative proposals may have on e-commerce.

---

[17] See LEH Memorandum 1998, in Dutch: Kamerstukken II, 1997-1998, 25 880, nos. 1-2.

[18] See Aanwijzingen voor de regelgeving, Stcrt. 26 November 1992, 230 (in Dutch).

[19] See *supra* n. 17, at pp. 180-181.

[20] Ibid.

[21] ILIS Memorandum 2000.

[22] UK e-Government Unit, *The Principles of e-Policy Making*, <http://e-government.cabinet office.gov.uk/assetRoot/04/00/60/79/04006079.pdf>.

One of the eight e-policy principles deals with self-regulation: 'Consider self and co-regulation options.' This principle means that to encourage trust and the fast, effective resolution of problems, the Government is pursuing a policy of promoting co-regulation between providers, users, and regulators. The British government sees its role as defining goals from a public-interest perspective and ensuring that there is an adequate and up-to-date framework of law where necessary. If possible, the Government will look at providers and users and stimulate non-legislative arrangements like codes of conduct, guidelines, and voluntary schemes for dispute resolution. In general, such arrangements provide a more rapid and flexible answer to changing market needs and achieve more international consensus than is possible through legislation. However, the Government warns that self-regulation or co-regulation is not a cost-free option.

5.2.2.4   *United States*

In the earlier years of Internet regulation, the US government indicated a strong preference for self-regulation, particularly in the area of commerce. The very first principle of the White House's 1997 *Framework for Global Electronic Commerce* is headed: 'The private sector should lead':

> 'Though government played a role in financing the initial development of the Internet, its expansion has been driven primarily by the private sector. For electronic commerce to flourish, the private sector must continue to lead. Innovation, expanded services, broader participation, and lower prices will arise in a market-driven arena, not in an environment that operates as a regulated industry.
> Accordingly, governments should encourage industry self-regulation wherever appropriate and support the efforts of private sector organizations to develop mechanisms to facilitate the successful operation of the Internet. Even where collective agreements or standards are necessary, private entities should, where possible, take the lead in organizing them. Where government action or intergovernmental agreements are necessary, on taxation for example, private sector participation should be a formal part of the policy making process.'[23]

The same approach was taken by the Department of Commerce:

- Governments must allow electronic commerce to grow up in an environment driven by markets, not burdened with extensive regulation, taxation or censorship. While government actions will not stop the growth of electronic commerce, if they are too intrusive, progress can be substantially impeded.
- Where possible, rules for the Internet and electronic commerce should result from private collection action, not government regulation.

---

[23] The White House, *A Framework for Global Electronic Commerce*, 1 July 1997, <http://www.technology.gov/digeconomy/framewrk.htm>.

However, there is a role for the government in providing a legal framework:

- Governments do have a role to play in supporting the creation of a predictable legal environment globally for doing business on the Internet, but must exercise this role in a non-bureaucratic fashion.[24]

Several American agencies give attention to self-regulation. An example is the Federal Trade Commission (FTC), which addresses various issues related to regulatory problems in the area of electronic communications, such as fraud on the Internet, buying on-line, spamming, and Internet auctions. In July 2000, the FTC published a report on On-line Profiling, in which it supported an industry plan drafted by the Network Advertising Initiative (NAI),[25] to self-regulate consumer privacy protection in this area. However, at the same time, the FTC concluded that legislation seemed necessary to enforce the industry guidelines.[26]

It seems that, over the years, the US has gradually shifted from vehemently stressing self-regulation as a starting point to a more nuanced point of view, in which government regulation is increasingly seen as a useful tool in ICT regulation. In fact, 'the end of self-regulation' may even be discerned when looking at the host of regulatory initiatives the US has taken in the past few years in the area of ICT.[27]

5.3 What Does It Mean?

5.3.1 Key characteristics

We started this chapter by introducing the concept of self-regulation by presenting Jorg Ukrow's definition. Many other definitions have been suggested, but we are not concerned here with a precise definition. For the purpose of this chapter, a brief discussion of the key characteristics of the concept will suffice.[28] In general, self-regulation could be described as the regulation and co-ordination of behavior (of

---

[24] Department of Commerce, *The Emerging Digital Economy*, April 1998, p. 50, <http://www.technology.gov/digeconomy/EmergingDig.pdf>.

[25] The Network Advertising Initiative (NAI), a coalition of America's largest profile marketers, authored an industry plan, the NAI guidelines, and established a basic set of rules for notice of on-line information collection activities, consumer consent to such information collection and future marketing uses, consumer access to information held by on-line marketers, and security protection with respect to such information.

[26] Federal Trade Commission, *On-line Profiling: A Report to Congress. Part 2: Recommendations.* July 2000, <http://www.ftc.gov/os/2000/07/on-lineprofiling.htm#III.%20RECOMMENDATIONS>.

[27] Geist 2003, p. 351.

[28] For a more detailed analysis of self-regulation, see Baldwin & Gave, 1999, in particular, Chapter 10.

individuals or groups) through rules of societal organizations or through the application, compliance checking and enforcement of those rules.[29] There may or may
not be a specific legal basis for those rules.

Self-regulation can therefore be characterized through its constituent elements,
such as self-rule-making, self-jurisdiction, and self-enforcement. Self-rule-making
indicates that the interest groups, social organizations, or stakeholders themselves
draft the rules. This may imply that one interest group or organization draws up the
rules, but it is also possible that several groups representing different interests formulate the rules together. The rules that eventually come about are applicable to the
members of the interest group or social organization that has drafted the rules (self-
jurisdiction). If the rules are binding for the members, such bindingness is often
based on an agreement to abide by such rules. Finally, the group or the organization
may take measures against those members that do not abide by the rules in order to
make sure that they do so henceforward (self-enforcement). Self-enforcement may
also involve the monitoring or supervision of adherence to the rules in order to
detect possible breaches of the rules.

5.3.2   Typology and the relation to government regulation

Self-regulation is often contrasted with government regulation. The most prevalent
and typical form of government regulation is legislation. Legislation is the result of
a democratic process on a constitutional basis by which rules are enacted that are
binding on the territory of the pertinent state, and these rules are binding precisely
because of the very procedure by which they came about. The above definition
perhaps suggests that self-regulation and government regulation are two distinct
and mutually exclusive, alternative forms of regulation. From an analytical perspective, this may very well be true but, in practice, government legislation and
self-regulation are often each other's complement in the regulation and co-ordination of behavior. In literature, much attention has been paid to the relation between
self-regulation and legislation, and a number of basic forms of self-regulation have
been distinguished, based on their relation to government regulation: pure self-
regulation, proxy self-regulation, legally stipulated self-regulation, and co-regulation.

In the case of pure self-regulation,[30] the initiative for self-regulation rests fully
on the interest group. Government remains neutral to the outcome of their initiatives. Of course, the rules thus drafted may not contravene existing national legislation. Examples of pure self-regulation are domain-name dispute resolutions
mechanisms, such as ICANN's UDRP,[31] or standards, for example, the Model Code
for the Protection of Personal Information, approved as a 'National Standard of
Canada' by the Standards Council of Canada.[32]

---

[29] Eijlander 1994, p. 94.
[30] Eijlander & Voermans 1999, p. 71.
[31] See <http://arbiter.wipo.int/domains/>.
[32] Bennett & Raab 2003, p. 127.

Proxy self-regulation is accomplished without an explicit obligation to do so, except where government puts pressure on interest groups to realize self-regulation. Because public interests may be at stake, the government guards over these interests in the background. An example of proxy self-regulation is a code of conduct about mergers and takeovers in the (newspaper) publishing business, for example, to prevent an oligopolistic market structure.[33] Such an implicit threat of government regulation may also very well have been an important factor in the establishment, in the later 1990s, of Internet hotlines for illegal and harmful content. At the time, ISP liability was still very much in discussion; content issues may well have tipped the balance towards a stricter liability for Internet Service Providers. Thus, for instance, Dutch ISPs took the initiative to create a Dutch hotline for child pornography; they wanted to be seen doing something against child pornography on the Internet.

Pure self-regulation and proxy self-regulation do not *as such* fall within a legal framework. Types of self-regulation that are being accomplished within an existing legal framework are called stipulated self-regulation.[34] Legally stipulated self-regulation can be characterized as follows: the legislature sets the framework conditions within which the self-regulation has to be accomplished. Within the framework, citizens, companies, and social organizations have considerable freedom in drafting their rules. However, government has a more active role than with pure or proxy self-regulation. The ways and extent of stipulated self-regulation may differ. The legislator can merely prescribe the procedure for the realization of self-regulation and, for example, make provisions for dispute resolutions. In other cases, the legislator can also prescribe conditions for the results of the self-regulation, or the legislator can prescribe the minimum issues that have to be regulated.

Three types of stipulated self-regulation can be distinguished, according to the types of legislation that support self-regulation.

1. *A statute attaches legal consequences to self-regulation.* The legislator may oblige a certain group to draft self-regulation and stipulate what legal consequences are attached to the self-imposed rules, to what legal issues the self-regulatory rules are applicable, or what the legal status is of enforcement or other decisions of a self-regulatory body. It is, possible, for example, to obtain a legal order with which a decision of a self-regulatory body can be executed. Disciplinary law is but one example of this type of self-regulation.

2. *A statute prescribes procedures for self-regulation and for the legal consequences of the self-regulation.* Sometimes, the legislator offers the possibility to generate self-regulation, according to a specific procedure. As a result, the drafted self-regulation results in legal consequences. An example is the drafting of codes of conduct on data protection in a certain sector. Various Data

---

[33] See *supra* n. 30, at p. 72.
[34] Ibid.

Protection Acts in Europe, following the Directive on the protection of personal data, allow Data Protection Authorities to declare that the code of conduct conforms with the law, thus giving legal effect to the code, but only if certain procedural criteria are met, such as sufficient representation (see also section 5.4.2).

3. *A statute lays the foundation for new legislation if self-regulation is not forthcoming.* Sometimes, the law makes a provision for legislation, for situations where self-regulation is not achieved or does not measure up. An example of this is the DRM provision about Digital Rights Management (hereinafter: DRM) in the Copyright Harmonization Directive:[35] 'In the absence of voluntary measures taken by rightholders, including agreements between rightholders and other parties concerned, Member States shall take appropriate measures to ensure that right holders make available to the beneficiary of an exception or limitation provided for in national law.'[36] That is, if industry self-regulation does not sufficiently safeguard the interests of users of copyrighted material to benefit from the legal exceptions to the copyright, states should enact legislation to safeguard those rights. Another example is the statement of the Joint Committee on the British Draft Communications Bill, which noted that the Office of Communications (OFCOM), the communications regulator which was created by the Communications Act, should retain back-stop powers and the statutory right to re-impose detailed regulation where self-regulation fails to comply with agreed standards.[37]

Although the extent of stipulated self-regulation may vary, there is a difference between self-regulation and legislation with open norms or vague rules. By using open norms, the legislator leaves the specific interpretation and effects of the legal framework to the addressee and in last resort to the courts. This does not have to result in self-regulation.[38]

Finally, co-regulation is a kind of regulation that is characterized by the cooperation between government and the private sector. Government and social organizations are equal partners in initiating discussions about social problems and solving them. Co-regulation is a communicative way of decision-making, where the government is not the central actor who defines problems and initiates solutions. It is a kind of policy-making with open negotiations between interested parties about the nature, the extent, and the seriousness of certain problems and the directions and options for solution.

---

[35] Directive 2001/29/EC of the European Parliament and of the Council of 22 May 2001 on the harmonization of certain aspects of copyright and related rights in the information society, OJ L 167/10, 2001.

[36] Art. 6 para. 4 Directive 2001/29/EC, OJ L 167/10, 22.6.2001.

[37] Joint Committee Report, para. 71. See McKean & Hinton 2002.

[38] See *supra* n. 30, at p. 74.

As ICT law advances through the years, a gradual increase can be discerned in preference for co-regulation. In a 2000 inventory of government positions on ICT regulation,[39] we concluded that co-regulation is prominently present in several policy documents across Europe, at least in the Netherlands, Germany, France, and the United Kingdom, relating to e-Commerce and Internet policy. In 2001, in the European Commission White Paper on European Governance,[40] the Commission clearly saw a role for co-regulation, but would only allow this instrument to be used if certain conditions were met (see sections 5.2.1.1 and 5.5). Even in the US, there is a tendency to think that government should play a more important controlling part in realizing ICT policy, together with the industry and other social organizations. The OECD has also shown appreciation for co-regulation.[41]

5.3.3   Advantages and disadvantages of self-regulation

It is clear that self-regulatory initiatives have both strengths and weaknesses. In general, the advantages of self-regulation appear to be efficiency, flexibility, an incentive for compliance, and reduced costs for government. American scholars in particular have paid considerable attention to the benefits of self-regulation, given that private ordering is considered, in the US, to be 'politically more attractive than new government regulation in this modern era of hostility towards the state.'[42] Hence, the concepts of 'private' and 'public' ordering in relation to the on-line world have been extensively explored and discussed.[43] Here, we briefly touch upon the key arguments in favor of self-regulation.

Drafting and adapting the rules is often less time-consuming when this is done through self-regulation than by drafting and implementing legislation. For with self-regulation, the process of setting the rules draws on the specific expertise of the actors involved. Also, the rules usually evolve gradually. The effect of this appears, among other things, that the drafting process of self-regulatory mechanisms is usually not surrounded by intense lobbying as is the case with the development of legislation and international rules. Noteworthy is also that the rules established through self-regulatory instruments are not externally imposed and monitored by actors unfamiliar with the specifics of the context. Instead, the rules build on values that are internalized, meaning that the relevant parties are often already familiar with them. Given the absence of time-consuming formal procedures, it allows for easy adaptation to changing circumstances, new expertise, and changed views as regards the values, the monitoring options, and the enforcement mechanisms. Thus, self-regulation can turn out to be more efficient and flexible than legislation.

---

[39] Koops, et al., 2000.

[40] See *supra* n. 4.

[41] OECD Forum on Electronic Commerce, *Report on the Forum*, Paris, 12-13 October 1999, p. 11.

[42] Lemley 2000, p. 1546.

[43] See for an extensive discussion: Radin & Wagner 1998.

Another advantage relates to the above-mentioned internalized values on which self-imposed norms are often built. It is the very essence of self-regulation that the norms incorporated in the self-defined standards reflect the standards of the relevant group. Thus, since the parties involved in self-regulation have drafted the rules themselves, or close representatives have done so, there is usually substantial commitment among parties to observe their own rules. This works as an incentive for compliance.[44] Moreover, the adoption of self-defined standards could raise awareness among the partners. It is also relevant here that the rules established by the group itself may be more specific than laws issued by national or international governments. The participants in the self-regulatory scheme are likely to be more willing to comply with rules to which they themselves contributed than if the rules were addressed at a distant level by political motivations.

A further advantage of self-regulation is that the costs of self-regulation are low for government. Self-regulation leads to costs for the parties involved in complying with their rules. Government can supervise the performance of self-regulation, but those costs will in general be much lower than the costs for regulating the market.

Finally, it has been contended that self-regulation is more consistent with the specifics of the Internet architecture, i.e., an environment which tends to defy centralized control.[45] The characteristics of the on-line world make it difficult for governmental authorities to regulate and control this world. Moreover, it is argued that: 'preserving autonomy in cyberspace helps to maintain a critical balance of power between the public and private sectors, that serves the common good. The more on-line regulations we have, the greater the state's influence in the affairs of cyberspace, and this will inevitably mean more centralized structures of choice.'[46]

Of course, self-regulation does not only have advantages. A prominent weakness of self-regulation is that, in principle, the rules can be revised at will, and little is guaranteed. In other words, the flexibility for changing the rules may simultaneously be a disadvantage. In addition, there may be a lack of transparency. Where procedures exist for the publication of legislation, such procedures usually do not exist for self-regulation. At least, it seems more difficult for citizens to know of the creation, existence, and monitoring of self-regulatory schemes. Thus, the advantage that rules are based on internalized values may also be counter-productive because of a lack of external accountability for these values. The values may turn out to be selective or too narrow-minded, in that they fail to recognize other (societal) values. A consequence of self-regulation may also be that the power of the strongest or best-organized participating party will increase. This may turn out nega-

---

[44] The EU White Paper on Governance states about co-regulation: 'The result is wider ownership of the policies in question by involving those most affected by implementing rules in their preparation and enforcement. This often achieves better compliance, even where the detailed rules are non-binding.' European Commission, *European Governance. A White Paper*, Brussels, 25.7.2001, COM (2001) 428 final, <http://europa.eu.int/eur-lex/en/com/cnc/2001/com2001_0428en01.pdf>.

[45] See, for example, Spinello 2001, p. 167.

[46] Ibid., p. 168.

tively for other participants. Here, the lack of democratic control appears to be a disadvantage. Proper or legitimate use of the self-regulatory mechanism would therefore require that rules are set for the administration of the mechanism (for example, a trustmark) and that these rules are made publicly available. After all, only with such a transparency might people disadvantaged by the scheme be able to set matters right by recourse to the courts.

Another weakness may be the mechanisms' lack of clarity. As mentioned, the instrument of self-regulation allows for more open norms than is the case with legislation. The consequence of this could be that the rules set remain rather vague and unclear for the citizens and businesses. Often, no transparent criteria exist to offer guidance for being able to genuinely trust self-regulatory schemes. Especially when schemes originate from different countries, the lack of clarity could mean that no common guidelines exist for assessing the merits of the schemes or for monitoring and enforcing the standards set. Given the borderless context of the on-line world, this concern is of particular importance.

When considering the problems and promises of self-regulation, it is worth looking at the results of a study conducted by researchers from Oxford University. The study shows that most successful self-regulatory activity has taken place where there is a clear legal basis, such as in the field of illegal content on the Internet. Self-regulation therefore seems to have been less successful where public policy objectives are less clear, for example, in relation to trust of Internet content. Moreover, the study points out that there are significant problems with many existing self-regulatory models including:[47]

- a lack of clarity and transparency about key processes, such as rating of material;
- procedures of code renewal and revision;
- insufficient transparency and accountability in code production processes;
- a lack of sustainability of funding of self-regulatory initiatives; and
- a lack of knowledge by those who are subject to a specific self-regulatory model like codes of practice.

Unfortunately so far, not much empirical research data have been available on user experience, trust, and perception of self-regulatory activities. As a result, it is difficult to assess the effectiveness of self-regulatory models and activities compared to for instance other regulatory alternatives, or to evaluate their impact on social processes. The Oxford study generally observes that, according to available studies on user attitudes towards the Internet, trust seems to be static or even declining. Although the Internet is increasingly used for all kinds of activities (e-commerce, e-learning, entertainment, information, friendships, different forms of community

---

[47] PCMLP, *Self-Regulation of Digital Media Converging on the Internet: Industry Codes of Conduct in Sectoral Analysis*, 30 April 2004, University of Oxford, <http://www.selfregulation.info/iapcoda/0405-iapcode-final.pdf> (last visited October 2004).

building, etc.), user trust in this medium seems to be affected by software viruses, unsolicited e-mail (spam), inappropriate or harmful contact and content, threat of prosecution for breach of copyright, and even criminal activities on-line.[48] Moreover, user knowledge on trustmarks provided by self-regulatory bodies turns out to be very low in Europe: only 10 per cent of EU citizens in 2003 were aware of trustmarks.[49] Most EU citizens also do not know where to report potentially harmful content: 57 per cent of EU citizens do not know whom to contact and only 13 per cent are aware of a self-regulatory solution like an ISP or hotline, with the Dutch citizens highest at 26 per cent.[50]

5.3.4   Self-regulation in practice: How does it apply?

Having discussed some theoretical dimensions of self-regulation in the area of ICT, it is interesting to take a brief glance at the initiatives that have been established thus far, since the above discussion might give the impression that the field of self-regulation is neatly structured and transparent. In practice, however, initiatives diverge in territorial scope, in the groups to which they are applicable (certain industry sectors, or whoever wants to participate), the parties that set up and run the self-regulatory scheme (industry or consumer associations, individual companies), the character of those parties (not-for-profit or commercial), and the scope as regards the subjects covered (single-issue or multiple-issue schemes). It is outside the scope of this chapter to provide even a very general overview of all the initiatives that have emerged over the years. Nevertheless, to give an impression, we will give a few examples in the next section that show a range of initiatives and characteristics present in different forms of self-regulation.

5.3.4.1   *Codes, guidelines, and assessment schemes for on-line activity*

Self-regulatory instruments like codes of conduct, guidelines, seal programs, and voluntary schemes for dispute resolution usually have been created with the aim to regulate behavior in e-commerce environments. In several cases, they can be found in on-line public environments as well. In the last decade, many applications of these specific forms of self-regulation have seen the light.

A self-regulatory instrument frequently used by organizations is a code of conduct, a set of rules providing guidance on correct procedure and behavior for individuals. A well-known example the Code of Conduct for e-Commerce drafted by the Dutch Electronic Commerce Platform (ECP.NL).[51] This Code of Conduct has

---

[48] <www.selfregulation.info>, reporting of June 2004, p. 4 (last visited October 2004).

[49] Eurobarometer 2004.

[50] See *supra* n. 47.

[51] In October 2001, a new version 4.0 of the Model Code of Conduct was published. See also ECP.NL, *Model Code of Conduct (Draft 4.0 2001),* <http://www.ecp.nl/ENGLISH/publication/cocdraft4.0ENG.pdf>. The standards outlined in version 3.0 were drafted after consultation with Dutch

become a model for international organizations such as the Organization for Economic Co-operation and Development (OECD) and the United Nations (UN).[52] The object of this Model Code of Conduct is to create trust in electronic commerce by incorporating major principles in the code, such as reliability, transparency, confidentiality, and privacy. The Model Code of Conduct may serve as a checklist to assess the degree to which contracts, general terms and conditions, regulations, etc., help to increase mutual trust in e-business, but may also be perceived as an example or a source of inspiration for organizations in drafting codes of conduct for e-business.

Available at many web sites nowadays, privacy codes are another example of self-regulatory instruments. Based on generally acknowledged information privacy principles, these codes contain a set of rules to be followed by organization members or users of websites concerned. Specific examples of these privacy codes can be found for companies (for example, American Express), sectors or industry associations (for example, the Federation of European Direct Marketing Associations), organizational practice (for example, direct marketing associations), technology, (for example, smart card technology) and professional societies (for example, librarians).[53]

Web sites that require high levels of trust, such as those concerned with e-commerce transactions or health information, in many cases make use of a trustmark program to demonstrate that the content of their site meets a common set of standards. This set of standards is usually set out in a written code of conduct.[54] One example in this respect the TRUSTe trustmark, an on-line, branded seal, which is displayed by members of the TRUSTe's licensing program. Only those web sites that meet the privacy principles established by the On-line Privacy Alliance (OPA) and agree to comply with TRUSTe oversight and dispute resolution are allowed to display the TRUSTe seal. Members of the TRUSTe's licensing program are obliged to post a privacy policy on their web site, which discloses on-line information gathering and dissemination practices. In case of a privacy violation, they are contractually liable to an examination of their privacy practices.[55] A similar example that can be mentioned here is the introduction of hallmarks for secure e-commerce in specific geographical areas or sectors, like TrustUK.[56] However, the application of this self-regulatory instrument might lead to the development of trade barriers, as a higher level of consumer protection may be requested from specific companies.

---

representatives of all parties involved, including the business community and scientific research organizations, government agencies, and consumer organizations.

[52] The Centre for Trade Facilitation and Electronic Business of the United Nations (UN/CEFACT) adopted the Recommendation regarding 'E-commerce self-regulatory instruments' which included the Model Code of Conduct for Electronic Commerce (Draft version 3.0) as an example. See < http://www.unece.org/cefact/recommendations/rec32/rec32_ecetrd277.pdf >.

[53] See *supra* n. 32, at , p. 123.

[54] Bennett & Raab 2003.

[55] Ibid.

[56] <www.trustuk.org.uk> (last visited October 2004).

The Pan European Games Information rating system (PEGI) for video games and other media content can be mentioned as an example of self-regulation regarding content assessment. Implemented by the Interactive Software Federation of Europe (ISFE) in 2003 and with sixteen European countries participating since March 2004, the PEGI content rating system is a collaborative effort of national self-regulatory organizations and industry. The content rating system embodies five age categories (3, 7, 12, 16, and 18) and six content descriptors with warnings respectively regarding discrimination, drugs, fear, bad language, sex, or violence.

An example of what many authors perceive as a pure form of self-regulation are domain-name dispute resolutions mechanisms, such as the Uniform Domain Name Dispute Resolution Policy (UDRP) adopted by the Internet Corporation for Assigned Names and Numbers (ICANN) in 1999. The UDRP is based on recommendations made by WIPO. If a trademark holder thinks that a domain name registration infringes on his trademark, he may initiate proceedings under this Policy. The UDRP permits complainants to file a case with a resolution service provider, i.e., the WIPO Arbitration and Mediation Center, specifying the domain name in question, the respondent or holder of the domain name, the registrar with whom the domain name was registered, and the grounds for the complaint. Such grounds include the reason why a domain name is identical or similar to a trademark to which the complainant has rights; why the respondent should be considered as having no rights or legitimate interests in respect of the domain name that is the subject of the complaint; and why the domain name should be considered as having been registered and used in bad faith.[57] Respondents are given the opportunity to defend themselves against the complaint. Moreover, the WIPO Arbitration and Mediation Center appoints a panelist who decides on the potential transfer of the domain or domains.[58]

5.3.4.2 *Standards*

Standards are an example of self-regulatory arrangements which not only imply the availability of a common code but also a conformity assessment procedure. In 1996, the Model Code for the Protection of Personal Information was approved as a National Standard of Canada by the Standards Council of Canada.[59] This standard is based on ten principles, which organizations are advised to adopt in their entirety. Any public or private organization that processes personal data may adopt this voluntary instrument. Once adopted, however, the standard implies that certain obligations must be followed through in the event of organizational claims.

Other examples of standards or attempts towards standardization are negotiations towards a certifiable management standard for data protection through the

---

[57] <http://arbiter.wipo.int/center/faq/domains.html#16> (last visited October 2004).
[58] <http://arbiter.wipo.int/domains/> (last visited October 2004).
[59] See *supra* n. 32, at p. 127.

International Standardization Organization (ISO), later followed by similar attempts via the Comité Européen de Normalisation (CEN).[60]

5.3.4.3 *Netiquette*

Netiquette is considered to be the general network etiquette or etiquette of Internet users. Etiquette means, 'forms required by good manners or prescribed by authority to be needed in social or official life.' Netiquette is thus a set of basic rules for Internet users on how to behave properly on-line. Netiquette embodies the following set of guidelines for general behavior in various on-line environments:[61]

'Rule 1: Remember the Human: Do unto others as you'd have others do unto you.
Rule 2: Adhere to the same standards of behavior on-line that you follow in real life: Breaking the law is bad netiquette.
Rule 3: Know where you are in cyberspace: What's perfectly acceptable in one area may be dreadfully rude in another.
Rule 4: Respect other people's time and bandwidth: When you send email or post to a discussion group, you're taking up other people's time (or hoping to). It's your responsibility to ensure that the time they spend reading your posting isn't wasted.
Rule 5: Make yourself look good on-line: You will be judged by the quality of your writing. For most people who choose to communicate on-line, this is an advantage; if they didn't enjoy using the written word, they wouldn't be there. So spelling and grammar do count.
Rule 6: Share expert knowledge: The Internet was founded and grew because scientists wanted to share information. Don't be afraid to share what you know.
Rule 7: Help keep flame wars under control: Netiquette does forbid the perpetuation of flame wars. Flame wars are series of angry letters, most of them from two or three people directed toward each other, that can dominate the tone and destroy the camaraderie of a discussion group.
Rule 8: Respect other people's privacy: Of course, you'd never dream of going through your colleagues' desk drawers. So naturally you wouldn't read their email either.
Rule 9: Don't abuse your power: Knowing more than others, or having more power than they do, does not give you the right to take advantage of them. For example, sysadmins should never read private email.
Rule 10: Be forgiving of other people's mistakes: Everyone was a network newbie once. So when someone makes a mistake – whether it's a spelling error or a spelling flame, a stupid question or an unnecessarily long answer – be kind about it. If it's a minor error, you may not need to say anything. Even if you feel strongly about it, think twice before reacting. Having good manners yourself doesn't give you license to correct everyone else.'

---

[60] As described by Bennett & Raab 2003.
[61] These guidelines for on-line behavior were excerpted from Virginia Shea, *Netiquette*, Albion Books, 1994.

These Netiquette guidelines do not take into account all kinds of problems resulting from deviant on-line behavior, but provide basic principles that can be used to solve dilemmas in deciding upon on-line behavior. Netiquette rules can be further adjusted by any organization for their own users, clients, employees, etc.

5 3.4.4   *Public watchdogs and hotlines*

Internet does not only offer 'good' or lawful information and activities to its users, but also comprises illegal and harmful information, materials, or behavior. Examples in this respect are child pornography, discriminatory information, or illegal offers of medication. As traditional law enforcement turned out to be a complex matter for the deterritorialized, border-less Internet, self-regulatory instruments like public watchdogs and hotlines have been created as alternative solutions for this gap.

A public watchdog organization internationally considered as a model organization is the Internet Watch Foundation (IWF). In 1996 as public concern about illegal and offensive material on the Internet was increasing, the UK Department of Trade and Industry (DTI) facilitated discussions between ISPs, the London Metropolitan Police, the UK Home Office and an organization called the Safety Net Foundation. These discussions resulted in the 'R3 Safety Net Agreement', with R3 referring to the triple approach of Rating, Reporting, and Responsibility. This agreement resulted in the establishment of the IWF as the responsible body for implementing this voluntarily established arrangement for monitoring and tackling illegal and offensive content on the Internet. The IWF has three main roles:

1. It operates a hotline where UK Internet users can report on-line material which they believe might be illegal. If the IWF supports this view, it passes on the relevant information, either to the Metropolitan Police (if the alleged offence has been committed in the UK) or to the National Criminal Intelligence Agency (if the alleged offence has been committed in another country);
2. Together with other relevant organizations, it promotes voluntary systems for the rating of Internet content and the use of filtering techniques to enable parents, teachers and others responsible for children to prevent children in their care from gaining access to illegal, offensive, or inappropriate materials;
3. In partnership with many other organizations, the IWF has an education and awareness role so that some of the problems of Internet use, particularly the risks to children, and the mechanisms for dealing with these problems will become better known and understood.

The global nature of the Internet as well as the fact that over 90 per cent of all pornographic material accessed by UK Internet users is hosted outside the UK bring in the need for an international focus of the IWF in its activities. Consequently, the IWF strongly supports the Internet Hotline Providers in Europe (INHOPE) association as well as the Internet Content Rating for Europe (INCORE) organization.

In the Netherlands, ISPs united in the Dutch Foundation for Internet Providers (NLIP) developed a policy to be able to act against available materials on-line that under Dutch law are illegal. Part of this policy is the joint establishment by ISPs and consumers of hotlines [*meldpunten*] against child pornography, discrimination, and illegal content where on-line illegal materials can be reported. After notification, the hotline or ISP will test the reported content against existing Dutch laws and rules. The Dutch hotlines are only able to act in accordance with Dutch national legislation, and therefore only against offenders or information suppliers residing in the Netherlands. Notifications concerning offenders or information suppliers residing in other countries are reported to foreign watchdogs wherever possible.

Generally, the observation can be made that ISPs have been under pressure regularly to become more involved in monitoring, evaluating, rating, and removing Internet content. So far, they have resisted most involvement, arguing that they are mere conduits of information and that additional regulatory functions would burden them with unreasonable costs.[62] However, with policy and financial support of the European Commission and national governments, ISPs have evolved towards a new model of self-regulation in the form of Notice and Take Down (NTD) procedures operated through telephone hotlines. In twelve European countries, there are sixteen hotline services, at present, with the following general characteristics.[63]

- They operate primarily to facilitate removal and law enforcement in dealing with content that is clearly illegal in any medium. What is illegal, however, varies from state to state (for example, varying interpretations of hate speech, varying legal treatments of racist speech). The majority of complaints and actions relates to child pornography. Other forms of content taken down through hotlines include copyright infringement and defamatory and racist material.
- Complaints are roughly dealt with according to the following procedure: ascertaining if content is illegal; passing on relevant information to law enforcement; informing the ISP that the material is hosted on its servers, and take down of that content by the ISP.
- ISP hotline organizations have become involved in other forms of self-regulatory activities as well, for example, in the promotion of filtering, awareness, and rating technologies. Moreover, they have been proactive in raising awareness of other child-protection issues on the Internet, particularly with regard to chat-room danger and privacy.

5.3.4.5 *Technology as self-regulation*

Not only organizational solutions exist to arrive at self-regulatory arrangements, the technology itself also offers opportunities for self-regulation.

---

[62] <www.selfregulation.info> (last visited October 2004).
[63] See *supra* n. 47.

As an example, technological mechanisms exist that can anonymize information which is usually associated with certain individuals, such as anonymous remailers for electronic mail or anonymous browsers for Internet surfing. These Privacy Enhancing Technologies (PETs) can be found in other forms as well. Besides instruments for anonymity and pseudonymity, as mentioned, Bennett and Raab distinguish the following types of instruments that provide individual empowerment regarding on-line privacy protection:[64] encryption instruments (for example, e-mail encryption programs); filtering instruments (for example, filtering software to block and delete cookies); and Privacy Management Protocols (for example, privacy preference protocols like the Platform for Privacy Preferences (P3P) initiative, set-up by the World Wide Web Consortium).

Another technological development that provides a new form of self-regulation are Digital Rights Management Systems. These systems can automate permission as well as payment for the use of copyright-protected works. Secure viewers can also be used to assure that an owner's choice of restrictions will be self-executed.

5.4   WHEN SHOULD IT APPLY?

The self-regulatory schemes that have been established thus far – section 5.3 offers only a small selection of initiatives – appear helpful mechanisms in dealing with the variety of regulatory gaps on the Internet or complementing and reinforcing existing legal frameworks. In itself, the development of self-regulatory initiatives as well as their diversity appears welcome. However, the question arises to what extent and under what circumstances and conditions they may be helpful. While codes of conduct, seals, hotlines, trustmarks, and other instruments potentially add value to tackling the numerous problems that users face in the on-line environment, these instruments may also have their drawbacks. There is, for example, concern that there is no set of benchmarks by which parties can judge the relative merits of the instruments. Also, what self-regulatory initiatives can genuinely be trusted? Are the criteria for granting seals and trustmarks transparent, neutral and objective? What about the monitoring and enforcement of self-established rules? And what are the cross-border implications, given that the majority of the initiatives merely cover the situation in a specific country? So, is the rapidly multiplying variety in scope, geographical coverage, participation and oversight of the hundreds of ICT-related self-regulatory initiatives in itself a welcome development?

In the remaining part of this chapter we will aim to develop criteria to determine when self-regulation should – or should not – be considered and try to define in how and to what extent self-regulation should indeed be a starting point for ICT regulation. First, we will indicate some relevant criteria, starting with several lists

---

[64] See *supra* n. 32, at pp. 148-153.

of criteria suggested by policy documents. We will subsequently cluster these into seven broad criteria.

5.4.1 Criteria in policy documents

According to the Dutch government, self-regulation is the starting point (see 5.2.2.2), but not at all costs:

> 'Self-regulation as an alternative to government regulation is not suitable if fundamental norms and values of the democratic rule of law are at stake. In the case of the electronic highway, this holds especially with respect to protecting classical human rights of citizens and preventing and investigating infringements of the rule of law and state security. In these cases, agreements between parties cannot suffice and legislation will be necessary.'

Moreover, in order to be acceptable as an alternative to government regulation, self-regulation has to meet several elementary conditions:

- the relevant groups must be well-organized;
- relevant social interests must be equally protected;
- all parties must be sufficiently bound to the rules;
- enforcement of the rules must be sufficiently guaranteed.

In the long run, however, government regulation might become the starting point again.

This may be the case if:

- developments lead to replacement, i.e. when people can no longer do things off-line but can only perform them on-line. The government should then create guarantees for accessibility;
- technological turbulence decreases and stability is achieved. Then, to promote legal certainty, perhaps codification of norms established by self-regulation could take place.[65]

In the 2001 White Paper on European Governance, the European Commission also lists various criteria for private regulation in the form of co-regulation: 'Co-regulation implies that a framework of overall objectives, basic rights, enforcement and appeal mechanisms, and conditions for monitoring compliance is set in the legislation.' When can co-regulation be considered?

---

[65] See *supra* n. 17, at pp. 181-182.

'It should only be used where it clearly adds value and serves the general interest. It is only suited to cases where fundamental rights or major political choices are not called into question. It should not be used in situations where rules need to apply in a uniform way in every Member State. Equally, the organizations participating must be representative, accountable and capable of following open procedures in formulating and applying agreed rules. This will be a key factor in deciding the added value of a co-regulatory approach in a given case.

Additionally, the resulting co-operation must be compatible with European competition rules and the rules agreed must be sufficiently visible so that people are aware of the rules that apply and the rights they enjoy. Where co-regulation fails to deliver the desired results or where certain private actors do not commit to the agreed rules, it will always remain possible for public authorities to intervene by establishing the specific rules needed.'[66]

In the US Department of Commerce indicated criteria for regulating privacy in e-commerce:

'In order to empower consumers to have control of their own personal information, the US government is encouraging the private sector to establish codes of conduct and self-regulation. To be meaningful, the government believes that self-regulation must do more than articulate broad policies or guidelines. Effective self-regulation involves substantive rules, as well as the means to ensure that consumers know the rules, that companies comply with them, and that consumers have appropriate recourse when there is noncompliance.'[67]

Some other aspects emerge in the US FTC's recommendations on on-line profiling, where it concluded that legislation seems necessary to enforce industry guidelines.[68]

'As the Commission has previously recognized, self-regulation is an important and powerful mechanism for protecting consumers, and the NAI principles present a solid self-regulatory scheme. Moreover, NAI members have agreed to begin to put their principles into effect immediately while Congress considers the Commissions recommendations concerning on-line profiling.

Nonetheless, backstop legislation addressing on-line profiling is still required to fully ensure that consumers' privacy is protected on-line. For while NAI's current membership constitutes over 90% of the network advertising industry in terms of revenue and ads served, only legislation can compel the remaining 10% of the industry to comply with fair information practice principles. Self-regulation cannot address recalcitrant and bad actors, new entrants to the market, and dropouts from the self-regulatory pro-

---

[66] See *supra* n. 4, at p. 21.

[67] Department of Commerce, *The Emerging Digital Economy*, April 1998, <http://www.technology.gov/digeconomy/emerging.htm>.

[68] Federal Trade Commission, *On-line Profiling: A Report to Congress. Part 2: Recommendations*. July 2000. On the Internet: <http://www.ftc.gov/os/2000/07/on-lineprofiling.htm#III.%20RECOMMENDATIONS>.

gram. In addition, there are unavoidable gaps in the network advertising companies ability to require host Websites to post notices about profiling, namely Web sites that do not directly contract with the network advertisers; only legislation can guarantee that notice and choice are always provided in the place and at the time consumers need them.'

The Australian Taskforce on Industry Self-Regulation referred to a general guide as to whether self-regulation is appropriate: the Commonwealth Office of Regulation Review's Regulatory Impact Statement checklist. This checklist states that:

'self-regulation should be considered where:
• there is no strong public interest concern, in particular, no major public health and safety concern;
• the problem is a low risk event, of low impact/significance, in other words the consequences of self-regulation failing to resolve a specific problem are small; and
• the problem can be fixed by the market itself, in other words there is an incentive for individuals and groups to develop and comply with self-regulatory arrangements (for example, for industry survival, or to gain a market advantage).

In addition, for self-regulatory industry schemes, the checklist determines success factors to include:
• presence of a viable industry association;
• adequate coverage of the industry by the industry association;
• cohesive industry with like minded/motivated participants committed to achieving the goals;
• voluntary participation – effective sanctions and incentives can be applied, with low scope for the benefits being shared with non-participants; and
• cost advantages from tailor-made solutions and less formal mechanisms such as access to quick complaints handling and redress mechanisms.'[69]

This checklist is analyzed and elaborated in the report, with attention paid to, among other issues, adequate coverage, clarity, consumer and industry awareness, transparency, dispute procedures and sanctions for non-compliance, monitoring, reviewing, accountability, and costs. There can be no one-size-fits-all guidelines for self-regulation, but the 'appropriate form of self-regulation will depend on what is trying to be achieved, which will vary depending on the industry.'[70]

The World Summit on the Information Society's Declaration of Principles outlined key principles for building an inclusive information society.[71] One of these key

---

[69] <http://www.selfregulation.gov.au/publications/TaskForceOnIndustrySelf-Regulation/FinalReport/isr_part2-05.asp>.
[70] <http://www.selfregulation.gov.au/publications/TaskForceOnIndustrySelf-Regulation/FinalReport/isr_part2-06.asp>.
[71] World Summit on the Information Society, *Declaration of Principles*, Document WSIS-03/GENEVA/DOC/4-E (12 December 2003), p. 3, available at <http://www.itu.int/wsis/documents/>.

principles is to create an enabling environment, which gives an indication of when governments should intervene:

> 'The rule of law, accompanied by a supportive, transparent, pro-competitive, techno-logically neutral and predictable policy and regulatory framework reflecting national realities, is essential for building a people-centered Information Society. Governments should intervene, as appropriate, to correct market failures, to maintain fair competi-tion, to attract investment, to enhance the development of the ICT infrastructure and applications, to maximize economic and social benefits, and to serve national priori-ties.'

5.4.2   Main criteria

Various policy papers have thus listed sets of criteria for situations in which self-regulation can be considered and when government intervention is called for. These can be summarized as follows.

1.   Fairness
A broadly shared view is that regulatory rules should be fair. That is, social interests should be protected, particularly those of weaker parties who may not have been able to participate in the regulatory process or whose interests might be crushed under the weight of industry interests.[72] Equality, non-discrimination, fundamental rights and fair competition should be safeguarded if 'replacement' occurs, that is, if people can no longer fall back on traditional means and ways of doing things, situ-ations should be avoid in which certain groups in society fall behind, for instance, because they lack relevant ICT skills of the new communications media.

Fairness is one of the prime indicators for government involvement. If funda-mental rights are at stake or if certain groups threaten to be discriminated, self-regulation is not an adequate instrument. Safeguarding all relevant interests, particularly those of weaker parties cannot be left to private actors.

2.   Inclusiveness
A second criterion is the inclusiveness of the self-regulatory process: who partici-pates in drafting rules and do these participants constitute a sufficiently representa-tive sample of the relevant actors? For self-regulation to work, the stakeholders should be well organized in order to ensure that the people participating in the process know the needs and desires of their colleagues and the people they repre-sent.

Although this criterion is related to the first, in that the self-regulatory process works better if interest groups representing weaker parties participate, it is a sepa-

---

[72] Cf., the Law Council of Australia's comment that 'a minimum condition for successful self-regulation is the provision of industry funded independent consumer representatives, so that the vari-ous uneven elements of the consumers/producer relationship can be remedied', <http://www.self regulation.gov.au/publications/TaskForceOnIndustrySelf-Regulation/FinalReport/isr_part2-06.asp>.

rate issue. 'Fairness' looks at subject-matter and results, indicating that where complex balancing issues involving fundamental rights are at stake, self-regulation usually will not work and the government should keep a close eye on developments. 'Inclusiveness' is a criterion for those issues that, in principle, lend themselves well to self-regulation; it stresses that the effectiveness of self-regulatory rules will depend on the representativeness of the actors that take part in drafting the rules.

3. Compliance

Perhaps most often cited as a primary concern with self-regulation is the issue of compliance. To what extent and with what instruments can organizations that self-declare their standards of communication or behavior be held accountable if their initiatives fail to live up to the expectations of consumers, citizens, or other parties in the on-line world? What, for example, to do with businesses that apply privacy seals, but fail to provide the expected level of care? A crucial difference with government regulation is that, with self-regulatory rules, there is not a natural mechanism to ensure compliance. In principle, self-regulatory mechanisms do not establish law in the meaning of legal rules that are binding on all citizens in a certain country (for the very reason that self-regulatory mechanisms are not created by democratic means such as control by an elected parliament). Thus, a key disadvantage of self-regulatory schemes is their lack of adequate enforcement.[73] Hence, considerable attention must be given to enforcement mechanisms. Since the mere creating of rules does not make the self-regulating parties accountable for complying with the rules, various instruments may be considered to enhance accountability, such as monitoring committees and procedures, and complaint-handling and dispute resolution mechanisms.

In fact, a closer look at self-regulation initiatives reveals that various enforcement scenarios appear in practice. First, organizations may decide to enforce the self-declared rules themselves. Many responsible organizations indeed try to ensure the adherence to the norms they have set, either by sanctions (for example, by ejection from membership or by denying further use of a trustmark), by means of labeling, and by rating mechanisms. However, the characteristics of the on-line world make it difficult to effectively sanction parties who fail to respect these norms. Ensuring that the initiative passes from letter to action appears, in particular, to be difficult in light of the borderless environment in the on-line world. Also, since self-regulatory sources are often located only in a certain territory or that the initiatives are often limited to a group of actors who share a certain attitude towards professional behavior, the overall effect of self-regulatory initiatives may be questioned. For if an organization lacks the means, power, and authority to enforce its norms, then their value remains symbolic. Thus, a convincing case for self-regulation can only be made if the relevant parties to the self-imposed rules or standards formulate organizational compliance measures with inherently binding provisions,

---

[73] See on this in detail: Prins, Schellekens, 2004.

for example, in operational policies. But as the FTC has noted, unwilling actors must also be taken into account: 'Only legislation can compel the remaining 10% of the industry to comply with fair information practice principles. Self-regulation cannot address recalcitrant and bad actors, new entrants to the market, and drop-outs from the self-regulatory program.' That is to say, self-regulation works well with willing actors, but as long as a certain part of the market has an interest in not complying, self-regulation alone cannot do the trick. In the end, the effectiveness of self-regulation largely depends on the internal discipline of the organization or group of actors. Thus far, very little research has been done to measure the exact commit-ment of the partners in a self-regulatory scheme.

In a way, the issue of compliance mirrors the criterion of inclusiveness: the more involved all stakeholders are in drafting self-regulatory regimes, the better incen-tive they will have to comply with the rules. In other words, in domains and pro-cesses in which a high level of involvement of all relevant actors is ensured, perhaps less attention need be given to enforcement mechanisms. The reverse is also true: the less actors participate in self-regulation, the more compliance becomes an is-sue. In those cases, if insufficient legal instruments are or can be created for com-pliance, regulation is more a matter for government than for private parties.

4. *Transparency*

Almost equally frequently mentioned as a concern with respect to self-regulation is the transparency of the process of drafting rules or of the resulting rules them-selves. Contrary to (the theory of) democratic rule-making, self-regulation may be an obscure and behind-the-scene process. If the people affected by self-regulation are not made aware of the process, they cannot try and influence it to their benefit (compare also the criterion of fairness); and if the resulting rules are invisible or untransparent, they cannot complain if they are adversely affected.

Transparency is related to the effectiveness of the regulation: self-regulatory rules that are opaque (for example, seals or trustmarks with obscure criteria) will be less trusted and hence not readily followed. In that sense, transparency is also re-lated to compliance: since self-regulation is usually done by a selection of private parties, the non-participating actors will not be willing to comply, unless the pro-cess and rules are sufficiently transparent for them to adopt the rules voluntarily.

5. *Legal certainty*

Comparable to transparency is the issue of legal certainty: are rules sufficiently clear, unequivocal, and consistent to provide the legal certainty needed by actors in a certain field? As with legislation, this is an important issue. However, it is not easy to say whether legal certainty in general is an argument for or against self-regulation. In some cases, self-regulation is better suited to provide legal certainty, for instance, if the field is rapidly changing and flexibility in updating rules is called for. Moreover, self-regulation might be seen as a better instrument for very detailed rules, while legislation is more suited to general and more abstract rules. However, this argument is not backed up by legislative practice: large areas of the law are extremely detailed. Indeed, sometimes the law does need to be detailed in order to provide the right level of legal certainty, while self-regulation may equally well lose itself in vague rules that leave much room for interpretation. Hence, it should be considered whether the subject-matter and the actors involved in self-regulation are sufficiently able to draft clear and precise rules, or whether this particular subject-matter is more suited for government regulation to provide adequate legal certainty.

6. Context

This brings us to the more general criterion of context. As the Australian taskforce noted, much depends on what self-regulation tries to achieve, and this varies, depending on the industry and subject-matter. It also depends on the technology at issue, as the Dutch criterion of technological turbulence shows.

Also relevant is the international context: is the subject something which can be fairly well regulated in a national context? Is it an issue with a large variety of initiatives around the world? Is it something that calls for harmonization? Note that, like legal certainty, the international context is not necessarily something that favors self-regulation: although it might be said that, at an international level, self-regulation is easier to achieve than government regulation (compare chapter 6), it is not obvious that a multitude of private parties around the world can achieve harmonized rules better than governments. This, again, also depends on the subject-matter, the industries, and the technologies involved.

Another dimension of the context is politics: self-regulation is more suited to 'neutral' issues: issues that call for answers (what electronic signatures have sufficient legal validity?) rather than policy choices (should spam be allowed or restricted?).[74] If major political choices are at stake democratically elected governments should make them, not private parties.[75]

7. Efficiency

Last and perhaps least on a theoretical level, but foremost on a practical level, is the issue of efficiency. Government regulation is often regarded as cumbersome, time-consuming, and costly, while self-regulation is seen as swift, meager, and cheap. Moreover, self-regulation is more flexible and therefore better suited for regular updating with developments. This does not only relate to the process of regulation: self-regulation may also impose lower compliance costs on businesses because they themselves can better tailor the rules to their situation.

---

[74] In the terminology of our earlier report on internationalization: 'answering issues' are more suited to self-regulation than 'steering issues'. See Koops, et al., 2000, p. 173.

[75] Compare the Australian Taskforce's principle 34: Government involvement in self-regulation is justified when there is a public policy objective that would otherwise call for a regulatory response', <http://www.selfregulation.gov.au/publications/TaskForceOnIndustrySelf-Regulation/FinalReport/isr_part2-07.asp>.

This is not to say that self-regulation should therefore be the starting point, but it does mean that if other criteria do not indicate a clear preference for government regulation, self-regulation is the natural first choice. In other words, efficiency is a criterion that becomes prominent if the other criteria give insufficient guidance in choosing between self-regulation and government regulation.

5.5   How Can It Be Applied?

Taking the criteria listed above into consideration, it appears that there will seldom be a preference for pure self-regulation. If the subject-matter is not contentious, if the stakeholders participate in a transparent process with sufficient respect for all interests at stake, with compliance ensured by effective self-enforcement and a 100 per cent involvement of all market parties, and with awareness-raising mechanisms for consumers, then pure self-regulation is a good starting point indeed. But this will rarely be the case.

Nearly all policy documents as well as the literature stress that there is also a role for the government. Just what this role is, is less clear – there is a large variety of options and types of government intervention to chose from. The criteria outlined above may give a clue to the right level of government action.

In this section, we will indicate various roles for the government and mechanisms for enhancing the efficacy of self-regulation, which all can be deemed some type of co-regulation. We distinguish between legislative action, procedural action, and other facilitating action.

1.   Legislative action

1.1 Codification
A straightforward way of enhancing the efficacy of self-regulation is to codify in law the norms that have been created by self-regulation. It is one of the traditional types of co-regulation in the form of stipulated self-regulation (see section 5.3.2). This has been suggested by the Australian taskforce as one of their conclusions: '36. Government can assist in integrating schemes into the regulatory framework.'[76] It is also what the Dutch government suggested as an option when turbulent times have calmed down and self-regulatory norms have crystallized, in order to enhance legal certainty.[77]

Codifying self-regulatory rules does not only enhance legal certainty, but it also strengthens compliance, since legal norms are usually easier to enforce than self-regulatory norms. Of course, it should only be considered for self-regulation that is additional to and consistent with existing legal norms, and only if the subject-mat-

---

[76] <http://www.selfregulation.gov.au/publications/TaskForceOnIndustrySelf-Regulation/FinalReport/isr_part2-07.asp>.

[77] See *supra* n. 17, at p. 182.

ter is not contentious and the norms are widely shared by the stakeholders. If the self-regulation was flawed in some sense, for instance, if interests of vulnerable groups were insufficiently taken into account, the government should consider new or other regulation rather than codification.

1.2 Backstop legislation

In many cases, self-regulation will not by itself be completely satisfactory where, for instance, the criteria of fairness or inclusiveness are concerned. In such cases, 'backstop' legislation can be considered, as the FTC suggested: 'Backstop legislation addressing on-line profiling is still required to fully ensure that consumers privacy is protected on-line.'

Such backstop legislation can take various forms. It can be enacted pro-actively, as an incentive for market parties to develop self-regulation. Such legislation can offer incentives, such as providing legal certainty for parties that comply with standards to be developed by industry. Examples of this are the Directive on digital signatures (providing evidential value for signature schemes compliant with the Annexes criteria) and the 'safe harbor' that the US CALEA Act offers telecom carriers who comply with publicly available technical requirements or standards adopted by an industry association or standard-setting organization for interceptability of telecommunications (47 USC § 1006). Alternatively, the law may use a stick rather than a carrot and threaten with legislation if adequate self-regulation is not forthcoming. An example of this is the DRM provision in the Copyright Harmonization Directive:

> 'In the absence of voluntary measures taken by rightholders, including agreements between rightholders and other parties concerned, Member States shall take appropriate measures to ensure that rightholders make available to the beneficiary of an exception or limitation provided for in national law'.

Threatening with legislation if self-regulation does not meet the criteria determined by government, is one of the instruments mentioned by the Dutch government (see section 5.4.1).[78] Apart from pro-active legislation, backstop laws may also be enacted ex post, for instance, to push recalcitrant actors into complying with self-regulatory schemes developed by others. It should also be considered as soon as self-regulation appears not to work. As one of the conclusions of the Australian taskforce stated: 'The degree of government involvement will depend on the significance of the market failure or social policy objective being addressed and the consequences of self-regulation proving ineffective.'[79]

---

[78] Ibid., at p. 181.
[79] <http://www.selfregulation.gov.au/publications/TaskForceOnIndustrySelf-Regulation/FinalReport/isr_part2-07.asp>, conclusion 38.

1.3 General framework legislation

Rather than enacting pro-active or ex post incentives or retaliatory legislation, the government can also establish a general framework, for instance, with minimum standards or conditions, in which self-regulation can subsequently take place. 'In this hybrid form of self-regulation, the legislator takes the initiative and determines the frameworks in which the self-regulation has to take place. For example: only the further technical detailing is left to market parties and private normalization bodies. As far as such stipulated self-regulation constitutes further detailing of government responsibilities, a number of formal and procedural requirements will hold. These do not differ in the electronic environment from those in the traditional environment.'[80]

The framework may be more basic than to only leave room for 'technical detailing'. The framework could also consist of some basic norms that have to be safeguarded, while leaving open other issues and the way in which those norms will be satisfied. This could be a viable option with respect to codes of conduct, where there is currently a highly diverse landscape of – often conflicting – standards for conduct and on-line behavior. Illustrative is the variety in substantive rules included in the codes of conduct of the Web trader initiative established by the consumer associations in different European countries. The present situation made Endeshaw argue that: '[t]he functional diversity and overlap, on the one hand, and the conflicting standards among trustmarks, on the other hand, prompt a coherent solution.'[81] A possible solution is the e-Confidence program of the European Commission, which examines the possibility for drawing up common guidelines for e-commerce codes of conduct; these guidelines could be used by bodies responsible for monitoring and approving codes of conduct. Thus far, no Recommendation has been published; a second draft of the framework principles was produced by a group of business and consumer stakeholders and published for comment in early 2001.[82] A related initiative (also part of the EU e-Confidence project) is that of BEUC and UNICE to establish a set of requirements for trustmark schemes, the European Trustmark Requirements.[83]

Nevertheless, it could be questioned to what extent standardization and certification of trustmarks, codes of conduct, seals, and other self-regulatory initiatives should be a goal in itself. It could be argued that a diversity in schemes and their content is in itself welcome, because it encourages competition between standards and thus, over time, may enhance the quality and level of the standards. It would

---

[80] See *supra* n. 17, at p. 184.

[81] Endeshaw 2001, p. 225.

[82] The texts of the first and second drafts as well as the comments made by various organizations are available at <http://econfidence.jrc.it>. The second draft of principles contains ten general principles for generic codes of practice for the sale of goods and services to consumers on the Internet: Fairness and equity, Added value, Transparency, Openness and non-discrimination, Global dimension, Social responsibility, Compliance, Complaint handling and dispute resolution, Security, and Data protection.

[83] Also available at <http://econfidence.jrc.it>.

also provide consumers and businesses with a wider choice. What is more, setting certain standards for self-regulatory initiatives may not offer a definitive solution to the present landscape of highly different substantive rules. Even with a general framework of basic principles, disparity in national laws regarding the status and enforcement of self-regulatory initiatives will continue to affect the end result of the initiative. Individual countries may also try and compete on the use or non-use enforcement mechanisms. For example, despite the availability of guidelines, one country might decide to close the door to foreign initiatives (such as a foreign trustmark) and provide its own businesses with advantages. In its reaction to the second draft of the European Union Principles on E-Commerce Codes of Conduct, the US Federal Trade Commission expressed a view in line with this point: 'We have concerns that approval of codes could have a discriminatory effect on US businesses and could therefore deter the growth of an international electronic marketplace.'[84]

Perhaps needless to stress, framework legislation is always appropriate when fundamental rights are at stake (see the fairness criterion in section 5.4.2). As the final conclusions of the OECD Forum on Electronic Commerce stressed, it is the responsibility of national governments 'notably to protect vulnerable groups'.[85] This protection can only be achieved by legislation that sets basic standards for protection of weak parties and for fundamental rights.

1.4 Procedural legislation
Similar to creating framework legislation with basic substantive principles, governments could also enact legislation that sets procedural requirements for self-regulation. An example is the drafting of sectoral codes of conduct for data protection. The Directive on the protection of personal data encourages the drafting of codes of conduct for data protection,[86] and organizations can request the Data Protection Authority (DPA) to declare that, given the particular features of the sector or sectors of society in which these organizations operate, the rules contained in their code properly implement the Personal Data Protection Act or other legal provisions on the processing of personal data. However, the DPA may only consider requests

---

[84] Comments on the Second Draft Principles for E-Commerce Codes of Conduct made by the US Federal Trade Commission Staff, 18 April 2001, available at <http://econfidence.jrc.it>.

[85] OECD Forum on Electronic Commerce, *Report on the Forum*, Paris, 12-13 October 1999, p. 13. Likewise the 1997 Ministerial Conference in Bonn, in which the EU ministers concluded that the main role for the legislator is to safeguard fundamental norms and values in an electronic environment. European Commission, *Ministerial Declaration*, Ministerial Conference, Bonn, 6-8 July 1997, <http://europa.eu.int/ISPO/bonn/Min_declaration/i_finalen.html>.

[86] Directive 95/46/EC of the European Parliament and of the Council of 24 October 1995 on the protection of individuals with regard to the processing of personal data and on the free movement of such data, Recital 61. In practice, the benefit of such a 'conformity declaration' lies in the added certainty for those who work with personal data that their handling of personal data is lawful if and when they align their behavior with the code of conduct. Codes of conduct are in effect so complete in their coverage of subjects that those working with personal data in the pertinent sector need not have recourse to other legal sources.

where, in its opinion, the organizations that request recognition are sufficiently representative, and the sector or sectors concerned should be adequately defined in the code of conduct. Moreover, if the code includes a dispute resolution mechanism, a declaration of conformity can only be considered if sufficient guarantees for independence are given.[87]

1.5 Liability

Not purely a legislative action, but a traditional legal instrument nonetheless, is liability. The majority of the current self-regulatory initiatives aim at making promises to the outside world: they publicly claim – implicitly or explicitly – that users can depend on a certain level of privacy or consumer protection, a minimum standard of the quality and credibility of the on-line services, etc. This raises expectations with the general public and specific consumers. As a result, the presentation tends to enhance the standard by which the conduct of those applying the initiative is measured. The fact that the applicable norms, definitions, and responsibilities have been made explicit makes it, in general, easier to successfully win a liability case. In other words, when the claimed or expected results of the self-imposed initiative turn out to be not as expected or do not materialize at all, the self-regulatory parties may be held liable for any resulting damage.[88]

Of course, this will only be the case if a contractual relationship exists between the organization that initiated the self-regulatory scheme (for example, a code of conduct established by the representative body of ISPs) and a member of that organization (for example, an individual ISP). For example, an ISP may thus be accountable to the organization for any operation not in accordance with the code of conduct. On its part, the organization may be held liable if it did not exercise due care and skill in accepting new members, monitor its members' activities and take appropriate steps to remedy unwanted operations of members. In the absence of adequate monitoring and enforcement, the success of the code of conduct may be comprised and thus become less 'trustworthy', which could have negative consequences for the other members of the organization.

Contractual liability may also play a role in enforcing self-regulatory mechanisms in the relation between electronic businesses and consumers. For example, when a trustmark or seal is put up on the web site of an on-line shop, an aggrieved consumer who was misled may seek to pursue a contractual liability action.

However, this option would only seem available when the relationship between the on-line shop and the consumer is entirely contractual and the 'promises' behind the trustmark are somehow integrated into the contract. In all other situations, a contractual liability claim will not find any legal support. In certain situations, liability under tort law may then provide an alternative for enforcement. However, whether a consumer's claim succeeds will depend on many circumstances, such as

---

[87] See, for example, Art. 25 of the Dutch Personal Data Protection Act.
[88] Prins & Schellekens 2004.

the nature and explicitness of the 'promises', the additional claims as to the role the trustmark plays, the type of consumer.

It is in the absence of a contractual relationship that the lack of enforcement tools becomes most evident. As mentioned, self-regulatory mechanisms do not establish law in the meaning of legal rules that are binding on all citizens in a certain country. Thus, a third party that is not a participant in the self-regulatory scheme is, in principle, not obliged to follow any suggestions the body might make. In fact, it may do nothing. This is a rather unsatisfactory situation, given the numerous self-regulatory initiatives that have appeared in the past few years.

An interesting question would therefore be how self-regulatory initiatives could gain some external effect. In other words, could a code of conduct adopted by representatives of certain actors influence or even determine the required behavior of actors that are not a party to the code of conduct? Although the recognition of such an effect would not guarantee an optimal sanctioning and enforcement of violations of the private norms, it will certainly contribute to the efficacy of self-regulatory schemes. One step further would be a situation in which the norms adopted, such as standards for on-line consumer protection, may become a professional standard whereby contravention automatically constitutes a fault. This would create a situation in which self-regulation becomes a key source of law complementary to the rules issued by the government and could perhaps even replace the latter. Could a situation thus arise in which trust or quality criteria for on-line communication and transactions become more than just the professional standard, i.e., a *de jure* standard?[89] An answer to this question requires a discussion on the legal status of self-regulatory initiatives versus third parties. Thus far, private law has been either very reluctant in debating the status under private law of self-regulatory mechanisms or has even fully ignored such a discussion. Given the prominent role of self-regulatory mechanisms in an on-line environment, it appears high time that such a debate is put on the agenda.

2. Facilitating action

Legislation is not the only instrument of governments for regulation. In fact, they have a large variety of actions that may stimulate self-regulation or that can steer self-regulation in a direction that conforms better with the criteria for self-regulation. For instance, governments 'can assist in analyzing systemic problems in an industry and in facilitating the design of a self-regulatory response to address those systemic problems.'[90] The establishment of study groups or task forces, either directly or indirectly, for instance, through financial incentives, is an obvious way to stimulate self-regulation; the Dutch government's stimulation of the Electronic

---

[89] Prins & Schellekens 2005.
[90] <http://www.selfregulation.gov.au/publications/TaskForceOnIndustrySelf-Regulation/FinalReport/isr_part2-07.asp>, conclusion 35.

Commerce Platform is a good example of this,[91] as is the establishment of a public-private program on vulnerability on the Internet.[92]

In order to enhance the fairness of self-regulation, governments may also promote the interests of insufficiently represented or vulnerable groups,[93] for instance, by encouraging the self-regulatory parties to include representatives of consumer, human rights, and privacy organizations. Another procedural action is to facilitate some sort of monitoring mechanism, for example, a review or monitoring committee that checks whether the self-regulation complies with its own rules or with the general criteria for self-regulation (see section 5.4).

Perhaps most the important point is facilitating international adjustment: 'Government is uniquely placed to promote international cooperation and harmonization of self-regulatory initiatives.'[94] Many of these initiatives, after all, are national in character, resulting in an international kaleidoscope of potentially widely diverging rules. Moreover, since many ICT activities cross borders, it is a serious shortcoming when self-regulatory provisions are not applicable to users who are not subject to these rules. Therefore, it is important to pay attention to the international adjustment of self-regulatory programs, including trying to achieve co-operation between several countries to ensure effective enforcement of self-regulation. International adjustment can be achieved at different international forums, such as the OECD,[95] the Council of Europe, OAS and ASEAN, the UN,[96] or the ICC. It is not so much achieving regulation itself at these levels that is relevant in this context, but agenda-setting and awareness-raising: if sufficient attention within these international forums to diverging rules that emerge in a certain sector will be an incentive for market parties to work together to try and adjust their self-regulatory activities internationally.

3.   Additional actions

3.1 Raising awareness

One of the prime criteria for self-regulation is awareness, for in order to understand self-regulation and play by these rules, users must be aware of the existence and

---

[91]   See <http://www.ecp.nl>.

[92]   *Beleidsnota Kwetsbaarheid op Internet (KWINT)*. Kamerstukken II, 2000/01, 26 643, no. 30. The purpose of the KWINT program is to develop practical solutions for companies, citizens, consumers, and government, for a better protection against certain risks of Internet use: continuity of the Internet in the Netherlands, denial of service attacks, data integrity, authenticity, transparency of the Internet, abuse by personnel, and the exclusiveness of information. See <http://www.kwint.org>.

[93]   See *supra* n. 17, at p. 181.

[94]   <http://www.selfregulation.gov.au/publications/TaskForceOnIndustrySelf-Regulation/FinalReport/isr_part2-07.asp>, conclusion 37.

[95]   See, for example, OECD Working Party on Information Security and Privacy, *Report on Compliance with, and Enforcement of Privacy Protection On-Line*, 12 February 2003, JT00139173.

[96]   For example, the European Commission promoted the awareness and international co-operation against spam at the UN level for the World Summit on the Information Society in December 2003.

substance of the self-regulation. Governments can stimulate educational activities targeted at enhancing awareness. For example, the French Commission Nationale de l'Informatique et des Libertés (CNIL) has put a substantial information package on various aspects of spam on its web site.[97] The information package contains the results of its e-mailbox experience and the cases referred to judicial authorities, but also basic guidance on how to prevent spam, information on how to report spam, references of users' associations active in this area, etc.

Several government parties may be involved in the promotion of awareness: supervisory authorities, consumer protection agencies, ombudsmen, et cetera. These parties should focus on various steps to be taken, such as providing information about prevention and enforcement (do's and don'ts), users' rights, and complaint mechanisms. These awareness activities should not only be through web sites, but also through other means to reach the various audiences targeted, such as speeches, interviews, and e-mail alert services. Of course, governments carry only partial responsibility; involvement of industry and consumer associations is equally essential for raising effective awareness.

3.2 Enhancing enforcement

Another essential criterion for self-regulation, and the one in which government involvement may be most called for, is enforcement. Enhancing enforcement in various ways is one of the instruments the Dutch government mentioned for government action: 'cooperating in enforcing self-regulation, as for instance already happens with the Child-Porn Hotline'.[98]

An example is a project of the International Marketing Supervision Network (IMSN) that has resulted in a web site to gather and share complaints about cross-border electronic commerce;[99] among others, the Mexican Federal Consumer Protection Agency (Profeco) took part in this activity.[100] Government may also facilitate 'more interventionist' dispute resolution 'where businesses may be dealing with a large amount of complaints and/or dealing with complaints of a more serious nature', in which case 'an external dispute resolution scheme may be appropriate. An independent body capable of adjudicating and exercising sanctions can further strengthen an external dispute resolution scheme.'[101] Of course, governments can always provide legal backstop enforcement: 'The Code of Practice adopted by the

---

[97] See Commission Nationale de l'Informatique et Libertés, *Results of the Initiative Taken by the CNIL in Relation to Unsolicited Electronic Communications,* <http://www.cnil.fr/uk/Doc/CNIL-PR-spamming-VA.pdf>, February 2003.

[98] See *supra* n. 17, at p. 181.

[99] <http://www.econsumer.gov>.

[100] As mentioned in OECD Working Party on Information Security and Privacy, *Report on Compliance with, and Enforcement of Privacy Protection On-Line,* 12 February 2003, p. 10, available at < http://www.olis.oecd.org/olis/2002doc.nsf/43bb6130e5e86e5fc12569fa005d004c/26eb7e5a8a723451c1256cad004fbf8d/$FILE/JT00139173.PDF>.

[101] <http://www.selfregulation.gov.au/publications/TaskForceOnIndustrySelf-Regulation/FinalReport/isr_part2-06.asp>.

Fruit Juice Industry is supervised by an Industry Compliance Committee. Ultimate sanctions are law enforcement by the appropriate government regulatory bodies should the self-regulatory scheme be ignored or flouted by participants.'[102]

5.6   WHAT SHOULD IT MEAN?

Although they are often (implicitly) contrasted as opposites, self-regulation and legislation are not mutually exclusive. The existence of self-regulatory systems does not prevent the national or international legislature from taking initiatives. In fact, having studied a plethora of self-regulatory initiatives, we may even conclude that pure self-regulation is rare, and that most self-regulatory initiatives in some way have a back-up in formal legal rules or in other public regulatory instruments.

Therefore, 'the starting point is self-regulation' creates a wrong impression of a preference for (pure) self-regulation over government regulation, which effectively is a false dichotomy. The starting point should rather be turned around: 'ICT regulation should not be purely a government activity, but should also involve private parties.'

In what cases would this be a good starting point? We have listed several criteria to judge when and to what extent self-regulation can be considered a viable addition to government regulation. Primary criteria that should be safeguarded are fairness, inclusiveness, and compliance. Also, transparency, legal certainty, efficiency, and the context of the regulation play a part in deciding to what extent regulation should involve private parties. This means, for instance, that domains in which fairness and inclusiveness are at risk, for example, because fundamental rights and vulnerable groups are involved, and in domains where self-compliance is not a given, government regulation should be more prominent than self-regulation. Conversely, in non-contentious domains where there is a reasonable balance of stakeholders who have an interest in complying, there is ample room for private parties to self-regulate, with relatively little government activity in the background. It is noteworthy that many of the criteria for self-regulation are procedural rather than substantive ones.[103]

Supposing that some form of self-regulation is indicated, the next question is how private parties should be involved and what role there is for the government. The ways of involving private parties are numerous: codes of conduct, seals and trustmarks, hotlines, standardization, and incorporating norms into technology are some examples of regulation undertaken by the private sector. Governments can

---

[102] Ibid.
[103] Cf., Prins & Schellekens 2004, who call for the development and analysis of procedural criteria, such as: Do all interested parties get a relevant hearing in any way? Is there some form of a self-reflective mechanism to understand earlier mistakes and challenge and review of earlier adopted norms? Is there an opportunity for a wide range of views and arguments to be discussed in an open dialogue by different stakeholders rather than a narrow selection determined by market forces?

back-up such initiatives in a variety of ways, for instance, by enacting codifying, backstop, framework, procedural, or liability legislation. They have other instruments as well to protect fundamental values such as fairness and inclusiveness: they can stimulate fair procedures in self-regulatory processes, enhance international adjustment, or facilitate monitoring mechanisms. Moreover, they have a task in raising awareness and in enhancing enforcement, so that self-regulatory rules are indeed followed in practice.

This means that the best way of reading the starting point is: 'Co-regulation is the starting point'. This is not a revolutionary conclusion, nor is it particularly helpful in solving real-life regulatory problems in the field of ICT. The starting point says little about when and how what forms of co-regulation are to be chosen. This chapter has tried to give some clues for putting this starting point into operation, with a checklist of criteria and an indication of regulatory instruments. Still, numerous questions and trade-offs remain. A few of the questions that merit further analyses are the following: under what circumstances do self-regulatory rules have an external effect? To what extent would courts be willing to take into account self-regulatory standards to hold private actors liable? Should 'harmonization' of self-regulatory initiatives be considered to enhance legal certainty and international adjustment? What instruments are best suited for enhancing the fairness and inclusiveness of self-rule-making, and what instruments can best ensure self-compliance? Only when we have satisfactory answers to such questions can we really say that 'the starting point is co-regulation'.

Chapter 6
SHOULD ICT REGULATION BE UNDERTAKEN AT AN INTERNATIONAL LEVEL?

Corien Prins

6.1 INTRODUCTION

This chapter focuses on the starting point that ICT regulation should be undertaken at an international level. From most studies, books, and policy documents dealing with ICT regulation, it is clear that there is a vague need for international rule-making. Experts and policy makers have argued that international legal instruments require a harmonization of national rules that apply to ICT. However, numerous questions arise when trying to better define the vague notion of 'internationalization' the harmonization issue. What should the international regulatory instruments be focused on? Does the need for harmonization imply that rules and regimes should be harmonized by means of established institutions or can harmonization be accomplished through new bodies and methods in ICT governance? What issues could and should be addressed at an international level and how does the starting point relate to national sovereignty? Can regional, i.e., European harmonization be considered international rule-making? Numerous questions and points of discussion arise when considering and deliberating what a comprehensive international approach to ICT regulation would entail. This chapter seeks to contribute to the understanding of the interplay between ICT developments and international regulation. In examining the many issues that arise in relation to the practice and prospects of the internationalization of ICT law, the discussion below will show that the allocation of regulatory competences at national or international levels appears to be a highly complex and multi-dimensional issue.

In line with the general structure of the discussion in this book, the starting point is formulated at the outset of this chapter as it is often stated in policy documents, i.e., proposing a strong stand for international co-ordination and rule-making. While acknowledging that this does not fully encompass all dimensions mentioned in the different policy documents, the starting point for the purpose of the discussion is simply formulated as that ICT regulation should be undertaken at an international level. The discussion in this chapter starts with an overview (far from exhaustive) of e-policy documents that address the starting point that ICT regulation should be

B-J. Koops, et al. (Eds), Starting Points for ICT Regulation
© *2006, ITeR, The Hague, and the authors*

dealt with at an international level. Subsequently, the different components of the starting point and the meanings it has or that can be attributed to it will be dealt with. In line with the format of the discussion in the other chapters, illustrative cases will be presented that show how the starting point works in practice. Subsequently, oft-cited justifications for international harmonization and unification of legal rules in the area of ICT will be analyzed, discussed and commented upon. On the basis of this discussion and in order to assess whether and to what extent the starting point can be put into practice in concrete cases, the various pros and cons of international co-ordination and international rule-making will be distilled. An indication can then be given of how the principle can be adapted to various situations. The chapter will be concluded with an assessment of the extent to which the starting point is a useful one and a presentation of suggestions to define the starting point in its most useful form.

6.2   WHERE DOES THE STARTING POINT COME FROM?

As with many other developments in communication technology – telegraph, telephone, radio, television, and satellite – ICT has had a profound impact on the international regulatory arena. ICT and, more in particular, on-line communication have inspired numerous actors to engage in the international debate on how to regulate the new technological phenomena. The analysis provided in chapter 2 of this Volume shows that, throughout the world, policy documents either make subtle reference to or expressly stress the importance of regulatory initiatives at an international level. A brief look at the activities of the different international organizations and bodies shows that many issues are indeed dealt with at a level other than that of the individual countries. Often, the general line is that, in order to facilitate the development of ICT and to provide for adequate legal security, harmonization at an international level is desirable.

Before discussing four illustrative cases in more detail in the next section, we will now take a look at several policy documents that (briefly) mention the starting point or make (subtle) reference to it. In doing so, we distinguish between national, regional, and worldwide documents.[1] In addition to the examples mentioned below, there are of course numerous other statements and initiatives.[2] However, this is not the place to provide a detailed description of all the statements. Below some prime representative examples will be mentioned to illustrate the nature of the claims and the argument underlying the efforts to take up ICT regulation at an international level.

As regards policy documents of individual countries, in 1997 the US the Clinton-Gore Administration expressed a favorable attitude towards international rule-mak-

---

[1] The rather broad distinction between global and regional will be discussed in more detail in section 6.3.

[2] See chapter 2 for examples.

ing. By using the designation global in its policy memorandum, A Framework for Global Electronic Commerce, it implied preferring an international approach in solving problems.[3] Although the document expressly mentions a set of issues that should be left to the national legislature (provider liability, fraud prevention, content controls, and cryptography control), the need for international co-operation, throughout the document, action by international organizations and legal standardization generally is expressed. Although not a governmental document, it is worth mentioning the 2001 study made by a public policy think tank entitled, 'A Third Way Framework for Global E-commerce.'[4] According to one of the authors of the study all the ICT issues that have been debated in the US will to have be resolved at the international level as well: 'If consumers are wary of venturing into foreign cyberspaces or businesses are burdened by conflicting national law, we risk the creation of a digital Iron Curtain which may Balkanize the Internet, causing the World Wide Web to become Numerous National Nets.'[5]

In Japan, the Advanced Information and Telecommunication Society Promotion Headquarters of the Japanese government presented a revised set of basic guidelines to facilitate the establishment of an advanced information and telecommunication society in November 1998.[6] The guidelines call for international collaboration in formulating ICT policy. The report indicated that, given the globalization of the economy and of society, the Japanese government must work together with international organizations and other nations in the field of international harmonization and international standards wherever possible, demonstrating initiative in establishing international consensus. In discussing self-regulatory instruments, an Australian Taskforce concluded that 'there is a need for international harmonization of codes.'[7]

In European countries, the starting point is more or less explicitly mentioned in the two general policy documents on ICT regulation that were been formulated by the Dutch and UK governments. The Dutch policy memorandum *Legislation for the Electronic Highways* of 1998 states that: 'The rules and regulations should preferably be introduced at a global level, or at any event together with as many countries as possible.'[8] The government has indicated that particularly private law lends itself to these rules and regulations, as do standardization and legislation in the field of economic regulation. Generally, it is argued that all issues in which cultural atti-

---

[3] Framework for Global Electronic Commerce, White House 1997, <http://clinton5.nara.gov/WH/New/Commerce/index.html>.

[4] S. Ham and R. Atkinson, Progressive Policy Institute, Washington DC, March 2001.

[5] *Electronic Commerce & Law Report*, 21 March 2001, p. 296.

[6] Advanced Information and Telecommunications Society Promotion Headquarters, Basic Guidelines on the Promotion of an Advanced Information and Telecommunications Society, 9 November 1998, at: <http://www.kantei.go.jp/foreign/990209guideline-aits.html>, p. 3.

[7] Taskforce on Industry Self-Regulation, *Industry Self-Regulation in Consumer Markets*, August 2000, p. 32. Available at: <http://www.selfregulation.gov.au/publications/TaskForceOnIndustrySelf-Regulation/FinalReport/contents.asp>.

[8] LEH Memorandum 1998, p. 185.

tudes do not differ lend themselves to a global approach. In the 2000 follow-up memorandum on internationalization, the starting point is still considered workable, but its limits are also acknowledged: 'A starting point is the harmonization of regulations. Experience has taught us that when there are culturally-determined differences in legislation, harmonization is often unsuccessful. This must be taken into account.'[9] Whereas the Dutch statements emphasize the starting point as such, the UK e-Policy Principles do not explicitly support international rule-making and prefer to draw the attention to the possible international dimension and effects of the e-world: 'Take account of the global market place – the EU and international angle.'[10]

Although the French government has not mentioned the starting point as an explicit policy statement in governmental documents, various official reports refer to the necessity to regulate ICT at an international level.[11] The *Conseil d'Etat* mentioned electronic commerce (including taxation), international consumer protection standards, copyright protection, and personal data protection among the issues that require international co-operation.[12] The French government used an interesting argument in favor of international efforts in the debate on the regulation of domain names. The *Conseil d'Etat* stated that, from a European perspective, engaging in an international debate on the regulation of the Internet is about preserving some of the old world's ideals of cultural diversity and human rights driven action in the context of globalization.[13]

At the level of organizations that have a regional scope, the European Union has shown itself a prominent advocate of international rule-making. In one of the very first documents on ICT policy, 'Europe and the global information society. Recommendations to the European Council',[14] the High Level Expert Group emphasized the need for EU measures to ensure competitiveness for European enterprises on the international information services market. A common regulatory approach was considered crucial for the successful development of a competitive European information services market. Harmonization measures on issues such as the liberalization of the national telecommunication markets, standardization issues, intellectual property rights, privacy, and security of data transmission were placed high on the European agenda. Three years later, in Bonn, at the EU Ministerial Conference entitled 'Global Information Networks: Realising the Potential', Ministers of 29 European countries agreed upon a number of key principles, paving the way for further stimulating the use of global information networks in Europe. Besides the further development of national policy and action plans towards the use of interna-

---

[9]   ILIS Memorandum 2000, p. 21.

[10] <http://www.e-envoy.gov.uk/oee/oee.nsf/sections/guidelines-eprinciples/$file/index.htm>.

[11] Falque-Pierrot in 1996; *Conseil d'Etat* 1998.

[12] *Conseil d'Etat* 1998, p. 72, p. 109, p. 165.

[13] Idem, p. 14.

[14] This report, often referred to as the Bangemann report, dates from 1994. See <http://europa.eu.int/ISPO/docs/basics/docs/bangemann.pdf>.

tional information networks, the Ministers agreed upon strengthening their co-operation at the European and international level.[15] Two recommendations from the Bonn Ministerial Conference Declaration are of importance in view of this chapter's issue. Recommendation 46 refers to the regulatory point of departure that ICT regulation should be accomplished at an international level: 'Ministers agree to work together towards global principles on the free flow of information whilst protecting the fundamental right to privacy and personal and business data, building on the work undertaken by the EU, the Council of Europe, the OECD, and the UN.'

Recommendation 59, however, moderates this regulatory point of departure by determining the national level as the appropriate level for legislation and, where appropriate, international and global levels:

'Ministers advise that full use be made of multilateral forums to strengthen international cooperation, while ensuring that their activities are properly co-ordinated ... in order to identify and dismantle existing obstacles to the use of electronic commerce, to prevent the establishment of new barriers, and to establish a clear and predictable legal framework at national and, where appropriate, European and global levels.'

In recent years, the European Union has made a particularly strong case for global international regulation with respect to the governance of domain names. The European Commission's principal objection to a set of proposals made by the US Department of Commerce (in a Green Paper entitled 'A Proposal to Improve Technical Management of Internet Names and Addresses') was the lack of recognition of the need for an internationally co-ordinated approach to the governance of the Internet.[16] The Green Paper, in the opinion of the Commission was 'U.S.-centric' and sought to secure exclusive US jurisdiction over the Internet.

The starting point that ICT regulation should be undertaken at an international level was also used by the Council of Europe while working on the passage of harmonized rules on cybercrime. One of the aims of the Cybercrime Convention was to harmonize substantive criminal law for a number of offences. Also, the adoption, in early 2003, of an additional protocol to this Convention was clearly motivated by the desire to harmonize Member States' national laws on racism and xenophobia on the Internet.[17] In addition to mandatory international harmonization, the Council shows itself a proponent of international co-operation in applying self-regulatory mechanisms.

---

[15] See <http://europa.eu.int/ISPO/policy/isf/documents/declarations/Bonn-Ministerial-Declaration.htm>.

[16] See *International Policy Issues Related to* Internet *Governance* – Communication to the Council from the Commission, 20 February 1998, <http://www.infosociety.gr/policies/Internet/docs/governance.pdf>; Internet *Governance, Reply of the European Community and Its Member States to the US Green Paper*, 16 March 1998, <http://europa.eu.int/ISPO/eif/InternetPoliciesSite/Internet Governance/MainDocuments/ReplytoUSGreenPaper.html>.

[17] This Additional Protocol on racism and xenophobia was opened for signature in January 2003, <http://www.coe.int>.

'The Internet cannot be confined within an over-strict, inflexible national legislative framework, which would prove incompatible with rapid technological progress. In addition, any attempt to harmonise legislation at a European level would be doomed to failure (on account of cultural diversity and disparities between states as to the Internet's penetration, in particular in terms of user numbers). This therefore bears out the idea of co-operation as a means of seeking compromise solutions, flexible enough to be adaptable to everyone's circumstances and to keep pace with progress.'[18]

A final example of explicit attention for the starting point at a regional level is the Asia-Pacific Economic Co-operation (APEC). As was mentioned in chapter 2, a task force of this organization, with broad involvement by Asian governments, the Australian, New Zealand, and US government and industry, discussed international co-operation on charging arrangements for Internet services.[19] While the harmonization initiatives of APEC do take other international activities into consideration, they clearly seek to establish regional guidelines. Illustrative are the recent efforts in the area of privacy protection. In September 2003, APEC decided to develop a set of privacy principles. Although the OECD Guidelines and the Directive on the protection of personal data offered a starting point for the discussion among the APEC members, harmonization is to be established by means of a 'region-centric set of guidelines'.[20]

At a global level, mention can first be made of the OECD. The 1998 Ottawa Conference of the OECD Ministers stressed that member countries should consider possibilities to harmonize national legal frameworks at an international level and consequently further stimulate the developing international electronic environment. Among other things, Member States were called upon to give favourable consideration to the UNCITRAL Model Law on e-Commerce and take a non-discriminatory approach to foreign authentication.[21] The attacks of 11 September 2001, have had a major impact on the quest for international co-operation and regulation, something which is clearly visible in the recent activities of the OECD. On 25 July 2002, the OECD Council adopted guidelines for the security of information systems and networks with the aims to raising awareness about the risks to information systems and networks and to promote the international development of a culture of security, i.e., a focus on security in the development of information systems and networks and the adoption of new ways of thinking and behaving when using and interacting within information systems and networks.[22]

---

[18] Council of Europe, Secretariat memorandum prepared by the Directorate General of Human Rights, *Self-regulation and User Protection Against Illegal or Harmful Content on the New Communications and Information Services*, 24 April 2002, <http://www.coe.int>.

[19] To date, APEC has 21 members, combining a gross domestic product accounting for 47 % of world trade.

[20] See Electronic Commerce & Law Report, 17 September 2003, p. 865.

[21] In 1999, the OECD adopted the 'Guidelines for Consumer Protection in the Context of Electronic Commerce'. In 2003, the organization published the 'Guidelines for Protecting Consumers from Fraudulent and Deceptive Commercial Practices Across Borders'. See <www.oecd.org>.

[22] OECD, Guidelines for the Security of Information Systems and Networks. Towards a Culture of Security, 2002, p. 8.

Above, reference was already made to the work of UNCITRAL. This internationally recognized institution of the UN has a long history of promoting international collaboration in rule-making and has shown to be a successful forum for unifying Internet-related rules at a global level.[23] In particular, the Model Law on E-commerce has received a warm welcome and has served as a blueprint for subsequently adopted national and regional rules on electronic commerce.[24] The internationality and subsequent uncertainties and problems of the Internet have also been noticed by the World Trade Organization (WTO). In view of this, the WTO has promoted or considered international harmonization as well as international co-operation with respect to issues such as intellectual property rights, privacy and electronic commerce[25] as well as consumer protection.[26]

An organization that has a longtime tradition in advocating international rule-making and that has effectively adopted uniform rules at a global level is WIPO. In contrast to the model rules drafted by UNCITRAL, WIPO issues provisions that are binding upon the Member States. The challenges that intellectual property rights holders face in a borderless society with increasingly low threshold electronic copying and distribution facilities has triggered the Geneva-based organization to implement a vast set of rules harmonizing the copyright systems of numerous countries around the world. By means of its 1996 Copyright Treaty, WIPO has set the worldwide standard for rules on issues such as reproduction in an on-line environment and legal protection for Digital Rights Management systems (making it unlawful to circumvent DRM applications). The US (by means of the Digital Millennium Copyright Act) and Europe (through the May 2001 Copyright Harmonization Directive)[27] all closely followed the standards set by WIPO.

Whereas WIPO has shown to be rather successful in regulating an ICT-related topic at an international level, others have struggled or even failed in their attempts, despite their longtime experience in international rule-making. Illustrative is the unsuccessful work of the Hague Conference on Private International Law. In 1992, at the urging of the US, the Hague Conference – a treaty drafting body with 62 Member States – began work to draft a new Convention on Jurisdiction and the Recognition and Enforcement of Foreign Judgments in Civil and Commercial Mat-

---

[23] UNCITRAL also adopted various model laws not specifically dealing with on-line issues, such as the model law on International Commercial Arbitration. See <http://www.un.or.at/uncitral>.

[24] Various national laws, regulations, and projects dealing with E-commerce issues (among them the Uniform Electronic Transactions Act (UETA) in the US and various initiatives in European countries) were closely modelled after the UNCITRAL Model Law.

[25] See the WTO Ministerial Declaration, adopted 14 November 2001 in Doha. Available at: <http://www.wto.org/english/thewto_e/minist_e/min01_e/mindecl_e.htm>.

[26] See, e.g., the report 'Electronic Commerce and the role of the WTO', WTO Publications, March 1998, <http://www.wto.org/english/news_e/pres98_e/pr96_e.htm> as well as the work programme on electronic commerce adopted by the General Council on 25 September 1998, <http://www.wto.org/english/tratop_e/ecom_e/wkprog_e.htm>.

[27] Directive 2001/29/EC of the European Parliament and of the Council of 22 May 2001 on the harmonization of certain aspects of copyright and related rights in the information society, OJ L 167/10.

ters. Although the members have been working on the new jurisdiction treaty for more than a decade, many complex questions remain on the agenda. The key reason for the failure to reach an agreement appears the development of electronic commerce. By now, the US delegation has successfully persuaded the Hague Conference to address a much narrower set of issues than deliberated in the early stages of the drafting process.[28]

Finally, reference can be made to the ambitions of the International Telecommunications Union, the United Nation's telecommunications policy-making body, in organizing the World Summit on the Information Society (WSIS). The first meeting, held in Geneva in December 2003, was aimed at a better understanding of the information revolution and its impact on the international community. In explaining the reasons to hold the summit, ITU's Secretary General stated that a new global governance network is needed to handle issues of cyberspace.[29] Whereas he acknowledged the existence of national policies and law on Internet governance, the Secretary General said that their effectiveness is limited by national borders.[30] Although the Declaration of Principles entitled 'Building the Information Society: A Global Challenge in the New Millennium' issued on the occasion of the Geneva summit, acknowledges the essential role of international co-operation among governments, clearly there remains an important role for national and regional policy-making: 'The rule of law, accompanied by a supportive, transparent, pro-competitive, technologically neutral and predictable policy and regulatory framework reflecting national realities, is essential for building a people-centered Information Society.'[31]

The above clearly demonstrates that numerous actors in the international community acknowledge the importance of having harmonized rules in an electronic environment and thus strive for an international regulatory approach on a broad set of issues.

6.3   WHAT DOES INTERNATIONAL REGULATION MEAN?

In arguing that regulation should be undertaken at an international level, a number of queries and discuss items arise. These items can be divided into two groups:

---

[28] The relevant texts are available at: <http://www.hcch.net>.

[29] See the documents on the ITU World Summit at: <http://www.itu.int/wsis>.

[30] The US Government, in its participation in preparing the world summit, emphasized that it is a forum for heads of state to address consensus issues and not the place for complex technical debates. The US representative stated that his country is primarily interested in pursuing the goals of infrastructure development, education, and network security at the summit. Complex and disputatious policy considerations are not appropriate subjects for the summit. Instead, the heads of state should gather to demonstrate their agreement on broad principles. *Electronic Commerce & Law Report*, 19 February 2003, p. 169.

[31] Consideration 38. Document WSIS/PC-3/DT/6(Rev 3)-E, 9 December 2003. See also the Plan of Action issued on the same date.

- What exactly do we mean by *international level*?
- What observations can be made with respect to the term *regulation*?

6.3.1 'International level'

In assuming, as the starting point does, that the answer to the question at what level a regulatory framework for steering ICT developments should be designed is international, a first task should be to explore the concept 'international level'. A closer look at the concept reveals that it is a very broad and vague term. There is no distinct international 'ICT' body of law with its own sources and methods of rule-making deriving from principles peculiar or exclusive to ICT concerns. Instead, regulatory action at the international level has emerged in a rather *ad hoc* fashion, originating from the variety of international institutions and organizations that deal with specific ICT-related topics. Nonetheless, a distinct set of rules and regulations does now exist for the application and use of ICT. This section will endeavor to identify the sources of these rules and regulations as well as the organizations that are involved in international rule-making. We will start with the sources of international ICT rule-making.

A first remark that should be made is that, as has already been observed in the previous section, 'international' does not necessarily mean 'global'. The OECD is often referred to as a global organization. However, there are no OECD member countries in Central and South America and Africa. International co-operation and harmonization can also be established at regional or even sub-regional levels, whereby institutions such as the European Union, the North American Free Trade Agreement, the Council of Europe, and the Asia-Pacific Economic Co-operation are well-known examples. The membership or participation of countries in non-global international organizations may also be related to considerations other than regional ones. Economic (compare G8; non-Western countries), cultural, social, and technical as well as issue-related concerns (compare WIPO) may also determine the institutionalization of international co-ordination. It is furthermore important to observe that formal competence and a high level of country representation do not necessarily imply that an organization is an essential and powerful forum for international co-operation in relation to ICT issues. The actual regulatory role is not always derived from the formal power of an international organization. An organization conferred with considerable formal means may be unsuccessful in its efforts because it lacks the (political) means and influence to address certain problems, e.g., because the outcome of the project is of high economic relevance.

Finally, regulatory developments in the past decade shown that the international organizations that have proved important to the development of international ICT law are largely dominated by industrialized countries, with the US and the European Union countries usually taking the lead.[32] Closely related to this observation

---

[32] This is not surprising, considering that the concentration of Internet hosts and thus the use of the (commercial) on-line information and applications originates from or is directed at these countries.

is the issue of the so-called digital divide, a term coined to refer to the gap between geographic areas or individuals at different socio-economic levels in respect to their opportunities to access information and communication technologies.[33]

Since a range of organizations at different levels and geographical location is involved in international co-operation and rule-making in the area of ICT, a second issue here appears to be the hierarchy between these bodies. Addressing this issue is of importance given that various organizations deal with similar issues. The hierarchy of the law-making powers of the different regional, multilateral and global bodies is in several cases clear (for example the jurisdiction power of WIPO in relation to the EU or of the WTO in relation to the EU)[34]. In other instances, however, their mutual position is not formalized and there some degree of *de jure* or *de facto* competition between institutions may occur (for example, between the OECD and the EU on ICT-related issues in the domain of taxation). Often, more than one international body presides over a certain topic and conflicts may arise as a result of different perspectives on the interests at stake and thus on the different regimes the organizations enact. The issue of electronic signatures, however shows that institutions and organizations also built upon earlier work done by others. For example, the European Union, emphasized in its Directive on electronic commerce, the need to take into account the earlier work of the WTO, the OECD and UNCITRAL in the area of electronic commerce.[35] Also, the EU has put forward a paper to the WTO indicating the issues that it believes WTO members should consider in their regulatory activities in the area of electronic commerce.[36]

A third point to note is that rule-making at an international level does not necessarily mean that a subject should be brought to the international table where binding decisions on the issue are formulated. Of course, numerous issues (copyright, personal data protection, taxation, E-commerce, electronic signatures, liability of Internet Service Providers (ISPs), and certain content-related issues) show that imposed or formal harmonization by international institutions is significant in the area of ICT. However, the change of national legal rules under international influence may occur by means of other instruments than mandatory measures formulated in the international arena. Here the impact of spontaneous harmonization should be considered as well. Key impetus for such spontaneous (i.e., non-regulatory) harmo-

---

[33] For example, by October 2000, there were just over 94 million Internet hosts in the world. The share of hosts in the Member States of the OECD amounted to 95.6%. Just 4.4% were outside the OECD area. Source: OECD Communications Outlook, Information Society, Paris Cedex 2001, p. 272.

[34] Both the Member States and the EU itself are members of WIPO and the WTO. This double participation however, has, generated controversy as regards the competence of the respective members. See Eeckhout, 1997.

[35] Consideration 58, Directive 2000/31/EC of the European Parliament and of the Council of 8 June 2000 on certain legal aspects of information society services, in particular electronic commerce, OJ L 178, 17 July 2000.

[36] E-commerce: Contributions to the WTO. Communication from the European Communities and their Member States: Electronic Commerce Work Programme, 30 November 2000. Available at: <http://europa.eu.int>.

nization appears to be certain social and economic forces, such as competition between national legal orders. According to Ogus, such competition is even 'the chief engine for change'.[37] An ICT-related example might be the position of providers of certain ICT services. Domestic Certification Authorities (CAs), competing on the international market of digital signature services may, for example, find that their national (or proposed) legal system imposes on them higher costs (for example, because the national accreditation system requires a high security level) than the costs incurred by their foreign competitors operating under a more favorable accreditation system. They will apply pressure on their legislator to reduce the costs by demanding a regime similar to the ones enacted in other major countries. Another example is ISP liability. It could be argued that the European and global evolution of the rules on liability of Internet Service Providers is largely attributable to competition between national legal orders. In elaborating on the influence of competition in relation to international convergence of rules, Ogus also pointed to the impact of competition between suppliers of legal rules, among them lawyers who find it convenient to imitate legal principles developed in other jurisdictions.[38] The conclusion here may be that it is sometimes difficult to detect where, in the gradual process of change, a national rule becomes an 'international' rule.

In addition to the above reflections on the sources of the international rules and regulations, several issues in relation to the specific organizations that are involved in international rule-making should be discussed. As was shown in the first section, a plethora of actors of international origin addresses issues related to ICT. Today, an overwhelming and still growing number of regulatory forums at global, regional, national, and sub-national levels preside over countless provisions in seeking to exert control over the application and use of ICT. Decisions are taken within well-known bodies such as the WTO, ITU, WIPO, the Council of Europe and the United Nations, but also by ICT-specific organizations, such as ICANN,[39] ISOC,[40] IETF,[41] and IAB.[42] Depending on their scope and competences, the organizations deal with selected issues. In dealing with these issues, the institutions attempt to reconcile a wide array of interests (industry, consumers, service providers, right holders, enforcement authorities, and society at large), but are also criticized for taking a too unilateral perspective.[43] In addition to the various formal bodies, numerous informal (specialized) institutions, non-governmental organizations, civil society groups, and private sector bodies influence the international policy area, in some cases enacting so-called 'soft law' or co-operating in enforcing legislation. Examples here

---

[37] Ogus 2001, p. 27.

[38] For more detail: Ogus, 1999.

[39] Internet Corporation for Assigned Names and Numbers.

[40] Internet Society.

[41] Internet Engineering Task Force.

[42] Internet Architecture Board.

[43] The policy of ICANN is argued to be dominated by US interests. More in general, governance on the technical architecture of the Internet (the issuance of the numerous protocols and standards) is said to be 'An American Thing', Mayer, 2000, pp. 161-168.

are the GBDe[44] and INHOPE. The latter is the European Association of Internet Hotline Providers, in which various national hotlines involved in web site content control co-operate. An example at the global level is ICRA (Internet Content Rating Association), which brings together organizations representing Internet industry players with the aim of promoting and managing an international content rating system.

In some situations, it is even difficult to clearly point to a certain international origin (level) of global norms. Illustrative is the 'birth' of netiquette, that has influenced behavior in the on-line world and has even been recognized in court cases as well as in codes of conducts formulated by, for example, associations of ISPs.

A major problem, and thus challenge, for the majority of the institutionalized international bodies is their time-consuming and often bureaucratic processes. The average time from the initial submission of a proposal at the level of a specific international body to the actual implementation of the rules at a national level is often several years. Less formal international institutions may have an important role here. We have seen various examples of non-governmental regulatory forum (industry, consumer- and public interest groups, as well as other non-governmental actors) that quickly initiated or facilitated regulation schemes for certain ICT-related problems and questions. For example, in the field of personal data protection, useful examples exist of private sector initiatives that have developed guidelines geared towards facilitating on-line protection, of personal data in a cross-border context (such as the model agreement drafted by the International Chamber of Commerce). Closely related to this are the emerging new forms of international dialogue and co-operation between governmental and non-governmental actors. A successful impetus to cross-border co-operation in the area of criminal law, for example, was established by means of an international network of hotlines on child pornography and illegal content.[45] In private law, the work on introducing international minimum standards for on-line alternative dispute resolution can be mentioned. The present sources of international regulation are thus becoming highly diverse, and include many new, sometimes merely virtual, organizations. A key challenge in international ICT regulation appears to be to what extent formal regulators at regional and global levels can accommodate the involvement of a growing number of new actors representing a variety of perspectives and interests without sacrificing requirements of effectiveness, efficiency, and quality of international legislative processes.

In conclusion it can be stated that an adequate understanding of the concept 'international level' requires insight into the historical context and practice of international rule-making as well as the dynamics of the ICT regulatory context. The decision to opt for a particular forum will stem to a certain degree from the specific issue at stake (e-commerce, taxation, privacy, illegal and harmful content, cybercrime,

---

[44] Global Business Dialogue on Electronic Commerce, a global organization that aims to set common E-commerce standards and promote self-regulation, <http://www.gbde.org>.

[45] <http://www.inhope.org>.

etc.), but many other considerations are relevant as well. Gaining an understanding of the regulatory powers of specific international bodies and of how the institutions relate to one another requires that attention is given to the scope and competencies of the different forums. The regulation of ICT at a European level, for example, will be most directly conditioned by Community law and the issues covered in the different Pillars. Crucial to an assessment of the current state of international ICT law is also an understanding of the relevant political and economic powers, since the choice for a regional (European) or global forum appears to be largely determined by political and economic considerations. Also, the regulation of several issues (intellectual property law, personal data protection) has shown that the outcome was profoundly affected by political and economic pressures.

6.3.2 **Regulation**

Most of the documents mentioned in the first section that assert or refer to the starting point focus on an international *approach* or international *co-operation*. Some expressly mention *regulation* or a *regulatory* approach as the subject of the initiative. International *legislation* as such is scarcely mentioned. The use of the different terms relates to the focus of the starting point. One focus would be that regulation in its broad meaning should be established through an international institution, thus relating to the *level* of international rule making. The other focus is related to the international *effect* of, national, rules, thus focusing on the transboundary externalities of national rules and the subsequent necessity to co-ordinate activities in preventing distorting effects or realizing mutual goals and interests (consumer protection, privacy protection, legal certainty).

A related point is whether the international approach should aim at harmonization, procedural co-operation, approximation[46] or unification. In the few instances where the documents make explicit reference to a formal convergence of national legislative systems, the word harmonization is used. Clearly, full unification is seldom realized.[47] However, harmonization may, in certain circumstances, result in unification of individual themes and issues within the broader, harmonizing, framework. An example is the set of information requirements stipulated in Articles 5 and 6 of the Directive on electronic commerce.[48]

As was discussed in chapter 1 of this Volume, 'regulation' covers a broad range of instruments. The term includes more than just law (and it also includes economic, market, and technological steering instruments). In focusing on interna-

---

[46] A term used in the Council of Europe's Cybercrime Convention.

[47] Full unification between different legal cultures and traditions appears inherently impossible. Whether and under what circumstances national legal systems are capable of harmonization has been debated extensively in legal literature. For more detail, see section 6.4 of this Chapter.

[48] Directive 2000/31/EC of the European Parliament and of the Council of 8 June 2000 on certain legal aspects of information society services, in particular electronic commerce, OJ L 178, 17 July 2000.

tional regulation, it should also be borne in mind that there are different types of rule-making at an international level with different purposes. Certain regional (most prominently the European Union) as well as international bodies (WIPO) have issued a large body of binding harmonization measures with respect to ICT developments. The output of institutions such as UNCITRAL and the OECD is of a different nature. The measures adopted by these bodies serve as model laws or model rules that states are free to implement. They may also have an impact on court rulings in developing judicial doctrine. Even more informal are certain customs developed by the on-line community (e-customs) that, over time, may become a source of law.[49]

In his Article 'Of Governments and Governance', Froomkin distinguishes the following six mechanisms that form the spectrum of regulatory harmonization methods:[50]

- norms, usages of trade, *lex mercatoria*, that spontaneously develop within a transnational community (customary law);
- a jurisdiction's law that has become the *de facto* rule for other countries, perhaps due to regulatory arbitrage;
- a jurisdiction's law that is being copied by other jurisdictions;
- model laws drawn up under communal law reform projects (such as UNCITRAL model laws) and presented to states for enactment;
- legislative harmonization projects adopted by supra-national bodies that have been empowered to harmonize law;
- international, multilateral, treaties.

Often, international harmonization is a laborious consensus process. Illustrative are the Council of Europe's Cybercrime Convention and the European Union's Directive on the protection of personal data. Common international solutions to ICT problems can also be established by other, indirect and sometimes faster, means. This is the case when one nation or region seeks to persuade other nations to adopt its national/regional regime. Several examples show that, depending on the circumstances and the issue at stake, the path to such harmonization can be walked faster by means of persuasion. Successful persuasion can be achieved if a country dominates the international regulatory initiatives through a privileged (economic or technological) position and thus influences the outcome of the harmonization at an international level. Illustrative domains where a certain country or region induced other countries/regions to follow the lead of its law are intellectual property rights, domain names, and personal data protection. The bargaining power of the US in the area of international domain names (ICANN) is determined by its privileged (economic or technological) position.[51]

---

[49] For more detail, see Polanski, 2002.

[50] Froomkin, p. 4. Of course, mixtures of the above-mentioned methods are possible.

[51] Another example is the US position in the area of copyright. A glance at the US White Paper on Intellectual Property and the National Information Infrastructure shows that the suggestions on digital

A key instrument in indirect international convergence of legal rules and principles by means of strong persuasion is the reciprocity rule. In the 1980s the US used this stick approach in its 1984 Semiconductor Chip Protection Act.[52] The European Union used it in persuading the US to adopt its database and personal data protection regimes. Consideration 56 of the European Database Directive stipulates that protection is accorded to databases whose makers are nationals or habitual residents of third countries 'only if such third countries offer comparable protection to databases produced by nationals of a Member State or persons who have their habitual residence in the territory of the Community.'[53] A similar, highly debated, reciprocity rule was included in Articles 25 and 26 of the 1995 Directive on the protection of personal data. Here the EU required third countries to provide for 'adequate' protection if personal data were to be exported to such countries.[54] The key question here of course was to what extent third countries were allowed to use their own preferred regulatory instruments (self-regulation as opposed to legislation) in achieving the same result (adequate protection). The danger of using regulatory reciprocity is of course that countries turn to the WTO claiming that the reciprocity rule represents a non-tariff barrier to trade and violates international trade agreements.

A final point to be made here is the influence of market actors and public interest groups on the regulatory process at an international level. As regards the role of major multinational companies, Froomkin has described the process of what he calls 'regulatory arbitrage' these companies engage in: multinationals play nations off against one another as a way to get acceptance of rules that they prefer. As will be discussed in section 6.4, this argument is closely related to the so-called races to the top and races to the bottom (who, being pressured by market forces, will adopt the toughest or least restrictive rules that will become the baseline for applying pressure to obtain international adoption by others), which have been analyzed and discussed extensively in legal and economic literature.

6.4 How Does Regulation Apply?

An enormous increasing variety of policy activities from regional and international bodies has been witnessed during the past ten years. Hence, there are many illustrative cases of regulation that evidence the tendency towards international rule-mak-

---

copyright are virtually identical to the WIPO treaty proposals that were submitted in Geneva at more or less the same time by the Clinton Administration. Samuelson, 1999, p. 12.

[52] See § 912 (c) 1984 Semiconductor Chip Protection Act.

[53] Directive 96/9/EC of the European Parliament and of the Council of 11 March 1996 on the legal protection of databases, OJ L 077, 27 March 1996. See also Art. 11 of this Directive.

[54] Directive 95/46/EC of the European Parliament and of the Council of 24 October 1995 on the protection of individuals with regard to the processing of personal data and on the free movement of such data, OJ L 281, 23 November 1995.

ing. In this section four of these cases will be discussed and analyzed in more detail. They were chosen in that they provide a more in-depth indication of the various dimensions of the starting point as well as the pros and cons that the starting point gives rise to in practice. These cases will also yield inspiration for the discussion in section 6.5 on the various arguments on which international rule-making is based. The cases have been selected on the basis of differences in focus and subject-matter as well as differences in instruments used in establishing international rules.

6.4.1 Copyright

Copyright is a domain characterized by a long and strong tradition of regulatory co-operation at an international level, as is illustrated by the Berne Convention and the TRIPs agreement. Being the key international organization for copyright matters, WIPO faced numerous challenging questions with the advent of Internet. As has often been mentioned, the Internet is one large global copying machine and distribution medium. Techniques such as MP3, and, more recently, the peer-to-peer phenomenon show that finding, downloading and copying software, music files, and other forms of digital entertainment products have become child's play. However, the Internet is not only an uncontrollable copying instrument in the hands of millions of on-line actors. As a new commercial distribution channel, it also offers the information industry an enormous potential. To safeguard their position, the information industries began to lobby for changes to the law. The key aim was to preserve the same rights in the electronic context as enjoyed in the analogue world and to pursue harmonization on a global scale in realizing the new electronic rights. The powerful path taken was that of a multilateral treaty process. It was believed that the best instrument in realizing an Internet-proof copyright regime was binding harmonization through WIPO. Commentators in the US argued that a key reason for using this international process was that thus results could be achieved that were unachievable by ordinary national legislation.[55] After years of meetings, a treaty was produced by WIPO adapting copyright rules to digital works.[56] The provisions of this 1996 WIPO Copyright Treaty were subsequently implemented in the Member States, in the US by means of the Digital Millennium Copyright Act[57] and in the EU through the Copyright Harmonization Directive.[58] A glance at the harmonizing efforts shows that both WIPO and the EU struggled in striking a balance between copyright owners' interests and the broader public interests. A glance at

---

[55] Froomkin 1999. In the US, treaties are subject to ratification in only one House.

[56] World Intellectual Property Organization Copyright Treaty, adopted 20 December 1996, 36 ILM 65 (1997), WIPO Doc. CRNR/DC/94 (23 December 1996), <http://www.wipo.int/clea/docs/en/wo/wo033en.htm>.

[57] Digital Millennium Copyright Act, Pub. L. No. 105-304, 112 Stat. 2860 (1998), <http://www.loc.gov/copyright/legislation/dmca.pdf>.

[58] Directive 2001/29/EC of the European Parliament and of the Council of 22 May 2001 on the harmonization of certain aspects of copyright and related rights in the information society, OJ L 167/10.

the provisions included in Article 6 of the Copyright Harmonization Directive (dealing with a prohibition on circumvention devices) shows that the European legislature failed to provide the required uniformity and clarity in accommodating the fundamental contradiction between both interests. Article 6(a) of the Directive leaves it to the Member States, given the specifics of their national perspective on the relevant societal and economic interests, to determine the extent to which copyright owners may rely on technical measures to attain protection they are unable to achieve by means of the law.

The process of international regulation chosen in the area of copyright is characterized by the following. First, the mode of regulation used is the powerful instrument of a multilateral treaty at a global level, thus applying a forced and formal means of harmonization. Second, the level of harmonization is global with a subsequent implementation at regional (EU) and national level. On the general level, the countries sitting at the WIPO table all shared a common interest in addressing the digital copyright problems. In essence, at this level the goals to be achieved did not diverge between the relevant countries. Given the nature of the issue and the interests at stake, it could be successfully brought to a multilateral process designed to create some international set of rights and obligations. Undoubtedly, because of the economic interests at stake made that the top-down binding mechanism of an international treaty suited the players controlling the issue best. In contrast to, for example, content control, copyright is not primarily concerned with the preservation of national values. It is not an issue involving intrinsic sensitive political and cultural questions that vary from country to country. The issue is primarily about safeguarding economic interests at a global market. Even with respect to implications for the more fundamental issue of freedom of expression (debated in view of the measures on circumvention of technical protection systems) the views appeared to be shared between the representatives countries. Finally, the copyright issue appeared to be a topic where addressing the problems by means of marginal adjustments to the national regulatory framework (i.e., without altering fundamental principles of the national system) appeared sufficient.

Opting for harmonization by means of a multilateral treaty has the advantage that truly international solutions are found. Opting for the global mode of harmonization, however, also has its drawbacks. The WIPO Treaty clearly shows this. At the level of an international treaty, it is difficult to attain consensus on the fine details of the legal rules. Choosing for the global option requires striking a balance between the aim of realizing a uniform global copyright framework and the interest of accommodating national preferences. Also, political reality often requires compromises that are far from the best scholarly or practical solutions. According to Stephan, the political economy of the harmonization process 'results too often either in rules written for the benefit of particular industries and other interest groups, or in the suppression of conflict that in turn increases legal risk.'[59] The WIPO

---

[59] Stephan 1999, p. 744.

Treaty as well as the Directive clearly testify of these struggles. The end result is that the language of the broadly conceptualized rights of the WIPO Copyright Treaty is vague and fails to provide clarity on various points. On the other hand, the text allows Member States from different legal cultures some room to vary rights and exceptions according to their national preferences.

Apart from these observations, the following additional remarks can be made. The WIPO harmonization effort was clearly an intensely lobbied issue. The media and information industry, library associations, civil rights associations, and other groups each exercised considerable power to persuade the Member States' representatives to favour their interests. But apparently individual countries also highly influenced the discussions and imposed their perspective on the matter. Some clearly had a first-mover advantage: the US is claimed to have persuaded other Member States to adopt the rules proposed earlier by the Clinton Administration in the US White Paper on Intellectual Property and the National Information Infrastructure.[60]

6.4.2 Domain names and Internet governance

The administration of the Domain Name System (DNS) and subsequently the issuance of worldwide domain names has been a topic of much debate and numerous court cases. The problem with most domain name disputes relates to the interaction between the traditional concepts of the trademark system and the new (technologically determined) procedures on the administration of domain names. Conflicts arise because the trademark system is based on geographical and sectoral boundaries, whereas in the domain name system, these are irrelevant and only one single .com or .info name can exist. The key players in dealing with conflicts between most types of Internet domain names and trademarks are WIPO and ICANN. Being the key international forum on intellectual property matters, WIPO appeared the natural organization to take on the issue. ICANN (the Internet Corporation for Assigned Names and Numbers) has authority on matters relating to Internet governance, the technical management of the domain name system among them.[61] Although ICANN is often solely connected to the management of domain names, it should be noted that the power of ICANN reaches further. The corporation is also responsible for the distribution of IP addresses, the development of new standards for Internet protocols, and the organization of the root server system of the Internet.

The position and arrangement of ICANN is a rather peculiar one, being a private non-profit corporation under Californian law. ICANN's co-ordinating functions were accorded to the organization by the US government,[62] but it is not formally ac-

---

[60] Samuelson 1999.

[61] ICANN decides which new TLDs (Top Level Domains) should be introduced and oversees registrars issuing domain names. Originally these functions were carried out by various bodies including the US government.

[62] See *Memorandum of Understanding Between the U.S. Department of Commerce and ICANN*, <http://www.ntia.doc.gov/ntiahome/domainname/icann-memorandum.htm>. See also The Commerce

countable to any institution or government body. Also, no government officials or officials of a multinational entity or treaty organization may serve on the board of the organization.[63] Numerous experts and as well as officials have criticized the regulatory arrangement implemented with ICANN. Many have pointed to the problems arising out of the US jurisdiction, which makes that the corporation works under the shadow of US jurisdiction.[64] Criticism also focuses on the private character of the organization where it deals with issues that clearly affect the public interest of standards, interconnectivity, and the unity and control of the Internet system. Finally, authors question the legitimacy of this form of 'proprietary private law-making'.[65] To cite Froomkin:

'It is one thing to celebrate market-driven outcomes (corrected for market failures), and to value market-making technical standardization. It is quite another thing to tolerate private sector leadership when it clothes itself in the guise of 'bottom-up rule-making' but actually seeks to use government or government-like power to lock in advantages enjoyed by established firms, often at the expense of consumers or new competitors.'[66]

Hence, ICANN was faced with scrutiny from various sides and questions were posed as regards the accountability, democracy, and transparency of this mode of international governance.[67]

This and other criticism[68] appears to have been the impetus for the recent reform proposals, starting in February 2002, with a first document presented by ICANN's president Stuart Lynn.[69] In response, the Evolution and Reform Committee (ERC) was created to recommend on a framework for reform. In June 2002, this resulted in a report, 'The Blueprint for Reform', which contained several proposals, including on policy development (improve accountability and redress misuse of authority) and board membership (directors must reflect public, private, institutional, and individual interests and must be selected by a committee that is geographically and functionally diverse).[70] In recognition of the report's recommendations, ICANN

Department's White Paper on the Management of Internet Names and Addresses, 63 Fed. Reg. 31, 741, 31,750, 1998, <http://www.ntia.doc.gov/ntiahome/domainname/6_5_98dns.htm>.

[63] Art. VII s. 5.

[64] See Internet *Governance, Management of* Internet *Names and Addresses, Analysis and Assessment from the European Commission of the United States Department of Commerce White Paper,* Communication from the European Commission to the European Parliament and to the Council, 29 July 1998. COM (1998) 476, http://europa.eu.int/ISPO/eif/InternetPoliciesSite/InternetGovernance/MainDocuments/com(1998)476.html>. Also: Mayer 2000, p. 166.

[65] Froomkin 1999 and Froomkin 2002.

[66] Froomkin 1999.

[67] Commentators have pointed out the poor representational legitimacy of well-established international bodies such as the WTO panels as well because they are 'insulated from democratic pressures', Dinwoodie, 2000, p. 506.

[68] On the various points of criticism see Withers 2003, pp. 32-35.

[69] 'ICANN: A Case for Reform' available at: <http://www.icann.org>.

[70] Committee on ICANN Evolution and Reform, *ICANN: A Blueprint for Reform*, available at: <http://www.icann.org/committees/evol-reform/blueprint-20jun02.htm>.

set out the changes required in a detailed set of so-called Bylaws, which came into effect on 15 December 2002.[71] Since then critical voices have not been silenced, which inspired the ERC to propose various clarifications, corrections, and modifications.[72] In view of this chapter's focus, it is interesting to note that one author suggested: 'It may be asking too much of any organization to combine global inclusiveness with accountability, agility, and effective decision-making (…).'[73]

Irrespective of the question of whether the organization will always have its critics, the ICANN case shows that even a crucial issue like Internet control and Internet governance does not depend on the authority of a traditional international organization in which states are represented. Instead, this new mode of governance privileged the participation of individuals and groups rather than of states.[74] This is of course largely due to the way the Internet development process evolved: in the earliest days of the network, many individuals participated in building it and thus in debating the standards.[75]

However, the ICANN case also illustrates that an issue with a worldwide interest (Internet control) was given in the hands of an organization with a distinct link to only one single country: the US. Economic considerations and industry interests appear to have played a major role in opting for a governance arrangement that is not rooted in traditional ways of international co-operation and international law. The opinion that Internet governance is considered a technical issue and not a value-driven issue may also have contributed to the realization of an arrangement such as the ICANN structure.

6.4.3   Personal data protection

Where the international governance of domain names appears to be dominated by the US, it could be said that data protection *legislation* is a European phenomenon. The protection of personal data gained legislative recognition with the Council of Europe's Convention for the protection of individuals with regard to automatic processing of personal data, concluded on 28 January 1981.[76] The purpose of this Convention, as expressed in Article 1, is to secure in the territory of each party for

---

[71] <http://www.icann.org/general/archive-bylaws/bylaws-15dec02.htm>

[72] ERC's Proposed Clarifications, Corrections, and Modifications to New Bylaws, 8 February 2003, available at: <http://www.icann.org/committees/evol-reform/proposed-bylaws-corrections-08feb03.htm>

[73] Withers 2003, p. 35

[74] Mayer 2000, p. 167.

[75] For detailed information on the creation of Internet and the involvement of the many participating organizations, see Froomkin 2003.

[76] Convention for the protection of individuals with regard to automatic processing of personal data, Council of Europe (Convention No. 108), 28 January 1981, <http://conventions.coe.int/treaty/en/Treaties/html/108.htm>. The convention came into force on 1 October 1985 after ratification by five countries: Sweden, Norway, France, Germany, and Spain. Since then, almost all Member States of the Council of Europe have signed the Convention, and it specifically provides for the possibility of accession by non-Member States.

every individual, whatever his nationality or residence, respect for his rights and fundamental freedoms, and in particular his right to privacy, with regard to the automatic processing of the personal data relating to him. The Convention formulates a set of basic principles with respect to the protection of personal data of every individual in the territory of a Member State. These basic principles are also set out in the OECD Guidelines Governing the Protection of Privacy and Transborder Data Flows of Personal Data[77] and the 1995 European Directive on the protection of personal data.[78] The general ideas behind the three legal instruments are similar. They all more or less, try to reconcile the fundamental but competing values of privacy and the free flow of information. Characteristic for the EU approach is that the principles are effectuated by means of mandatory rules to be implemented in the European Member States. In the past decade, the EU has produced an extensive package of data protection provisions supplementing the 1995 Directive laid down in directives that specifically address privacy, directives on other issues that include privacy-related provisions, recommendations, as well as an express inclusion of the right to privacy in the Union's Charter of Fundamental Rights. The Charter not only proclaims a right to privacy similar to Article 8 of the European Convention for the Protection of Human Rights and Fundamental Freedoms (ECHR), but also contains in Article 8 a provision on the data protection (Art. 8).[79]

Not all countries have opted for a scenario similar to that in the EU. Around the world different systems of data protection have emerged. Some countries rely on a combination of legislation and self-regulatory measures. In Australia, for example, the government opted for so-called co-regulation and adopted a legislative context for flexible industry codes of conduct. The US has shown itself a prominent advocate of self-regulation.[80] Here, legislation is only considered in situations of clear misuse of personal data, in situations where specific types of data (health, financial) are processed or where certain groups seen as vulnerable (children) are involved. More recently, the regulatory climate has changed somewhat. Even the US largest high technology trade association (the American Electronics Association) now says that the federal government should take the initiative and work for international

---

[77] OECD Guidelines on the Protection of Privacy and Transborder Flows of Personal Data, 23 September 1980, <http://www1.oecd.org/publications/e-book/9302011E.PDF>.

[78] Directive 95/46/EC of the European Parliament and of the Council of 24 October 1995 on the protection of individuals with regard to the processing of personal data and on the free movement of such data, OJ L 281, 23 November 1995.

[79] Art. 8 of the Charter, on the protection of personal data, reads as follows:
1. Everyone has the right to the protection of personal data concerning him or her.
2. Such data must be processed fairly for specified purposes and on the basis of the consent of the person concerned or some other legitimate basis laid down by law. Everyone has the right of access to data which has been collected concerning him or her, and the right to have it rectified.
See also Art. 29 Data Protection Working Party, 'Recommendation 4/99 on the inclusion of the fundamental right to data protection in the European catalogue of fundamental rights', 7 September 1999, available at: <http://europa.eu.int/comm/internal_market/privacy/docs/wpdocs/1999/wp26en.pdf>.

[80] An overview of the different regimes around the world is presented in: *Privacy & Human Rights 2002: An International Survey of Privacy Laws and Developments*, EPIC, Washington DC 2002.

harmonization. The AEA president fears that without harmonization, consumers and businesses alike would lose.[81]

As with many other issues in the on-line world, personal data processing is emphatically a global issue. The developments of protection standards and instruments can therefore no longer be confined to individual or even regional jurisdictions. In recognizing this, the EU dictated its standard and instrument to the rest of the world. Based on the concept of reciprocity, Article 25 and 26 require that, prior to personal data about EU citizens being transferred to a third country, that country must have personal data protection equivalent to that in the EU Member States. Although representatives from outside the EU argued that the European data protection measures thus had an improperly extraterritorial effect and were protectionist,[82] the European stick approach has turned out to be rather successful.[83] The policy measures taken by India[84] and Canada are evidence to the fact that the European measure had a considerable impact.[85] The EU policy instrument has been powerfully felt in the US as well. The US was forced to negotiate with EU representatives on new data protection measures. After more than two years of negotiations, the EU and US agreed upon a set of privacy protection principles, the so-called Safe Harbor Principles, which companies can voluntarily sign up to. The EU recognized these principles as establishing adequate protection under its Directive.

In returning to the central theme of this chapter – the starting point that ICT regulation should be established at an international level – the following observations are in order. First, personal data protection is an issue with an international history of several decades. This history is however largely geographically restricted, viz. to Europe and international bodies with a primarily European representation. Nevertheless, the above also shows that the external influence of this regional harmonization is considerable. By means of regulatory reciprocity, the typically continental European Union data protection perspective has been exported across oceans. Hence, we could speak of a certain degree of global harmonization, established by means of an indirect instrument (regional pressure) instead of the direct mechanism of a recognized global forum.

A closer look reveals that the global harmonization concerns the minimum standard of protection, not so much the instruments used. Although it must be admitted that legislative protection measures are gaining support, the present harmonization

---

[81] *Electronic Commerce & Law Report*, 24 January 2001, p. 79.

[82] On this issue see Shaffer 1999.

[83] For a discussion on the EU and other privacy models around the world, see Yuill, 2003.

[84] The Indian government, for example, expressly indicated it drafted an EU-style data protection regime to attract business from Europe. *Electronic Commerce & Law Report*, 4 June 2003, p. 549.

[85] Noteworthy however, is the remark of Australia's Attorney-General, Williams, at the 25th International Conference of Data Protection and Privacy Commissioners. Williams said the European privacy policy is no model for a worldwide approach: 'We think that there is more than one model that can achieve the objectives of privacy protection, and we don't see that there is a need for the global community to be compressed into one model.' *Electronic Commerce & Law Report*, 17 September 2003, p. 866.

process has primarily occurred at the level of the underlying minimum goals, i.e., the basic data protection principles themselves. The Safe Harbor compromise refers only to a set of general principles accepted by all nations. The pluralistic set of modes of data protection regulation remains. Given the present diversity in legal traditions, legal conceptions[86] and political as well as economic considerations, the global variety in the area of personal data protection mechanisms will probably continue to exist for some time. The case of personal data protection, however, shows that international harmonization can be realized by accepting that a given legal system provides an equivalent solution (i.e., guaranteeing a certain level of data protection) formulated in terms of its own legal language and regulatory instruments.

A final remark is that the case of personal data protection is also a fine illustration of the role that soft law (codes of conduct, privacy policies, corporate rules, privacy seals and trustmarks) and the actors involved therein can play in establishing a certain degree of international protection.

6.4.4   Cross-border law enforcement

As will be discussed in section 6.6, states may for various reasons hold on to their national rules. Here, the notion of sovereignty plays a crucial role. Clinging to national rules and regulations means that states will also want to enforce their national laws in the global setting of the Internet. The problem that subsequently arises is that relevant concepts are interpreted differently between countries. For example, there is no internationally accepted definition of fraud. Apart from such problems of substantive law, challenges arise as regards enforceability in an international context, i.e., procedural questions that relate to mutual assistance, investigation powers, etc. Although the enforcement challenges arise in all areas of law and as such are not new,[87] the key challenges can be found in criminal law. Technically, searches for offenders can take place globally by using powerful programmes and interception of communications. Most states, however, present legal barriers on grounds of breach of territorial sovereignty. Due to the lack of international agreement on the power to conduct global searches, the capability of tracing an offender can be nullified. Thus, law enforcement agencies must count on national governments to pursue Internet crime across-borders and obtain information about an alleged or suspected criminal operating through the Internet.

By now, in many individual countries, laws or regulations have been issued that provide for mechanisms that enable law enforcement officials to obtain information from Internet providers. Various national rules as well as mutual assistance

---

[86] In Europe, neither privacy nor personal data protection is considered merely a commodity issue. Privacy is a fundamental right as well and this is reflected in the formal legal mechanisms used for the protection of this privacy.

[87] Cross-border enforcement is, of course, an issue that predates the Internet and, as a result, countries have established treaties to regulate enforcement competences.

rules between countries have also been issued on ways in which law enforcement officials can facilitate investigation of Internet-related activities in order to detect fraud and other criminal activities perpetrated over the Internet. However, no over-all initiatives are known within international organizations that aim at safeguarding enforcement of ICT law in general. In specific areas, initiatives do exist to ensure enforcement, and uniform procedures have been established for cross-border enforcement. The key example outside the area of criminal law is the enforcement procedure on domain names, established under WIPO. The European Union also has proposed a Directive on the enforcement of intellectual property rights[88] and the OECD has established guidelines to help law enforcement agencies protect consumer rights around the world.[89] The best-known example of international policy co-ordination and harmonization in the area of criminal law enforcement is the Cybercrime Convention established by the Council of Europe.

Interestingly, several initiatives dealing with enforcement have been established through self-regulatory means. Well-known is the international co-operation between hot lines. INHOPE, for example, is the European association of Internet hotline providers, in which various national hotlines involved in web site content control co-operate. An example at the global level is ICRA (Internet Content Rating Association), which brings together organizations representing Internet industry players with the aim of promoting and managing an international content rating system. At an international workshop on cross-border fraud hosted by the US Federal Trade Commission, the suggestion was made for law enforcement agencies of different countries to work out stopgap solutions in the form of memoranda of understanding or protocols. Such protocols may not only create a mechanism for disclosure of information by service providers to foreign law enforcement agencies, but set parameters as well (such as how long the agency may retain the information and whether it can make further disclosures to other parties).[90] Both government and private sector representatives at the workshop acknowledged that the complex problem of efficient and effective law enforcement on the Internet could only be completely resolved by international treaties. Mention can finally be made of the private sector initiative of the Organization for the Advancement of Structured Information Standards (OASIS). Early in 2003, it announced the establishment of the Legal XML Lawful Intercept XML Technical Committee. This new technical committee was charged with creating a universal, global system for supporting the discovery, sharing, and authentication of suspected criminal and terrorist evidence by law enforcement agencies.[91]

---

[88] Proposal for a Directive on measures and procedures to ensure the enforcement of intellectual property rights, COM (2003) 46 final, available at: <http://europa.eu.int/eur-lex/>.

[89] 'Guidelines for Protecting Consumers from Fraudulent and Deceptive Commercial Practices Across Borders', issued on 17 June 2003, available at: <www.oecd.org>. The guidelines contain principles regarding international law enforcement co-ordination, as well as specific information on how countries can best work together during the course of joint investigations.

[90] *Electronic Commerce & Law Report*, 26 February 2003, pp. 193-195. See <http://www.ftc.gov/bcp/workshops/crossborder/index.html>.

[91] See <http://xml.coverpages.org/LawfulInterceptTC.html>.

The law enforcement case shows that no truly global overall procedures are initiated under the regime of international organizations that aim at safeguarding enforcement of ICT law in general. The prime reason for this situation is the absence of harmonized substantive rules. The case of intellectual property rights shows that, when large parts of substantive law have been harmonized, the prospect of harmonization of procedural rules glooms up.[92]

In specific areas initiatives do exist to ensure enforcement, and uniform procedures have been established for cross-border enforcement.[93] However, the majority of the initiatives relate to areas where a certain level of general agreement exists as regards the goals to be realized (e.g., with respect to privacy and consumer protection). Also, the instrument used for the initiatives is not the most powerful among the regulatory modes that exist. Usually the international understanding takes the form of a guideline (e.g., OECD privacy guidelines), trustmark (EU trustmark on consumer protection), or standard (EU standard on on-line dispute resolution).[94] Thus far, the perhaps most promising tools for enforcement at an international scale appear to be global standards on technological enforcement methods as well as international co-operation between private initiatives (hotlines).

6.5   WHY STRIVE FOR HARMONIZATION?

Now that the illustrative cases of regulation have provided a more in-depth look at how the starting point works in practice, a more general description of the arguments oft-cited in favor of the starting point will be given. In gaining an adequate understanding of the arguments and justifications for the ICT-related starting point discussed in this chapter, it is first necessary to situate the debate on international policy-making within the larger debate about the impact of globalization on state regulation, because the broader process of globalization definitely has an impact on the contours, dynamics, and boundaries of international policy-making related to ICT.

The process of globalization has been discussed, analysed, and described extensively in theoretical literature.[95] To briefly summarize the discussions, it can be stated that globalization implies a speeding up of global interactions, highly facilitated by new information and communication mechanisms (among which ICT) that

---

[92] In the meantime, the EU is also working on the harmonization of certain issues of criminal laws: see Proposal for a Council Framework Decision on attacks against information systems. COM (2002) 173 final, Brussels, 19 April 2003.

[93] For example, the United States and Japan are reported to work on a bilateral co-operation convention to combat cybercrime. *Electronic Commerce & Law Report*, 23 July 2003, p. 716.

[94] The recent EU proposal for a Directive on IP enforcement is a first example of the use of a more powerful instrument.

[95] See among others: Strange, 1996; Cerny, 1995.

increase the 'velocity of the global diffusion of ideas, goods, information, capital and people.'[96]

The key characteristic of the process of globalization is that it results in 'a *stretching* of social, political and economic activities across frontiers such that events, decisions and activities in one region of the world can come to have significance for individuals and communities in distant regions of the globe.'[97] Globalization thus has a clear impact on the autonomy of individual states in regulating the effects of various social, political, and economic activities. When considering activities related to the use of ICT it can be noted that they clearly display the above characteristics of globalization. A picture emerges of a world in which national attachments are not, or less, important and fast global communication and interaction of information is the driving force of a global on-line economy. Such a global world and economy necessitates regulation on a worldwide level. Under the broader umbrella of globalization, more detailed arguments can be found that underlie the quest for international regulation. As will be shown, international institutions have used several of the arguments to justify their regulatory initiatives in the area of ICT. Some of these arguments relate to economic considerations, others are based on societal interests or focus on enforcement. Some arguments underscore the interest of stimulating certain processes, whereas others focus on protecting interests (consumer protection, privacy protection, societal and public interests). The various arguments cited in justifying the starting point will all be presented below from the perspective that ICT regulation should be established at an international level. The arguments will be supplemented with remarks that put them in a different perspective. Core arguments against the starting point will be discussed when assessing, in section 6.6, whether and to what extent the starting point can be put into practice in concrete cases.

6.5.1 Legal certainty

The on-line world is a market that knows no frontiers and is constantly changing. In such a global environment, the relevant players should not be dependent on (extremely) divergent legal systems they know nothing about. Differences between national law systems are not desirable and harmonization of national laws is necessary to provide sufficient legal certainty. Illustrative are the arguments brought forward by the European Commission in Consideration 5 of the Directive on electronic commerce:

> 'The development of information society services within the Community is hampered by a number of legal obstacles to the proper functioning of the international market which make less attractive the exercise of the freedom of establishment and the free-

---

[96] Held, et al., 1999, pp. 15-16.
[97] Ibid. (emphasis in original).

dom to provide services; these obstacles arise from divergences in legislation and from the legal uncertainty as to which national rules apply to such services (...).'

The Commission used the argument also in its Green Paper on the conversion of the Rome Convention of 1980 on the law applicable to contractual provisions into a Community instrument and its modernization.[98] Mention can also be made of the arguments underlying the drafting of a model law on electronic commerce in the context of the UNCITRAL. This project was mainly directed at removing improper legal obstacles in the global market by adopting a set of uniform international rules. Promoting the predictability of the law and increasing its practical applicability were key considerations.

To some, the argument of promoting legal certainty is founded on the logic that a global market and thus global market players need uniform regulatory regimes.[99] Nevertheless, other authors have argued that diversity in rules may bring important benefits as well. 'The lawyers' blind concern for legal certainty diverts their attention away from the important benefits of competition between legislators. Such competition may initiate more efficient rules.'[100]

Another basic presumption underlying the argument of promoting legal certainty is that all legal regimes are relatively similar in tradition and in the regulatory instruments used. This is clearly simplistic. As has been mentioned in earlier chapters, the level of legal certainty that can and will actually be realized may vary greatly, depending on numerous factors, such as the level and scope of regulation, the legal tradition, the subject-matter, and the discretionary powers of Member States in implementing and interpreting the international rules. Hence, in order to know what degree (and what kind) of harmonization is realistic in aiming at legal certainty, it should be closely assessed just what level of legal certainty is called for, given the economic interests at stake and the factors and circumstances that influence the actual realization of harmonization.

Faced with the problems and disadvantages of far-reaching international harmonization, several international bodies have adopted a less stringent position in addressing the problem of legal uncertainty and have tried to find a middle road between international uniformity and national diversity of regulation. International rulemaking is here confined to implementing minimum standards of protection or minimum rules. A precondition here is that all affected jurisdictions should indeed agree on a certain threshold. Illustrative is UNCITRAL's light regulatory touch approach, underlying, for example, the project focusing on electronic signatures. The aim of

---

[98] Brussels, 14 January 2003, COM (2002) 654 final.

[99] This argument was, for example, brought forward after an Australian federal court ruling (Kabushiki *Kaisha Sony Computer Entertainment Inc.* v. *Stevens* [2002] FCA 906) made it clear that the Australian position on technological protection measures does not reflect the approach taken in the US and Europe. While the latter adopted broad definitions in their copyright regimes that encourage technological innovation to prevent copyright piracy, the Australian Copyright Act limits copyright holders in their actions against hackers of technological protection measures.

[100] Van den Bergh 1998, p. 130.

the model law is to set down a minimum package of conditions that Member States involved must implement if electronic signatures are to be considered legally valid. The approach leaves it to Member States to decide what is right by national law if the conditions are violated. In addition, the model law leaves plenty of room for self-regulation. At the EU level also, the minimum level approach has been used in several directives.[101]

What should be considered finally is that legal certainty can be realized by other means than mandatory intervention of international organizations. To the extent that this is allowed under the private international law of their home country, companies involved in e-commerce or other dealings related to ICT can choose the jurisdiction whose rules provide the most legal certainty on a specific issue.[102]

6.5.2   Balanced competition on markets

Differences between national legal systems can affect the conditions of how products and services are presented at the various markets. This implies that the competitive positions of the market players in the different countries are not balanced. In other words, variations in national regulatory regimes would adulterate the best possible working of the global on-line market. Harmonization of law is an instrument in harmonizing market conditions. The argument is a popular one in justifying the regulatory initiatives of the EU. The argumentation of the European Commission is that differences in national laws may obstruct competition within the internal market for information services. For example, competition between ISPs might be asymmetrical in the situation that in one country unclear standards exist as regards ISP liability (which may constitute an incentive for not making any effort to know about content) whereas, in another country, the problem is solved (e.g., through case law) and clear guidelines exist as regards the situations where control over content is required (thus requiring the ISP to implement filtering software). In looking at the various Directives issued in the area of ICT, the argument of imbalanced competition is advanced to justify almost all measures. It can be found, for example, in the EU 'telecom package', issued in July 2000. The European Commission adopted this package of legislative proposals in order to strengthen competition in the emerging electronic communications markets in the EU. The proposed Directives (all adopted in 2002) aimed at creating a level playing field across the EU in facilitating market entry through simplified rules and ensuring harmonized application through strong co-ordination mechanisms at the European level.[103] It is

---

[101]   See Green Paper on the Rome Convention, Brussels, 14 January 2003, COM (2002) 654 final, p. 29.

[102]   Although it must be acknowledged that the applicability of the present body of private international law to on-line transactions does not provide the required legal certainty as well. Problems, e.g., arise when applying the traditional methods for tracking down the place of business or the place where a contract was concluded. See Mankowski 1999; Van der Hof 2002.

[103]   European Commission, Press Release IP/00/749, 12 July 2000, Brussels. See <http://europa.eu.int/ISPO/infosoc/telecompolicy/press/ip00-749en.htm>.

the argument of imbalanced competition that also seems to be an important basis of the European Directive on the protection of personal data.[104]

The argument of imbalanced competition due to differences in national legal systems implies that there is a close relationship between the harmonization of legal regimes, on the one hand, and market entry conditions, on the other. Legal subject-matters outside the domain of ICT, however, show that such a relationship is often very difficult to prove. In general there is a lack of empirical evidence to what extent variations between national legal systems obstruct market competition and what the positive effect of harmonization measures would be. Illustrative is the report of the European Commission on the practical effects of Directive 85/374 on liability for defective products.[105] In this report, the European Commission acknowledges that the effect of the European Directive on liability for defective products on the harmonization of market conditions cannot be proved. First, 'only little information about the application exists and statistics, if available, are not complete.' In addition, the harmonization legislation is often merely an additional layer to an already existing body of (substantive and procedural) national law. In the words of the Commission: 'In most Member States, the national rules implementing the Directive are applied alongside other liability regulations in the majority of the cases.'[106] Thus the 'traditional' legislation stays intact irrespective of the European measures and it is the 'traditional' body of law that, to a large extent, influences the actual market conditions. Illustrative for the domain of ICT law is the regime on liability of ISPs under the European Directive on electronic commerce. One of the cornerstones of the new European regime is that – being considered essential to the functioning of the open networks of the Internet, should be exempted from liability for the mere facilitation of communications. Articles 12 to 15 of the Directive on electronic commerce delineate exceptions to Internet Service Providers liability for the transfer or storage of illegal information in a communication network, provided that the ISPs role is a merely technical one and is limited to the technical process of operating and giving access to the network. In introducing this regime, the Directive only provides for possibilities that free ISPs from liability in case of mere conduit, caching, and hosting and in doing so, does not establish liability itself. This issue is left to the national liability regime of the individual Member States.

A final point that should be mentioned when considering the argument that differences between national legal systems have an adverse effect on the conditions under which products and services are presented at the different markets is that the absence of an integrated economic market does not by definition imply that market conditions vary. The US market appears a prime example that an integrated eco-

---

[104] Compare the arguments of the Commission in Consideration 7 of the Directive. Also Consideration 2 of the Council Regulation of 22 December 2000 on jurisdiction and the recognition and enforcement of judgments in civil and commercial matters, OJ L 012, 16 January 2001.

[105] Report from the Commission on the application of Directive 85/374 on Liability for Defective Products, Brussels, 31 January 2001, COM (2000) 893 final.

[106] Ibid., p. 8.

nomic market can exist where market conditions (here, the competing legal systems of the different states) are not the same.[107]

6.5.3 Administrative burden

A third argument is that harmonization would lead to a simplification of the rules applicable in an on-line world. Companies and other actors engaged in international on-line activities will be better informed or acquainted as to the applicable legal rules. This may save on information costs and thus result in a reduction of the overall costs that companies incur when conducting on-line business. Benefits from uniform international rules can also arise from a reduction in court costs in case a dispute arises. A reduction of costs appears to be of importance for the further development of new markets because in the end consumers will pay the costs. It is this argument that, for example, seems to be a basis of the proposal for a Directive in the area of indirect taxation (VAT).[108] The argument was also forwarded in the debate on the revision of the Brussels Convention of 1968[109] and the ongoing discussion on the revision of Article 5 of the Rome Convention of 1980.[110]

As with the argument of imbalanced competition mentioned earlier, no empirical support has been given for this justification of harmonization and it has therefore been criticized by various authors.[111] The exact impact of international harmonization efforts on costs appears highly difficult to assess.[112] Many other factors and developments have their influence on administrative costs and no research seems available on the potential impact of harmonization measures on price setting. The introduction of an expanding and increasingly complex body of (albeit harmonized) law may very well leads to an increase in costs instead of a decrease (an often-heard claim with respect to the European Directive on the protection of personal data). The cost of accommodating a concept foreign to a national legal culture (legislation, case law, training) could outweigh the claimed information and administrative advantages of harmonized rules.

In any event, the argument that international rule-making results in a reduction of administrative costs, would require a cost-benefits analysis that not only shows the benefits of a simplification of the applicable rules between the different countries but at least also includes the different costs.

---

[107] Faure and Hartlief, 2003, p. 173.

[108] See the Explanatory Memorandum COM (2000) 349 final. The argument is only one of many other motives underlying this Directive. The Directive, for example, also wants to provide a competitive edge to EU suppliers (the US therefore considered challenging the European rules in the WTO for being unfair to non-European countries).

[109] The Brussels Convention was replaced (as of 1 March 2002) by Regulation 44/2001, OJ L 12, 16 January 2001.

[110] See Green Paper on the Rome Convention, Brussels, 14 January 2003, COM (2002) 654 final.

[111] See, for example, Van den Bergh, 1998.

[112] Curran 1994, p. 96.

6.5.4   The race to the bottom

Another argument presented in favor of international harmonization of laws is that companies may (ab)use differences between national laws for the very reason that they will persuade national policy makers (and thus legislatures) to create a favorable climate for investment in their country by adopting low legal standards. This would lead in a downward spiral of legal standards as companies search for competitive advantage and as countries cater to their needs by progressively weakening their jurisdictional standards to attract global investment ('race to the bottom').[113]

A prominent example in the domain of ICT is the politically complex issue of VAT for on-line services. Clearly, the applicable VAT tariff has an effect on the costs of on-line services and different VAT regimes give companies an incentive to relocate their on-line activities to the most favorable jurisdiction. Thus there seems to be a competitive advantage for states to have an attractive VAT regime and they could use tax regulation as an instrument to compete for global investment. The intention of the European Union, expressed in the late 1990s, to introduce a so-called 'bit tax' (which would be charged on transmissions of bits of digital information) was clearly a step to slow the race-to-the-bottom within the EU and provide for a unified European answer to the attractive investment climate in the US.[114] In 2002, the EU issued a Directive on VAT and e-commerce, changing the circumstances under which liability of VAT rising for digital products imported into the EU from outside (e.g., the US). The prime goal of the Directive is to level the playing field between EU and non-EU suppliers so that any supplies made to customers based outside the EU will not give rise to VAT and supplies made into the EU will.[115] However, the Directive does not tackle the far more fundamental problem of the diverging VAT rates between the EU Member States.

As shown in various publications, the race-to-the-bottom argument is not an easy one to defend[116] and a number of critical questions can be raised. A primary question to be answered here is how much exactly is known about competition between legal systems. What are the advantages and disadvantages of such competition? And what is more: do companies base the decision of where to establish a branch on the legal regime applicable in a certain country or do other, economic, factors play a more prominent role? The answer to this question will vary depending on the subject of the regulation (VAT, liability, privacy[117]) and the specific activities the company is involved in. Even if everything is harmonized, differences

---

[113] More in detail Van den Bergh, 1998.

[114] See also 'EU Digital VAT Directive Raising Concerns For U.S. Retailers, Consumers, Allen Says', *Electronic Commerce & Law Report*, 2 July 2003, p. 661.

[115] Council Directive 2002/38/EC of 7 May 2002, OJ L 128, 15 May 2002, pp. 41-44.

[116] As discussed by Ogus, empirical support for the prediction is weak: 'Studies tend to show that races to the bottom are rare' (Ogus 1999, p. 414).

[117] For an extensive discussion of the race-to-the-bottom thesis and personal data protection measures, see chapter 10 of Bennett and Raab, 2003.

influencing market conditions that are outside the scope of law will continue to exist, for example, differences in infrastructure, level of technological development, and knowledge. More in general, it seems that no or hardly any empirical evidence is available providing an adequate insight into the extent to which legal considerations play a role in an ICT company's decision to establish a branch in a certain country. It therefore, also remains unclear on what basis and to what extent countries can indeed successfully compete with their legal systems in stimulating the ICT industry to favor their country.

Finally, besides potential races to the bottom, there are also races to the top. Under this scenario, individual states contest over the most stringent rule that will act as an instrument for applying pressure to get international adoption by other countries. The illustrative example mentioned in legal literature is the Clinton Administration's effort to persuade other countries to adopt the anti-circumvention rules laid down in the Digital Millennium Copyright Act as an appropriate implementation of the WIPO Copyright Treaty.[118]

6.5.5   No room for nationally oriented perspectives

The on-line world is a society without traditional boundaries and borders, characterized by a high mobility. The global problems and threats that arise in such a society need global answers, meaning that, in such a society, there is no room for something like German, Italian, or Canadian perspective on interests such as freedom of speech, free flow of information, etc. Given the characteristics of the Internet and the interests at stake, certain issues can no longer be dealt with according to the own national preferences of each individual country. Illustrative is the question of the liability for information and content distributed on the Internet. Such liability has arisen in various countries in relation to claims in tort, defamation, intellectual property infringement, and breach of content regulation laws. The *Yahoo* case (first decided in France and subsequently in the US) has shown that the present situation in which the respective courts came to opposite conclusions as regards the liability of an ISP for facilitating the distribution of neo-nazi material leaves certain actors in the on-line world with highly unsatisfactory situations. Given the free and borderless distribution of information on the Internet, it is argued that worldwide uniform liability criteria should apply to those who provide or distribute information. Another issue is the need to criminalize the dissemination of certain on-line content, such as racist and xenophobic material.

The key challenge here is of course: is there, or must there be such a thing as, a European or global perspective on, for example, free speech? In arguing that there should be something as global freedom of expression or a worldwide level of consumer protection, it is assumed that all actors in the on-line world have the same preferences. Clearly, this is too simple. National preferences regarding the level of

---

[118] Samuelson, 1999, p. 13.

protection differ and why should the preferences of citizens in one country prevail over the standards of other jurisdictions? One answer is that widely held perceptions of human rights must be observed and that thus the lower standards fail to meet the generally accepted standard. Another argument is that diverging standards on what counts as racist or xenophobic speech will result in a 'zoning' of the on-line world, meaning that access to content may be (technically) restricted based on the user's citizenship and domicile. This would leave the on-line community with Americans being able to access certain content that Europeans no longer can.

Nevertheless, in many situations, it will be difficult to determine the overall international standard to be applied. If harmonization appears to be the best approach, how should the standard be constructed: do we look for the greatest common denominator? Or should we choose a top-down (compromise) approach? Given the depth of the contrasts between US and European law on the issue of freedom of expression, the chance of a worldwide uniform perspective on racism, hate speech, discrimination and xenophobia seems highly remote. Illustrative are the discussions while drafting the Council of Europe's Cybercrime Convention. Although there were powerful reasons to believe that international harmonization was required with respect to criminal offences, the Cybercrime Convention shows that harmonizing legislation in the field of content-related offences on the Internet requires an enormous effort and may, for some issues, not even be viable[119] due to national legislative characteristics as well as national preferences and traditions.[120] Although, early in 2003, the Committee of Ministers decided to open for signature an Additional Protocol against racism and xenophobia on the Internet, it remains to be seen how many countries (Member States as well as non-Member States) will adopt the rules that require them to criminalize the dissemination of certain content.[121] It is expected that the US, for example, will not sign the protocol since it conflicts with the First Amendment.

Not only the discussions on content-related problems, but also the issues related to personal data protection and contract formation are evidence of the problems.

Harmonization in the area of electronic contracting may, for example, in view of the conceptual differences between national civil law regimes on the concepts of 'writing' and 'offer and acceptance', require some governments to accept rather foreign principles. In the end, the contrast between laws in dealing with these and other issues is closely related to differences in societal values, preferences, and (legal) tradition. In addition, various other factors may influence a country's perspective on a certain issue.

---

[119] With the exception of child pornography.

[120] Another problem appears to be that the harmonization efforts for offences conducted in the on-line world are likely to affect international intervention and thus harmonization of rules applicable to the physical, off-line world.

[121] The Additional Protocol was opened for signature on the occasion of the Committee of Ministers' Parliamentary Assembly session in January 2003, <http://www.coe.int>.

'For example, different countries with varying educational practices and literacy rates may permit or prohibit quite different copying practices. The manner in which authors are compensated may differ from country to country depending upon established labor and employment practices. The ways in which works are exploited, and thus need to be protected, may hinge upon social customs unique to particular countries. The extent of reasonable copying privileges may reflect the level of access to public libraries. Commitments to free expression, and hence use of a work in that cause without the need for permission, may vary in intensity depending upon the political development of the society in question. Unqualified respect for the integrity of artistic works might be affected by different notions of property. Moreover, market mechanisms necessary to support schemes for compensating authors might be more feasible in certain cultures than in others.'[122]

The close relationship between law and society, between law and legal culture, is what makes harmonization of certain issues a potentially insurmountable problem. Many authors have argued that harmonization of different legal cultures (such as those of the civil law systems of continental Europe, on the one hand, and those of the common law systems of the Anglo-American world, on the other) is inherently impossible.[123] Interesting in this light is the statement of the European Commission when emphasizing the importance of its *eEurope* initiative:

'The EU effort is designed to build on and to strengthen the 'European social model', including a high level of social protection. It is also meant to preserve Europe's cultural and linguistic diversity. (...) The Internet may turn the world into a global village, but the EU is committed to ensuring that in this village every culture and every language maintains its role at local level.'[124]

6.5.6   A minimum level of legal security or protection

It has been argued that, considering their specific position, some parties acting in a global on-line environment must in any event be accorded a certain minimum level of protection. For example, it is generally understood that the 'legitimate expectations of the consumer' constitute a worldwide minimum level for the protection of the consumer.[125] A similar expectation operates in privacy law,[126] in contract law, and in the field of the law on misleading advertising.[127] Illustrative is the 2001

---

[122] Dinwoodie 2000, pp. 513-514.

[123] For law is 'a polysemic signifier which connotes *inter alia* cultural, political, sociological, historical, anthropological, linguistic, psychological and economic referents.' Legrand 1997, p. 116.

[124] European Commission, *Towards a Knowledge-Based Europe. The European Union and the Information Society*, Brussels, October 2002, p. 4, <http://europa.eu.int/comm/publications/booklets/move/36/en.pdf>.

[125] Howells and Wilhelmsson 1997, pp. 18-19.

[126] On the concept of *a reasonable expectation of privacy*, see *Katz* v. *United States*, 389 US 347, 1967.

[127] See C-210/96 (*Gut Springenheide GmbH and Rudolf Tusky* v. *Oberkreisdirektor des Kreises Steinfurt – Amt für Lebensmittelüberwachung*): 'In order to determine whether a statement (...) is

Green Paper on Consumer Protection, arguing for 'a comprehensive, technology-neutral, EU framework directive to *harmonise national fairness rules* for business-consumer commercial practices.'[128] In setting an example for a minimum international standard on consumer protection in the area of electronic commerce, the OECD issued the Consumer Protection Guidelines in December 1999.[129] A soft law example here is the work of the European Commission on a standard for an EU trustmark for e-Commerce.[130] In the area of personal data protection mention, can be made of the suggestions by the French government to establish, by means of a international treaty at a worldwide level, a set of minimum data protection principles, which could provide for a uniform mechanism among different countries for enforcement of consumer protection standards. These minimum principles could be further elaborated in the relevant countries by means of self-regulation.[131] Finally, the argument underlying the 2002 EU regulatory framework for the electronic communications infrastructure and services is that: it is aimed to 'ensure that a minimum of services are available to all users.'[132]

In adopting this argument, international rule-making is confined to implementing minimum rules and combines the best of both, i.e., national and international regulation as well as formal and informal regulation. Such a hybrid regulatory structure in which public and private parties combine their efforts is advocated, among others, by Perritt, who believes that formal law should set minimum general standards and provide enforcement power, while multiple 'private regulatory regimes can work out detailed rules, first-level dispute resolution, and rule enforcement machinery.'[133]

6.5.7 Effective enforcement

As has been said before, the on-line world is no longer a world determined by traditional, nationally controllable means of communication. The unique nature of the Internet, being a highly decentralized world in which anyone can (anonymously) circumvent, in often obscure patterns, local and national government-influenced distribution channels. This not only challenges the substantive national regulation, but its enforcement as well. Developments in numerous domains show that na-

---

liable to mislead the purchaser (…), the national court must take into account the presumed expectations which it evokes in an average consumer who is reasonably well informed and reasonably observant and circumspect' (European Court reports 1998, I-04657).

[128] *Green Paper on European Union Consumer Protection*, 2 October 2001, COM (2001) 531 final. Emphasis added.

[129] *Guidelines for Consumer Protection in the Context of Electronic Commerce* and available at: <http://www.oecd.org/pdf/M000014000/M00014340.pdf>.

[130] The standard is expected to take the form of a recommendation. *Electronic Commerce & Law Report*, 29 January 2003, pp. 90-91.

[131] *Conseil d'Etat* 1998, p. 44.

[132] See <http://europe.eu.int/information_society/topics/telecoms/regulatory/new_rf/print_en.htm>.

[133] Perritt 2000, p. 574.

tional enforcement measures have limited or no effect. The well-known *Radikal* and other cases decided by German courts on illegal content illustrate the problems and limits. Although the courts found that the information and material (neo-Nazi material, among them) was illegal under German law, it was subsequently available on servers hosted in various countries around the world.[134] The enforcement problems the music industry faces with applications such as Napster and KaZaa is another illustration. In the on-line world, with its lack of geographic borders and where it is practically impossible to trace the sources from which music files are distributed and the destinations to which they are downloaded, national enforcement instruments no longer offer a solution. The global impact of viruses, denial-of-service attacks, and hacking are other signs that the traditional (often geographical) barriers for invasive operations have become blurred, and different (global) modes of enforcement are in order. However, international harmonization of enforcement is not only required to ensure that certain actors cannot evade the legal rules. An international approach could also address on-line jurisdiction problems such as those that arise when information published in one country is available in another, with tougher libel laws. Introducing liability exemption (immunity) systems under national or regional (compare the provisions in Art. 12-14 of the Directive on electronic commerce) will not prevent legal action against them in foreign courts (including courts outside the region). In December 2002 the Australian high court asserted jurisdiction over a US-based publisher solely on accessibility of the publisher's web site in Australia.[135] In rejecting the arguments of the US publisher, Justice Callinan said that 'what the appellant seeks to do, is to impose upon Australian residents for the purposes of this and many other cases, an American legal hegemony in relation to Internet publications.' In recognizing this complication, the UK Law Commission concluded around the same period that an international treaty is needed to address the problem of these 'unlimited global risks'.[136]

Undoubtedly, there are areas where harmonization on enforcement can be realized. The adoption of the Council of Europe's Cybercrime Treaty shows that in the area of criminal law, certain issues related to the arsenal of investigative powers in an electronic environment have been successfully addressed at the international level. States also co-operate in an international network of national contact points available 24 hours a day and seven days a week to directly deal with and co-ordinate requests for mutual criminal assistance. This network can give an impetus to further-reaching forms of cross-border co-operation. As regards enforcement in private law, mention can be made of the EU rules on the evidentiary value of electronic signatures and the copyright rules on circumvention measures of Digital Rights Management (DRM). Other initiatives (such as in the area of on-line dispute resolution) show that national governments and international institutions have indeed

---

[134] See Kühne 1999, p. 188.

[135] *Dow Jones & Co* v. *Gutnick*, 2002 HCA 56, 10 December 2002. See *Electronic Commerce & Law Report*, 18 December 2002, p. 1226; *Electronic Commerce & Law Report*, 8 January 2003, p. 5.

[136] See <http://www.lawcom.gov.uk/files/defamation2.pdf>.

given considerable thought to the necessity and options of ensuring enforcement of ICT law in the international context.

A closer look at international regulation on enforcement issues shows few ideas have been put forward about an integral approach to enforcement. The examples show that the present initiatives are based on the pragmatic line to simply look for the best approach in each given case. In those areas where the interests to be protected are broadly shared internationally, there appears to be the best likelihood of an international approach to enforcement.

Practice also shows that it is often the private sector or a non-governmental organization that takes the lead in realizing successful international co-operation on enforcement. Illustrative is the international approach in combating child pornography, for which an international network of hotlines is at work.[137] Co-operation between national contact points in addressing enforcement of illegal and harmful content at an international level has also shown to be promising. In private-law matters, various successful trustmark projects (for enhancing consumer protection and personal data protection) have been launched.

6.5.8 Interests of developing countries

The argument for harmonization throughout the world is often heard in relation to the welfare of developing countries and countries with economies in transition. Developing countries have much to gain in terms of domestic economic welfare and individual consumer welfare, and ICT appears to be a key instrument for new social and economic potential. Also, the Internet is considered an important facilitator for the freedom to hold opinions without interference and to seek, send, and receive information and ideas regardless of frontiers. As such access to the Internet is seen as a fundamental human need, and every individual around the world should have the opportunity to freely participate and no one should be excluded from the benefits of the Information Society.[138] In order to achieve this goal, the promotion of effective participation by developing countries in international ICT forums is an issue on the agenda of many international forums.[139]

Reducing the present digital divide between the developed and developing countries must be achieved by means of various strategies. Securing access to the Internet for everyone is only one of them. Strengthening the economic environment and the conditions, for example, for investment that apply is another prerequisite for bridging the divide. Interests of security and integrity of the infrastructure and communication are also considered key enabling factors.

---

[137] <http://www.inhope.org>.

[138] See the Plan of Action and the Declaration of Principles of the World Summit on the Information Society, Geneva, December 2003.

[139] Various ICT-related initiatives are, for example, taken within the New Partnership for Africa's Development (NEPAD).

A line of argument is that developing countries will attract foreign investment and technology transfers if investors from other countries believe that ICT products, E-commerce processes, and trade secrets will be adequately protected. To achieve this, harmonized global rules appear a prerequisite. With respect to intellectual property rights, the case of harmonization has often been made in these terms. For example, it was suggested to support the harmonization efforts under the TRIPs agreement.

However, strength of the argument that harmonization could be in the long-term self-interest of developing countries does not appear to be straightforward. Some have argued that empirical evidence that developing countries indeed benefit from worldwide policy equivalence is sketchy and anecdotal. They argue that a more appropriate response might be to negotiate specific guarantees with investors, rather than increasing the level of protection.[140] Also, harmonization may not always be beneficial to all countries, in particular those developing countries that benefit from imitation (intellectual property rights) or free havens (privacy and taxation). International harmonization that results in higher substantive and procedural standards may here very well be seen as a welfare-reducing instrument. Hence, the overall trade-offs between innovation and welfare, on the one hand, and welfare as a result of imitation, on the other hand, differ from country to country.

6.5.9   Infrastructure is a global thing

Cyberspace is, in the words of Mayer, merely a technical product.[141] Setting technical standards and using certain technologies implies making policy choices. Experts have even argued that technical standards mirror cultural preferences.[142] When viewed in light of the starting point addressed in this chapter, it seems that regulation of issues related to the technical infrastructure should by definition be addressed at a global level given the fact that the technical infrastructure spans the entire world. As has been discussed in earlier sections, the technical management of the Internet is indeed in the hands of various international bodies.

However, there is no denying that the issue is far more complex, the ICANN domain name and Internet governance scenario being a case in point. As mentioned in section 6.4.2, economic considerations and industry interests appear to have played a major role in opting for a governance arrangement that is not rooted in traditional ways of international co-operation and international law. The fact that Internet governance is a technical issue and not a value-driven one may also have contributed to the present arrangement in which a single economic power turns out to be the key player instead of an international body in which various countries are represented.

---

[140] Trebilcock, Howse, 1998, p. 19. The authors argue that the TRIPs agreement as a stand-alone instrument seems likely to reduce welfare in many developing countries.

[141] Mayer 2000, p. 161.

[142] Ibid., p. 162.

6.5.10   Code as international law

Technological control mechanisms, applications, and standards (regarding access, digital signatures, filtering programmes, digital rights management systems, etc.) influence behaviour in the on-line world. To some, technical means are therefore the only effective way to control behavior in an on-line world.[143] By means of the technological control mechanisms individuals or groups can impose rules or their preferences on persons or entities present in other countries. In other words, such control mechanisms have an extraterritorial effect, which undoubtedly will result in the development of international norms and usages. Technology may could turn out to be a very effective and fast mode of harmonization.

Undoubtedly this development has advantages in enforcing music piracy, protecting personal data and addressing illegal and harmful content. There are of course disadvantages as well. In a scenario where this type of private international 'law-making' threatens to become the standard and present other users with a *fait accompli,* questions arise as regards its legitimacy in view of transparency and democratic values. Freedom of information and freedom of expression are interests too valuable to leave to the international 'forum' of those who have the power over technological content control. Thus, the growth of the use of control mechanisms requires in its turn a discussion on what role international institutions have in facilitating or restricting these mechanisms as well as in formulating uniform conditions for their use.

Above, the argument was presented that technology may turn out to be a very effective and fast mode of harmonization, given that technological control mechanisms have an extraterritorial effect. The reverse opinion may also be defended, viz. that technological control provides nations with a tool to enforce their local laws. In analysing the French court ruling in the *Yahoo* case,[144] Reidenberg argues that technological means such as filtering tools empower individual states to enforce their public policy and national values within their territory. Reidenberg thus concludes that 'sovereignty still matters in cyberspace.'[145]

6.6   BOUNDARIES AND LIMITATIONS OF INTERNATIONAL RULE-MAKING

Now that the oft-cited arguments justifying the starting point have become clear and have been commented upon, it is time to focus on the question of what considerations need attention when putting the starting point into practice. In answering this question, careful notice should of course also be given of the boundaries and limitations of international rule-making.

---

[143] For more detailed information, see also chapter 3 of this Volume.

[144] T.G.I. Paris, 22 May 2000, *UEJF and Licra* v. *Yahoo! Inc. and Yahoo France* available at: <http://www.juriscom.net/txt/jurisfr/cti/yauctions20000522.htm>.

[145] Reidenberg 2002, p. 271.

6.6.1   Formal and recognized limits of international rule-making

A key concept in determining the limits of regulation at an international level, is sovereignty. The exclusive power of individual nations to regulate certain issues is closely linked to this classical concept. As has been discussed in literature, the concept of sovereignty is founded upon the very existence of territory: the principle whereby a state is deemed to exercise exclusive power over its territory can be considered a fundamental axiom of classical international law.[146] Internet, however, challenges sovereignty. In 1996, Johnson and Post were among the first to consider the problems of sovereignty in the on-line world. They argued that this world should be its own jurisdictional entity because it is a world that cannot legitimately be governed by territorially based sovereigns. In contending that cyberspace should be deemed a distinct place for purposes of law-making sovereignty, they concluded that this world should be its own jurisdictional entity. The law applicable to interaction in cyberspace 'will not, could not, and should not be the same law as that applicable to physical, geographically-defined territories.'[147]

Irrespective of whether this radical position is true, practice clearly shows that Internet erodes the concept of sovereignty because it undermines and sometimes even eliminates a national government's ability to control the politics, economics, and culture within its territory. Of course, it is clear that the advent of the Internet is not the only factor that challenges a state's main competences in relation to sovereignty. Already, the more general process of globalization has shown the inapplicability of absolute territorial sovereignty. The rise of borderless on-line communication and the subsequent problems related to both substantial and procedural law, however, gives rise to new questions as regards the boundaries of the powers in national and international decision-making as well as interference in 'domestic' affairs. Often, Internet communication cannot be attributed to a single territory and often national regulatory measures of a certain state affect the activities of Internet users outside the regulatory jurisdiction of that state.

The discussion on the limits of national sovereignty in view of on-line communications must be held along two lines. The first point of discussion is a nation's actual capacity and ability to exercise control over its national territory. Developments in the area of enforcing content-related matters indicate that on-line communication threatens the sovereignty of states from a practical point of view. On-line activities appear to be unsusceptible to traditional physical control mechanisms, thus limiting the *actual* power of an individual state to act. International co-operation therefore seems crucial to solving enforcement-related problems. The second, but entirely different, point relates to the question to what extent state sovereignty

---

[146] Zekos 1999.

[147] Johnson, Post, 1996, p. 1367. See also Goldsmith, 1998, p. 475. See, however, Bergman contending that the concept of sovereignty is based on more than just territory. He argues that such a limited conception fails to account for the wide variety of community affiliations and social interactions that defy territorial boundaries. Bergman, 2002, Part IV.

in the area of legislative activity on substantive law should be justifiably diminished, i.e., that the formal regulatory power of individual nations on substantive issues is relocated to supranational bodies and institutions. The answer to this question appears to be closely related to the specific nature of the issue at stake. The interests of global on-line communication processes as well as the transboundary effects of such communication, for example, cannot overrule sovereignty on issues closely related to a nation's cultural, political, and social 'identity'. Certain differences in social and cultural values as well as legal traditions between nations must be recognized, meaning that certain value-driven issues are less suitable for harmonization by means of formal international legislation. Given the recognized value of cultural and normative pluralism, no single country or legal tradition can monopolize the norms and values that determine whether certain information may or may not be freely accessible on the Internet.

However, an appeal to national sovereignty seems less appropriate where it concerns issues related to economic interests (E-commerce, e-signatures, and intellectual property rights). Here the argument of transboundary effects of electronic communication could justify that regulation can no longer be addressed at a national level, but must be dealt with at an international level.

Apart from the worldwide recognized concept of sovereignty, more specific arguments may be brought forward to limit the power of certain international bodies. Of importance are the limitations laid down in the constituting agreement of a certain organization. Illustrative here is the European Union. The EC Treaty determines the competence of the Union. The subject-matter that must be addressed at the European level relates primarily to economic and financial issues, whereby the regulatory power of the EU has been expanded under recent treaties, such as the Treaty of Amsterdam. As for the distribution of competences between individual Member States and the EU, the so-called subsidiarity principle enshrined in Article 5 of the EC Treaty plays a primary role: EU harmonization measures that do not fall within the exclusive competence of the Union must always be compatible with this principle.[148] The question therefore will be: for what reasons is a certain subject-matter better regulated at a European level rather than at a national level? A key argument often found here is the transboundary effect of a certain problem. Nevertheless, in the past numerous legislative projects of the EU have been criticized for their interference in matters which do not belong to the competence of the Union. Clear illustrations can be found in non-ICT related areas such as environmental law and spatial planning,[149] but also in the area of on-line communication. The European Directive on electronic commerce, for example, has been criticized for its

---

[148] The Article provides: 'In areas which do not fall within its exclusive competence, the Community shall take action, in accordance with the principle of subsidiarity, only if and insofar as the objectives of the proposed action cannot be sufficiently achieved by the Member States and can therefore, by reason of the scale or effects of the proposed action, be better achieved by the Community'.

[149] Freriks, Peters, Robbe and Verschuuren 2002, pp. 5-10.

effects on issues that do not belong to the competence of the Union.[150] The different provisions included in the Directive have an effect on criminal and contract law as well.

In addition to the limits that follow from the EC Treaty, the competence of the EU is determined by the so-called *rule of reason,* providing Member States with the necessary leeway to implement certain provisions in the general national interest, such as consumer protection, public order, security, and health. An ICT-related topic where any legislative activity will surely be affected by this is on-line gambling.[151]

Given the above considerations, the conclusion must be that the Internet does not by definition imply the end of the national legislature as a player in setting the rules for on-line communication. On the contrary, given the concept of sovereignty and the competence of international organizations, in various situations and for various reasons, harmonization of national rules is not desired or appears not feasible. Nevertheless, numerous issues can or even must be dealt with at an international level. The subsequent question is therefore what considerations must be taken into account when determining the issues that should be on the international table.

6.6.2   The nature of the issue at stake

A first point of attention appears the nature of the issue at stake. Above, we already noted that, given the concept of sovereignty, justified reasons for leaving certain problems better regulated at a national level relate to value-driven considerations. In addition, attention should be given to a distinction made by Ogus between homogeneous and heterogeneous products.[152] The first type relates to those areas of law where there is unlikely to be a significant variation in preferences between different jurisdictions. The best examples can be found in 'facilitative' law (areas of law which provide mechanisms for ensuring mutually desired outcomes). With the second type, heterogeneous products, preferences between countries and regions vary. They vary with respect to the level of legal intervention, the price to be paid for the intervention, and the interests to be protected. The examples here relate to 'interventionist' law (areas of law in which defined interests are protected or party autonomy is superseded, such as consumer law, data protection law, and criminal law). Such examples may also be found in areas that involve intrinsic (political) questions and therefore vary from country to country (public, tax, and criminal law).

The distinction between homogeneous and heterogeneous products is somewhat related to the one made earlier in view of ICT regulation between regulations that primarily try to answer practical questions in order to create legal certainty (e.g.,

---

[150]   At least considering the Articles on legislative competence it was based upon.

[151]   As regards the importance of EU regulatory measures in the area of on-line gambling, see the questions posed by the European Parliament as well as the answers of the Commission. OJ C 31, 5 February 1999 (questions E-1190/98) and OJ C 350, 11 December 2001 (questions E-1571/01).

[152]   Ogus 1999, pp. 410-415.

'Can I use a digital signature to sign a contract?') and regulations that aim at influencing behaviour (e.g., 'Do not use encryption that may hamper investigation').[153] With 'answering issues', the addressees, in principle, care less about a particular outcome as long as a choice is made by the government, whereas with 'steering issues', addressees have a clear preference for a particular outcome. Of course, in trying to understand the relationship between the nature of the issue at stake and the likelihood of effective international harmonization, it is impossible to cling to a dualistic approach. Regulation is never completely answering or completely steering. The relationship is thus often diffuse, complex, and pluralistic, meaning that it depends on many factors, among them the specifics of the context or the stage of developments).

Nevertheless, it is clear that in thinking about how the starting point can be put into practice, consideration should be given to the nature of the issue at stake and the subsequent reasons for addressing the issue at an international level. In the case of primarily answering regulations, i.e., those aimed at stimulating certain behavior, international rule-making appears favorable, whereas more steering regulations, aimed at protecting certain interests and values, should only be undertaken once it has become sufficiently clear what 'steering goals' are envisioned and what are the best means to achieve those goals.

6.6.3 The nature of differences between national solutions

As mentioned in the previous section, an argument for harmonization is that differences between national systems may adversely affect competition, legal security, etc. An issue that should be considered here relates to the nature of the differences between national legal systems. Do the differences between national regulatory systems result from 'real' differences, where the outcomes of application diverge between legal systems, or are they mere 'superficial' differences? In the latter situation, functional similarities may be masked by differences in the conceptual structures of respective national systems.[154] As discussed in section 6.4.3, the adequacy requirement laid down in the European Directive on the protection of personal data fostered the discussion on whether individual states should be allowed to use their own preferred regulatory instruments (self-regulation as opposed to legislation) in achieving the same result (adequate protection). The following statement can be found in an OECD document on the issue:

'There is a broad consensus on the important role of privacy protection in building trust in the on-line environment. Effectively protecting privacy on-line and ensuring the continued transborder flow of personal data are shared objectives. The means by which those objectives may be achieved are viewed differently in member countries. There is agreement however, that there is no single uniform solution. A mix of regula-

---

[153] Koops, et al., 2000, p. 173.
[154] See Ogus 1999, p. 409.

tory and self-regulatory approaches blending legal, technical and educational solutions that suit the legal, cultural and societal context in which they operate holds the promise to provide effective solutions that, beyond the objective of building bridges, go to the actual integration of different elements into viable solutions.'[155]

In line with this, Samuelson has proposed to work towards achieving 'policy interoperability' at an international level: 'That is, agreeing on goals a policy should achieve, while recognizing that nations may adopt somewhat different policy means to implement the goals.'[156] Such an approach may foster a co-operative environment between nations and be especially important to those countries seeking to preserve the uniqueness of their social values within the framework of thriving global E-commerce, as she argues. It would also allow room for 'flexible approaches that can be tailored to the unique economic needs of each country, while simultaneously avoiding the threat that incompatible national regulatory regimes will derail the unique benefits of convergence and globalization that the Internet offers.'[157]

Hence, in further exploring the way in which the starting point can be put into practice, we may conclude that ample consideration should be given to the question of whether harmonization can be realized by other means, for example, because the given legal system provides an equivalent solution formulated in terms of its own legal language and concepts. When accepting the distinction between functional aspects, on the one hand and, conceptual aspects, on the other hand, and subsequently recognizing that different policy tools can be used to realize the same policy goals, the transaction costs in co-ordinating and realizing international harmonization could be dramatically reduced.

6.6.4 Different mechanisms in realizing harmonization

In its 2001 White Paper on European Governance, the European Commission paid considerable attention to the use of policy tools other than the often-used directives. In recognizing that 'legislation is often only part of a broader solution', it considered tools such as guidelines, recommendations, and co-regulatory mechanisms.[158] In formulating Action Points, the Commission stated that it will 'promote the use of new tools at global level as a complement to 'hard' international law.'[159] Today, practice already provides numerous examples of other tools than formal legislation. The previous sections have illustrated that harmonization by means of formal international legislative measures is the only mechanism available to realize the starting

---

[155] OECD, *Privacy Online: Policy and Practical Guidance*, 21 January 2003, p. 4, <http://www.olis.oecd.org/olis/2002doc.nsf/43bb6130e5e86e5fc12569fa005d004c/942914d87a941e54c1256cad004ed52a/$FILE/JT00137976.PDF>.

[156] Samuelson 1999, p. 13.

[157] Ibid.

[158] Commission of the European Communities, *European Governance. A White Paper*, Brussels, 25 July 2001, COM (2001) 428 final, p. 20.

[159] Ibid., p. 27.

point. Self-regulation mechanisms, technical instruments, customs, and codes of conduct appear to be powerful modes for international co-operation and harmonization as well. An example at the global level is ICRA (Internet Content Rating Association), which brings together organizations representing Internet industry players with the aim of promoting and managing an international content rating system. Under this system, web authors rate the content of their own sites. In the meantime, Germany, the UK, and Ireland have expressed their support to the association's activities and draw inspiration from ICRA's work to develop effective systems in this field. Use of 'walled gardens' by some operators is a further means of working towards an international standard of content on offer.[160] Mention can also be made of the work of the GBDe and Consumers International (the global federation of consumer organizations) to establish guidelines for alternative dispute resolution systems. Sometimes formal bodies and private initiative work together in realizing certain ambitions. The EU work on a European trustmark, for example, follows up on a range of national trustmark initiatives, including TrustUK in Britain, Webtrader in The Netherlands, and L+belsite in France and hopes to bring in standardization and compatibility with global initiatives. The EU trustmark also builds on guidelines issued by the European Consumers Association, BEUC, and the pan-EU industry confederation UNICE.[161]

What is more, actual stimulation by whatever body does not appear to be necessary to achieve a (certain degree of) harmonization. First, practice shows that law systems sometimes react to and learn from activities in other systems. Illustrative is the domain of spectrum management. While closely guarded as a domestic policy topic, the issue has traditionally enjoyed much international collaboration and observation over the years.[162] Second, international policy makers and legislatures have an easy instrument with the so-called country-of-origin principle. The use of this well-established principle of European law has resulted in a *de facto* harmonizing effect since companies will settle in a Member State that imposes the least restrictive legal requirements on an activity, thus forcing other Member States to implement a similar level of requirements to uphold an attractive climate for businesses. The country-of-origin principle can be found in the Directive on electronic commerce.

6.7   RELEVANCE OF THE STARTING POINT

The key question underlying the discussion of this chapter's starting point is whether and to what extent international co-operation or even international harmonization

---

[160] Council of Europe, Secretariat memorandum prepared by the Directorate General of Human Rights, *Self-regulation and user protection against illegal or harmful content on the new communications and information services*, 24 April 2002, <http://www.coe.int>.

[161] *Electronic Commerce & Law Report*, 29 January 2003, pp. 90-91.

[162] Ryan 2003.

can be regarded as a suitable starting point in addressing the variety of legal problems created by the Internet. In exploring the nature and the demand for the claim
that ICT regulation should be undertaken at an international level, the foregoing has
shown that a straightforward answer to this question cannot be given. There is no
such thing as a leading principle in dealing with the global dimensions of Internet,
nor can any single perspective on international rule-making monopolize the abun-
dant variety of problems and issues that arise in relation to the on-line world. Does
this mean that no clear or even subtle indications can be given as regards the status
of the starting point? Is it a case of sitting down and waiting because:

> 'No one really knows whether the nation-state is dying or thriving, whether globaliza-
> tion is truly a new phenomenon or a lot of hype, whether the Internet defies territorial
> borders or whether geographical boundaries can be reinscribed into cyberspace,
> whether the world is fragmenting into subnational conflicts, or conversely, whether it
> is moving towards an era of global cooperation and international governance. Or per-
> haps a cosmopolitan future awaits us, when people will come to interpret themselves
> without using the nation-state as their principal frame of reference?'[163]

Nevertheless, several general principles can be recognized when considering the
need for an international approach, apart from what the exact modes of this approach must be (legislation, self-regulation, standards, etc.). First, if the problem at
stake is 'trade-related' in the sense of distorting cross-border data flows, information transactions, for example, due to legal insecurity, different legal standards,
etc., an international approach appears in order.

Second, it can be concluded that if value-related issues are at stake, an international approach should not by definition be seen as not viable or hopeless. If on-line
communication, and therefore the applicable national regulations dealing with value-
related issues (including precarious issues dealing with the freedom of speech),
impose unacceptable externalities on other countries, national states cannot close
their eyes or hide behind the national sovereignty argument. States at least have to
face the transboundary implications of their national rules and regulations. This
could mean that all value-related issues should in principle be allowed on the agenda
of international bodies. Of course, the prime criterion in subsequently addressing
the issues at an international level is that international policy co-ordination would
indeed reduce the 'costs' of the transboundary implications.

Apart from these two broadly formulated principles, several other relevant considerations are important.

Acceptance of an international solution
Clearly, any international 'solution' to the problems faced in the context of ICT
must be accepted. Of course, various conditions may adversely affect the acceptance of the solution. There is the fact that the interests of the relevant parties differ

---

[163] Berman 2002, p. 529.

and it is hardly realistic that all of them can be satisfied by finding one solution to the problem. Moreover, some legal systems give rise to greater friction when they are adapted to technological developments than others, depending on the interaction between the different sources of law (legislature, judiciary, bureaucracy, doctrine, etc.).[164] Certain areas of the law are more likely to adapt to international influence (commercial law). Certain legal cultures may be more receptive to international change than others. A country that, from a historical perspective was intensely involved in international trade will more efficiently adopt and accept international rules or rules from foreign jurisdictions than countries without a history of such involvement. Furthermore, admittedly the political reality at an international level often requires compromises that are far from the best scholarly or practical solutions, hence the risk that the international outcome as opposed to a national solution less adequately or effectively addresses or solves the problem. Also, technological turbulence makes the future implications of certain developments far from clear, thus leaving international bodies, and in particular legislative bodies, with the problem of what exactly can or should be regulated.

These and other conditions play a role in the acceptance of international policy co-ordination or policy-making and therefore need careful consideration when discussing any international approach.

Clarity of Competence and Content
The success and failure of international rule-making also depends on clarity as regards both competence and content. As was shown in the first section of this chapter, an overwhelming and still growing number of regulatory forums at global, regional, national, and sub-national levels preside over countless provisions in seeking to exert control over the application and use of ICT. Often, more than one international body presides over a certain topic and conflicts may arise as a result of different perspectives on the interests at stake and therefore on the different regimes the organizations enact. Combined with the fact that the hierarchy between the bodies is not always formalized or clear, this result in situations where, *de jure* or *de facto,* some degree of competition between institutions may occur. Hence, adequate co-ordination and mutual account of earlier work is essential. That this is not an easy task is illustrated by the fact, that even within one single body, the – fragmented – measures issued may contradict one another. A brief look at the regulatory measures that have been taken at the EU level shows there is an increase in the amount and complexity of rules applicable to on-line activities. Illustrative are the various rules that apply to the processing of personal data. In addition to the Directive that specifically deals with personal data protection issues,[165] other directives with only an indirect connection to privacy govern the use of personal data as

---

[164] Sacco 1991, p. 343.
[165] Directive 95/46/EC of the European Parliament and of the Council of 24 October 1995 on the protection of individuals with regard to the processing of personal data and on the free movement of such data, OJ L 281, 23 November 1995.

well. Although the Directive on electronic commerce[166] does not specifically apply to privacy issues,[167] several of its provisions do affect the processing of personal data. Articles 5 and 6, dealing with information requirements, allow consumers to obtain the name, geographic address, phone number and e-mail address of the organization that processes their personal data. The Directive on electronic commerce also deals with unsolicited commercial communication (spamming). In contrast to the regime introduced with the 2002 Directive on privacy and electronic communications,[168] Article 7 of the Directive on electronic commerce includes an 'opt-out' regime. The failure of the European legislature to come up with a general system for unsolicited commercial communications leaves data subjects with considerable uncertainty when it comes to enforcing their rights.

Regard should also be had for the Directive on the protection of consumers in respect of distance contracts, otherwise known as the 'Distant Selling Directive'.[169] This directive also contains transparency rights of consumers (Arts. 4 and 5) and yet another rule on unsolicited commercial communication (Art. 10). Finally, the Directive on electronic signatures contains a provision on collection of personal data.[170]

In recognizing the problems, the European Commission, in its White Paper on European Governance, formulated several reform proposals in doing away with the landscape of conflicting and fragmented rules and introducing more effective and coherent regulatory frameworks. A first visible result of a more critical position towards legislative activity and the methods used is the package for electronic communications as adopted in 2002. It significantly reduced the number of EU rules and regulations that had been issued in the previous decade in the area of telecommunications.

Goals, tools, and effects

Lawyers and economists often consider the 'success' of (international) rule-making in different terms. The discussion in section 6.5 showed that economic theory stresses transaction costs and evaluates regulatory activity in terms of efficiency, ends, and means. Lawyers and legislatures often value other considerations, such as the symbolic value of regulatory initiatives as well as the openness and democratic legitimacy of the legislative process. Effectiveness and the time involved in finally

---

[166] Directive 2000/31/EC of the European Parliament and of the Council of 8 June 2000 on certain legal aspects of information society services, in particular electronic commerce, OJ L 178, 17 July 2000.

[167] See Art. 1, under 5, Directive on electronic commerce.

[168] Directive 2002/58/EC of the European Parliament and of the Council of 12 July 2002 concerning the processing of personal data and the protection of privacy in the electronic communications sector, OJ L 201, 31 July 2002.

[169] Directive 97/7/EC of the European Parliament and of the Council of 20 May 1997 on the protection of consumers in respect to distance contracts, OJ L 144, 4 June 1997.

[170] Directive 1999/93/EC of the European Parliament and of the Council of 13 December 1999 on a Community framework for electronic signatures, OJ L 13/12, 17 January 2000.

adopting and implementing the measures appears less important. Of course all considerations mentioned are important by themselves. However, they often prove to be difficult to combine.

Opting for international rule-making must be based on clear insight in the (economic, normative) reasons that underlie such rule-making and that thus justify harmonization or even unification of rules and regulations. In view of the arguments discussed in section 6.5, a clear understanding is required of the specific objectives to be achieved (providing clarity, protecting interests, fostering innovation, etc.). Consideration should be given to preferences as regards these objectives. Do they diverge (for example, e-market development concerns as opposed to consumer-protection interests) between national states and how strong an argument would such a divergence be in favor of heterogeneous legal rules and against harmonization? In particular, when addressing issues at a worldwide level, it is clear that depending on the stage of economic and technological development in the various countries, heterogeneous preferences may exist as to the goals to be achieved.

Linked to this is the extent of the harmonization in view of the objectives to be realized. Can they be achieved by implementing marginal adjustments to the national regulatory framework without altering the fundamental principles of the national system?

Another conclusion that can be drawn from the discussion in this chapter is that a distinction must be made between the goals and the tools. Can harmonization be realized by other means, for example, because the given legal system provides an equivalent solution formulated in terms of its own legal language and concepts? What is the expected future impact of the possible tools and, where available, what can be learned from past experience? Furthermore, attention should be given to the broader implications of the international rules for the respective national systems as a whole. For example, when transborder considerations constitute an argument for harmonization, the question arises whether such harmonization should be restricted to the transborder incidences. What are the effects of the harmonization efforts on the situations that have no on-line – and thus cross-border – dimension? This relates to the on-line/off-line problem discussed in chapter 3 of this Volume.

We have also seen that, irrespective of the discussion on whether national or international substantive rules apply in the on-line world, enforcement of rules is of crucial importance and effective enforcement can only be realized when nations combine their efforts and – in whatever manner – work together. In this chapter, several examples have been given of situations in which the international co-operation in enforcing rights and obligations appears to have been successful. However, many other situations reveal the complex problems of enforcement in a world without geographical boundaries. By now several cases, the famous Yahoo ruling among them (decided in France and the US), have shown the many questions that arise when international agreement lacks criteria in determining whether a nation can enforce its national norms on Internet dealings that impose externalities on all countries around the world. Hence, even where the interest of sovereignty prevails and countries are free in setting their norms and standards, they cannot close their eyes to the transboundary implications of their national rules and regulations. Even in these situations, states must continue to take into account the international aspects of what they do. An approach based on a merely national sovereign style would be short-sighted, given the unique world Internet provides.

6.8   CONCLUSION

In this chapter, the often-heard starting point has been explored that ICT regulation should be taken up at an international level. On the basis of the discussion, it can be concluded that the interplay between ICT developments and international regulation is highly complex. Having examined various questions and issues that arise in relation to the practice and prospects of the internationalization of ICT law, it can be seen that the questions surrounding the allocation of regulatory competences at national or international levels are multi-dimensional, and no common approach seems available. What is more, many relevant issues have not been dealt with: little is known of the exact interaction between international and national ICT law, of the effects of international law in the practical national legal order, and of the fundamental principles of national regimes. Developing a perspective on the benefits or perhaps even necessity of international rule-making is fraught with difficulties because the exact outcome and implications of harmonization at a national level are unknown.

Although the Internet may be a global phenomenon, the assumptions regarding the meaning, use, and limitations of this in principle unbounded network vary between countries, regions and individuals and are as such determined by 'borders'. The rich diversity of assumptions reflects historical, cultural, and economic realities that have evolved over many decades and do not disappear overnight. For this reason, it is unrealistic to think that irreconcilable differences resulting from these realities can be abrogated by international negotiation. Achieving regulatory models for the Internet requires recognition of the variety of historical, cultural and economic realities. Hence in dealing with ICT rule-making at an international level, the question is how social, cultural, economic, and individual identity and diversity can be balanced with the obvious advantages of harmonization (legal security, minimum level of fundamental rights, etc.).

It is at this point that an interesting new development requires our attention, for recent developments indicate that a new paradigm of 'borders' for the on-line world is slowly gaining importance. The once borderless on-line world is slowly starting to reorganize itself into 'regions'. Companies, organizations and private persons are now using technology or contractual arrangements to restrict the availability of their information or communication services. For example, Internet Service Providers block the transmission of unsolicited commercial information (spam), companies that offer on-line betting and games of chance bar residents of certain countries

from participating in the gambling activities via its web site and publishing companies allow only lawful users to access and use copyrighted works available within
protected areas. Thus, the once borderless world may again turn into a world with a
certain type of borders. This time other mechanisms than geographical borders and
judicial tools become crucial in blocking the access to certain information and actors, either because the information itself is not welcome, the person is a resident of
a certain country or the distributor of the information fails to meet the standards set
by the gatekeeper (e.g., an ISP). In other words, various actors now have the technical and contractual tools and thus the power to determine what is to be considered
'authorized' access to a certain area (domain) within the on-line world.

Slowly, these tools will creep into the on-line world and may thus ultimately
determine the new context of the virtual world in which questions of 'internationalization' will have to be posed and answered. Of course, this development will con-
fronts us with challenging new questions.

Chapter 7
CODE AS LAW?[1]

Simone van der Hof and Kees Stuurman

7.1 INTRODUCTION

The emergence of the information society in the last decades has brought along questions and concerns in many legal areas like private law, privacy law, copyright law, criminal law. Moreover, the borderless character of the Internet[2] as the most important technical component of this information society has raised more generally issues, which go beyond the different fields of law, most notably with respect to jurisdiction.[3] The legal questions and challenges that have arisen as a result of technological innovation can be summarized on the basis of four tendencies:

Internationalization

Internationalization has been taking place for centuries; however, the use of ICTs has been a strong catalyst with respect to this tendency. On-line contacts and activities more often and more easily occur at an international level; laws which regulate those contacts and activities, however, usually a national character and can vary amongst different legal systems. Unless it is clear what specific rules apply and how they apply in a particular international situation, users face and legal uncertainty when acting on-line in a legally significant way.

Deterritorialization

The tendency of deterritorialization is strongly related to internationalization and may lead to problems when attempting to link digital information flows to certain geographic locations. On-line activities are disconnected from physical locations,

---

[1] The concept of 'code as law' is part of the broader concept of 'regulation by technology'. This chapter decribes the background of 'code as law', its origins, meaning, and the application as well as a critical analysis of this concept.

[2] In this chapter, we will focus mainly on the Internet as an important component of the concept of 'code as law'.

[3] On legal questions and challenges see Van Klink & Prins 2002, pp. 1-35.

B-J. Koops, et al. (Eds), Starting Points for ICT Regulation
© *2006, ITeR, The Hague, and the authors*

since, from a technical point of view, the location where actions take place is irrelevant, may be unknown, or can be easily manipulated. Governments, therefore meet difficulties in exerting influence by regulating on-line activities and enforcing laws.

Both the tendency towards internationalization and to deterritorialization have resulted in questions and challenges with respect to jurisdiction in several areas of law.

Dematerialization

Traditional law dates back from an era when trade involved the physical delivery of goods and services. Nowadays, legal relationships evolve more and more around digitally traded information as a result of the dematerialization tendency. Some of the traditional concepts utilized in laws may give rise to legal uncertainty (e.g., contracts, signatures, general terms and conditions, property) or vulnerable positions (e.g., consumer fraud and privacy) with respect to on-line activities, which governments and ICT users/providers feel need to be addressed.

Technological turbulence

The tendency towards technological turbulence concerns the enormous pace in which technological developments happen in quick succession and the demands on traditional law as a result of these developments. In order for traditional law to be able to capture and regulate on-line behavior efficiently and in a timeless way, observance of technological neutrality as a basic assumption for lawmaking is often called for (see chapter 4 of this Volume).

The legal questions and challenges have resulted in debates and different movements particularly amongst American legal scholars on how to regulate the Information Society and its most important technical component, the Internet. Problems, particularly in the field of jurisdiction, as a result of these tendencies have led some American legal scholars to believe that law in the traditional sense has lost its meaning as an instrument to regulate the new 'place' called Cyberspace.[4] This new 'place' is defined by computer screens and passwords and not by geographic borders, which would result in erosion of 'the ability of physical location to give notice of which sets of rules apply.'[5] Therefore, Cyberspace needs its own rules, separate from the laws that regulate the physical, off-line world. Presently, this view on regulating the Information Society, however, has turned obsolete, because both the off-line and on-line world 'involve people in real space in one territorial jurisdiction transacting with people in real space in another jurisdiction in a way that sometimes causes

---

[4] See Post 1995, Johnson & Post 1996.
[5] Johnson & Post 1996.

real-world harms'[6] and the Internet is not a separate place but 'merely' a means of communication. Traditional laws, therefore, still apply in Cyberspace, although a review or alteration of its rules may, in some instances, be necessary or even essential in order to address and mitigate the risks and disadvantages of ICTs.[7]

Another movement, which emerged in reaction to the legal issues as a result of technological developments in the very same period, however, had a different effect on the role of law in Cyberspace and raised the question of what regulates the Internet besides laws and social norms. It acknowledged, for instance, that legal regulation is an important, but not the only means of regulating ICTs. The way in which the hardware and software of a system is designed can impose rules on users as well and technological and legal regulation of ICTs should be used complementary in order to solve policy and legal issues in the Information Society and more specifically with respect to the Internet. This notion of hardware and software design as a separate kind of regulation is called the concept of 'code as law'.[8]

'Code as law' is an interesting concept, as it can, and does, in a sense, accommodate the above-mentioned tendencies. Code is international and borderless in character, because it is, in principle, not bound to certain territories or, more specifically, nations.[9] It therefore defies legal and political challenges as a result of internationalization and deterritorialization. The concept of 'code as law' is symptomatic of the dematerialization tendency and can assist in solving legal issues raised as a result of dematerialization by effectively directing technological developments in a certain way.[10] Finally, since code is technology and is itself part of technological turbulence, it can, if used appropriately, anticipate or go along with other technological developments sooner and perhaps more effectively than legal regulation as regards addressing the legal challenges of ICT

7.2   THE MEANING OF 'CODE AS LAW'

In this section, we will explore the core elements of 'code as law' by focusing on the content, source, and implications of 'code as law'.

7.2.1 Content

The term 'code' in 'code as law' mostly refers to software code, although the line between software and hardware code is sometimes tenuous. Software code can be defined as a set of written instructions, which, when executed, causes computers to

---

[6] Goldsmith 1998, p. 1200.

[7] On conceptual deficiency, see Van Klink & Prins 2002, pp. 5-35.

[8] Also referred to as 'code as code' or 'lex informatica'.

[9] Although some nation states are obviously more involved in code writing than others and may, therefore, be seen as dictated 'rules', see also section 7.2.

[10] See section 7.3.

perform certain actions or tasks in a specific manner. Code, although initially fo-cused on achieving certain basic functionalities (e.g., providing word processing or web browsing functionalities), can receive a normative connotation when simulta-neously directing and influencing human behavior in a specific manner. The ways in which human behavior is influenced and directed, thus, depends upon the con-tents and design of these written computer instructions.

With respect to the Internet,[11] two main levels of regulation by code can be distinguished:

- The regulation of the structure and operation of the technical infrastructure, which essentially include protocols and other specifications for the function-ing of the network infrastructure and applications;
- The regulation of the application of the infrastructure, regarding for example, which access, services and information provided, and use can be distin-guished.

The concept of 'code as law' strictly concerns the first kind of regulation and refers to the process of setting legal norms through decisions on the contents and design of the technical infrastructure and applications. However, at the same time, the decision on the way in which code is written has an effect on the second category, i.e., the use of the infrastructure. Moreover, these decisions on functionalities of the technical infrastructure are dictated not only by purely functional issues like capac-ity and efficiency, but also, and perhaps more importantly, by issues concerning the desired use of the technical infrastructure essentially from a freedom viewpoint (e.g., freedom of information, anonymity) at one end of the scale and of control (e.g., identification, content management) at the other. In other words, the way in which the technology is designed and programmed implicates choices on matters such as freedom, for example, free access to networks for all without any restric-tions, or control, for example, controlled access for a limited number of people and monitoring of on-line activities. Both kinds of regulation are, thus, in complex cor-relation with each other and it is particularly with respect to this interaction that concerns with respect to 'code as law' are expressed. These concerns will be dealt with in the next sections.

The legal debate on 'code as law' emerged in the United States in the mid-1990s amongst legal scholars such as Reidenberg, Mitchell, and Lessig.[12]

In 1993, Reidenberg already stated that 'technical standards are set in ways that (…) define fair information practices'[13] and 'technical choices lead to normative decisions about fair information practices. Yet, the technical dimension subtly in-troduces these standards through network architecture itself, rather than through a

---

[11] Internet infrastructure and applications provide good examples of the concept of 'code as law' and are, therefore, important components of the concept.

[12] For an overview of related US literature, see <www.ilpf.org/events/selfreg/freemarket.htm>.

[13] Reidenberg 1993, p. 288.

broader debate on the norms.'[14] He goes on to say that '[t]he technical paradigm locates control of information practice in the network infrastructure. Technical organizations rather than government define norms for integrity and interoperability.'[15] In 1998, Reidenberg further elaborated on what he called, 'Lex Informatica' as a new, extra-legal[16] regulatory regime to information flows.[17] Lex Informatica is constituted by information policies embedded in network designs, standards and system configurations, but also by user preferences and technical choices.[18] Reidenberg distinguished between two types of substantive rules with respect to Lex Informatica:

- Immutable policies: these policies are embedded in the technology standards and cannot be altered;
- Flexible policies: these policies are embedded in the technical architecture and allow variations through configuration decisions.[19]

Lex Informatica has features, which to a certain extent run parallel to those of legal rule-making. For example, Lex Informatica, as law, consists of substantive default rules as well as rules which allow for flexibility and customization.[20] However, an important distinction between the two rule-making systems lies, in enforcement, which is *ex post* in legal systems and can be *ex ante* in technological regulatory systems. Thus, Lex Informatica supports 'automated and self-executing rule-enforcement'.[21]

In 1995, Mitchell referred to the code as a code phenomenon: 'Code is the law' on the electronic frontier. 'Just as Aristotle, in *Politics*, contemplated alternative constitutions for city-states (…) so denizens of the digital world should pay the closest of critical attention to programmed polity. Is it just and humane? Does it protect our privacy, our property and our freedoms? Does it constrain us unnecessarily or does it allow us to act as we may wish?' Mitchell recognizes that control of code is power, since it allows the controller to structure people's lives by either including or excluding people from certain spheres and either allowing or disallowing certain activities and behavior.[22]

In 1996, Lessig brought up the changing and makeable nature of Cyberspace that is constituted by software and allows embedding policy choices in the techno-

---

[14] Ibid., p. 301.

[15] Ibid., p. 303.

[16] Other extra-legal regulatory regimes are economic regulation, regulation by social norms, and self-regulation.

[17] Reidenberg 1998.

[18] Ibid., p. 555.

[19] Ibid., p. 568.

[20] Ibid., pp. 569-573.

[21] Ibid., p. 572.

[22] See Mitchell 1995, pp. 111-112.

logical architecture from a constitutionalist perspective.[23] Unlike laws and social norms, software code can enforce control directly since it does not depend on the co-operation of individuals who must abide by the rules.[24] By creating dimensions of discrimination in Cyberspace ('zoning'), a wide range of behavior can be controlled.[25] In 1999, Lessig further elaborated on the concept of 'code as law' and more specifically his concerns on and objections to code as a 'perfect tool of control' designed and created not by governments but by commerce.[26] In his view, governments should complement the efforts of commerce to create an architecture of trust by regulating the architecture of the Internet in order to make on-line behavior regulable. In this way, they can safeguard certain public values, such as privacy and free speech, in which the interests of commerce is less obvious or less great, as well as the political process in which choices and decisions are made on the way in which the network should ideally operate.[27]

In 2004, Reidenberg went one step further even and stated that Lex Informatica is inherently unfair and the state has to and will increasingly intervene by issuing laws which impose responsibilities on codewriters and seek assistance from the private sector in law enforcement in instances where there is unfairness in the resulting code.[28] Thus, private code will increasingly be subject to public policy influences.

7.2.2   The origin of 'code as law'

Different parties are involved in the design and creation of the hardware, software, and technical standards, which determine technical infrastructures and applications and, thus, constitute code that regulates behavior or, more generally, has legal consequences. These parties have a more direct or indirect influence on the design of technical architectures, which constitute the Internet and other ICTs. Direct influence is asserted when organizations actually determine the functionalities and specifications of code. Indirect influence is asserted when organizations direct technological developments by setting certain parameters. for example, in legal regulations to be implemented in software design.

The design of code and, direct influence on code can be exercised at different levels. On the one hand, there are several private organizations which are interrelated and in charge of the technical Internet architecture, such as: the World Wide Web Consortium (W3C), the Internet Society (ISOC), the Internet Engineering Task

---

[23] In the same year, Katsh developed the concept of 'software worlds' and discussed the role of software as a 'shaper' of these worlds, because it can 'impose conditions, set limits, and control the options as well as the behavior of users', see Katsh 1996, p. 344.

[24] Lessig 1996, p. 32.

[25] Ibid., p. 35.

[26] See generally Lessig 1999.

[27] Lessig 1999, pp. 43-44, 59.

[28] Keynote speech on 'Software Equality and the Law', IViR/TILT Roundtable on 'Code as Code' and 'Commodification of Information', Amsterdam, 1-2 July 2004.

Force (IETF), the Internet Engineering Steering Group (IESG), the Internet Architecture Board (IAB), and the Internet Research Task Force (IRTF). More specifically with respect to domain names and IP addresses, ICANN, IANA, and RIPE NCC are the central organizations to set standards for the Internet.[29] These organizations are mainly non-profit and of an international character, although US involvement in these organizations is still predominant and some regions (e.g., South-America, Africa) are presently hardly represented. Most of these organizations (with the exception of ICANN, where the federal US government is still involved) are independent of any government, especially the federal US government, and subject to self-regulatory schemes. The driving forces in and behind these organizations are professional technologists, who are the actual individuals shaping the Internet technology.[30]

On the other hand, the Internet provides many applications which ordinary and professional Internet users use to enjoy or utilize the possibilities of the Internet.[31] The applications level of the Internet consists of all of the software programs and files which provide functionalities for Internet users in the area of information security, communication, information provision, transactions, etc.[32] Most applications are designed and created commercially (proprietary software). Thus, it is the software engineers, increasingly those of large companies, who initially determine what rules code shall consist of. According to Lessig, at this level, commerce creates what he calls technological architectures of control.[33] Next to this, there is a movement against proprietary software, which dedicates itself to the development and further enhancement of what is called open code (as opposed to the closed code of commercial enterprises). Within this movement, the development of free software[34] or open source software is promoted to share source code for the sole purpose of improving the software not for commercial gain.[35] Although subject to the intellectual property regime, open code is, in a sense, not 'owned' by a certain company, or programmer or by anyone else for that matter.[36] Although the basic assumptions of the open code movement are fundamentally different from those

---

[29] For an overview of these organizations, see Koops & Lips 2003, pp. 267-269.

[30] See Koops & Lips 2003, pp. 290-292, although development of Internet technology is directed through open standardization procedures, which means that any individual can theoretically contribute to technology developments. The processes and organizations are unknown however, such that involvement is restricted to professional technologists.

[31] See Lessig 1999, p. 104, 'application space'.

[32] Protocols for these applications are, however, determined by the above-mentioned private organizations.

[33] Lessig 1999, pp. 6, 30-42.

[34] Not to be confused with freeware, which is free of charge, yet copyright protected software, whereas free software does not necessarily have to be free of charge and can be public-domain software.

[35] Although, in most instances, it is allowed to sell copies of open source or free software, royalties are not.

[36] Nevertheless, informal and other control exists within the open source and free software communities; see further McGowen 2001, p. 263.

with respect to proprietary software, it is still software engineers that design and create code and, thus, set the coded rules that govern the behavior of users.

Moreover, code can be indirectly influenced, when, for instance, legislators set certain parameters within the realm of which code can or is allowed to be written. In other words, the ways in which code can ultimately be used must then comply with certain requirements or safeguard the observance of particular fundamental rights or public interests and such conditions must, therefore, be built into or rather underlie code. An example of such a way of indirectly regulating code is the obligation to allow for technical wiretapping of public telecommunications lines.[37] Another example can be found in European data protection legislation, where those natural or legal persons who process personal data have an obligation to provide adequate technical and organizational security measures in order to protect such data.[38] In all these examples,[39] legislators aim to protect certain interests, which or will be insufficiently protected or not at all when left solely to code writers or the market at large. The interests concerned in the examples mentioned here are, those of law enforcement and intelligence services (investigation and national security interests) and individuals (privacy and consumer protection interests) respectively. In this way, legislators have aimed to have these interests expressed through and in technology.

7.2.3   Implications of 'code as law'

'Code as law', as was mentioned before, fits well within the tendency towards internationalization and deterritorialization, since it defies national borders and more generally territorial signposts and may therefore be considered an effective way of 'regulating' ICTs. Yet, for this same reason, 'code as law' has raised questions with respect to democratic legitimacy. In his book 'City of Bits', Mitchell, for instance, raises the following question with respect to 'code as law': 'How shall the writers of the rules[40] be answerable?'[41] As was shown in the previous section, it is in large part the professional technologists (and, in most instances, the companies these people are employed with) that determine the design of code and set the software rules that govern behavior on the Internet. One of the main concerns with respect to 'code as law', thus, is that there are no democratic checks and balances on the rule-making of software writers, as there are on writers of laws in democratic state settings. There is no parliament with representatives from the people that will ultimately be affected by the rules, which controls the process of code writing and balances

---

[37] See, e.g., Art. 13.1 of the Dutch Telecommunications Act.

[38] See Art. 17 of Directive 95/46/EC of the European Parliament and of the Council of the European Union of 23 November 1995 on the protection of individuals with regard to the processing of personal data and on the free movement of that data, OJ 1995, L 281.

[39] For examples see also Lessig 1999, pp. 44-49.

[40] See also section 7.4.1 Code: Rules or rules of law?

[41] Mitchell 1995, p. 112.

interests from various groups of people and organizations. The code writers are in principle free to write the rules they think are most functional in order to achieve certain purposes. Moreover, they have no obligations as governments do to observe public interest; they (may) have a different and less strict attachment to fundamental rights, and can write code that merely and completely serves commercial and/or functional interests instead. Although government and commercial/functional interests may in some instances coincide (e.g., each may be concerned with trust in e-commerce, although the view on how to achieve trust may again differ), they diverge in many other instances; sometimes even taking (well-) balanced interests in traditional laws down.[42]

In the case of the development of the technical Internet architecture a certain democratic legitimization was initially given albeit unilaterally, i.e., with respect to one country only, because of the involvement of the US federal government. Until the mid 90s, when the USA largely released its direct control on these issues to the private not-for-profit organizations mentioned in the previous section; only formally retaining control with respect to ICANN activities. The underlying ideas were that technical standards should be developed and set by the market and that the Internet should not be regulated by government regulation but (self-)regulation at an international level (tendency of horizontalization).[43] At present code with respect to Internet architecture, is in principle also, predominantly determined by private organizations both non-profit and commercial, without any democratic control on the process in which the coded rules are set. What is more, these democratic processes do not even exist in the international arena where Internet technology and Internet applications are developed.[44]

The reasoning that the concept of 'code as law' lacks democratic legitimacy needs some refining, since, as was indicated in the previous section, governments can still take charge of or direct technological developments by participating in the relevant organizations involved in code-making or by indirectly influencing code through legal regulation in cases where such fundamental rights or public interests are at stake and where they are not sufficiently or adequately observed by code writers. This brought Lessig to his plea that governments should be more involved in influencing code. In discussing the values of cyberspace, in this respect, Lessig speaks of two kinds of values: substantive and structural ones. Legitimization of control concerns the second one: in order to guarantee substantive values (e.g., free speech, privacy) and prevent a too one-sided power of one regulator, checks and balances on government, or more generally, rule-making bodies are

---

[42] For example, see section 7.3.1 on DRM. See, however, the US Digital Millennium Copyright Act of 1998 and Directive 2001/29/EC of the European Parliament and of the Council of 22 May 2001 on the harmonization of certain aspects of copyright and related rights in the information society, OJ 2001, L 167, which both reflect the interests that DRM aims to protect.

[43] Koops & Lips 2003, p. 295.

[44] Ibid., pp. 296-299.

necessary.[45] He argues that governments can regulate the Internet architecture, as it has regulated other technologies in the past, in order for behavior on the Internet to be regulable as well.[46] Since the nature of the Internet can be changed and molded, so to speak, governments need to define what nature they want the Internet to have. The lack of democratic legitimacy and control may be, for instance, compensated by rules (e.g., technology-neutral requirements with respect to access, the provision of services and information and the use of these services) issued as a result of democratic processes. A concern that can be raised when government influence on technology and particularly on Internet architecture and applications does exist and is exercised is the fact that, very often, it is unilaterally exerted by the Western world and, more in particular, the United States, yet the effects of such influence may very well be of a global nature.[47,48] Ultimately, this may be the major concern that needs to be addressed, rather than the lack of democratic legitimacy with respect to coded rules.

In discussing the lack of democratic legitimacy and control regarding the process of technological choices, it should, furthermore, be borne in mind that, in a broader perspective, this criticism is not new. Even in cases in which the technological development was deliberately aimed at implementing existing rules, an apparent lack of transparency and checks and balances has been identified.

A chief example is the European 'New Approach' to regulating product requirements. In the mid-1980s, the EU abandoned the per product approach of setting detailed product standards and shifted towards a system in which European legislation was restricted to setting 'fundamental requirements' (such as safety, health protection, and environmental protection). Elaboration of these requirements took place by means of reference to European technical standards as developed by the European standardization bodies CEN, CENELEC, and ETSI. Although in theory not mandatory, in practice these European technical standards became binding.[49] Effectively, part of the regulatory powers of the Commission and the Council of Ministers of the European Union were delegated to private institutions, lacking a democratic legitimization and applying standardization procedures that did not meet the standards of accessibility, transparency, and independent control as considered fundamental to a democratic legislative process.[50] The choice for the New Approach was deliberate and the direct result of the complexity of the European deci-

---

[45] Lessig 1999, p. 7.

[46] Lessig 1999, pp. 43-60. Whether governments should or should not make regulations, and under what conditions is another question altogether. In order for government Internet architecture regulation to be transparent, i.e., 'open code' free and open source software, presents important constraints, Lessig 1999, pp. 108, 223-225.

[47] See Koops & Lips 2003.

[48] However, in some cases, the tide may ultimately turn, as can be observed with respect to the regulation of copyright under WIPO auspices where Third World countries have started to throw off the yoke of Western domination.

[49] Stuurman 1995, p. 160.

[50] Stuurman 1995, p. 190; Breulmann 1993, p. 189.

sion-making process and the lack of technical know-how and capacity of the national governments.

The lack of democratic guarantees and controls in the application and development of technology that is identified in the 'code as law' approach, although of significant importance, is hence not an entirely new phenomenon, nor is it exclusive to cyberspace. This could be relevant when considering solutions for this problem. What does make regulation through code clearly different from legal regulation and other forms of regulation, such as self-regulation, and is, therefore, of paramount importance to include in such considerations is the inevitability of code. Whereas individuals have a certain autonomy to either comply with legal rules or not, code does not allow any civil disobedience because non-compliance is no longer an option. This characteristic of code already contributes to a controlled society and it is important to consider the desirability and legitimacy (including issues of transparency and foreseeability) of the implications of code in that respect.

7.3 How Does 'Code As Law' Apply?

7.3.1 Digital Rights Management (DRM)[51]

The development of the information society has immensely challenged copyright regimes. As a result of the tendency towards dematerialization and the rapid growth of the communications networks bandwidth, it is easy and cheap to copy data and, more particularly, digital copyrighted works. Consequently, the need to control the use and distribution of copyrighted works has fuelled the development of technologies with which to enforce copyright.

DRM systems restrict access to digital files, e.g., media files, for intellectual property protection purposes and controls the ways in which these files can or cannot be used. For instance, the use of digital files can be subject to licenses which set conditions for usage, such as expiration date and cost. An example of a DRM system is Microsoft's Windows Media Rights Manager (WMRM), which allows secure distribution of digital media files, such as music and videos, over the Internet. The software can be built into applications (e.g., streaming audio or video applications) and web sites and must be used in combination with Windows Media Player or other players supporting WM files (such as WinAmp and RealPlayer). Rights owners and content distributors (e.g., record labels, on-line retailers, radio stations, etc.) can distribute encrypted digital media. Users (e.g., consumers) need to obtain a license with a key in order to access and use the files. These licenses may contain different kinds of conditions. For example, the files may be used a certain number of times or during a certain period of time. Use of these files can, furthermore, be uniquely restricted to a PC, although rights may also be set in such a way that the

---

[51] This case is taken from Lips, Van der Hof, Prins & Schudelaro 2004.

consumer can distribute the files to a portable player or portable media in order to play them on another computer (the number of transfers can, however, be restricted). When a user attempts using a protected file for which no license has been provided, they are directed to a license acquisition URL where a license can be downloaded to the computer. At the moment, Microsoft is the most important player on the DRM digital media market.[52] Since over 450 million WM Players (which is included in the Windows OS) have been installed and other players are also compatible with WM files, support for WMRM is widespread.[53]

Therefore, DRM is an interesting tool for copyright owners (and, more generally, the content industry) to securely distribute and exploit copyrighted works on the Internet and attempt to regain some of the copyright control that has leaked away as a result of the dematerialization tendency. However, it is said that other new technologies, such as P2P, make these attempts to regain control obsolete as the DRM on DVDs experience has shown.[54]

DRM systems in general and Windows DRM in particular have been critically evaluated for several reasons. First of all, DRM may pose threats to the privacy of users of digital files distributed through DRM. These systems may lead to a standard practice where these users are required to identify themselves to content owners and, thus, prevent anonymous consumption. Moreover, DRM can allow for profiling of users' preferences by attaching personal information to identifiers, which are assigned to media files or players. For example, WM Player uses an embedded Globally Unique Identifier (GUID) in order to track users. In addition, it generates a log file of the content a user uses. Moreover, WM Player allows for automatic downloads of security-related updates to the OS, which may prevent copying and/ or playing of secure media files. Microsoft can, thus, control components of the users' operating systems unnoticed and without consent. The practice of linking identifiers and personal information may, furthermore, lead to price discrimination.[55] Finally, DRM does not recognize fair use of copyrighted works. Under the fair use doctrine in US law, for instance, unauthorized use of copyrighted works is allowed in some instances, for purposes such as teaching, research and, making comments, parodies, or news reports. Also, many lawyers believe that making a personal copy of a CD or ripping one's audio CDs (converting CDs into MP3 files) is fair use although these cases are not fully settled as yet.[56] Other national copyright laws have other or similar exemptions to copyright exclusive rights.

---

[52] See Rosenblatt 2004.

[53] In the field of DRM, there are competing standardization practices, one of which, eXtensible Rights Markup Language (XrML) from ContentGuard, is applied in Microsoft's DRM Technology, see <www.drmwatch.com/special/article.php/3095201>. This standard competes with the DRM standard of the Open Mobile Alliance, <www.openmobilealliance.org/>.

[54] Lohmann 2003.

[55] See the Digital Rights Management and Privacy page of the Electronic Privacy Information Center (EPIC) at <www.epic.org/privacy/drm/>.

[56] See EFF FAQ on Fair Use at: <www.eff.org/IP//eff_fair_use_faq.html>.

The DRM example shows how code not only supports the enforcement of laws, in this case copyright law, by providing content owners with a tool to exploit their copyrighted works, but sets new rules as well.[57] Where copyright law aims to strike a balance between owners' rights and the public, DRM technologies are one-sidedly favorable to the interests and rights of copyright owners by fully ignoring the fair use doctrine and more generally exemptions to exclusive rights of content owners. Moreover, DRM may also be biased from a privacy perspective, when users have no choice but to release personal data in order to use the DRM systems, and transparency and control with respect to the use of these data is lacking.

7.3.2 Privacy enhancing technologies

Privacy and, more particularly, personal data protection are persistent issues in legal as well as technical regulation of ICTs. For example, the DRM example shows that there are privacy concerns when consumers have no choice but to release personal data in order to be able to listen to music offered through DRM systems or use these per se. However, according to EPIC, alternatives exist that would provide copyright protection and at the same time protect privacy and it argues that these alternative, non-privacy invasive solutions have not been explored adequately with respect to DRM.[58] With this remark, we are entering the area of privacy-enhancing technologies (PETs). There have already been many initiatives to develop PETs in order to protect consumers' and citizens' privacy and personal data. PETs are usually understood to be technologies that utilize encryption in order to protect identities when acting or transacting on-line.[59] PETs minimize or eliminate the processing of identifiable data and, thus, enable anonymous or pseudonymous transactions between, for example, consumers and on-line businesses.

Nowadays, there are numerous technologies for enhancing privacy.[60] These technologies can have different functions, such as:

- preventing unauthorized access to communications and stored files;
- automating the retrieval of information about data collectors' privacy practices and automating users' decision making on the basis of these practices;
- automating audits of data collectors' privacy practices;
- filtering unwanted messages;
- preventing automated data capture through cookies, HTTP headers, web bugs, spyware, etc.;
- preventing communications from being linked to a specific individual; and

---

[57] See also Lessig 1999, pp. 126-127.

[58] *Supra* n. 36.

[59] On PETs see for instance Hes & Borking.

[60] For many examples of available technologies see EPIC Online Guide to Practical Privacy Tools, <www.epic.org/privacy/tools.html>.

- facilitating transactions that reveal minimal personal information.[61]

In some cases, attempts have been made to provide standardized solutions in this area, an example of which is P3P, the Platform for Privacy Preferences Project, developed by the World Wide Web Consortium (W3C). It aims to give users more control over their personal data when visiting web sites. P3P-enabled web sites make information on how personal data is handled available in a standard, machine-readable format, which can be read automatically by P3P-enabled browsers and subsequently compared to the user's set of privacy preferences.[62] However, P3P has met with criticism for several reasons, such as that 'P3P fails to comply with baseline standards for privacy protection' and 'is a complex and confusing protocol that will make it more difficult for Internet users to protect their privacy. P3P also fails to address many of the privacy problems specifically associated with the Internet.' [63]

Another standardization was initiated by the European Committee for Standardization's Information Society Standardization System (CEN/ISSS). CEN/ISSS established a group called Initiative for Privacy Standardization in Europe (IPSE). IPSE was established under a European Commission mandate with the objective, among other things, to investigate the case for standardization, as a means to help business and other market actors to implement the relevant privacy and data protection legislation (e.g., the Directive on protection of personal data). The IPSE Steering group[64] was established in order to carry out an expert study in that field and published a report with recommendations, one of which is to 'report on and create a process to assess the impact of technologies on data protection, including privacy enhancing technologies (PETs).'

From a 'code as law' perspective, it seems obvious that PETs implement and provide rules with respect to the protection of privacy of citizens/consumers and of personal data. PETs may, thus, support privacy and data protection legislation or provide different,[65] perhaps even stricter protection than legal rules. A complexity with respect to code and privacy,[66] however, is that there are legitimate as well as

---

[61] Faith 2003, p. 80.

[62] See <www.w3c.org/P3P>.

[63] EPIC & Junkbusters Pretty Poor Privacy, An Assessment of P3P and Internet Privacy, June 2000, at: <www.epic.org/reports/prettypoorprivacy.html>; see also D. Mulligan, A. Schwartz, A. Cavoukian, M. Gurski, P3P and Privacy, An Update for the Privacy Community, March 2000, at: <www.cdt.org/privacy/pet/p3pprivacy.shtml>.

[64] The Steering Group consists of national data protection officers, and representatives from industry and business stakeholders, standardization organizations, and consumer associations.

[65] For instance, allowing consumers to negotiate personal data protection with Internet businesses, as is the idea behind P3P.

[66] See also Koops & Leenes 2004, who, with respect to 'code and privacy', point at the relevant distinction between code in the neutral sense of (e.g., privacy-threatening) technology and code in a normative sense (e.g., re-establishing disturbed balances by using PETs). They conclude that code does only seldom contain privacy-related rules.

totally unacceptable uses of personal data, the specifics of which would have to be translated into technical architectures to control the processing of personal data.[67] All in all, PETs in practice still seem a long way off.

7.4 'CODE AS LAW' IN A BROADER PERSPECTIVE

7.4.1 Code: Rules or rules of law?

The term 'code as law' has at least a twofold meaning. It implies not only that the technical shaping of cyberspace creates new rules but also that these rules are, or at least function as, rules of *law*.

To a large extent, Internet code consists of technical standards, represented in software and data structures. These standards are technical rules that have been developed in a mainly private standardization process. Do these rules constitute *rules of law* or do they have a different status? The answer to this question is complex. One way of approaching this issue is to determine the legal status of technical standards, a major ingredient of 'code'.

The question of the legal status of technical standards is not a new one. It has been addressed extensively, particularly in the German legal literature, even as early as the 1970s.[68] The German authors generally assume that, in positivistic terms, technical standards *as such* are not legal norms. This view is widely supported for other jurisdictions as well.[69]

Technical standards however, can obtain a formal legal validity when they are being incorporated or referred to in legislation. Legal relevance of technical standards can also arise due to the fact that standards are being used widely, for instance, within a certain profession. This might result in recognition of certain standards as a custom or standards being accepted as a relevant interpretation of, for instance, an open statutory safety standard. The latter can be relevant in, for instance, liability cases. Technical standards can also factually result in certain patterns of behavior. In those cases, without being legally binding, technical standards still have *de facto* validity.[70]

Anybody who wants to access and use the Internet has to abide by the standards as set by the relevant organizations. Ultimately this compliance is not prescribed by law, but is primarily a factual reality. This is changed neither by the fact that certain Internet-related standards could be used, for instance, in contracts to describe the services available and obligations of access providers or software developers, nor by the fact they are being used in other legally binding documents.

---

[67] Prins 2004, section 7.
[68] See Stuurman 1995, p. 131 et seq. for an overview of the various views.
[69] Schepel & Falke 2000, p. 181.
[70] Marburger 1979, p. 299.

Asscher[71] concludes that, in the discussion about the legal nature of code, we first need to discuss the criteria that will be used in the analysis. Against this background, he takes a broader approach to the underlying question of the legal nature of code, and included in his analysis, next to Lessig's approach, various concepts of law, including both legal-positivists such as Hart and natural law or moral theories, in particular those of Fuller.

Lessig claims that, since code regulates human behavior, the comparison between code and law is appropriate.[72] In a legal-positivistic approach following Hart's concept of law, it is necessary to look for rules in code.[73] Fuller, a natural law theorist, claims that law is subject to a procedural morality consisting of eight principles.[74]

Based on a combination of Fuller's criteria and those developed by the European Court for the Protection of Human Rights (ECtHR) in cases concerning the restriction of fundamental rights, Asscher concludes that in particular the answers to the following questions will provide a relevant analysis of code as a regulating mechanism:

1. Can rules be distinguished in the code?
2. Can they be understood, i.e., is it understandable how code works and what it does? If so, are those rules transparent? Are they accessible to the general public?
3. Can the rules be trusted? Is there a guarantee that rules are not changed during the game? Are code rules reliable in the sense that they are predictable?
4. Is there a sovereign; an authority that makes the code rules?
5. Is there a choice? Can consumers/citizens choose not to obey the rules? Can citizens/consumers freely choose another system of law/code?

An application of these questions in the fields of free speech, privacy, and intellectual property shows that the answers to these questions depend on a number of factors, including the relevant domain as well as the organizational and technical level on which they are being applied. The mere statement that 'code is law' however, is not supported by these analyses.[75]

Even if from a legal-theoretical point of view, the rules created in shaping cyberspace do not qualify as rules of law in the traditional sense, they have yet to show to be of importance in regulating cyberspace.

---

[71] Asscher 2000, p. 11.
[72] Asscher 2004, p. 14.
[73] Ibid., p. 14.
[74] Ibid., p. 12.
[75] Lambers 2004, p. 47 et seq.; Helberger 2004, p. 46 et seq.; Leenes & Koops 2004, p. 40.

7.4.2   Code as law: A new phenomenon?

The concept of 'code as law' in essence refers to the various aspects of regulation by means of information technology. Various authors have welcomed the concept of 'code as law' as a more or less fundamental new approach.

Although the novelty certainly holds for the appreciation of the role of information technology, there are other elements of 'code as law' that are not as new as they initially might appear. This particularly holds for: (1) technological developments as a source of 'rules' and (2) the use of technology in enforcement of rules.

7.4.2.1   *Technological developments as a source of 'rules'*

The fact that technological choices impose certain 'rules' on the behavior of users of the technology is not a new phenomenon. Technology creates new degrees of freedom, but also restricts certain behavior. Compared to walking, driving a car will expand your reach very significantly, but it will also restrict your degree of freedom to a certain extent (e.g., generally no access to off-road areas).

The set of rules linked to a certain technology is in part a direct result of the characteristics of the technology itself (e.g., no off-road driving), and, on the other hand, a consequence of the application of concepts such as striving for safety.

Technological developments influence many aspects of our society. This influence partly comes in the form of practical rules allowing, restricting, or directing certain behavior. Opinions differ as to the extent of this influence. In the view of technological determinists, the effects of technological developments are even far reaching. In its most extreme form, technology dominates the social, political, and economic life ('the technological society').[76]

Information and communication technology (ICT) is key to many aspects of our current society. Internet has gained importance in an unprecedented short period of time. ICT has penetrated almost every aspect of our society. It is being used in every service provided to us, both in a private and a professional capacity. Today, its importance is even growing due to developments such as broadband and mobile Internet. Further impact on human behavior can be expected, for instance, due to the development of 'location based services'.

7.4.2.2   *The enforcement of rules by means of technology*

Examples
Enforcement of rules by means of technology is not a new phenomenon, nor is it exclusive to ICT. Examples of the enforcement of rules by means of technology can be found in everyday life, for instance, in the street (e.g., speed bumps, crash barri-

---

[76] Bimber 1994, p. 82, referring to the views of Jacques Ellul as expressed in his book, The Technological Society (Vintage: New York 1964).

ers, roadblocks and the like, separating, slowing down, and guiding traffic). A speed limiting device in a car is a more complex example. We can also refer to the mechanical enforcement of a safety rule for machine operators, e.g., the use of both hands in operating a cutting machine, aimed at preventing amputation.

Therefore, ICT does not seem to take a special position. This also holds for the interests at stake, given the examples set out above (mechanical solutions used to enforce rules, personal safety v. ICT to protect copyrights and privacy).

Technological enforcement: Incomplete by nature?
The above examples demonstrate the application of a certain technology to contribute to the compliance of individuals to specific rules. The technological measures taken, however, do not constitute a full representation of said rules. As an example, a speed limiting device will not allow the truck driver to exceed the pre-programmed speed limit, even in those circumstances where this is essential to avoid an accident. Similarly, the devices preventing the copying of software generally do not take into account that, under certain circumstances, a consumer has a legitimate right to make a copy of the software.

In these examples, the rules as embedded in technology represent only a certain aspect of the underlying legal rule. At the same time they create a factually binding new rule (e.g., never allowed to drive faster than 100 kms/h) that, in some cases, violates other aspects of the underlying rules of law (e.g., the exception for home copying of software) or higher legal principle (e.g., the duty to avoid damages).

In relation to anti-copying devices, relevant circumstances for its interpretation include the nature of use, the type of user (professional, consumer, library, etc.), as well as the applicable law. The development of an anti-copying device will require the interpretation of the relevant rules. An incomplete implementation might distort the delicate balance between copyright and the freedom of information (faire use, freedom of speech).[77]

Traditional, mechanical enforcement instruments, usually safeguards, have, by nature, very limited 'intelligence'. Technological enforcement of a legal rule will, in most cases, assuming it can be realized at all, require the use of a more or less complex expert system. Particularly when taking into account all relevant aspects of such enforcement, including its exceptions and norms of a higher hierarchical order. Currently ICT still falls short of providing smart solutions with a balanced reflection of a rule of law that takes into account an adequate range of relevant aspects of the rule of law concerned, the relevant circumstances for its interpretation, and economic and technical constraints (costs/benefit analysis, scale, scope of application, large scale distribution, security, etc.)

---

[77] Van Dalen & Lambers 2003, p. 5, point at this risk in relation to the US 'broadcast flag' system, a technical feature aimed at preventing unauthorized redistribution of digital television signals.

The legislator is well aware of these shortcomings, as is shown, for instance, in the explanatory memorandum to the bill amending the Dutch implementation of the Copyright Harmonization Directive.[78]

The ratio and legality of using technological constraints
In discussing the pros and cons of taking ICT regulation to an international level, Prins, in chapter 6 of this Volume, points at the fact that companies, organizations, and private persons can use technology or contractual arrangements to restrict the availability of their information or communication services, for instance, because the information itself is not welcome, the person is a resident of a certain country, or the distributor of the information fails to meet the standards set by gatekeepers, such as ISPs, e.g., with respect to spam or virus protection. Prins concludes that various actors now have the technical and contractual tools and, thus, the power to determine what is to be considered 'lawful' access to a certain area (domain) within the on-line world.

In analyzing this development, it should be kept in mind that the drivers for access constraints have very different backgrounds and consequences.

In part they are seen by right holders as an effective means to deal with illegal copying, and hence to recapture 'lost territory'. Next to contributing to compliance, however, these systems can also easily result in violation of the law. An example is price differentiation in artificially separated markets or other forms of blocking free trade. This can result in violation of or interference with among other things, the principle of exhaustion of copyrights or competition rules. As mentioned above, an incomplete implementation of copyright law might distort the delicate balance between copyright and the freedom of information (fair use, freedom of speech).

The use of this type of technology can also be the result of mandatory legislation or, be stimulated by legislation. An example of the latter is the use of the 'broadcast flag', a technology enabling closed circulation of television programs. Recently, the US Federal Communications Commission (FCC) has imposed the application of broadcast flags on the producers of equipment (TV sets, computers) for receiving digital television signals.[79] The obligatory application of protective technologies however, is rare. The broadcast flag is only the second example; the first, the obligatory application of the Serial Copy Management System under the US Audio Home Recording Act 1992, proved to be a failure. In all other cases, US and EU legislation on this matter has explicitly stipulated the non-mandatory nature thereof.[80]

---

[78] TK 28482, nr. 3 (MvT), p. 55: 'Apart from the fact that, currently, it is technically hardly possible to ensure that a protective system respects statutory exceptions such as those for quotes or news reports(…)' (translation C.S.)

[79] FCC 4 November 2003, Report and Order and Further Notice of Proposed Rulemaking, no. MB 02-30, <www.efff.org/IP/DRM/HDTV/20031104_fcc_order.pfd>. Van Dalen and Lambers 2003, p. 2 et seq.

[80] Van Dalen & Lambers 2003, p. 3. Art. 6 of the EU Copyright Directive (Directive 2001/29/EC, OJ L 167/10) is an example.

Another example of mandatory blocking of access can be found in on-line gambling. In various countries, including the Netherlands, strict legislation prohibits offering on-line gambling services. In Dutch case law, this legislation has been upheld and found to be in compliance with the EU Treaty provisions on the freedom of providing services.[81] The court decisions also provide a practical standard for the measures to be taken to prevent Dutch citizens from taking part in on-line gambling as offered by these sites (e.g., no payments to Dutch bank accounts).[82] The governments of Singapore and China have also imposed mandatory access constraints in attempts to control inbound and outbound Internet traffic. The conclusion that the use of access constraints should be compliant with the relevant legislation will be easily supported.

Above, we concluded that currently ICT seems to fall short of providing smart solutions taking into account an adequate range of relevant aspects of the rule of law concerned, the relevant circumstances for its interpretation, and economic and technical constraints (costs, scale, scope of application, security). Does this imply that the current access constraint solutions are unlawful? The answer seems to be negative. In the off-line world, the case of speed limiting devices currently on the market points in that direction. The same holds for anti-copying devices that are being used to protect software and DVDs.

The Copyright Harmonization Directive even provides an explicit answer. Given the current technically inherent imperfections of anti-copying devices, the legislator has to choose between either an effective protection of protective devices or fully respecting the exceptions of the copyright laws. In the EU, as in other jurisdictions, the legislator has chosen in favor of protecting the technical devices. In the US, Australia, and Japan, this choice has, been balanced by the introduction of a 'right to hack', allowing the user of a copyrighted work, in specific circumstances, to circumvent protective devices.[83] The prohibition in the Copyright Harmonization Directive is absolute. Under certain circumstances however, the rightholder can be forced to facilitate lawfully permitted, but technically blocked, use of the copyrighted work.[84]

Technological constraints: The boundaries of unlawfulness; control mechanisms
When the conclusion is that technical enforcement solutions are allowed even if they are an incomplete representation of the relevant rules, the next question is: what are the limits in this process? Or to put it differently, how incomplete can a technical enforcement mechanism be before it becomes unlawful? A related ques-

---

[81] In its most recent decision in this case, however, the court has pointed out that the Dutch anti-gambling policy may, in practice, be insufficiently restrictive to justify a prohibition of foreign gambling services in accordance with Art. 49 of the EC Treaty, see Rechtbank Arnhem [Arnhem District Court], 2 June 2004, 98631/HA ZA 03-606.

[82] Hof Arnhem [Arnhem Court of Appeal] 2 September 2003, zaaknummer 03/319 03/325 (*De Lotto* v. *Ladbrokes*).

[83] Koelman 2003, p. 255.

[84] Ibid., p. 254.

tion is, of course, how the development and control of those applications is controlled.

We will discuss various relevant mechanisms. In some cases, the distribution and application of technology will be subject to a license, as in the case of export of encryption technology. However, the rationale in that case is, quite different from, for instance, a balanced application of copyright laws. If there is no institutionalized mechanism for preventive control of protective systems with the view to the legitimacy of its functionality, interests groups could play an important role, for example, by filing claims against the application of certain types of access constraint.

Apart from discussions with developers and suppliers or filing claims, in some cases, the standardization process might allow for exercising user influence. This will only apply in formal standardization processes, where user participation and influence are generally recognized weak spots.[85] In industry standardization (*'de facto* standardization'), user participation is hardly ever sought. If the technological constraints are made obligatory, such as in the case of the US 'broadcast flag', the checks and balances inherent to the applicable system of rule-making apply. Interestingly, the European Commission is of the opinion that obligatory application of systems for conditional access is contrary to Article 49 of the EU Treaty (freedom of services).[86]

In their analysis of the introduction of the US 'broadcast flag', Van Dalen and Lambers' question whether the measures as imposed by the FCC could be adequately justified in the European setting, given Article 10 of the European Convention on Human Rights and the ECtHR's decision in the *Autronic AG* case,[87] which brings the means to receive electronic signals within the scope of Article 10. Furthermore, the imposed measure is currently not necessary in view of the limited bandwidth available, which precludes illegal distribution of digital television signals. Moreover, they conclude that the measure proposed is inadequate in view of the purpose defined; it will only provide protection against *casual copying*, whereas it is aimed at *indiscriminate redistribution*. Also other, less damaging alternatives exist, such as fingerprinting or watermarking data. Finally, they point at the risk that the US decisions might inspire also the European legislator or develop into a *de facto* standard. The US measures will also restrict the export capabilities for European producers, while the US export capabilities remain unharmed.[88]

7 4.3 Internet-related decision-making v. other forms of standardization

The development of Internet 'code' is a form of technical standardization. As set out above, a distinction can be made between the level of the architecture of the

---

[85] Schepel & Falke, p. 111 et seq.; Stuurman 1995, p. 90.
[86] Van Dalen & Lambers 2003, p. 5.
[87] Case 15/1989/175/231.
[88] See *supra* n. 86, at p. 6.

Internet and the level of the applications. The latter is the domain of software developers, including monopolists (such as Microsoft) and consortia (such as MPEG). To the extent that standards arise, they are *de facto* standards. In most cases, they are proprietary. An exception is open source software, although being in essence proprietary, its restrictive effects are waived by means of the open source licenses used.

On the architecture level, as set out above, the main players are the World Wide Web Consortium (W3C), the Internet Society (ISOC), the Internet Engineering Task Force (IETF), the Internet Engineering Steering Group (IESG), the Internet Architecture Board (IAB), and the Internet Research Task Force (IRTF). With respect to domain names and IP addresses, ICANN, IANA, and RIPE NCC are the central organizations to set standards for the Internet.

The Internet standardization process seems to a large extent to be independent of the traditional, formal standardization processes as going on within, amongst others, CENELEC, ETSI, IEC, and ANSI. These traditional standardization processes have serious difficulties in meeting adequate standards for access, transparency, and availability of information about the process and its results.[89]

The *accessibility* of these Internet-related standardization processes does not seem to be significantly better than holds for the process as organized by the traditional standardization bodies. Although technology easily facilitates the factual participation in the standardization process, the necessary participation in meetings, the necessary expertise, availability, labor, and travel costs are traditionally blocking factors that apply here as well.

The large number of organizations involved, their mutual interwovenness and open objectives seem to indicate that, as in traditional standardization processes, *transparency* is a point of concern. The same seems to hold for the *availability of information* regarding the standardization agenda, participants, elements, structure and outcome of the process. As a result, participation is in general limited to technical professionals.[90]

Compared to the traditional ICT standardization processes, Internet-related standardization processes therefore do not seem to offer significantly better procedural guarantees for the protection of democratic values.

7.4.4   'Code as law' in a changing world; The Internet in transition

The last few years have seen a significant transition in the use, positioning and perception of the Internet:

a)   There is a very significant increase in the number of statutes and regulations applicable to electronic communications which, given its key role, are par-

---

[89]   Schepel & Falke 2000, in particular p. 111 et seq. and p. 161 et seq.
[90]   Koops & Lips 2003, p. 292.

ticularly relevant for Internet use. The role of self-regulation has changed from being an alternative in the absence of formal rules, into supplementing, clarifying and explaining formal rules. The cross-border and global nature of the Internet is no longer a reason for the absence of the legislator;

b) From a network for exchanging information between researchers, the Internet has become a global communications network for virtually all groups in society;

c) Internet has become a part of the societal, economic, and even political reality. Internet has turned into a part of the 'public space' of our society;

d) There is a rapidly growing awareness of the risks involved in using the Internet, for both the private sphere (privacy, spam, viruses, hackers) as for the public sphere (criminality, terrorism). Internet innocence is lost completely. There is growing pressure on governments to take countermeasures.

In summary, we are now being confronted with 'Internet 2.0' or even higher.[91] This development has various consequences for the appreciation of 'code as law'.

In the mid-1990s, the US government has initiated the privatization of the Internet. The development of Internet standards was up to the market.[92] This by the way also implied that the standardization process was no longer subject to the democratic control mechanism applicable to the US decision-making process.

The developments described above under c. (Internet has become a part of the public sphere) and d. (Internet's innocence is lost), however, provided a strong counterforce against the intended effect (market control) of handing over the control with respect to the technological development of the Internet to private organizations. Governments were given (perceived) valid reasons to take a different attitude towards the Internet. This included not only active use of the Internet for spreading or blocking information and even warfare, but also for monitoring the Internet and, if necessary, active involvement in its technological development.

In the aftermath of '9/11' and 'Madrid', many governments even began to perceive the Internet as vital to their national security. Although this development is driven by the fear for terrorists, it should be borne in mind that, in relation to the Internet, there are many other major interests at stake (such as fighting child pornography and the growing economic damage of viruses) that will continue to put pressure on governments to become more pro-active in monitoring Internet traffic and its technological development. This is likely to have serious consequences for the freedom of private organizations to decide about the technological shaping of the Internet.

Although greater government involvement could in theory, provide better safeguards with respect to democratic decision-making, the background for the renewed governmental interest in the development of the Internet probably indicates other-

---

[91] Inspired by Michael Geist's 'Cyberlaw 2.0'.
[92] Koops & Lips 2003, p. 295.

wise. Not only is there still a US dominance of the process,[93] inadequately reflecting the global nature and importance of the Internet, also the driving forces (national security interests) probably will not add significantly to solving the lack of democratic control and legitimacy in the process of developing Internet code, either.

7.4.5 'Code as law': How to solve the problem

Given the interests at stake and the number of players involved, a significant improvement of democratic control and legitimacy of the development of Internet code, including relevant non-Western influence, will be very difficult, if not impossible, to achieve. The technological development of the Internet has consequences in many different areas (culture, society, economy, national security, economy, etc.). In all these areas, different players, issues, and interests are at stake.

Given the structure and use of the Internet, any approach will have to be international and preferably global. If we look for examples of global democratic co-ordination, then the United Nations is the prime source of inspiration.[94]

Within the UN framework, different regulatory bodies have been established for global co-ordination in various fields, such as the FAO (agriculture), UNESCO (culture), and the UNHCR (humanitarian help). This type of specialization is, in general, a prerequisite for bringing together the right organizations, persons, and know-how, and mastering the complexity of problems, processes, and implementation solutions. One of the key characteristics of the Internet standard setting process is, however, that most of the standards are at least potentially of equivalent relevance for the economic, cultural, military, security and other similar interests at stake. This seems to stand in the way of breaking down the standardization process in a UN type of approach.

Improving democratic control and legitimacy of the development of Internet code requires changes in both the architecture of the whole standard setting process (type, number of organizations involved and their interdependency), as well as in the structure, processes and legitimacy of each of the individual organizations involved. A short term solution is therefore not very likely.

7.5   CONCLUDING REMARKS

'Code as law' refers to a rather diffuse concept. The views concerning its range and meaning are very different. In order to keep the discussion focused, it is important

---

[93] Ibid., p. 295 et seq.

[94] Koops & Lips (Koops and Lips 2003, p. 308) refer, *inter alia*, to the ITU, as based on the ITU treaty, as a possible direction for finding solutions. They note, interestingly, that the ITU has tried to become involved in the development of the Internet. The organization, however, has failed to do so, having been overtaken by the many Internet-specific organizations that have arisen from the development of the Internet itself.

to make a distinction between at least two of the following aspects: (a) the use of code by the government and private parties as an enforcement instrument (for example, DRM) and (b) the regulatory effect of primarily Internet-related code which has been developed by private organizations.

Enforcement by technology is not a new phenomenon, although, more than in the past, fundamental rights (freedom of speech; access to information) seem to be at stake. Introducing code as an enforcement instrument makes it a legal instrument and therefore current guarantees should be taken into consideration during its development and implementation. It is particularly difficult to achieve a complete representation of the regulations within the present level of technology. This is the case, for example, with legitimate exceptions in copyright legislation.

It is uncertain whether code actually *is* law. Nevertheless, code does have a certain regulatory quality, although the views regarding the actual effect and impact vary.

Consequently, attention must be given to the fact that there is a lack of democratic control and legitimacy in the process of developing Internet code.

In the aftermath of '9/11' and 'Madrid', national security and defense interests, similar to the driving forces that created the Internet, have returned as an important perspective for at least monitoring and may be even partly controlling the development of the Internet. Although the precise impact of this development is still unclear, this form of renewed government interest in the development of Internet code is not likely to mitigate the concerns as expressed.

The role of code and the fundamental interests potentially at stake continue to legitimatize a critical approach to the process in which code is being developed, even when 'code is not law'.

Chapter 8
CONCLUSION

Maurice Schellekens, Bert-Jaap Koops and Corien Prins

8.1 INTRODUCTION

ICT places the law for new and complicated challenges. In order to come to grips with these complex issues, policy makers have formulated a number of starting points they hope are helpful in addressing them. We have held the starting points against the light in order to answer the question we set out to answer:

> 'Can prevalent policy statements about ICT regulation count as general ICT regulatory starting points or principles, which enable us to deal with current and future ICT developments from a global regulatory and legislative perspective? Is it possible to formulate a general perspective on the status and usability of these starting points?'

To address these questions, we have divided this chapter into three sections. In section 8.2, a summary is given of the pros and cons of the various starting points as we have outlined them in the various chapters. This yields a fragmented picture with too many obstacles for the starting points to be embraced unreservedly. There are good reasons to uphold them, but there is also much to advise against their application. In the next section 8.3, the starting points will be analyzed as regards their usefullness for e-regulation. We will discuss a potential use for them and indicate some approaches that might make the sweeping starting points more concrete and more practical to use in certain situations. We will end, in section 8.4, with an agenda for further research.

8.2 THE STARTING POINTS: ADVANTAGES AND DRAWBACKS

The starting points discussed and analyzed in the previous chapters were drafted by policy makers and legislators. Especially in the context of the 'craft' of drafting statutes, the starting points make sense. With respect to the five starting points this can be illustrated as follows.

B-J. Koops, et al. (Eds), Starting Points for ICT Regulation
© 2006, ITeR, The Hague, and the authors

- *Off-line = on-line*: If the law for the on-line environment can fit in with the existing system of the law, advantages in consistency, legal clarity, and legal certainty can be gained.
- *Technology neutrality*: Rules that are technology-neutral enjoy a certain longevity. This diminishes the pressure on legislators.
- *Self-regulation*: Technological turbulence makes the object of regulation unstable. The government simply cannot keep up with technical developments, so, it is only reasonable that those who are part and parcel of the turbulent developments take up a role in regulation.
- *Internationalization*: ICT enlarges the geographical scope of behavior, which therefore acquires an international dimension. It is therefore plausible to aim to adapt the geographical scope of the laws governing this behavior accordingly. If this were to succeed, the law in place would cover the behavior it governs both in legitimacy and scope.
- *Code as law*: acceptance and enforcement of a rule depends upon the factual context in which the rule holds (or is meant to hold). Since technology (code) is becoming one of the major determining factors for such a context, it is plausible that attention is paid to the 'normativity' of a technology.

Although, from the perspective of the drafting official, this analysis looks promising on the face of it, the critical appraisal of the starting points in the various chapters of this book has shown that there is much more to these starting points than meets the eye. The complex problems of regulating the information society involve more than is expressed by the starting points. When looking at the aspects in which strike the eye, the starting points are lacking at least the following issues.

- The starting points, as seen from the craftsman perspective described above, are very clean. They are 'empty' principles that say nothing about content or substantive values. Policy questions regarding the shape that the information society should take are not touched upon.
- There is a non-trivial step between theoretical proclamation and practical realization. There are often numerous practical, mundane reasons why the starting points do not work in real life.

Fundamental problems
The transition from an industrial society to an information or based society is, as has been pointed out, not a development that is neutral to the law. New relationships between legal subjects develop, new interests emerge that may need legal protection, new values develop. The information society is opening a new world of aspirations. People want life to be 'better' in the information society than it was in the industrial society. We may think that the law can and must contribute to the shaping of the information society. It is clear that this is a much wider perspective. It also holds more capacity for differentiation in views about the starting points,

since views about what is the most desirable development of the law in the information society are diverging, too. The starting points are not isolated from thoughts about aspirations for the information society.

Moreover, the starting points suggest that normative systems developed for the information society can be analyzed from the perspective of one unified and coherent legal system that can be logically ordered. Thinking about e-regulation along the lines of a set of starting points thus suggests a fixed instrumentalist notion of the law and the regulatory system. However, as has been shown in the previous chapters, the on-line society shows highly complex patterns of continuous interaction between many different public and private regulators in different areas. Several of the described conflicts in the on-line world resemble challenges in other fields (e.g., cross-border trade, transnational crime and migration, environmental pollution). Legal theorists argue that these and other global developments begin to change the present-day concept of law. Representatives of legal pluralism suggest that law in our modern society is plural rather than monolithic and that it is private as well as public in character.[1] Moreover, theorists emphasize that a pluralistic concept of law would also offer more room for legal traditions that have evolved in other countries than those based on western jurisprudence.[2] The acceptance of legal pluralism would mean a shift in focus from strictly defined and hermetically closed legal systems to legal discourses that are attentive both to the plurality of norms and the ways in which they are organized in and around practices.[3] For the on-line world this would mean that in seeking to regulate the information society, the focus should not be on deciding what starting point is to be applied, but on mechanisms whereby several starting points may operate together in different ways, depending on the specific context.

- *Off-line = on-line*: Unrestrained application of this starting point would mean that the law for the information society modelled on of the industrial society, whereas it is not obvious that the paradigm of the latter can be upheld in the information society. Moreover, it is not evident that values that have been cherished or choices that have been made in the past should still hold in a new context where several aspects of life are substantially different from the past.
- *Technology neutrality*: Application of this starting point could mean that sustainability is valued higher than legal certainty in the short run. It may also lead to sweeping legislation that has undesirable consequences for specific technological developments.
- *Self-regulation*: Self-regulation builds on the assumption that the citizens of the information society are capable and willing to regulate their own affairs.

---

[1] Galanter 1981.
[2] Jones 1998.
[3] See Melissaris 2004, p. 58.

But where does the responsibility end that actors are meant to take them-selves? Is self-regulation ultimately compatible with legitimacy and with en-forceability?

- *Internationalization*: How do we deal with social, cultural, and economic di-versity? In what situations can diversity be sacrificed for utilitarian purposes, such as more effective legal rules? Is it something to be fostered, and if so, in what situations? Some issues are deeply rooted in historic, cultural, and economic values or rest on long traditions. There is a fundamental conflict between fostering such national values and traditions and creating interna-tionally applicable regulation.
- *Code as law*: Technology can well be used as an instrument for enforcement. Yet the specifics of a technology, such as a lack of choice and transparency of built-in norms, may mean that what is intended as enforcement of existing rules effectively creates new rules or norms. Thus, code as law raises funda-mental questions as to the legitimacy of using technology as a normative in-strument.

These are broad and fundamental questions, to which no simple answers exist.

Practical problems
The problems that the law faces are not restricted to inconclusive fundamental is-sues. There are also more mundane, practical stumbling blocks that hamper the application of the starting points. The starting points describe a desirable state of affairs. What practical considerations have to be taken into account when realizing regulation according to the starting points?

- *Off-line = on-line*: The idea of establishing the same norms on-line as those that hold off-line, is appealing, but this starting point says nothing about how the two are to be compared. Just how are we to know when a comparison be-tween off-line and on-line situations is apt, or when such a comparison over-looks fundamental differences and thus leads to inequitable on-line rules?
- *Technology neutrality*: Similarly to the previous point, this starting point fails to indicate just to what extent regulation should be technology-neutral. In its most useful interpretation, the starting point holds that a balance must be struck between sustainability of regulation and legal certainty – but the prin-ciple gives no clue how to strike such a balance. Again, the gap between theory and practice is wide.
- *Self-regulation*: Whether self-regulation is possible depends very much on whether there are parties who are willing and able to take this up. Even if par-ties are willing to engage in self-regulation, it is questionable whether organi-zational or institutional embedding allows for continuity over a long period of time, and whether self-enforcement can be sufficiently relied upon to main-tain the self-imposed rules. In practice, self-regulation works well in a limited

number of circumstances, but it usually only works when there is some form of combination with government regulation. The starting point does not says what is the right form of combining self-regulation with government regulation.

- *Internationalization*: we still live in a world of sovereign states, whose co-operation is needed in order to bring about international regulation, and who can withhold their co-operation at will and may have many – respectable or less respectable – reasons to do so. The deterritorialization of the Internet may, moreover, give national states some power to create national rules that differ from international trends. Given the prevalence of a considerable variety of norms, traditions, and values, this means that the widely shared wish to fine-tune regulation on an international level is difficult to put into practice.

- *Code as law*: The idea of using technology as an enforcement instrument may appeal to many but, in practice, it is hard to build norms into technology that are sufficiently flexible to deal with the subtleties of legal, democratically-established norms. Therefore, code as law in practice is often a sweeping technology that cannot cope with delicate balances of interest. Moreover, if governments nevertheless wish to pursue this direction, do they really have the expertise to take part in standardization institutions and steer technology developments?

Thus, while the starting points seem plausible answers to the challenges posed to the law by ICT developments, upon closer scrutiny, there appear to be many fundamental and practical issues that make clear that the starting points oversimplify the reality of regulation.

8.3   CAN THE STARTING POINTS BE USED?

In the previous section, it was shown that there are certain reasons to uphold the starting points, but also that there can be many circumstances in which a diversion from the starting points is desirable. From the various chapters, we see a fragmented picture emerges. With respect to some starting points (technology neutrality, code as law), a cautiously positive stance is taken. It is not so much that the starting points are very much brought into practice, but they do embody an idea that needs encouragement, because it is a good approach in certain circumstances. The status as a starting point reinforces this. With respect to other starting points (international regulation, off-line = on-line), a more critical stance is taken. The authors of these chapters recur to the rationales behind the starting points and found out that the rationales are weak or can also be reached by other means than the starting points suggest. The starting points also often seem to suggest more traditional paths that do not need further encouragement. The formulation as a starting point then soon tends to give an absolute ring to the suggested way of action – as if every cross-border problem warrants regulation at the international level. In both respects – there are alternatives, and the approach is really nothing new – these starting points do not seem to really have a function. There is no need to encourage what is being done anyhow, and where functioning approaches exist and work, it is often best not to meddle with them.

Nevertheless, the starting points should not be too readily dismissed as useful principles for e-regulation, simply because they are too sweeping or too obvious to be considered a solution for all e-regulation problems. Given the wide store of maxims, mantras, and myths that people use in everyday life, there seems to be a use for broad, general statements that have a ring of truth about them. The question therefore is: might there still be some use for the starting points we have analyzed?

8.3.1   The starting points as a procedural checklist

A first issue is how the starting points should be regarded: can we give them the status of guidelines, legal principles, or e-regulation principles? In our view, the analysis has shown that there are simply too many obstacles for the starting points to be regarded as general principles. Evidently, the starting points cannot be used for all e-regulation problems. Moreover, it is unclear under what conditions a starting point can be applied: this depends on an evaluation and balancing of a number of factors. The application of the starting points is never straightforward. This enormously reduces their value as general guidelines or principles. *A fortiori*, the starting points cannot be seen as binding legal principles – they are merely policy statements without any legal status.

Therefore, the idea of regarding each starting point as a valuable principle in itself must be abandoned. Not one starting point can lay claim to universal usefulness; there is no one-size-fits-all guideline for e-regulation. However, in their combined effect, they may be of more value: ICT regulation is rather a matter of finding a way to combine starting points.[4] This combination of principles could take the form of a checklist for e-regulators.

Given the fragmented nature of the usability of the starting points in real life, and their character of openness – or emptiness – that does not provide any guidance for substantive regulatory directions, we ultimately tend to regard the starting points as a procedural checklist. When addressing e-regulatory problems, the parties involved should have a look at each starting point, and consider whether it helps them to find a method of solving their problem. The method may be, for instance, to look at similar issues in the off-line context and to derive some normative guidance from the rules established there (using the 'off line = on line' starting point as a heuristic method), or to gather a group of involved parties around the table from as many countries as can be expected to share a roughly similar value pattern in the specific context of the problem (using both the internationalization and the self-regulation starting points as a heuristic method).

---

[4] See also Mayer-Schönberger 2003 and Smith 2001.

8.3.2 Making the starting points more concrete

The law in the books does not always reflect the law in action. The above-mentioned rather academic suggestions on how to regard the starting points are, of course, politically weak by nature. Ultimately, regulatory choices will depend on political arguments and calculations based on commercial pressures or public objectives. Thus, in the political arena, the suggestion to regard the starting points as a procedural checklist will, in the end, be no restraint for legislators wanting to follow any political or economic agenda.

As mentioned earlier, the framework that we have implicitly used in this book for dealing with the starting points in the various chapters was to test the pragmatic value of the starting points: do they actually work, and can we indicate under what conditions they work? The qualified answer is that most starting points may actually work well in certain cases if they are interpreted and elaborated in certain ways. The analysis has yielded some useful insights into the situations in which, and the conditions under which, addressing e-regulation problems may benefit from the starting points. We can illustrate this by looking at e-regulation from four perspectives: from the purpose of regulation, from the means of regulation, from the context of regulation, and from the enforcement of regulation.

The purpose of regulation
In a number of chapters, it was shown that the purpose of a regulation elicited the need to apply a starting point and use it as a method to achieve regulation. The chapter on internationalization drew attention to a more or less social goal of law to offer a legal counterweight in imbalanced situations or to reinforce the position of weaker parties. Sometimes, regulation at the international level has an added value in this respect. For example, if a balanced competition on markets is to be achieved, the international level has an added value if markets transcend the territory of an individual state. The interests of the peoples of developing countries also offer an example. The international level can bring about the leverage needed to give them access to and effective participation in the Internet. In the technology-neutrality chapter, non-discrimination of certain technologies and the unhindered development of ICT was shown to be goals that highlight the need to observe technology neutrality in regulating. A similar argument can be found in the chapter about the equivalence of off-line and on-line. The choice between 'strong' or 'weak' protectionist aims and purposes may also influence the decision on whether or not to opt for self-regulation. For example, when opting for a strong level of consumer protection, legislation appears to be preferred over self-regulation. A final example of the purpose-driven use of the starting point is 'code as law': particularly when the purpose of regulation is enforcement of both existing as well as claimed rules or values, the use of technological enforcement instruments comes into view.

The means of regulation

Regulation has many forms and means. Three starting points in fact already indicate certain general forms of regulation: self-regulation, international regulatory instruments, regulation through technology. The analysis in the chapters dealing with those starting points give several indications of more concrete regulatory means, and the conditions that favor those more detailed forms of regulation. For instance, codes of conduct and trustmarks could be backed-up by government regulation in the form of backstop legislation or a general legislative framework.

The other two starting points do not target specific forms of regulation, but they do indicate means of regulation: try and reinterpret off-line regulations to cover on-line situations; create higher-level forms of regulation that abstract away from specific technologies. The chapters analyzing these starting points have indicated various more concrete strategies for fulfilling these desiderata. For instance, multi-tiered legislation, open-ended formulations, and mixed approaches are strategies to create legislation that offers both sufficient legal certainty for concrete technologies, and at the same time is flexible enough to deal with future developments. Frameworks of substantive principles could be drafted, perhaps even at supranational levels, to make concrete what is valued both off-line and on-line, and thus could help to make more correct analogies between off-line and on-line situations.

The context for regulation

The context is a key determining factor when it comes to deciding whether a specific starting point can be used, and if so, in what way. We have seen, for instance, that the starting point of regulation at an international level depends very much on the national contexts that are the basis of an effort to harmonize: to what extent do nation states cling to their sovereignty, are the issues to be regulated heterogeneously or homogeneously, are differences between nations real or superficial, and to what extent are regulatory preferences created by culture? At the same time, the technology-neutrality starting point focuses more on contextual issues like the urgency with which a regulation is required, the technological turbulence, or the degree to which the legal system allows courts to interpret laws.

Another illustrative situation where the context determines the way in which a certain starting point is applied, relates to the cross-border effect of the on-line problem at hand. The conflict between France and the US in the Yahoo case on Nazi memorabilia, for example, illustrates that differences in culture as well as in legal traditions are determining factors in deciding upon regulatory courses of action. The case also illustrates that e-regulation must ideally take into account not only its own cultural and legal context, but also its impact on other countries that are affected by the regulation. Here, the cultural and legal context influence the use of the internationalization starting point.

The enforcement of regulation

A final perspective is the enforcement of regulation. This actually relates closely to the previous three perspectives, since enforcement depends on the purpose, means, and context of regulation. In certain situations, enforcement instruments may be chosen that appear to be merely of a symbolic nature, e.g., private-law sanctions for disregarding personal-data protection obligations. However, in other situations, full-scale enforcement is needed as the obligation of a democratic state to sustain the rule of law. This also touches upon the issue of legitimacy: a choice for self-regulation, for example, is more legitimate if enforcement can be ensured within the self-regulatory context. Likewise, enforcement through technology itself can be viewed as legitimate if the 'code' enforces existing, democracy-based rules and does not superimpose other rules of itself.

From the perspective of enforcement, the starting points can thus be made somewhat more concrete. The starting point of internationalization, for instance, can be used and interpreted better in contexts where enforcement is viable at an international level; if, on the other hand, enforcement remains closely tied to territory, as will often be the case in for example criminal law, internationalization seems less useful as a starting point. 'Off-line = on-line' can be applied by looking at enforcement: where the available enforcement instruments and enforcement levels differ considerably in the on-line environment, such as in copyright law, different rules and regulation forms can be chosen in order to maintain a similar level of protection.

8.4   FUTURE OUTLOOK

The usability of the starting points appears to be smaller than the policy makers who came up with them perhaps may have hoped. Does this mean that it is better to forget about them, or is there still a way forward with the starting points? We think there is. We have argued that the starting points, in their entirety, are useful as a procedural checklist. People facing e-regulatory challenges can use this checklist to find heuristic methods for solving their problems. This heuristic approach would do justice to the legal pluralism that is required in the current complex and international information society.

The evaluation and concretization that we have aimed at for each starting point has yielded various suggestions for bridging the gap between the sweeping theory of each starting point and the unruly practice of real-life regulatory problems. Perhaps it is possible to draft a much more concrete checklist on the basis of our analysis, which would contain specific situations, contexts, sectors, and topics with an indication of useful applications of one or more starting points for each of these. This is a challenge for further research.

Still, one thing is blatantly absent and that is content. As we have pointed out, the starting points are procedural guidelines: they point to a method, but are empty as to what substantive direction regulatory decisions might take. Values are absent, and if there is one thing that is characteristic of regulation, it is that regulation is normative: it tells society which direction to take, it tells citizens, governments, consumers, and businesses alike what to do and what to leave undone. A checklist for e-regulation that fails to contain any indication of the direction that the information society is to take is a poor instrument for regulation developers.

Interestingly enough, it is precisely that many policy developers are trying to achieve. The World Summit for the Information Society, for instance, addressed many topics with an aim of providing substantive guidance as to where the information society should be heading. Most policy documents, of the European Union, the US, and Australia, for instance, also try and formulate basic values that policies and regulation should safeguard. Such policy documents are often topic-related, sector-driven, or context-specific: they do not address e-regulation at large, but real-world problems in certain areas of the information society. Another challenge, then, for further research, is to survey substantive principles and values that are explicitly or implicitly upheld in e-policy documents around the world. We expect that a similarly fragmented picture will emerge from such a survey, with values and ideals highly varying across continents and countries, and also across contexts, sectors, and topics, but nevertheless it seems useful to attempt some form of cataloguing of the substantive starting points that are considered to be relevant in the various domains of e-regulation.

Ideally, the results of such a substantive survey could be matched against our findings about the procedural starting points, in order to try and create a more balanced – and therefore perhaps more useful – checklist of starting points for e-regulation. It may turn out to be a doomed attempt but, to use a Dutch proverb, you are sure to miss if you never shoot.

For now, we have to make do with the limited usefulness of the starting points as we have outlined them in this book, as at most a procedural checklist for e-regulation. They are sweeping statements, often untrue and invalid, but sometimes useful. Sweeping statements have a function in themselves: they smooth complex situations by creating the impression that eternal truths exist, that there are ways to tackle every problem, and that always, somewhere, solutions exist. Perhaps, in order to cope with the myriad of e-regulation issues that the world currently faces, people simply need myths.

Chapter 9
SELECTED COMMENTS ON THEMES DEVELOPED IN THIS VOLUME

9.1   FOUR MYTHS ABOUT REGULATING IN THE INFORMATION SOCIETY –
       A COMMENT

Herbert Burkert

9.1.1   Introduction

One of the first things lawyers learn in their Legal Writing Course is to avoid terms like 'obviously'. Arguments are either convincing in themselves, in which case 'obviously' is not needed, or they are not obvious, in which case obviously is a dangerous camouflage only inviting deconstruction. Societies, however, need their assumptions on what is 'obvious' to avoid infinite regress. But they know better than to call these assumptions obvious; they avail themselves – to use Roland Barthes' intriguing concept – of myths, concepts which employ common notions, words, and pictures, give them meaning, and create a powerful association which surpasses the signs used, and their obvious meanings to create an unquestionable truth.[1] In the same way, the Information Society has created its own set of myths to simplify discourse and to immunize itself against criticism. Some of these myths are about regulating in the Information Society, and some of them will be commented on: the myth of technological neutrality, the myth of 'internationalization', the myth of 'code as code', and finally the myth of 'self-regulation.'

Before addressing these myths, two notes of caution seem to be necessary. Many of the phenomena I touch upon are associated with the Information Society in a manner that suggests causation as regards its main characteristic: information and communication technology. It is said, for example, that information and communication technology has caused (or at least significantly accelerated) internationalization. This in itself might constitute one of the myths of the Information Society; it seems sufficient to me to simply state that there is a *parallel* between the elements which we associate with the Information Society and, for example, internationalization.

---

[1]   Barthes 1957, p. 197 et seq.

B-J. Koops, et al. (Eds), Starting Points for ICT Regulation
© *2006, ITeR, The Hague, and the authors*

The other note refers to method. Whenever members of the 'law community' talk about phenomena of the kind mentioned, they should clarify the mode in which they are addressing issues. Is what they talk about meant to be descriptive, for example, do we see certain traits which reflect spatial or conceptual extension beyond the local, regional and national toward something international or even global as evidence of internationalization? Or is it that they hold and argue that internationalization is something that *should* be achieved, in other words, is the approach normative? Finally, are phenomena addressed because there is a discrepancy between what has been observed descriptively (A) and what has been demanded normatively (B) so that it is time to formulate strategies on how to move from (A) to (B), in short, is the discourse political? While, for reasons of space, I will not address all three levels for all four myths, I will at least try to keep these levels apart.

9.1.2   The myth of technological neutrality

Now and then, legislators in the Information Society are reminded to remember technological neutrality. Legislators claim that their regulations are indeed technologically neutral. Particularly when they resort to criminal law, a regulatory tool which offers itself whenever there is doubt, since it is symbolically potent but does not seem to involve costs, at least not directly, legislators claim to make sure that the world, and particularly its values, as we have known it will continue even if some appearances may have changed. In short, what has held off-line should, indeed, hold on-line.

Is this a correct description of what has happened in, for example, Internet regulation so far? If we look at the recent regulatory package of the European Union on electronic communication, we must concede that this package by its very term 'electronic communication' tries to group various technologies under one heading. Such an attempt, not fully successful upon closer analysis, seeks to combine, different technologies under one heading for certain competition-oriented aspects. Such an approach, however, is technologically sensitive rather than technologically neutral because it seizes upon the specific competition-related aspects of one group of technologies which seem to have characteristics in common which they do not share with other technologies or previous stages of those technologies.

But what about the area of Internet contents regulation, an area where that myth seems to flourish? The lower court judge who, in that famous Internet provider case in Munich some years ago, was chastised for applying the standards appropriate for booksellers who order books upon request of their customers to Internet providers, might see it differently. The consensus that at least Internet *access* providers should profit from a lower standard of responsibility had been reached rather quickly. Not necessarily everything that has been done on-line may lead to prosecution as easily as it would if it had been done off-line. On the other hand, looking at the plethora of copyright regulation in recent years, the more appropriate formula, seems to be that what still may be possible off-line, should certainly not be allowed on-line. And as a final example, we might look at the law of domain names. Domain names on the Internet can be treated like trademarks, indeed an example of some sort of neutrality; but trademarks on the Internet, in most jurisdictions, cannot co-exist, as trademarks in the off-line world, in different geographical areas.

These remarks are not meant as an entry point to a discussion on the merits of such regulatory approaches; rather they serve as simple reminders of the fragility of the 'off-line/on-line'-adequacy.

But would such an adequacy principle be desirable from a normative point of view? The equality principle requires that what is equal is to be treated equally, and whatever is different has to be treated differently. Technology provides a significant difference, in particular information and communication technology. ICT has changed information handling in our societies, making such handling less dependent on restrictions of quantity, distance, and complexity. This technology has removed what once were tacit, inherent barriers to the use of organizational power, to name just one set of its effects. Legislators always have the technologies of the day in their minds when they regulate. It is one of the tacit but nevertheless present assumptions in their minds on which they build their concepts. Consequently, to maintain the function of checks and balances in our societies, technology-specific responses to such changes in the power structure are needed. One such approach has been data protection (privacy) regulation. It has to be conceded that in the process of developing this concept of regulation, many legislators, included non-electronic automated and even manual data handling under the application of such laws. This happened under the urgent suggestion from the data processing industry, which claimed technological neutrality and feared discrimination against electronic data processing. This fear was justified: data protection legislation has to discriminate against electronic processing because of the specific risks of this technology. 'Paper-related' technologies were thus included, where they did occur, not because of some neutrality principle, but because even these paper-related technologies posed a threat in an environment that already contained electronic processing and was moving fast towards full electronic automation.

Why then has the 'off-line/on-line adage' received so much prominence when it has been observed so little? Times of change create special burdens for legal systems. Legal systems are more strongly pressed to provide orientation and at least mid-term stability and predictability. Legal systems are prepared to cope with change. Laws are by definition abstract rules of the past for concrete cases which occur in the future. However, in times of change, the law is confronted to a larger extent with the changing faces of phenomena, and it takes more time to evaluate which of the changes are essential and which are accidental. Again, this is an everyday task of the law, called interpretation, but with technological change, this task grows in quantity and complexity. However, the law takes its time; it is a process to deliberately slow down processes to be able to reflect on them. Times of change, however, are also used by all those forces which were frozen into the political compromise of past legislation. This is their moment to test whether these compromises still hold.

With technological change, new players also enter the scene claiming their own share. The time the legal system takes to adjust is therefore highly politically charged; court decisions are criticized, the patience to wait for high court decisions is running out, the legislator is under pressure to show to be in command. This is the time for symbolic legislation, which regardless to what extent it serves new interest groups or appeases the old ones, has to be seen to meet the challenge. One way, not the only one, but perhaps the most favored way, is to show that the old values will survive in the new world. Whatever real changes a new technology may bring, the 'Law of Suppression of Radical Potential'[2] has been shown to contain them, to integrate them, at least symbolically, into the old value system. This is the role of the 'off-line/on-line' myth. It is under this umbrella then that the new technology may eventually produce change. However, by then, it will no longer be noticed as change, the new shares will already have been distributed, and a new political compromise will have been frozen into law.

9.1.3 The myth of internationalization

Internationalization, or its younger brother globalization, are often attributed to information and communication technology but both phenomena are, in fact, examples of that need for caution mentioned in the introduction. They are not new phenomena, nor is law particularly inapt to deal with them. The International Law of Trade has a long history. Private International Law, which in spite of its name, has always been national law, has seen many successful attempts at harmonization. International trade law practice has heavily and successfully relied on the almost universal principles of contract law and on the processes of arbitration. There is the great example of European Union Law as a dynamically stable body of regional law.

What is changing, however, or to be more precise, what might be changing, are the parties affected by internationalization. Small and medium-sized companies and individual consumers as well as individual entrepreneurs may be exposed in larger numbers to the international effects of law. This implies a qualitative change: concepts of national or regional consumer protection, for example, are on their way to being introduced into international trade law which still builds on the classical contractual assumptions of equal and informed parties.

Currently, in spite of the heated battles at The Hague, all this remains speculation. It still remains to be seen to what extent economic restraints will lead to alternative solutions for conflicts in commercial exchanges (cutting losses, using trusted third parties, gestures of good will, alternative dispute resolution).

However, this trend in 'democratizing' the subjects of international law has another effect on internationalization, this time on internationalization as a process of rule-making. Being a possible subject of international law this raises interest to learn about how international law comes about. This is a process that can be dated

---

[2] Winston 1986, p. 23 et seq.

back to developments in another area where there has been a spill-over from national legislation into neighboring legislation: the area of environmental law, which, together with human rights, provided the source from which Non-Governmental Organizations started to grow. Their impact on the many national debates on internationalization helped to understand another aspect of internationalization: Internationalization proved itself to be a useful process for governments to introduce national change which they could not achieve directly as an international obligation which they had to follow to honor international law agreements. International agreements in turn have the advantage of being binding and leaving no space for modification: they are either accepted by national parliaments or they are rejected. Any possible parliamentary influence therefore shifts to the time of negotiation; negotiations, however, to be effective, are a prerogative of governments.

Democratizing such processes is painful and time consuming. In the European Union, for example, it took a very long time till national parliaments had developed institutions and political processes to exert some influence on their governments' position in the Council, a process which is not equally effective in all Member States and which still has a long way to go.[3]

In the end then, the 'democratization' of the potential subjects of international law at the era of ICT may lead to a democratization of the making of international law. Then again, this attempt to get a better hold on internationalization may prove to be elusive. In fact, neither the forums, nor the subjects, nor the actors of international regulation and of Internet-related regulation are particularly easy to grasp. There is an ongoing process of political 'forum shopping', of testing this international organization or that international organization and whether it could produce desired outcomes within a given time. There has been a time for the OECD, there has been a time for the WTO, there may be a time for the ITU, or at least with regard to some issues. There may be a time for all of them. There is space for multilateral, bilateral and, for some players, even unilateral approaches. While the pressure to democratize international rule-making may have increased, so have the possibilities of governments to change subjects, forums and participants. For governments, however, these processes have become more complicated. They, too, have to deal with more and different players in different arenas.

This increasing complexity also raises the chances of success for dedicated epistemic communities, communities, sharing cultural backgrounds and political beliefs, to use the interconnectivities of these multi-player, multi-issue, multi-forums games for dedicated interest-oriented efforts even if they operate outside governments or traditional power elites. They might use their expert knowledge for coalition building across interest divides, at least for a given period in time. The so-called 'cryptography' debate has provided some evidence for such potentialities.

Within such complex frameworks, there is an equal opportunity, however, for government approaches which build on unilateral strategies, provided such govern-

---

[3] Kohler-Koch 2003.

ments have access to sufficient resources or, at least, are perceived as having access to resources. So in parallel to the de-fragmentation of internationalization as just described, we come across equal evidence for attempts at hegemonial solutions.

What seems left of the myth of internationalization is therefore either de-fragmentation (including democratization) or hegemonial aspirations, or both.

9.1.4 The myth of 'Code as Code'

'Code as Code' is a comment again on the relationship between information and communication technology and law. It is a critical comment, building strongly on myths which exist about law. Law, this comment seems to imply, is too slow. When it finally does come into play, the 'hard' technical architecture/infrastructure with its own 'laws' is already in place, and law as a 'soft' social process can do little about it but further stabilize these architectures or seek minor remedies against its excesses.

This understanding of law and its technological environment is not new; it at least dates back to the early days of technology assessment when there was still hope that if law would only intervene early enough in the design of technological systems, it might have a stronger impact.

My interest here is not to review once again this understanding of the role of law in relation to technological change. Chances are that the answers reveal a similar dialectic tension as regards internationalization or technological neutrality.

It seems more interesting, however, to ask why such an old theme has been revitalized just now, and why it is now that it has received so much attention. Again, I would hold that it is the mythical quality of this concept that has been able to catch the attention.

'Code as Code' reconfirms, as I have shown, a commonly held suspicion about the effectiveness of the law. However, it is even more interesting because of what it does not say explicitly, but what it insinuates, and it is equally interesting because of what it remains silent about. 'Code as Code' renders governments as regulators insignificant; industries decide on architectures, either depending on their market power, unilaterally or by standardization among themselves, with governments formally providing the final stamps of approval. Even when competition law, that tends to favor standardization cartels anyway, tries to reign in unilateral solutions, it usually comes too late: as usually happens in network economies, *de facto* standards have been created by explicitly open, non-discriminatory practices to achieve lock-ins, at least they do so in the end.

Furthermore, by pointing to the 'hard' architecture, 'Code as Code' propagates a new sort of technological determinism, only this time, it is of course an enlightened determinism. There are indeed builders of these architectures, and it is not just the architecture which builds inevitable structures. Whatever these builders do, they seem to bypass governments, and whatever might be done to participate in architecture building would have to be done outside traditional regulatory processes as well. In short, whatever values can be embodied will be or should be decided on the basis of their sustainability in the market place.

'Code as Code', in this reading, finally reveals itself not as a neutral new approach to supplement other regulatory approaches in the Information Society. Rather, 'Code as Code' is a cultural code in itself by which assumptions of a specific society at a specific time seek to make their impact on other regulatory cultures which are still based on different assumptions. In short, 'Code as Code' might be read just as another myth joining the myth of internationalization in an attempt at unilateralism. It should be added, to avoid misunderstandings, that such attempts are not restricted to the United States. The European Union, with its reciprocity clause in the Database Directive, has shown similar tendencies, even if, in that particular case, perhaps with the silent agreement of the United States, that had intended to use this clause for its own internal interests.

9.1.5 The myth of 'Self-Regulation'

As so many myths, 'Self-Regulation' is a semantic puzzle: What the term seems to refer to is very often neither regulation, nor is it, in its effects at least, restricted to the 'selves' exercising it. Self-Regulation almost always implies regulatory overspill which withholds from those being spilled upon a say in further spilling. 'Self-Regulation' might rather be understood as a term for an already existing practice seeking legitimacy, with the expectation that its official recognition might eventually lead to a de-legitimation of other current practices still conflicting with those seeking self-regulation. A more adequate term that might help to demystify 'Self-Regulation' is the term used by Claire Cutler, Virginia Haufler and Tony Porter in a 1999 publication: *Private Authority and International Affairs.*[4] Of course, private authority lacks the charm of 'Self-Regulation' which borrows its name from the positive connotations of democracy which, after all, is nothing but a form of 'Self-Regulation'.

Private authority, to remain more precise then, has to be reckoned with. Regulation in complex economic systems is negotiated regulation; and if negotiated regulation failed, negotiated application will remain. Building on private authority saves resources and may even have efficiency gains. But building too strongly on private authority reveals a dilemma; it makes the Information Society appear too easily as a neo-feudal society, a perception that, by the way, has gained some popularity among those criticizing recent approaches to copyright and related rights in the Information Society.[5]

One way to balance this perception is the introduction of concepts like 'co-regulation'[6] which insists on the state setting the rules and boundaries of private authority, remaining silent, however, on the influence of private authority already

---

[4] Cutler, Haufler & Porter 1999.
[5] Drahos & Braithwaite 2002.
[6] Price & Verhulst 2000, pp. 133-198.

on the design of these frameworks. Furthermore, private authority, as a regulatory tool, suffers from deficiencies common to current regulatory tools in the public sector even more strongly, while it lacks some of the possible remedies for the latter. In an Information Society, governmental regulatory approaches are increasingly under pressure to become more transparent. The application of private authority remains, what it calls, 'private', and only in those instances when it endangers the very functioning of markets; competition law procedures, which very strongly rely on negotiation themselves, might bring such authority into the open, and even then basic materials, in the interest of business secrecy, would remain under seal.

Against such a background, it is very difficult to create sufficient trust for 'Self-Regulation', in its current format, to spread more widely in the Information Society, except as an ideological catchword.

9.1.6   Final observation

Technological Neutrality, Internationalization, Architecture and Self-Regulation are, not, of course, as they may seem by now, the Four Horsemen of the ICT Regulation Apocalypse. However, these terms do more than just describe characteristic traits of regulation in the Information Society. They contain a normative agenda precisely by avoiding a discussion of normative values, by setting tools in the place of goals. Like true myths they hide their own agenda under the layer of the apparent. As I have tried to show, internationalization, technical neutrality, architecture and self-regulation, with their tool approach, tend to marginalize other tools with which to build a more democratic society. The four myths tend to hold on to the existing structures of regulation, to current patterns in the distribution of information, communication channels, and processing capacities. At the same time, ironically, through their conservative character, they cannot avoid becoming more visible against the background of the progressive technological possibilities they themselves proclaim and thus they reveal their own deficits and fragilities even more clearly.

It will be up to the law community in the Information Society to bring such inconsistencies out into the open and to make its choices on which trends to favor, and which to avoid.

Chapter 9
SELECTED COMMENTS ON THEMES DEVELOPED IN THIS VOLUME

9.2 ICT AND CO-REGULATION: TOWARDS A NEW REGULATORY APPROACH?

Yves Poullet

In December 2003,[1] the World Summit on the Information Society (WSIS) adopted the 'Declaration of Principles' which was presented as a first attempt at a Global Information Society Constitution.[2] Certain provisions of this Declaration directly address the question of how to regulate the Information Society. The answer is clearly 'co-regulation', although the concept is not defined. Beyond this assertion, the text prescribes a clear partitioning of the roles of the different actors in the regulatory process.

1. The management of the Internet encompasses both technical and public policy issues and should involve all stakeholders and relevant intergovernmental and international organizations. In this respect it is recognized that:

a) The policy authority for Internet-related public issues is the sovereign right of States. They have rights and responsibilities for international Internet-related public policy issues;
b) The private sector has had and should continue to have an important role in the development of the Internet, both in the technical and economic fields;
c) Civil society has also played an important role in Internet matters, especially at the community level, and should continue to play such a role;

---

[1] The World Summit on the Information Society was organised by ITU in Geneva (10-12 December 2003). As previously decided, this first meeting will be followed-up by a second meeting, to be held in Tunis in 2005. The World Summit was the result of difficult, numerous, and intense discussions at regional and global levels. The text of the 'Declaration of Principles' is available at the ITU website: <http://www.itu.int/dms_pub/itu-s/md/03/wsis/doc/S03-WSIS-DOC-0004!!MSW-E.doc.>.

[2] The language used to introduce the Declaration is very enlightening on this point: 'We, the representatives of the peoples of the world, assembled in Geneva from 10-12 December 2003 for the first phase of the World Summit on the Information Society, declare our common desire and commitment to build a people-centred, inclusive and development-oriented Information Society.'

B-J. Koops, et al. (Eds), Starting Points for ICT Regulation
© 2006, ITeR, The Hague, and the authors

d) Intergovernmental organizations have had and should continue to have a fa-
    cilitating role in the co-ordination of Internet-related public policy issues;
e) International organizations have also had and should continue to have an im-
    portant role in the development of Internet-related technical standards and
    relevant policies.

2. I will come back to this important assertion but before doing so, some clarifi-
cation on the concept of co-regulation is needed.

Co-regulation is a multifaceted and ambiguous concept encompassing multiple
ways to ensure what the OECD,[3] in 1998, called the 'effective mix' of public and
private sectors in regulating the Internet. This first approach to the concept underlines the fundamental role of co-regulation as regards the 'effectiveness' of the
regulation, which is, as Ost and Van de Kerckove have excellently demonstrated,
only one of the three criteria as regards the legal validity of a normative instrument
beside the two other criteria: legality and legitimacy.[4]

3. In a previous essay[5] elaborating on these three criteria in the field of ICT regulations and taking fully into account the plurality of the norms,[6] particularly self-
regulation, I have proposed to redefine these three criteria as follows:[7]

a) Legitimacy is 'source-oriented'[8] and underlines the question concerning the
    authors of a norm. To what extent might the legal system accept a norm
    elaborated without involvement of the actors designated by the Constitution
    or by constitutional rules? This quality of the norm means that the authorities
    promulgating the norm must be authorized to do so by the community or
    communities of the persons who will have to obey this rule. This legitimacy
    is obvious as regards the traditional State authorities acting in conformity
    with the competence attributed to them by the Constitution. It is less obvious
    when the regulation is the expression of private actors, as is the case with
    self-regulation, particularly when certain obscure associations or even private
    companies are able to impose their technical standards.
b) Conformity is 'content-oriented' and designates the compatibility of the nor-
    mative content with fundamental social values, those undoubtedly embedded

---

[3] In Provision 50 of the WSIS Declaration of Principles, the Secretary General of the United
Nations is asked to set-up 'a working group on Internet Governance, in an open and inclusive process
that ensures a mechanism for the full and active participation of governments, the private sector and
civil society from both developing and developed countries, ... to ... make proposals for action, as
appropriate, on the governance of the Internet by 2005.'

[4] Gérard, Ost & van de Kerchove 1996.

[5] Poullet 2001.

[6] About the *pluralisme normatif*, which means the various possible sources of the norms and their
recognizance by the legal systems, see Coipel 2002 and Vivant 1996.

[7] Poullet 2001, p. 145 et seq.

[8] On this distinction between source-oriented tests, content-oriented tests, and effectiveness-ori-
ented tests, see Summers 1985.

in the legal texts but also beyond those considered as ethical values to be taken into account by the legal system, not only those unquestionably embedded in legal texts, but also those considered to be ethical values to be taken into account by the legal system. Again, this criterion is quite easy to satisfy and to verify for traditional texts issued by governmental authorities insofar as these texts must take into consideration of already existing rules with superior values. It seems more complicated to satisfy this criterion when compliance with existing legislative texts is not systematically checked insofar as these texts do not exist or are not clearly identified. Indeed self-regulation is often a way to avoid the traditional and constitutionally provided regulatory methods of rule-making.

c) Finally, effectiveness is 'respect-oriented'. To what extent will a norm be effectively respected by those to whom the norm is addressed? The question on the information about the existence of the norms, about the sanctions, and the way by which they might be imposed are therefore central for determining the effectiveness of a norm. This criterion refers in particular to the fact that the addressees of the norm must be aware of the content of the norm but also that the cost of a norm's non respect must be foreseeable by its addressees who are so stimulated to follow the rule.

On that point, it is quite clear that technology, as Joel Reidenberg[9] has pointed out, and self-regulatory mechanisms like code of conduct labeling systems or ODR might bring additional ways for promoting and enforcing the normative instruments.[10]

4.   These criteria will definitely be interesting in order to appreciate the legal validity of the different mechanisms designated by this concept. Certain mechanisms are more or less clearly defined. Among the more clearly defined mechanisms, count the French approach which has been defined in the context of the setting-up of the 'Forum des droits de l'Internet'[11] and the European vision which has been

---

[9] Reidenberg 1998. On the same point, my remarks about the relationship between law and technology in Poullet 2004, and finally, Lessig's fundamental reflections in Lessig 1999.

[10] Notably Marais 2002. About the characteristics of the Internet which justify a self-regulatory decentralized approach rather than the traditional top-down approach based on a legislative and nationally bounded approach, see Post & Johnson 1997: 'The ideal of national debate among wise elected representatives regarding the overall public good may be replaced, on-line at least, by a new architecture of governance that allows dispensed and complex interactions among groups of individuals taking unilateral actions and seeking more local goods and solutions. Instead of attempting to rely even upon the best of our democratic traditions to create a single set of laws imposed on the net from the top down, we may all be better off if we allow the emergence of diverse and contending rule sets, in distinct areas of the net, which pull and tug against each other (and that help to recruit or drive off potential participants) – with the result that an optimal overall combination of rules arises.'

[11] The Forum des Droits de l'Internet is a non-profit organization created with the financial support of the French Government. This Forum was created on the basis of the famous C. Paul's Parliamentary report, submitted at the request of the French Prime Minister to the Parliament in July 2000. About the history of the Forum's setting-up, see Falque-Pierrotin 2002 (I. Falque-Pierrotin is the Chair-

described in the Inter-institutional agreements on Better Law-Making recently approved by the European Parliament.[12] These mechanisms can be seen as a 'third way' next to legislation and self-regulation.

Apart from these two approaches, a wide variety of co-regulatory mechanisms has to be considered, which means a combination of private and public normative interventions in order to regulate the Information Society. We shall introduce these different approaches.

5.   Paul's Parliamentary Report already defined 'co-regulation' as a method and not as a normative source.[13] It justified recourse of this method as follows:

> 'Si les institutions démocratiques veulent remplir leur rôle sans se trouver court-circuitées par la réalité, elles doivent être capables de traiter les questions posées avec la rapidité et la pertinence nécessaires. Elles doivent le faire en écoutant davantage, en collaborant mieux avec l'ensemble des acteurs et des parties prenantes aux débats. Elles doivent savoir se focaliser sur les sujets dont les enjeux sont essentiels et où leur intervention est décisive, et laisser différentes formes – pas uniquement marchandes – d'autorégulation s'exercer là où elles suffisent à répondre aux attentes sociales. Il s'agit donc, non pas de définir une nouvelle forme de régulation, mais de trouver une méthode adaptée aux temps nouveaux.'

So, co-regulation aims at organizing a co-operation on rights and usage issues raised by the Information Society development between all stakeholders. Co-regulation is a consensus-building process giving all the players the opportunity to express their views and to agree on certain solutions which will have to be enacted in the legal system by state intervention. These legal solutions insofar they have been discussed between all actors will be more easily implemented and respected. The Forum's mission can be deduced from this aim:

- to submit opinions on the problems brought about the use of ICT technologies;
- to inform and sensitize the public on these issues;
- to organize, notably through a public forum discussion, a broad discussion on crucial topics among all parties interested;
- to make its best efforts to reach a consensus and, finally to address recommendations to the 'legislation' if needed.

Co-regulation in this sense is a pre-normative process. It intervenes in the preliminary phase and appears as a way to reinforce the legitimacy of State intervention

---

man of the Forum). See also the Forum's website: <http://www.foruminternet.org>. The French example was followed in Belgium through the creation by the Ministry of Economy in 2001 of the Internet Observatory (see the Observatory's website: <http://www.internet-observatory.be>).

[12] The European Parliament Decision of 9 October, 2003 (OJ C 81 E/84, 31.3.2004) is based on the Commission White Paper 'European Governance' (COM (2001)428 final).

[13] Ch. Paul's Report, *supra* n. 11, at p. 17.

insofar as the decision taken by the State after this consultation process will take into account the interests of all the players. At a certain point, this co-operation in the drafting of regulation will ensure its better effectiveness since each partner present during the preparatory phase will commit itself to respect the consensus searched and since enacted.

6.   The European conception of co-regulation considerably enlarges the role of co-regulation and envisages this mechanism not as a way to prepare future public regulation but as a tool to refine the content of the regulation enacted by the public bodies and to concretely implement it. On this point, I would like to comment very briefly the recent Inter-institutional agreement called 'Better Law-Making', concluded between the three legislative authorities of the European Union: the European Parliament, the Commission, and the Council of Ministers in order to improve the legislative production and the quality of European legislation.[14] In doing so, the Agreement underlines the essential place of co-regulation.

Without denying the interest of close co-operation between public and private players in the preliminary phase, the European Agreement clearly distinguishes this preliminary discussion from the co-regulatory mechanisms. The first concern is envisaged through the obligation imposed upon the European bodies to ensure the participation of all stakeholders at any step of the legislative process. As pointed out by the White Paper, 'the quality, relevance and effectiveness of EU policies depend on ensuring wide participation throughout the policy chain – from conception to implementation. Improved participation is likely to create more confidence in the end result and in Institutions which deliver policies'.[15] The White Paper thus suggests a 'more effective and transparent consultation at the heart of EU policy-shaping' through multiple channels: advisory committees, hearings, on-line consultations, etc.

The recently adopted inter-institutional agreement gives a precise definition of co-regulation: 'Co-regulation means the mechanisms whereby a Community legislative act entrusts the *attainment of the objectives* defined by the legislative authority to parties which are recognized in the field (such as economic operators, the social partners, non-governmental organizations, or associations).'

7.   This definition induces a clear partitioning of the responsibilities of the State, on the one hand, and of the co-regulation, on the other hand in the regulatory pro-

---

[14] The agreement (2003/2131(ACI)) does envisage all the societal issues and not only those raised by the Information Society development, even if these specific issues are mentioned as a test case by the White paper, *supra* n. 12.

[15] White Paper, *supra* n. 12, at p. 9. In that consultations process, the White Paper insists on the need to involve civil society: 'Civil society plays an important role in giving voice to the concerns of citizens and delivering services that meet people's needs. (White Paper, p. 14; see also: Opinion of the Economic and Social Committee on 'The role and contribution of civil society organizations in the building of Europe' (OJ C 329, 17.11.99, p. 30).

cess: the legislative authorities have to identify the *essential public policy objec-tives* when the means, by which they are met, are established by the public and the private sectors together. The private sector is mainly responsible for defining the means whereas the end result and objectives are identified by the legislative instruments. In short, the private sector must answer the question of 'how to implement them'. This partitioning of responsibilities is precisely the one also promoted by the WSIS Declaration of Principles when this Declaration asserts: 'Policy authority for Internet-related public policy issues is the sovereign right of States ... The private sector has had and should continue to have an important role in the development of the Internet, both in the technical and economic fields'.

It is therefore clear that public and private ordering mechanisms are not on the same footing. There is a sort of hierarchy insofar as co-regulation is viewed not as a substitute to public intervention but as a way to achieve (choice of the means) the end results imposed by the framework fixed by the State.

8. At the same time, through the provision quoted, the EU Agreement imposes certain limits upon the public legislator: 'The three institutions recall the Community's obligation to legislate only where it is necessary .... They recognize the need to use, in suitable cases or where the Treaty does not specifically require the use of a legal instrument, alternative regulation mechanisms.' The text clearly confirmed the double 'subsidiarity' of the legislative approach:[16] the first one was already asserted as a fundamental principle of the European Union functioning by Article 5 of the European Treaty and means that: the European Union institutions may only act on matters that might not be more adequately ruled at another inferior level.[17] According to that statement the subsidiarity principle clearly states that local solutions are still needed and must be preferred to international or global solutions, even if this international or European level might establish the general framework wherein these local solutions will take place and interoperate: 'Think globally, act locally'. In other words, local or sectoral solutions are the best way to take into account the cultural and business peculiarities of each situation and to develop adequate solutions otherwise, the regulation will be reduced to an enumeration of vague and broad common principles.

The second subsidiarity principle is quite new.[18] It provides not to legislate when other means to achieve the public objectives might be met in other ways, particu-

---

[16] On this principle, see Delpérée 2002.

[17] About this first traditional meaning, see Verhoven 2002.

[18] On that point see Timsit's reflections (Timsit 1996) about this new normative approach 'Lorsque l'Etat moderne est apparu, il a en effet trouvé sa traduction dans une droit qui conservait des origines historiques de son Auteur, l'Etat, le caractère mystique et abstrait dont celui-ci était paré. C'est ce droit qui a été le premier corps du droit- un droit abstrait, général et désincarné que j'appelle le droit-réglementation.... Abstrait et désincarné il ne correspond plus aux exigences de la gestion des sociétés post-modernes. Trop complexes pour être gérées aussi généralement, abstraitement et pour ainsi dire d'aussi loin, elles requièrent un autre droit – actuellement en formation – qui se caractérise, au contraire par son adaptation au concret, son rapprochement des individus, son adéquation au contexte exact des

larly self-regulation,[19] or to legislate only to the extent necessary to establish these public objectives, leaving the decision to the private sector as regards the right way to reaching these: co-regulation. Thus the second meaning of the concept envisages the subsidiarity principle as a way to validate and to specify the limits of the co-existence of the traditional regulatory model: the public one and the 'modern' ones: self-regulation and co-regulation. Everything that can be better addressed by co-regulatory or self-regulatory solutions must be fixed so addressed. Many prestigious authors have broadly asserted the complementarity of the two regulatory models.[20]

9.   Two exceptions are foreseen by the text: 'These mechanisms will not be applicable where fundamental rights or important political options are at stake or in situation where the rules must be applied in a uniform fashion in all Member States.' As regards the second exception, it may be feared that, under the pretext of ensuring a really unique market for Internet services, the European legislator pleads for having detailed legislation, leaving no place for co-regulatory or self-regulatory mechanisms. The second exception is questionable. Recently, in order to fight illicit or harmful content on the Internet, which undoubtedly is a question of public order, the European Council Declaration on Freedom of Communication on the Internet adopted on 26 May 2003,[21] has urged all Member States to encourage self- or co-regulation as regards Internet content regulation. About privacy, Directive 95/46 asserts that a code of conduct must be promoted and it is quite clear that self-regulatory mechanisms including technological solutions will ensure the needed data protection more efficiently than certain legislative texts.[22]

---

sociétés qu'il prétend régir. Concret, individualisé, contextualisé, c'est un droit que j'appelle de régulation. Le paradoxe est que ces deux corps du droit-de réglementation et de régulation- le second n'a été jusqu'à présent, ni connu, ni reconnu...' (p. 377).

[19] About the different merits of self-regulation compared to State regulation, read the sound synthesis and the references by C. Lazaro (Lazaro 2002).

[20] See recently Trudel 2002: 'Pour y obtenir des énoncés normatifs efficaces, il faut exprimer le droit en ménageant des ouvertures vers les autres normativités.' Cf., also Slaughter 1997, Reidenberg 1996, Katsch 1995. This principle of complementarity is developed broadly in environmental regulation where one call on the assistance of a multiplicity of self-regulatory and co-regulatory initiatives beyond the legislative intervention. On this point, see notably Jadot 2002.

[21] On 26 May 2003, the EU Council decided to extend by two years the previous Decision and Action Plan for promoting the safer use of the Internet by combating illegal and harmful content on global networks. The Decision focuses on the need to reinforce a certain number of actions which might be deemed as co-regulatory measures insofar as their enforcement will require full support, including financial and administrative support of the States, thus completing and improving the existing network of hotlines, ensuring co-operation between self-regulatory initiatives, development of quality site labels, benchmarking of filtering software and services, promotion of self-rating systems, etc. On that issue see our remarks on the progressive trend towards an EU co-regulatory system, d'Udekem-Gevers & Poullet, 2001.

[22] On the valuable interdependence of law, technology and self-regulation as regards privacy protection, see Reidenberg 2001: 'Each of the distinct forms of regulation embody inherent limitations that preclude adequacy for effective protection of Privacy.'

Perhaps, through this restriction, the Agreement wanted to recall the Council of Europe Convention principle whereby limitations to fundamental liberties might be enacted only through legislation in the formal sense. However, that principle does not forbid the possibility of co-regulatory measures next to the legislative material and compliant with it.

10. Other remarks might be made on the basis of the text. As regards the application of the triple criterion of the legal validity of a norm, the following can be stated:

- As regards the 'legitimacy' criterion: the text requires the representativeness of the parties involved and the transparency of the procedures followed within the co-regulatory process.
- As regards the 'conformity' criterion, the principle of 'added value' is repeated. The mechanisms may be used on the basis of criteria defined in the legislative Act. The idea is again to fight against the rigidity of the legislative solutions and for a supple mechanism for ensuring a continuous adaptation to the problems and sectors concerned. The European Commission ensures conformity also through mechanisms of notification, even control.[23]
- Finally, as regards the 'effectiveness' criterion, the co-regulation mechanism is deemed as being the way to attain the objectives defined by the legislative authorities. The main 'added value'[24] of self-regulation or co-regulation relies on this criterion insofar as co-regulation might set-up better adapted enforcement mechanisms more rapidly and efficiently (through label, accreditation, standardization, and ADR mechanisms) than the traditional judicial remedies.

11. The European approach of co-regulation is fundamentally a 'top-down approach'[25] rather than a 'bottom-up approach' following the distinction proposed by the Mandelkern Report written for the German Bundesministerium des Innern (BMI).[26] Under the 'top-down approach' or 'new approach',[27] that the essential

---

[23] 'These measures may provide, for example, for the regular supply of information by the Commission to the legislative authority on follow up to application or for a revision clause under which the Commission will report at the end of a specific period.' (Interinstitutional Agreement, n° 21 in fine).

[24] The 'added value' principle has been enacted quite clearly by the 'e-confidence forum' set-up by DG Sanco in order to define key principles as regards the acceptability of the self-regulatory methods (code of conduct, labelling system and ODR). As regards these principles, see the e-confidence website at: <http://econfidence.jrc.it/default/show.gx?Object.object_id=EC_FORUM0000000000000 00D>. These principles and, more broadly, the attitude of the EU authorities *vis-à-vis* self-regulation were commented on in: Poullet 2001a.

[25] On that point see, A. Massimo, The 'Better Regulation' Action plan and the Framework Action 'Up-Dating and Simplifying the Community Acquis', Rome, October 2003, available at: <http://www.astrid-online.it/qualitate/regolazion/Riunione-d/Iniziative/EC-Presentazione-Roma_def.ppt>.

[26] Mandelkern report, Moderner Staat – Moderne Verwaltung: Der Mandelkern-Bericht: Auf dem Weg zu besseren Gesetzen, available at: <http://www.staat-modern.de/dokumente/sm_bestellservice /,-548850/dok.htm>.

[27] As asserted in the European White Paper, COM (2001) 130 final, p. 7.

objectives, fundamental mechanisms, and mechanisms as regards the implementation and control of these objectives must be regulated by Governmental regulations and, insofar as it is possible, by legislation.

By contrast, the 'bottom-up approach'[28] designates any self-regulatory mechanism at a certain moment transformed or taken into account by Public Authorities. Schultz and Held[29] distinguish four cases illustrating the two approaches:

- A legislative text provides the co-regulatory mechanisms and encourages actors of the private sector involved to transpose by self-regulation the objectives pursued by the legislation (top-down approach).
- Self-regulatory mechanisms are surveyed or controlled by the State (top-down, bottom-up approach).
- Self-regulatory mechanisms developed in a first step beyond all intervention by the State are integrated within a legislative text (bottom-up, top-down approach).
- Public and private actors co-operate under diverse arrangements. Through their mixed interventions, which are placed on an equal footing, a better enforcement is given to certain rules (bottom-up, top-down approach).

The three last mechanisms clearly escape from the too strict definition given by the European text. However, they are illustrated by other ICT regulation mechanisms as will now be demonstrated, and must be considered 'co-operative approaches to regulation' following the OECD expression.[30]

12. The Australian way to regulate Internet content is often quoted as the perfect example of a co-regulatory approach. It illustrates perfectly the top-down approach suggested by the European Union by giving plenty of room for private actor intervention and free developments. In mid-1999, the Australian Parliament passed new laws aimed at regulating content on the Internet and setting up the Australian Internet Content Regulation Scheme.[31] In summary the scheme:

- enables the industry to set out procedures for itself through codes of practice, registered by the Australian Broadcasting Authority (ABA), which aim to provide a balanced and responsible approach to certain content issues;

---

[28] Palzer 2002; White Paper, *supra* n. 12, at p. 9.

[29] W. Schulz and T. Held, Regulierte Sellsregulierung als Form modernen Regierens, Hans Budow-Institut für Medienforschung, Hamburg, October 2001, available at: <http://www.tauss.de/sys_files/1030028087.54/Gutachten-Bredow-Institut>.

[30] Co-operative Approaches to Regulation, PUMA (Public Management) Occasional Papers, OECD, 97, available at the OECD website: <http://www.oecd.org/>. The Paper analyzes different cases of co-operation between public and private bodies in different sectors (chemical sector regulation, environmental regulation, and food safety regulatory issues).

[31] On the Broadcasting Services Amendment Act 1999 see, n° 90 amending the Broadcasting Services Act 1992. The text is available at: <http://www.scaleplus.law.gov.au/>. About the genesis of this text and a comparison with other approaches, see Granger 2000.

- includes a complaints system in which any person in Australia can complain to the ABA about offensive content they have accessed on-line;
- provides for an investigation process where the ABA is required to investigate the complaints and, based on classification decisions from the Office of Film and Literature Classification (OFLC), determine whether the content complained about falls into prohibited categories. If it does, the ABA may notify to the Internet Content Host (hereinafter: ICH) who hosts the content, requiring it to stop hosting the content. If the prohibited content is hosted overseas, the ABA notifies the makers of approved filters;
- includes a graduated scale of sanctions against ISPs and ICHs who fail to comply with the codes, notices to take down content, or ABA directions; and
- includes a community advisory body called NetAlert.[32] Its role and that of the ABA is to educate and inform the public about managing access to content on the Internet.

13.   The second case is 'TRUST UK'.[33] The multiplication of labeling systems in UK has provoked as elsewhere, confusion about the quality of each label. To tackle this problem the UK government[34] created a consortium (joint venture) together with consumer and business representatives in order to accredit the labeling systems which are committed to abiding the Trust UK Code of Practice. A Trust UK Complaint form has been drawn up so that consumers can appeal if neither the Web Trader nor their Code Owner have been able to resolve the problem.

This scheme was proposed in the White Paper 'Modern Markets: Confident Consumers', issued by the British Government,[35] and as an alternative to direct intervention by the State. Under this scheme, it is assumed that the private stakeholders will bear the entire responsibility for implementing the solution outlined by the public authorities after having consulted all interested parties. It is also clear that if the system were to fail, it would be the responsibility of the government to take-up its regulatory role again.

14.   The last case is quite controversial and its complete analysis would definitely go beyond the scope of this study. I do limit myself to a few reflections.

The WIPO Internet Domain Name Process might be considered another way of co-regulation or, as Froomkin[36] called it, as a 'semi-private process', which means 'a cooperative endeavour between a public body and private interests that is designed to create a body of rules enforced by some mechanism other than direct promulgation by the public body'.[37]

---

[32]   About Netalert, see website: <http://www.netalert.net.au/00051-What-is-Co-regulation.asp>.
[33]   See the Trust UK website at: <http://www.trustuk.org.uk/>.
[34]   About the history of Trust UK, see De Bruin 2002, p. 146 et seq.
[35]   Available at: <www.dti.gov.uk/consumer/whitepaper>.
[36]   Froomkin 2000 and 2000a.
[37]   According to Froomkin, semi-private rule-making should not be confused with either negotiated rule-making. A Government agency or other public body meets with representatives of the group

The Uniform Dispute Resolutions Procedures rules were drafted by an international public body not as an intergovernmental resolution[38] or convention but as a simple Experts' Report finally approved ICANN,[39] a US private non-profit organization. Without repeating all the details of the WIPO drafting procedure, broadly criticized by a number of authors, it may be concluded with Froomkin that: 'A semi-private process led by a public body (like the WIPO Internet Domain Name Process) risks combining some of the worst features of both traditional regulation and private ordering: opaque decision-making is easy. In some cases, the process may be managed by a body acting outside its jurisdiction. The public-private blind may also insulate the process from judicial review since it falls outside the categories that courts would tend to think of as within their purview'.[40]

All these issues might be also raised as regards the functioning of ICANN itself. The origin of ICANN demonstrates the deep link between the US government and this 'independent' private body.[41] This US governmental control is still present even if, according notably with European Union pressure,[42] a more democratic way of rule making ensuring a better participation of the different continents and a

---

that will be affected by the regulation, and seeks to find agreement on rules that can be promulgated and enforced by the Government. True self-regulation excludes the participation of a public body.

[38] As a follow-up to the US White Paper: 'Statement of Policy on Management of Internet Names and Addresses' (U.S. Department of Commerce, 1998), the World Intellectual Property Organization (WIPO) initiated an international process to develop recommendations on certain intellectual property issues associated with Internet domain names (First Internet Domain Name Process: Compatibility between trademarks and domain names (started 8 July 1998, ended 30 April 1999); Second Internet Domain Name Process: Compatibility between certain names and domain names (ended 3 September 2001). It is quite interesting to underline the adoption by the WIPO during this process of the Request for comment (RFC – 1 and 2) procedure which is typically used by private bodies like ICANN, IETF and private standardization bodies and the fact that governments (especially the European Commission, see the EU Commission Reply – 29 October 1998) have intervened in the context of this procedure. Source: The Management of Internet Names and Addresses: Intellectual Property Issues, Final Report of the WIPO Internet Domain Name Process, 30 April 1999, ANNEX II, List of Governments, Organizations and Persons Submitting Formal Comments: <http://arbiter.wipo.int/processes/process1/report/index.html>.

[39] It must be underlined that only the WIPO secretariat was involved in the drafting of the rules. The rules were forwarded to ICANN without first being approved by the WIPO General Assembly. ICANN adopted the UDR Policy aimed at settling disputes arising out of abusive registration and use of domain names.

[40] The comparison between this WIPO rule-making and the US Federal Agencies' rule-making is quite interesting on that point. According to the Administrative Procedure Act, certain requirements have to be taken into account by the Agencies. So the obligations: 1. to issue a notice of the proposed rule-making and to ensure its large publication 2. to give to everyone the opportunity for comments, 3. to consider there comments and motivate the attitude of the Agency *vis-à-vis* these comments. Finally, it must be underlined that each person affected by the Agency's decision might challenge it before the Court and that for different reason ('arbitrary and capricious rule', 'outside of the reasonable'). On all these points, see Froomkin 2000a.

[41] See Mounier 2000; Iteanu 2002; Froomkin 2002, quoting S. LYNN, ICANN President: 'Each of ICANN's accomplishments to date have all depended, in one way or another, on government support, particularly from the United States' and Delmas 2002.

[42] On these pressures, see Delmas 2002.

more transparent way of deliberating has been progressively installed.[43] It is quite interesting to underline that one of the major modifications introduced has been the setting-up of a Governmental Advisory Committee (the GAC). This creation illustrates that co-regulation might lead to a reversal of the traditional hierarchy insofar as governmental authority has a simple consultative voice in the ICANN's process of rule-making. Very severely concerned is Albert[44] 'This ultimately means we are left with a self-regulatory organization managing core resources of the Internet, directly controlled neither by the governments of this world, nor by the users of the virtual world. Instead at the end of the day ICANN is controlled by the industry protecting their profitable monopolies and to make everybody outside the US even more concerned about the future of self-regulation by representatives of the unilateralist US Administration.'

15.   These criticisms highlight the dangers linked with certain co-regulatory schemes. The main fear is what economists call the 'regulatory capture',[45] i.e., the fact that the regulatory power is given to certain bodies in a non-transparent way. This may be the case when decisions are taken in a non-transparent way. Insofar as co-regulation could create confusion between public authorities' and private bodies' competences, this fear might be founded. The risk of seeing rule-making deeply influenced by the interests of a specific group as regards the content of the rule leads to a 'spill-over effect.'[46] Another concern is definitely the difficulty to ensure that 'those who are affected by conduct that is the subject of particular rules must have some voice in determining the content of their rules.'[47] This 'legitimacy' question of certain co-regulatory norms especially when the co-regulation is not organized by the law itself, is not easy to solve. It requires a transparent rule-making process and all the opportunities given by the Internet to reach a maximum of transparency and open debate.[48] It is quite clear that intervention in certain co-regulatory schemes of public bodies like GAC or WIPO might create a false appearance of legitimacy, which would be an additional risk.

---

[43] Read the interesting debate between Palfrey, Chen, Hwang, Eisenkraft: 'Public Participation in ICANN' and Mc Laughlin: 'The Virtues of Deliberative Policymaking: A Response to 'Public Participation in ICANN'.

[44] Albert 2003.

[45] On that issue, see Brousseau 2001 and Mueller 1998.

[46] So a number of authors have denunciated the fact the WIPO rules focus mainly on the protection of IPR holders and have not sufficiently taken into account other general interests like competition and privacy questions (see notably Mueller 1999).

[47] Post & Johnson 1997 and 1999. These authors emphasize the absolute need to control the spill-over effects of self-regulation or co-regulation by a systematic assessment of the different rules adopted by the self-regulatory bodies.

[48] See the constant reference to the procedural Ethic developed by Habermas as a way to solve the legitimacy problem raised by these new normative approaches, in Froomkin 2003, p. 800, and Maesschalk & Dedeurwaerdere 2002.

16.   In conclusion, my intention is definitely not to reject any form of co-regulation. On the contrary, certain schemes like those promoted by the WSIS and the European Union, might bring what is needed by the Internet: more decentralized and adapted regulatory framework allowing each community to take its own responsibility and providing certain added value to the legal framework enacted by national or even international constitutional authorities. Other forms of co-operation between public and private authorities do not have to be excluded but, in these cases, respect for the three fundamental criteria of legitimacy, conformity, and effectiveness must be scrupulously evaluated.

Chapter 9
SELECTED COMMENTS ON THEMES DEVELOPED IN THIS VOLUME

9.3   COMMENT ON 'SHOULD ICT REGULATION BE UNDERTAKEN AT AN INTERNATIONAL LEVEL?'

Dan L. Burk

9.3.1   Introduction

In chapter 6 of this Volume, Prins outlines an argument for the international co-ordination and harmonization of laws governing Internet activity. In this ambitious undertaking, Prins attempts to outline the situations in which international rule-making will be most viable, and the criteria that indicate prospects for effective international rule-making. At the same time she sounds a cautionary note, arguing that successful international regulation will require a clear understanding of the purposes that justify harmonized or unitary regulation. As a practical matter, she argues for an incremental and flexible approach that respects and preserves to the extent possible the fundamental principles of national regulatory systems.

This case for Internet regulation at the international level is in many instances compelling, however, as Prins recognizes, enthusiasm for an international regulatory approach must be tempered by caution over the potential costs and drawbacks of centralized hierarchical control. Improperly applied, international Internet regulation threatens to negate the very benefits that make the network most valuable, and could in fact negate the very benefits that the regulation is intended to preserve.

In this comment, I briefly discuss two related cautionary models implicated by Prins' argument for international regulation. I begin by more fully developing the inter-jurisdictional competitive principles touched upon in her analysis; I then extend the basic concepts of that model to discuss implications of international regulation in light of network effects in the market for law. I conclude that these models point to only a limited and particularized case for international regulation in order to preserve the benefits of decentralized innovation in law. Consequently, in any given instance, the case for harmonized international regulation must be evaluated according to its potential for curtailing the competitive benefits of localized regulatory innovation.

B-J. Koops, et al. (Eds), Starting Points for ICT Regulation
© 2006, ITeR, The Hague, and the authors

9.3.2 Law as a product

In 1956 Charles Tiebout published his now classic paper modeling local provision of public services on a theory of inter-jurisdictional competition that closely resembles market competition for provision of private goods.[1] Tiebout theorized that if citizens are free to migrate between jurisdictions, competition for desirable citizen immigrants will arise. Local communities will offer to potential immigrants the most attractive packages of goods and services at the lowest tax rate possible. Similarly, migrants will relocate to jurisdictions offering the maximum package of public goods at the tax rate that the migrant is willing to pay. Local communities may even tailor their offerings to appeal to particular types of immigrants, and immigrants would be expected to sort themselves out into groups of similar means and tastes by jurisdiction.[2]

The production of local public goods and services might thus resemble the production of private goods in a competitive market: competitive pressure from other jurisdictions will prevent any given jurisdiction from offering too much or too little in the way of public services.[3] Jurisdictions that offer too much will experience an influx of immigrants from less generous jurisdictions; jurisdictions that offer too little will experience an exodus to more generous jurisdictions. Migration in or out of the jurisdiction will continue until parity with competing jurisdictions is reached.[4] These forces therefore act as a check on over production or under production of local public goods. By 'voting with their feet', or exiting, citizens force efficiency in allocation of resources to such goods.[5]

Business firms were not part of Tiebout's original model, but his insight was quickly expanded to encompass strategic preferences of local governments regarding such firms. Just as in the consumer/citizen model, businesses too may 'vote with their feet', locating their operations in jurisdictions that offer the most attractive set of local public goods.[6] This in turn implies that jurisdictions may tailor their offerings to attract businesses, or to attract certain kinds of desirable businesses, or even to repel undesirable businesses.[7] In this 'market' for business migration, the 'price' of migration may take a variety of forms: jurisdictions may offer anything from tax incentives, land grants, and liability waivers to museums, sports arenas, and public transportation systems.[8]

Local law comprises an important component of each jurisdiction's competitive package. Regulation with economic effects may be tailored to foster and attract certain industries. For example, environmental regulations may be eased in order to

---

[1] Tiebout 1954.
[2] McGuire 1974.
[3] Stiglitz 1983, p. 18.
[4] Stigler 1972, p. 93.
[5] Mueller 1979, pp. 126-127.
[6] Easterbrook 1983, p. 28.
[7] Easterbrook 1983, p. 43; Rose-Ackerman 1981, p. 157.
[8] Breton 1991, p. 42.

lower the operating costs of favored industries. Patent and copyright laws may be strengthened in order to maximize the economic return to industries that generate new innovation. Corporate and partnership laws may be designed to accommodate investment and control structures amenable to certain industries. Indeed, development of desirable law 'products' may be even more important to attract and retain high-value businesses activity than it is to attract and retain high-value individuals.

We would therefore expect that competition for business and for desirable immigrants will prompt jurisdictions to compete with one another to offer the most attractive law 'products' – in effect, creating a market for law. Optimally, such competition will tend toward not only the production of law that is differentiated to suit certain business profiles, but also to produce better and more efficient regulation – the threat of losing businesses to another jurisdiction will tend to weed out the inefficient legal regimes. However, as Prins notes, it is also possible for this race to the top to become a 'race to the bottom'. The Tiebout model assumes that jurisdictions are tightly compartmentalized so that no external costs or benefits accrue from the local provision of public services.[9] If jurisdictions are 'leaky', then individuals could perhaps enjoy the positive benefits of a neighboring jurisdiction's policy without actually incurring the cost of migrating there.[10] More significantly, in a world of 'leaky' borders, jurisdictions could lower the costs to local firms by imposing all or part of those costs on neighboring jurisdictions.[11] This would serve to attract firms, but not necessarily by generating a net gain in efficiency.

Consequently, in a world of 'leaky' borders, the race to the bottom might best be characterized as a race to externalize – for jurisdictions to seek ways to gain at the expense of their neighbors. Because the costs are imposed upon others, jurisdictions will tend to overspend on law 'products', offering incentives for which they themselves need not pay the costs. The Internet of course is a source of transborder leakiness, at least for digitized products and for data migration. This raises the concern that that the Internet may trigger such races to externalize costs, providing a conduit for local costs to be imposed upon other jurisdictions.

Thus, to take a recent, prominent, and hotly debated example, one possible characterization of the peer-to-peer music file-sharing phenomenon, whereby digitized music, software, and sometimes movies are shared via the Napster, Kazaa, or other services, is that implicating a race to the bottom. Much of the supply of such files comes out of jurisdictions with lax copyright law or lax enforcement; and indeed, businesses supplying software for such file-sharing have taken advantage of the attractive incorporation law and legal immunity provided by small and somewhat obscure jurisdictions such as the Pacific island of Vanatau. Lurking in permissive jurisdictions, these entities free-ride off of the creativity fostered in protective jurisdictions, using the Internet as a conduit to bleeds legitimate incentives away from the owners and producers of valuable creative works.

---

[9] Inman & Rubinfeld 1997, p. 83.
[10] Stiglitz 1983, p. 48
[11] Romano 1993, pp. 5-6.

But in branding such a scenario an inefficient 'race to the bottom' we must exercise care. Early analyses of incorporation races among jurisdictions in the United States branded this race a 'race to the bottom', a race to benefit corporate officers at the expense of shareholders. Later, more careful analyses suggest that it may in fact have been a 'race to the top', a competition among jurisdictions to produce the best package of corporate law 'products'. In making such characterizations, the perspective adopted may dictate the conclusion.

Thus, in our peer-to-peer file sharing example, a rather different story might be told on the same facts: in this version, off-shore encouragement of peer-to-peer entrepreneurship becomes a race to the top, forcing a bloated and complacent U.S. entertainment industry to revise its archaic and outmoded business models. On this view, consumer adoption of digital technology has outstripped the recording label's sluggish pace of change, creating a gap between consumer demand and the outmoded product provided by entertainment firms. Peer-to-peer entrepreneurship filled that gap, providing not only innovative distributional services, but models for traditional entertainment firms to emulate. Without the harsh market discipline of file sharing, the authorized music downloading services now beginning to cater to consumer demand might never have been launched.

Law Cartels

Much like a classic private-sector economic cartel, governments that participate in an international agreement may be able to avoid 'ruinous competition' in the market for law as a good. By standardizing the law product, they may succeed in effectively fixing the 'price' for business migration. Taking copyright as an example in the Internet context, enforcement of high protectionist standards would prevent cartel nations from lowering their 'price' to attract information distributors – that is, so-called 'pirates'. Fixing the price for information distributor migration would in turn allow domestic producers to avoid foreign information competition, and engage in monopoly overcharge for information products.[12] On an international scale, this type of monopoly overcharge effectively taxes non-producing nations – particularly developing nations – to support the information producers of the developed world.[13]

Such collusive international activity may be highly advantageous to politicians at the national level.[14] First, through collusion with foreign politicians, domestic politicians can protect themselves against superior foreign law products. Exodus of firms to more attractive regulatory regimes may place domestic politicians and bureaucrats under pressure to streamline local regulation, perhaps at the expense of favored but inefficient rent-seeking constituents.[15] Such streamlining may, how-

---

[12] Easterbrook 1983 p. 39.
[13] Ibid., p. 39.
[14] Vaubel 1991, p. 32.
[15] Breton 1991, pp. 39-40.

ever, be avoided by agreement with foreign counterparts to co-operate in suppressing formulation of more efficient regulation in their respective jurisdictions.

At the same time, local politicians may use an international agreement to deflect domestic voter dissatisfaction over domestic special interest legislation, by characterizing the local protectionist measures as a necessary part of international co-operation. This in essence facilitates *intra*-jurisdictional externalization of regulatory costs: rather than shifting costs to other jurisdictions, costs are shifted to a different constituency within the jurisdiction.[16] Thus, international collusion may prevent not only 'exit' from correcting political improvidence, but may also suppress the 'voice' of internal constituents from prompting correction.

Returning to our example of peer-to-peer technology, we might query whether the active campaign for increased intellectual property protection in the face of widespread file sharing fits this model. Indeed, this characterization suggests that the fierce lobbying and advocacy campaigns waged by the entertainment industries have merely been rent-seeking, attempts to preserve their current business position by legislative fiat, which may be had for a small investment in lobbying activity – cheaper than making the sizeable investment necessary to restructure their outmoded business model. If this characterization is correct, elevating the results of such lobbying efforts to the international level only encourages socially inefficient behavior by removing the possibility of more efficient extraterritorial competition.

However, the success of national protectionists, or any other group of price-fixers, requires a stable cartel, and cartels of any sort are notoriously unstable.[17] Such instability results in part from a sort of 'Prisoner's Dilemma' version of the 'race to the bottom' effect. Cartels extract monopoly profits by agreeing to restrain output so as to be able to push prices to monopoly levels that would be impossible to maintain if the members engaged in production at competitive levels. Cartel members therefore have a strong incentive to cheat: if a cartel member engages at competitive level production while competitors restrain output, the cheater can reap enormous profits. But since all members of the cartel are tempted by this same possibility, one member is unlikely to be able to cheat without triggering cheating by all the other members, leading back to competitive pricing and loss of the profits that prompted the cheating.

In the case of private economic cartels, a collusive organization is believed to be most feasible and stable where the quality of the product is homogeneous, the price elasticity of demand for the product is low, barriers to entry are high, all suppliers of the product have similar cost functions, and there is a dominant supplier who can act as price-leader.[18] In the case of international collusion over Internet law 'products', several of these requirements may be met by the configuration of participation in law production.

---

[16] Trachtman 1993, p. 57.
[17] Stigler 1977.
[18] See *supra* n. 14, at p. 33.

First, it would appear that the universe of law producers on an international scale is largely closed, forming something of a barrier to entry. New nations do not arise with particular frequency, and when they do, the circumstances of their inauguration – such as revolution or social upheaval – will likely deter information producers from relocating to take advantage of whatever new law products they choose to offer. Additionally, accumulation of 'legal capital' poses a barrier to jurisdictions attempting to enter the law product market. In Roberta Romano's classic analysis of the 'race to the top' for incorporation law in the United States, firms that incorporated in Delaware repeatedly referred to the large body of settled case law on corporations as a reason for incorporating there.[19] Similarly, nations with a long history of well-developed information law may be especially attractive to information distributors seeking to locate their operations, especially if the jurisdiction sports 'specialty courts' with a high degree of expertise. The certainty offered by a well-developed body of relevant law may in many instances offer greater business value than would relaxed regulation of information distribution. New entrants into the information law market may have their work cut out for them in order to displace the law products of well-established jurisdictions.[20]

Price-leadership or 'dominant firm' effects may also be seen in the market for law products. The number of sovereign states is relatively large, but certain nations, particularly the United States, are able to exert considerable diplomatic and economic pressure toward conformity.[21] By promulgating its copyright and patent law products as a proposed standard for inclusion within the Berne treaty revisions, or TRIPs trade agreements, the United States was attempting to co-ordinate the international market for such law products. The European Union has taken much the same approach in promulgating its standards for data privacy protection and proprietary database protection.

Barriers to product substitution may also exist. The price elasticity of demand for law products has in the past been tied to firm location, depending on the type of law in question. The incorporation law of one state may be an acceptable substitute for that of another, because a firm need not physically move to make the substitution. However, when firms must physically move to substitute law 'products', they may be locked into one legal standard by the cost of migration. The Internet itself, by increasing firm mobility, increases the ability of law 'purchasers' to substitute one jurisdiction's law product for another. By substantially lowering or eliminating that cost, the Internet destabilizes the ability of nations to collectively set an international standard for intellectual property law.

If the conditions for a stable intergovernmental cartel can be attained, the expected damage to innovation and competition will follow naturally from the principles outlined in the literature on law as a product. First, by homogenizing national intellectual property systems, an international agreement forces international busi-

---

[19] Romano 1985, pp. 258-261, 274-275.
[20] Romano 1993, p. 40.
[21] Hamilton 1996, pp. 615-616.

nesses to operate in a world where 'one size fits all'. Opportunities for jurisdictional experimentation and innovation are curtailed.[22] New information industries that might have arisen under innovative schemes may be stifled. Established information industries will be confined to an international norm, rather than offered the opportunity to select from a diversity of systems that which is best suited to their operation. As a corollary effect, information firms will be exposed to greater business risk because they will be less able to diversify across jurisdictions.[23] Thus, the international inefficiencies resulting from an international intellectual property cartel may be no less serious than the inefficiencies resulting from lack of co-ordination.

Law Centralization

Prins has elaborated how, in some situations, certain types of defection may be desirable in order to create inter-jurisdictional law competition, but how in other situations defection may lead to an undesirable race to externalize. If in fact co-operative strategies prove impossible or unworkable, rational competitors may have yet another option. If 'horizontal' co-operation between jurisdictions proves unstable, the creation of a 'third party' standing in a vertical relationship to the competitors may be necessary.[24] Charles Tiebout recognized this in his original model by noting that where externalities exist, centralized decision-making, rather than inter-jurisdictional competition, may be required to achieve an efficient outcome. This principle may also be stated in game theoretic terms: because states know that their own rational short-term competitive preferences will inevitably lead to their own detriment in the long-term, states may choose to voluntarily surrender all or part of their decision-making power to a third party.

The 'third party' approach is in essence the strategy adopted by the individual states of the United States in acquiescing to the constitutional compact that creates a centralized federal government'[25] similar benefits may be found in the federal compacts of Canada and Australia,[26] and to some extent that of the European Union.[27] Interestingly, it is also much the strategy adopted by the GATT signatory nations in creating the World Trade Organization (WTO).[28] However, any movement toward centralization should preserve to the extent possible the benefits of inter-jurisdictional legal diversity. For example, in the United States, the benefits of interstate competition have also been preserved to the extent deemed practical.[29] Because competitive benefits will be lost in whichever markets are centralized, centralization must be considered a drastic measure to be taken only where no such

---

[22] Vaubel 1991, p. 29.
[23] Idem.
[24] Breton 1991, pp. 48-49.
[25] LeBoeuf 1994.
[26] Sproule-Jones 1975.
[27] Buchanan 1995/1996, pp. 266-267.
[28] Komuro 1995.
[29] Epstein 1987, p. 1454.

efficiencies are to be had; that is, where externalities prevent the development of competition in the first instance.[30] Therefore, international centralization for Internet-related information rights should likewise be approached with a minimalist attitude, if at all. As Prins points out, this requires a careful consideration as to which areas truly generate externalities that would undermine information product creation, and then careful limitation of the central authority to those areas.[31]

9.3.3 Law as a standard

The model of Internet law centralization as an international law cartel implicates another set of economic models related to the standards-setting for technical compatibility. On this view, the 'harmonization' process for international Internet law essentially comprises a standards-setting process, establishing uniform legal standards across multiple jurisdictions. Standards-setting is a necessary exercise for technical design; as any traveler carrying an electrical appliance has discovered, the costs of non-uniform technical standards can be profound: voltage, current, and plug configuration vary enormously among different jurisdictions, requiring either expensive duplication of compatible appliances, or a panoply of adapters and transformers allowing a non-compatible appliance to interoperate with the local standards. Co-ordination of technical design, even among competitors, is often necessary to avoid the costs and inconvenience associated with such technical incompatibility.

As an international network, the Internet presents not only issues related to such actual compatibility of technical products, but also to the virtual compatibility of legal products. Both sets of issues arise as a consequence of so-called 'network effects'. Network effects may arise in situations where the value of a system increases as users are added.[32] Purchasers of such goods find the good increasingly valuable as others also purchase the good. Typically, the increased value accrues to subsequent adopters, and accrues as a positive externality.[33] For example, a telephone system is of relatively little value if it has only two subscribers; each subscriber can call only one other person.[34] The system is of greater value if it has more subscribers, because each subscriber can then communicate with many others. Those who subscribe to the system after it has accrued a large number of subscribers may obtain a more valuable service than those who subscribed early, when there were few other subscribers. At the same time, the value of the service to the early subscribers grows as additional users sign on to the network.

This insight can be generalized to other types of human artifacts with shared compatibility: languages, for example, may be thought of as goods having network

---

[30] Breton 1991, p. 46.
[31] Posner 1992, p. 635.
[32] Katz & Shapiro 1985.
[33] Liebowitz & Margolis 1994, p. 135.
[34] Katz & Shapiro 1985, p. 424; Liebowitz & Margolis 1994, pp. 139-140.

effects. The ability to 'interoperate' internationally with a wide diversity of individuals is illustrated by the benefits of speaking Greek in the ancient Western world, Latin in the Medieval Western world, or English in the current global era. As another common example, many commentators have noted that computer operating systems tend toward a uniform standard because of the natural benefits of a uniform standard: users need only invest in learning the characteristics of the system once, technical support for a single standard is simple to provide, and producers of compatible software applications need only develop products to function with a single platform.

The Internet itself, not surprisingly, is a prime candidate for display of such network externalities: network access becomes more valuable as it becomes more ubiquitous.[35] Much of the success of the Internet itself is due to the creation of a new type of physical network: the internetworking protocols on which the Internet operates allow disparate types of computer hardware, running many different software systems, to interact on a single network. Thus, users with previously incompatible equipment can now join the same system and interoperate. Additionally, any given application run on the network may show a different kind of network effect from usage: e-mail, for example, is a more valuable service if it can be used more widely. Similarly, the World Wide Web becomes more valuable as it accumulates more reference linkages, allowing more information to be indexed and accessed.

Both types of network activities are simultaneously possible because the Internet exhibits more than one type of network effect, a point that may require some brief explanation. Katz & Shapiro have distinguished between actual and virtual networks.[36] Actual networks may be characterized as those that physically interoperate with one another; virtual networks as those that share common features without direct interoperation. To the extent that the Internet generates benefits to users by having their machines physically connected to the network, allowing interaction between users, it represents an actual network. Whereas the benefits accruing from similarity of software platforms or, for that matter, from the content on the system, comprise a virtual network of shared compatibility. By providing a common technical standard, the Internet generates both types of beneficial effects.

The creation of a common standard is often beneficial, and indeed may be critically important, where network efficiencies can be realized. At the same time, the potential downside of any standards setting process is profound.[37] Networks may also produce negative effects, as the cost of leaving the network, even when it would be socially desirable to do so, may be prohibitively high. The likelihood of 'lock-in' to an inefficient standard remains a disputed, but nonetheless serious consideration.[38] The concern in such situations is that once a standard is adopted, net-

---

[35] Lemley & McGowan 1998, p. 551.
[36] Katz & Shapiro 1994, p. 95.
[37] Shapiro 2001, p. 88.
[38] Leibowitz & Margolis 1994; Leibowitz & Margolis 1990.

work effects may raise the cost of changing to a newer or better alternative causing the standard to become permanently entrenched. This may possibly occur where the short-term costs of switching away from the old standard are greater than the long-term benefits of the new standard – indeed, it has been argued that development of new standards may be deterred if network effect raise the short-term cost of development and deployment is above the perceived savings of a new standard.

As a consequence, the development of standards carries potential risks to competition, related to the potential negative consequences of network effects. Eventually, the prevailing standards in a networked industry might be displaced by the promulgation of new or better standards, but there is a serious danger of anti-competitive manipulation of the standards-setting process, or the standard itself, to achieve some form of market dominance.[39] Standard-setting organizations, for example, may sometimes cloak anticompetitive cartel-like activity if their membership is limited and conditions permit them to control adoption of the standard.[40] Either within or without an organizational setting, it has been argued that a dominant industry player may be able to arrange 'tipping' of the market toward a desired standard; presumably, a proprietary standard that can be controlled or exploited by that producer. Network effects may be manipulated in these situations to 'lock' users into the standard, frustrating new entry or technological improvement

Law may also be characterized as a system with network effects, displaying the same standardization issues familiar from analysis of technological standards. Legal harmonization facilitates a virtual network of compatible legal standards. Efficiencies may be realized when inter-jurisdictional legal standards are adopted, just as they may be when inter-jurisdictional electrical or telecommunications standards are adopted. Such legal compatibility allows individuals and entities to invest once in learning the legal system, then apply that investment across multiple jurisdictions. Indeed, it might be said that law interoperates with law from other jurisdictions, particularly as capital, goods, and individuals interact or move across borders – such movements or transactions may be simultaneously subject to the legal standards of multiple jurisdictions, potential for incompatible standards to impose conflicting demands on the inter-jurisdictional actor.

Where legal standards differ, or are incompatible, compliance with applicable law becomes expensive and uncertain. These uncertainties have long been a focus of concern for Internet-related activities, although this type of interaction is not unique to Internet activity. Indeed, large bodies of adaptive jurisprudence have grown up around routinely encountered questions of jurisdiction and choice of law conflicts – negotiating these complex systems of rules is a daunting task even to those knowledgeable in their mysteries, and a nearly impossible proposition to the average person or business entrepreneur. The Internet greatly facilitates such interaction, connecting individuals and institutions from differing jurisdictions and raising

---

[39] Besen & Farrell 1994.

[40] Lemley 2002.

the level of virtual movement. Perhaps more importantly, the low costs of accessing the network also makes such interactions relatively cheap, placing them within the purview of small businesses and average citizens – no longer are transnational interactions relegated to a relatively few highly-capitalized firms. However, this new cheap access also means that inter-jurisdictional conflicts affect those least likely to have expertise or skill in negotiating inconsistent legal regimes.

This rise of Internet-based 'virtual' interaction illustrates the interconnection of legal and technical networks, and implies that law interoperates with technology. The interconnected technological system of the network may be considered as an extension of the legal systems arrayed at the periphery of the net. The technological system of the network provides a common standard for inter-jurisdictional interoperation of diverse legal systems. But it must be understood that just as the network is agnostic toward the applications, platforms, or devices arrayed at its periphery, so too is it indifferent to the legal networks that it interconnects. The open architecture and 'end to end' design of the network may connect devices with otherwise incompatible operating systems, or it may connect jurisdictions with otherwise incompatible legal systems: whether it is Unix-based machines interoperating with Windows-based machines or protectionist-based copyright interoperating with access-based copyright, the network treats them all the same. The result is that the network may bridge legal systems with radically different goals and expectations.

Indeed, most of the legal controversies surrounding the Internet may be characterized as arising out of this interconnection of incompatible legal systems. A variety of Internet-related controversies have erupted ranging from the promulgation of pornographic materials to the sharing of software or music files. The design of the network, lacking the natural impediments intrinsic to traditional media, actually facilitates the distribution of problematic information.[41] Responses to electronic dissemination of pornography, or of private information, or of copyrighted works are essentially attempts to either legally or technically retrofit the network to comply with the local legal regime.[42] Restrictions on such uses may be implemented via legal prohibitions or via equivalent technologies, such as content filters or digital rights management systems, or with some combination of legal and technical prohibitions.

Attempts to retrofit the network to local standards via technological or cultural add-ons are in essence attempts to adapt a foreign standard to interoperate with local systems, much as the traveler may attempt to retrofit a non-conforming device to local voltage, current, and plug configuration by means of adapters and transformers. As with electrical adapters and transformers, the cost of such inconvenience could be lowered, and a variety of other efficiencies realized, by establishing a single international standard for international legal interoperation, at least interoperation facilitated via the Internet. But while this approach offers the ben-

---

[41] Burk 1999.
[42] Idem.

efits of standardization, it carries with it the same dangers indicated above: there may be serious long-term costs if Internet law becomes 'locked' into a single standard, particularly if dominant nations act strategically in establishing that standard. As in the case of technical standards, in standardizing law there is a real danger that creation of a dominant standard will suppress competition and entry into the market for law products. There is already some evidence that this is occurring in international harmonization regarding privacy and intellectual property, where the United States and the European Union have largely eliminated any competing regulatory systems.[43] In this environment, such dominant law producers may well monopolize the market for Internet law for the foreseeable future.

9.3.4   Conclusion

I have suggested here that the costs and benefits of internationalizing Internet law can be evaluated by adapting models drawn from the economic analysis of cartel theory and standards-setting, as law may be considered not only a product, but a standard. The equation of law with interoperable technical standards should hardly come as a surprise. Students of technological meaning have long held that technology comprises reified norms.[44] At the same time, law is largely the formal statement of those norms.[45] The normative meanings of these two cultural artifacts interact in a complex relationship, both re-shaping and reinforcing one another. More recently, legal scholars including Reidenberg and Lessig have suggested and extensively explored the interchangeability of law and of technological constraints in achieving social policy objectives.[46] This conceptualization of law is in some sense the logical endpoint of the economic approach conceiving law as a product: if law is an economic good that competes with similar goods from other producers, so too is law a product that interoperates with similar products from other producers, as well as with other systems of complementary or competing products, even if they take the form of technological standards.

---

[43] See Burk 2004
[44] Latour 1992; Latour 1988, p. 306.
[45] Posner 2002.
[46] Lessig 1999; Reidenberg 1998.

LITERATURE

AALBERTS AND VAN DER HOF 2000
Aalberts, B. and van der Hof, S., *Digital Signature Blindness, Analysis of Legislative Approaches to Electronic Authentication*, Deventer: Kluwer 2000, <http://law.uvt.nl/simone/ds-fr.htm>.

ALBERT 2003
Albert, C., From Global Elections to Self-Regulation without the Public: How ICANN Fails to Fulfil its Basic Promise, *PCMPL Self-Regulation Review*, 2003, <http://www.selfregulation.info>, <http://www.selfregulation.info/iapcoda/0310xx-selfregulation-review.htm>.

ASSCHER FORTHCOMING
Asscher, L., Code as law. Discussion paper ITeR Workshops Code as Code, as held in Amsterdam on 1 and 2 July, 2004 *Draft 1.2.*

BALDWIN AND CAVE 1999
Baldwin, R. and Cave, M., *Understanding Regulation. Theory, Strategy, and Practice*, Oxford: Oxford University Press, 1999.

BARTHES 1957
Barthes, R., *Mythologies*, Paris: Seuil 1957.

BENNETT AND RAAB 2003
Bennett, C.J. and Raab, Ch.D., *The Governance of Privacy. Policy Instruments in Global Perspective*, Dartmouth: Ashgate 2003.

BERMAN 2002
Berman, P.S., The Globalization of Jurisdiction, *University of Pennsylvania Law Review*, 2002, pp. 311-529.

BESEN AND FARRELL 1994
Besen, S.M. and Farrell, J., Choosing How to Compete: Strategies & Tactics in Standardization, *Journal of Economic Perspectives* 1994, pp. 117-131.

BIMBER 1994
Bimber, B., Three Faces of Technological Determinism, in: Smith, M.R., and Marx, L., '*Does Technology Drive History? The Dilemma of Technological Determinism*', MIT Press 1996, pp. 79-100.

BLOK 2002
Blok, P., *Het recht op privacy. Een onderzoek naar de betekenis van het begrip 'privacy' in het Nederlandse en Amerikaanse recht*, The Hague: Boom 2002.

BONN MINISTERIAL CONFERENCE 1997
<http://europa.eu.int/ISPO/bonn/Min_declaration/i_finalen.html>.

BRETON 1991
Breton, A., The Existence and Stability of Interjurisdictional Competition, in: Kenyon, D.A. and Kincaid, J., *Competition Among States and Local Governments: Efficiency and Equity in American Federalism*, Washington, D.C.: The Urban Institute, 1991, pp. 37-56.

BREULMANN 1993
>   Breulmann, G., *Normung und Rechtsangleichung in der Europäischen Wirtschafts-gemeinschaft*, Duncker and Humbolt: Berlin 1993.

BROUSSEAU 2001
>   Brousseau, E., Régulation de l'Internet; l'autorégulation nécessite t'elle un cadre institutionnel?, *Revue économique*, n° hors série: Economie de l'Internet, Brousseau, E. and Curien, N. (eds.), October 2001.

DE BRUIN 2002
>   De Bruin, R., *Consumer Trust in Electronic Commerce, Time for Best Practice*, Kluwer Law International, Vol. 17, 2002.

BUCHANAN 1995
>   Buchanan, J.M., Federalism and Individual Sovereignty, *Cato Journal* 1995/96, pp. 259-268.

BURK 1999
>   Burk, D.L., Cyberlaw and the Norms of Science, *Boston College Intellectual Property and Technology Forum* 1999, <http://infoeagle.bc.edu/bc_org/avp/law/st_org/iptf/commentary/content/burk.html>.

BURK 2004
>   Burk, D.L., Privacy and Property in the Global Datasphere: International Dominance of Off-the-shelf Models for Information Control, in: Sudaweeks, F. and Ess, Ch. (eds.), *Proceedings of the Fourth International Conference on Cultural Attitudes Toward Technology and Communication* 2004, pp. 363-374.

BURK AND LEMLEY 2002
>   Burk, D.L. and Lemley, M.A., 'Is Patent Law Technology-Specific?', *Berkeley Technology Law Journal* 2002, pp. 1155-1206.

CASTELLS 1996
>   Castells, M., *The rise of the Network Society*, in: The Information Age: Economy, Society and Culture, Vol. I, Blackwell Publishers: Cambridge, MA 1996.

CASTELLS 2001
>   Castells, M., *The Internet Galaxy. Reflections on the Internet, Business, and Society*, Oxford University Press: Oxford 2001.

CLINTON AND GORE 1997
>   Clinton, W.J. and Gore Jr., A., *A Framework for Global Electronic Commerce* 1997, <http://www.nyls.edu/cmc/papers/whgiifra.htm>.

COIPEL 2002
>   Coipel, M., Quelques réflexions sur le droit et ses rapports avec d'autres régulations de la vie sociale, in: *Gouvernance de la société de l'information*, Cahier du Crid, n° 22, 2002, p. 44 et seq.

COMMISSIE GDT 2000
>   Commissie Grondrechten in het Digitale Tijdperk, *Rapport* 2000, <http://www.minbzk.nl/search/contents/pages/00008117/rapport_gdt_5-00.pdf>.

CONSEIL D'ETAT 1998
>   Conseil d'Etat, *Internet et les réseaux numériques* 1998, <http://www.Internet.gouv.fr/francais/textesref/rapce98/accueil.htm>.

CURRAN 1994
>   Curran, Ch., 'The Burden of Proof and the Liability Rule for Suppliers of Services in the EEC', *The Geneva Papers on Risk and Insurance* 1994, pp. 85-98.

CUTLER, HAUFLER AND PORTER 1999
Cutler, A., Haufler, V., and Porter, T., *Private Authority and International Affairs*, Albany: State University of New York Press 1999.

VAN DALEN AND LAMBERS 2003
Van Dalen, O.L. and Lambers, R., De broadcast flag en fundamentele rechten, Verplichte kopieerbeveiliging in de Verenigde Staten, *JAVI* 2004, nr. 1, pp. 2-8.

DELMAS 2002
Delmas, R., Internet, une gouvernance imparfaite, in: Chatillon, G., *Le droit international de l'Internet*, Brussels, Bruylant 2002, p. 279 et seq.

DELPÉRÉE 2002
Delpérée, F. (ed.), *Le principe de subsidiarité*, Brussels: Bruylant, 2002.

DINWOODIE 2000
Dinwoodie, G.B., 'A New Copyright Order: Why National Courts Should Create Global Norms', No. 149 *U. PA. L. Rev.*, pp. 469-490.

DRAHOS AND BRAITHWAITE 2002
Drahos, P. and Braithwaite, J., *Information Feudalism, Who Owns the Knowledge Economy?*, London: Earthscan 2002.

DUTCH MINISTRY OF JUSTICE 1998
Dutch Ministry of Justice, 'Legislation for the Electronic Highways. Management Summary', February 1998, in: Koops, E.J., Prins, J.E.J. and Hijmans, H. (eds.), *ICT Law and Internationalisation*, Kluwer Law International, 2000.

DUTCH MINISTRY OF JUSTICE 2000A
Dutch Ministry of Justice, 'Internationalisation and Law in the Information Society', in: Koops, et al. (eds.), *ICT Law and Internationalisation. A Survey of Government Views* 2000, The Hague: Kluwer Law International 2000a.

DUTCH MINISTRY OF JUSTICE 2000B
Dutch Ministry of Justice, *Memorandum Internationalisation and Law in the Information Society*, 2000b, available at <http://www.justitie.nl/Images/11_5538.pdf>.

EASTERBROOK 1983
Easterbrook, F.H., Antitrust and the Economics of Federalism, *Journal of Law and Economics* 1983, pp. 23-50.

EECKHOUT 1997
Eeckhout, P., 'The domestic legal status of the WTO Agreement: Interconnecting Legal Systems', *Common Market Law Review* 1997, pp. 11-58.

EIJLANDER 1994
Eijlander, Ph., 'Zelfregulering in soorten en maten', in: Eijlander, Ph., et al., *Wetgeven en de maat van de tijd*, Zwolle: Tjeenk Willink 1994.

EIJLANDER AND VOERMANS 1999
Eijlander, Ph. and Voermans, W., *Wetgevingsleer*, Deventer: W.E.J. Tjeenk Willink, 1999.

ENDESHAW 2001
Endeshaw, A., 'Legal Significance of Trustmarks', *Information & Communications Technology Law*, 2001, pp. 204-230.

EPSTEIN 1987
Epstein, R., The Proper Scope of the Commerce Power, *Virginia Law Review* 1987, pp. 1387-1455.

EUROPEAN COMMISSION 1994
European Commission, *Europe's way to the information society. An Action Plan*, July 1994.

EUROPEAN COMMISSION 2003
European Commission's Information Society Directorate-General, *Towards an Information Society for all*, September 2003.

FAITH 2003
Faith, L., The Role of Privacy Enhancing Technologies, in: *Considering Consumer Privacy: A Resource for Policymakers and Practitioners* 2003, <www.cdt.org/privacy/ccp>.

FALQUE-PIERROTIN 2002
Falque-Pierrotin, I., Le Forum des droits sur l'Internet: un instrument de gouvernance, in Chatillon G., *Le droit international de l'Internet*, Brussels: Bruylant 2002, p. 284 et seq.

FAURE AND HARTLIEF 2003
Faure, M. and Hartlief, T., 'Naar een harmonisatie van aansprakelijkheidsrecht in Europa?', *NJB* 2003, pp. 170-177.

FRERIKS, PETERS, ROBBE AND VERSCHUUREN 2002
Freriks, A.A., Peters, Th., Robbe, J., Verschuuren, J.M., *De invloed van het Europees recht op het ruimtelijk bestuursrecht*, Kluwer: Zwolle 2002.

FRISSEN 1996
Frissen, P.H.A., *De virtuele staat. Politiek, bestuur, technologie: een postmodern verhaal*, Academic Service: Schoonhoven 1996.

FRISSEN 1998
Frissen, P.H.A., Public Administration in Cyberspace, in: Snellen, I.Th.M. and van de Donk, W.B.H.J. (eds.), *Public Administration in an Information Age. A Handbook*, IOS Press: Amsterdam 1998.

FROOMKIN 1999
Froomkin, M., 'Of Governments and Governance', *Berkeley Technology Law Journal*, No. 2, 1999, <http://www.law.berkeley.edu/journals/btlj/Articles/vol14/Froomkin/html/reader.html>.

FROOMKIN 2000
Froomkin, M., Semi-Private International Rule Making, in: Marsden, C.T. (ed.), *Regulating the Global Information Society*, London-New York: Frontledge 2000, p. 211 et seq.

FROOMKIN 2000A
Froomkin, M., Wrong Turn in Cyberspace: Using ICANN to Route Around APA and the Constitution, *Duke Law Journal* 2000, p. 17 et seq.

FROOMKIN 2002
Froomkin, M., 'Form and Substance in Cyberspace', *The Journal of Small & Emerging Business Law*, Vol. 6:93, pp. 93-124.

FROOMKIN 2003
Froomkin, M., 'Habermas@Discourse.Net: Toward a Critical Theory of Cyberspace', *Harvard Law Review*, No. 3, 2003, pp. 751-873.

FULLER 1969
Fuller, L., *The Morality of Law*, Revised Edition, New Haven and London: Yale University Press 1969.

G7 1995

G7, *Conclusions of G7 Summit 'Information Society Conference'*, February 1995, DOC/95/2.

GALANTER 1981

Galanter, M., Justice in Many Rooms: Courts, Private Ordering, and Indigenous Law, *Journal of Legal Pluralism and Unofficial Law* 1981, No. 19, pp. 30-42.

GEIST 2001

Geist, M., 'Is There a There There? Towards Greater Certainty for Internet Jurisdiction', *Berkeley Technology Law Journal* 2001, <http://papers.ssrn.com/sol3/papers.cfm?abstract_id=266932>.

GEIST 2003

Geist, M., 'Cyberlaw 2.0', *Boston College Law Review* 2003, pp. 323-358.

GÉRARD, OST AND VAN DE KERCHOVE 1996

Gérard, Ph., Ost, F., Van de Kerchove, M., *Droit négocié, droit imposé?*, Bruxelles: Faculte's universitaires Saint-Louis 1996.

GOLDSMITH 1998

Goldsmith, J.L., Against Cyberanarchy, *University of Chicago Law Review* 1998, pp. 1199-1250.

GOLDSMITH 1998

Goldsmith, J.L., 'The Internet and the Abiding Significance of Territorial Sovereignty', *Indiana Journal of Global Legal Studies*, p. 475.

GRANGER 2000

Granger, G., Liberté d'expression et réglementation de l'information dans le cyberspace, in: Unesco (ed.), *Les dimensions internationales du droit du cyberespace*, Economica: 2000, p. 89 et seq.

HAANAPPEL 1990

Haanappel, P.P.C., *New Netherlands Civil Code. Patrimonial Law*, Deventer: Kluwer 1990.

HALL 1998

Hall, P., *Cities in Civilization. Culture, Innovation, and Urban Order*, Weinfield & Nicolson: London 1998.

HAMILTON 1996

Hamilton, M.A., The TRIPS Agreement: Imperialistic, Outdated, and Overprotective, *Vanderbilt Journal of Transnational Law* 1996, pp. 613-634.

HELBERGER FORTHCOMING

Helberger, N., *Code and (intellectual) property*. Discussion paper ITeR Workshops Code as Code, as held in Amsterdam on 1 and 2 July 2004 *Draft*.

HES AND BORKING 1998

Hes, R. and Borking, J., *Privacy Enhancing Technologies: The Path to Anonymity* (rev. edn.), Registratiekamer: Achtergrondstudies en Verkenningen 1998.

HOSEIN AND ESCUDERO PASCUAL 2002

Hosein, I. and Escudero Pascual, A., 'Understanding Traffic Data and Deconstructing Technology-neutral Regulations', *UNECE* 2002, <http://www.it.kth.se/~aep/publications/unece-latest-escuderoa-hoseini.pdf>.

HOWELLS AND WILHELMSSON 1997

Howells, G.C. and Wilhelmsson, Th., *EC Consumer Law*, Aldershot: Ashgate 1997.

ILIS MEMORANDUM 2000
>   The Netherlands Ministry of Justice, 'Internationalisation and Law in the Informa-
>   tion Society', in: Koops, B.J., Prins, J.E.J. and Hijmans, H. (eds.), *ICT Law and
>   Internationalisation*, The Hague: Kluwer Law International 2000, pp. 21-68.

ILIS MEMORANDUM 2000
>   Nota Internationalisering en recht in de informatiemaatschappij, *Kamerstukken II*
>   1999/2000, 25 880, no. 10.

INMAN AND RUBINFELD 1997
>   Inman, R.P. and Rubinfeld, D.L., The Political Economy of Federalism, in: Mueller,
>   D.C., *Perspectives on Public Choice: A Handbook*, Cambridge: Cambridge Uni-
>   versity Press 1997, pp. 73-105.

ITEANU 2002
>   Iteanu, O., L'ICANN, un exemple de gouvernance originale ou un cas de law intel-
>   ligence?, *Homo Numericus* 2002, <http://www.homo-numericus.net>.

ITU 2001
>   ITU, *Effective Regulation Case Study,* Singapore: 2001.

JADOT 2002
>   Jadot, B., Le pouvoir de gérer les questions d'environnement, faire confiance a
>   priori au 'privé' ou au 'public', in: Delpérée, F. (ed.), *Le principe de subsidiarité*,
>   Brussels: LGDJ-Bruylant 2002, p. 212 et seq.

JOHNSON AND POST 1996
>   Johnson, D.R. and Post, D., Law and borders, The rise of law in Cyberspace, Sym-
>   posium: Surveying Law and Borders, *Stanford Law Review* 1996, pp. 1367-1402.

JONES 1998
>   Jones, R., The Internet, Legal Regulation and Legal Pluralism, The Changing Ju-
>   risdiction, *13ᵗʰ Annual BILETA Conference*, Dublin 1998, <http://www.bileta.ac.uk/
>   98papers/jones.html>.

KAHIN 1997
>   Kahin, B., 'The U.S. National Information Infrastructure Initiative: The Market,
>   the Web, and the Virtual Project', in: Kahin, B. and Wilson III, E.J. (eds.), *National
>   Information Infrastructure Initiatives. Vision and Policy Design*, 1997, The MIT
>   Press, Cambridge, Massachusetts, pp. 150-189.

KASPERSEN 1996
>   Kaspersen, H.W.K, Aansprakelijkheid van Internet-Providers, *Computerrecht* 1996,
>   pp. 9-13.

KATSH 1995
>   Katsh, E., *Law in a Digital World*, New York, Oxford University Press 1995, p. 20
>   et seq.

KATSH 1996
>   Katsh, E., Software Worlds and the First Amendment: Virtual Doorkeepers in
>   Cyberspace, *University of Chicago Legal Forum* 1996, p. 335.

KATZ AND SHAPIRO 1985
>   Katz, M.L. and Shapiro, C., Network Externalities, Competition, and Compatibil-
>   ity, *American Economic Review* 1985 pp. 424-440.

KATZ AND SHAPIRO 1994
>   Katz, M.L. and Shapiro, C., Systems Competition and Network Effects, *Journal of
>   Economic Perspectives* 1994, pp. 93-115.

Van Klink and Prins 2002
Van Klink, B.M.J. and Prins, J.E.J., *Law and Regulation: Scenarios For The Information Age*, Informatization Developments and the Public Sector Series, No. 7, Amsterdam, Berlin, Oxford, Tokyo, Washington DC: IOS Press 2002.

Kloosterhuis 2002
Kloosterhuis, H., *Van overeenkomstige toepassing. De pragma-dialectische reconstructie van analogie-argumentatie in rechterlijke uitspraken*, Amsterdam: Thela Thesis 2002.

Koekkoek, et al. 1999
Koekkoek. A., Zoontjens, P., Koops, B.J., et al., (2000), *Bescherming van grondrechten in het digitale tijdperk. Een rechtsvergelijkend onderzoek naar informatie- en communicatievrijheid en privacy in Zweden, Duitsland, Frankrijk, België, de Verenigde Staten en Canada*, Tilburg: 2000, 258 p.

Koelman 2003
Koelman, K.J., *Auteursrecht en technische voorzieningen. Juridische en rechtseconomische aspecten van de bescherming van technische voorzieningen*, *ITeR-reeks* nr. 57, 2003.

Koger 2001
Koger, J.L., 'You Sign, E-SIGN, We All Fall Down: Why the United States Should Not Crown the Marketplace As Primary Legislator Of Electronic Signatures', *Transnational Law and Contemporary Problems* 2001, pp. 491-516.

Kohler-Koch 2003
Kohler-Koch, B., *Linking EU and National Governance*, Oxford: Oxford University Press 2003.

Komuro 1995
Komuro, N., The WTO Dispute Settlement Mechanism: Coverage and Procedures of the WTO Understanding, *Journal of International Arbitration* 1995, pp. 81-171.

Koops, Prins and Hijmans 2000
Koops, B.J., Prins, J.E.J. and Hijmans, H., *ICT Law and Internationalisation. A Survey of Government Views*, The Hague: Kluwer Law International 2000.

Koops, et al. 2000
Koops, B.J., Prins, J.E.J., Schellekens, M., Gijrath, S. and Schreuders, E., 'Governments on Internationalisation and ICT Law. The Positions of Germany, France, the United Kingdom, and the United States', in: Koops, B.J., Prins, J.E.J. and Hijmans, H. (eds.), *ICT Law and Internationalisation. A Survey of Government Views*, The Hague: Kluwer Law International 2000.

Koops 2002
Koops, B.J., *Strafvorderlijk onderzoek van (tele)communicatie 1838-2002. Het grensvlak tuusen opsporing en privacy*, Deventer: Kluwer 2002.

Koops and Lips 2003
Koops, B.J. and Lips, A.M.B., Wie reguleert het Internet? Horizontalisering en rechtsmacht bij technische regulering van het Internet, in: Franken, H., e.a., *Zeven essays over informatietechnologie en recht*, *ITeR-reeks* nr. 63, 2003, p. 261.

Kühne 1999
Kühne, H.-H., 'Strafbarkeit der Zugangsvermittlung von pornographischen Informationen im Internet', *NJW* no. 3, 1999, p. 188.

KUNER 2003

Kuner, C., Enabling a Legal Framework for the Information Society: Summary of Presentation 2003, Geneva, Presentation at the Enabling Environment Roundtable, WSIS Prepcom 2.

LAMBERS 2004

Lambers, R., Speech control through network architecture, *Discussion paper IteR Workshops Code as Code*, Amsterdam 2004 Draft 0.9.

LATOUR 1988

Latour, B., a.k.a. J. Johnson, Mixing Humans and Non-Humans Together: The Sociology of a Door Closer, *Social Problems* 1988, pp. 298-310.

LATOUR 1992

Latour, B., Where are the Missing Masses? The Sociology of a Few Mundane Artifacts, in: Bijker, W.E. and Law, J. (eds.), *Shaping Technology/Building Society: Studies in Sociotechnical Change*, Cambridge MA: MIT Press, 1992 pp. 225-258.

LAZARO 2002

Lazaro, Chr., Synthèse des débats, in *Gouvernance de la société de l'information*, Cahier du Crid, n° 22, 2002, Bruylant-Bruxelles, p. 161 et seq.

LEBOEUF 1994

LeBoeuf, J., The Economics of Federalism and the Proper Scope of the Federal Commerce Power, *San Diego Law Review* 1994, pp. 555-616.

LEE 2003

Lee, A., 'Regulating the Internet: Comments on the Second Draft of the U.K. Communications Bill', *World Internet Law Report* 2003 (3), pp. 19-21.

LEENES AND KOOPS FORTHCOMING

Leenes, R. and Koops, B.J., *'Code' and Privacy. Discussion Paper IteR Workshops Code as Code'*, Amsterdam 2004, Version 18 June 2004.

LEGRAND 1997

Legrand, P., 'The Impossibility of 'Legal Transplants'', *Maastricht Journal of European and Comparative Law*, no. 4, 1997, pp. 111-124.

LEH MEMORANDUM 1998

The Netherlands Ministry of Justice, *Legislation for the Electronic Highways*, February 1998, Management Summary in English in: Koops, B.J., Prins, J.E.J. and Hijmans, H. (eds.), *ICT Law and Internationalisation*, The Hague: Kluwer Law International 2000, pp. 5-20.

LEH MEMORANDUM 1998

Nota Wetgeving voor de elektronische snelweg, *Kamerstukken II*, 1997/98, 25 880, nos. 1-2.

LEMLEY AND MCGOWAN 1998

Lemley, M.A., and McGowan, D., Legal Implications of Network Economic Effects, *Cal. L. Rev.* 1998, pp. 479-611.

LEMLEY 2000

Lemley, M.A., 'Comments. Private Property', *Stanford Law Review*, p. 1545.

LEMLEY 2002

Lemley, M.A., Intellectual Property Rights and Standard-Setting Organizations, 90 *Cal. L. Rev.* 2002, pp. 1889-1976.

LESSIG 1999

Lessig, L., *Code and Other Laws in Cyberspace*, Basic Books, New York, 1999.

LIEBOWITZ AND MARGOLIS 1990
Liebowitz, S.J. and Margolis, S.E., The Fable of the Keys, *Journal of Law and Economics* 1990, pp. 1-25.

LIEBOWITZ AND MARGOLIS 1994
Liebowitz, S.J. and Margolis, S.E., Network Externality: An Uncommon Tragedy, *Journal of Economic Perspectives* 1994, pp. 133-150.

LIPS, PRINS, VAN DER HOF AND SCHUDELARO FORTHCOMING
Lips, A.M.B., Prins, J.E.J, Van der Hof, S. and Schudelaro, A.A.P., *Issues of Online Personalisation in Commercial and Public Service Delivery,* Wolf Legal Publishers: Tilburg 2005.

LIPS 2001
Lips, A.M.B., 'Designing Electronic Government Around the World. Policy Developments in the USA, Singapore, and Australia', in: Prins, J.E.J. (ed.), *Designing E-Government. On the Crossroads of Technological Innovation and Institutional Change*, The Hague: Kluwer Law International 2001.

LIPS AND FRISSEN 1997
Lips, A.M.B. and Frissen, P.H.A., *Wiring Government. Integrated Public Service Delivery through ICT in the UK and the USA*, NWO/ITeR-series, Vol. 8, Samsom BedrijfsInformatie bv: Alphen aan den Rijn/Diegem 1997, pp. 67-164.

LIPS, FRISSEN AND PRINS 1998
Lips, A.M.B., Frissen, P.H.A. and Prins, J.E.J., 'Regulatory Review through New Media in Sweden, the UK and the USA: Convergence or Divergence of Regulation', *The EDI Law Review* 1998, pp.123-257.

LITAN 2001
Litan, R.E., *Law and Policy in the Age of the Internet*, Working Paper AEI-Brookings Joint Center for Regulatory Studies 2001, <http://www.aei.brookings.org/>.

VON LOHMAN 2003
Von Lohman, F., *Digital Rights Management: The Skeptics View*, Electronic Frontier Foundation, <www.eff.org/IP/DRM/20030401_drm_skeptics_view.pdf>.

MAESSCHALK AND DEDEURWAERDERE 2002
Maesschalk, M. and Dedeurwaerdere, T., Autorégulation, Ethique procédurale et Gouvernance de la société de l'information, in: *Gouvernance de la société de l'information*, Cahier du Crid, n°22, 2002, Bruylant-Bruxelles, p. 77 et seq.

MANKOWSKI 1999
Mankowski, P., 'Das Internet im Internationalen Vertrags- und Deliktsrecht', *RabelsZ* 1999, pp. 203-294.

MARAIS 2002
Du Marais, B., Autorégulation, régulation et co-régulation des réseaux, in: Chatillon, G., *Le droit international de l'Internet*, Brussels, Bruylant 2002, p. 296 et seq.

MARBURGER 1979
Marburger, P., *Die Regeln der Technik im Recht*, Carl Heymans Verlag: Köln 1979.

MASKUS 2002
Maskus, K.E., 'Regulatory standards in the WTO: Comparing Intellectual Property Rights with Competition Policy, Environmental Protection, and Core Labour Standards', *World Trade Review* 2002, 1:2, pp. 135-152.

MAYER 2000
Mayer, F.C., 'Europe and the Internet: The Old World and the New Medium', *EJIL* 2000, pp. 149-169.

MAYER 2003
> Mayer-Schönberger, V., The shape of governance: analyzing the world of Internet regulation, *Virginia Journal of International Law* 2003, pp. 605-673.

MCGOWAN 2001
> McGowan, D., Legal Implications of Open-Source Software, *University of Illinois Law Review* 2001, p. 241.

MCGUIRE 1974
> McGuire, M., Group Segregation and Optimal Jurisdictions, *Journal of Political Economy* 1974. pp. 112-132.

MCKEAN AND HINTON 2002
> McKean, R. and Hinton, P., 'The Draft Communications Bill – Door is Left Ajar for Regulation of Internet Content', *World Internet Law Report* 2002, p. 18.

MELISSARIS 2004
> Melissaris, E., The More the Merrier? A New Take on Legal Pluralism, *Social & Legal Studies* 2004, pp. 57-79.

MITCHELL 1995
> Mitchell, W.J., *City of Bits: Space, Place, and the Infobahn*, Cambridge Mass.: MIT Press 1995.

MITCHELL 2000
> Mitchell, W.J., *E-Topia. 'Urban life, Jim – but not as we know it'*, 2nd edn., MIT Press: Cambridge, MA 2000.

MOUNIER 2000
> Mounier, P., Les maîtres du monde, *Homo Numericus*, 2000, <http://www.homo-numericus.net>.

MUELLER 1979
> Mueller, D., *Public Choice*, Cambridge: Cambridge University Press 1979.

MUELLER 1998
> Mueller, M., *The 'Governance' Debacle, How the ideal of Internetworking Got Buried by Politics,* <http://www.open-rsc.org/essays/mueller/govdec/> and <http://www.isoc.org/inet98/proceedings/5a/5a_1.htm>.

MUELLER 1999
> Mueller, M., ICANN and Internet Governance, Sorting through the Debris of Self-Regulation, *Info* 1999, pp. 497-520.

NICOLL 1999
> Nicoll, C.C., 'Singapore: The Intelligent Island', *The EDI Law Review* 1999, pp. 123-141.

NOIE 1998
> National Office for the Information Economy, *A Strategic Framework for the Information Economy. Identifying Priorities for Action* 1998, <http://www.noie.gov.au/projects/framework/reports/dec98_strategy.htm>.

NOIE 2000
> National Office for the Information Economy, *Second Progress Report – May 2000. Strategic Framework for the Information Economy. Action Plans* 2000, <http://www.noie.gov.au/projects/framework/reports/May2000_update.htm>.

NOIE 2000
> National Office for the Information Economy, *Strategic Framework for the Information Economy. Action Plans* 2000 Second Progress Report, <http://www.noie.gov.au/projects/information_economy/strategic_fr.../May2000_update.html>.

OECD 1998
OECD Ministerial Conference in Ottawa, *Building Trust for users and consumers* 1998.

OECD 1999
OECD Ministerial Conference in Paris 1999.

OECD 2002
OECD, *Guidelines for the Security of Information Systems and Networks. Towards a culture of security* 2002, OECD Publications.

OGUS 1999
Ogus, A., 'Competition between National Legal Systems: A Contribution of Economic Analysis to Comparative Law', *International and Comparative Law Quarterly* 1999, pp. 405-418.

OGUS 2001
Ogus, A., 'The Contribution of Economic Analysis of Law to Legal Transplants', in: Smits, J. (ed.), *The Contribution of Mixed Legal Systems to European Private Law*, Insertia: 2001, pp. 27-37.

PALZER 2002
Palzer, C., La coregulation en Europe: conditions générales de mise en œuvre des cadres corégulateurs en Europe, *IRIS plus* 2002.

PERRITT 2000
Perritt Jr., H.H., 'Economic and Other Barriers to Electronic Commerce', *U. PA. J. Int'l Econ. L.*, p. 563, <http://www.kentlaw.edu/perritt/publications/U.PA.J. INTLECONLAW.htm>.

POLANSKI 2002
Polanski, P.P., 'A New Approach to Regulating Internet Commerce: Custom as a Source of Electronic Commerce Law', *Electronic Communication Law Review*, 2002, pp. 165-205.

POSNER 1992
Posner, R.A., *Economic Analysis of Law*, Boston: Little, Brown & Co., 1992.

POSNER 2002
Posner, E.A., *Law and Social Norms*, Cambridge, MA: Harvard University Press 2002.

POST 1995
Post, D.G., Anarchy, State and the Internet: An Essay on Law-Making in Cyberspace, *J. Online L.*, 1995.

POST AND JOHNSON 1997
Post, D. and Johnson, D.R., The New Civic Virtue of the Net, <http://stlr.stan ford.edu/STLR/Working Papers/97 Post 1/>.

POST AND JOHNSON 1999
Post, D. and Johnson, D.R., Chaos Prevailing on every Continent: A New Theory of Decentralized Decision-Making in Complex Systems, *Chicago-Kent Law Review* 1999, p. 1055 et seq.

POULLET 2001
Poullet, Y., How to Regulate the Internet : New Paradigms for Internet Governance, in *Variations sur le droit de la société de l'information*, Cahier du CRID, n° 20, 2001, p. 130 et seq.

POULLET 2001A

Poullet, Y., Vues de Bruxelles: Un droit européen de l'Internet?, in Chatillon, G. (éd.), *Le droit international de l'Internet*, Brussels : Bruylant 2002, p.165 et seq.

POULLET 2004

Poullet, Y., Technology and Law: From Challenge to Alliance, in: Gasser, U. (ed.), *Information Quality Regulation: Foundations, Perspectives, and Applications. Festschrift für W. Kilian*, Baden-Baden: Nomos 2004.

PRICE AND VERHULST 2000

Price, M. and Verhulst, S.G., The Concept of Self-Regulation and the Internet, in: Waltermann, J. and Machill, M. (eds.), *Protecting Our Children on the Internet. Towards a New Culture of Responsibility*, Gütersloh: Bertelsmann Foundation Publishers 2000.

PRINS 2004 FORTHCOMING

Prins, J.E.J., *Property and Privacy: European Perspectives and the Commodification of our Identity*

PRINS AND SCHELLEKENS, 2004

Prins, J.E.J. and Schellekens, M.H.M., 'The Chilling-Effect of Liability Law on Initiatives to Enhance the Reliability of On-Line Health-Related Information', *European Journal of Health Law* 2004, pp. 201-207.

PRINS AND SCHELLEKENS, 2005

Prins, J.E.J. and Schellekens, M.H.M., 'Fighting Untrustworthy Internet Content: In Search for: Regulatory Scenario's', *Information Polity*, 2005 (forthcoming).

RADIN AND POLK WAGNER 1998.

Radin, M.J. and Polk Wagner, R., 'The Myth of Private Ordering: Rediscovering Legal Realism in Cyberspace', *Chicago-Kent Law Review* 1998, p. 1295.

REIDENBERG 1993

Reidenberg, J.R., Rules of the Road For Global Electronic Highways: Merging the Trade and Technical Paradigms, *6 Harvard Journal of Law & Technology* 1993, p. 287.

REIDENBERG 1996

Reidenberg, J.R., Governing Networks and Cyberspace Rule Making, *Emory Law Journal* 1996, p. 911.

REIDENBERG 1998

Reidenberg, J.R., Lex Informatica: The Formulation of Information Policy Rules Through Technology, *Texas Law Review* 1998, pp. 553-593.

REIDENBERG 2001

Reidenberg, J.R., Privacy Protection and the Interdependence of Law, Technology and Self-Regulation, in: *Variations sur le droit de la société de l'information*, Cahier du Crid, n° 20, Brussels, Bruylant 2001, p.130 et seq.

REIDENBERG 2002

Reidenberg, J.R., 'Yahoo and Democracy on the Internet', *Jurimetrics J.* 2002, pp. 261-280.

REMMELINK 2000

Remmelink, J., 'Skeelers en skates', *Verkeersrecht* 2000, pp. 44-47, <http://www.verkeerskunde.nl/artikelen/skeeler_remmelink.htm>.

ROMANO 1985

Romano, R.A., Law as a Product: Some Pieces of the Incorporation Puzzle, *Journal of Law, Economics, and Organization* 1985, pp. 225-267.

ROMANO 1993
Romano, R.A., *The Genius of American Corporate Law*, Washington, D.C.: American Enterprise Institute 1993.

ROSE-ACKERMAN 1981
Rose-Ackerman, S., Does Federalism Matter? Political Choice in a Federal Republic, *Journal of Political Economy* 1981, pp. 152-165.

ROSENBLATT 2004
Rosenblatt, B., 2003 in Review: Online Content Services, *DRMWatch* 2004, <www.drmwatch.com/ocr/article.php/3294461>.

RYAN 2003
Ryan, P.S., 'The Court as a Spectrum Regulator: Will there be a European Analogue to U.S. Cases NextWave and GWI', *German Law Journal*, No. 2, 2003, <http://wwwgermanlawjournal.com>.

SACCO 1991
Sacco, R., 'Legal Formants: A Dynamic Approach to Comparative Law', *American Journal of Comparative Law* 1991, pp. 1-34 (Part I); pp. 343-401 (Part II).

SAMUELSON, 1999
Samuelson, P., '*Five Challenges for Regulating the Global Information Society*', conference paper, Warwick 1999, p. 12, <http://www.sims.berkeley.edu/~pam/papers/5challenges_feb22_v2_final_.pdf>.

SAMUELSON 2000
Samuelson, P., 'Five Challenges for Regulating the Global Information Society', in: Marsden, Chr. (ed.), *Regulating the Global Information Society*, Routledge, 2000, <http://www.sims.berkeley.edu/~pam/papers/5challenges_feb22_v2_final_.pdf>.

SAROCCO 2002
Sarocco, C., Elements and Principles of the Information Society, 25 August 2002, ITU, a background resource for the WSIS, available at: <http://www.itu.int/osg/spu/wsis-themes/Access/BackgroundPaper/IS%20Principles.doc>.

SHAFFER 1999
Shaffer, G., 'The Power of EU Collective Action: The Impact of the EU Data Privacy Regulation on US Business Practice', *European Law Journal* 1999, pp. 419-437, <http://www.wisc.edu/wage/papers/PowerEUCollectiveAction.pdf>.

SCHELLEKENS 2001
Schellekens, M.H.M., *Aansprakelijkheid van Internetaanbieders* (dissertation Tilburg), The Hague: Sdu 2001.

SCHEPEL AND FALKE
Schepel, H. and Falke, J., *Legal Aspects of Standardization in the Member States of the EC and EFTA. Volume 1: Comparative Report*, Luxembourg 2000.

SHAPIRO 2001
Shapiro, C., Setting Compatability Standards: Cooperation or Collusion, in: Cooper Dreyfuss, R., et al. (eds.), *Expanding the Boundaries of Intellectual Property: Innovation Policy for the Knowledge Society*, New York: Oxford University Press 2001.

SLAUGHTER 1997
Slaughter, A.M., The Real New World Order, *Foreign Affairs* 1997, pp. 183-184.

SMITH 2001
Smith, B.L., The third industrial revolution: policymaking for the Internet, *Columbia Science and Technology Law Review* 2001, pp. 1-134.

SMITS 1998
> Smits, J.M., 'A European Private Law as a Mixed Legal System: Towards a Ius Commune through the Free Movement of Legal Rules', *Maastricht Journal of European and Comparative Law* 1998, p. 328.

SPINELLO 2001
> Spinello, R.A., 'Morality, Markets, and the Internet', in: Bykum, T.W., et al. (eds.), *The Social and Ethical Impacts of Information and Communication Technologies* 2001, pp. 162-173.

SPROULE-JONES 1975
> Sproule-Jones, M.A., *Public Choice in Federalism in Australia and Canada*, Canberra: Australian National University 1975.

STEPHAN 1999
> Stephan, P.B., 'The Futility of Unification and Harmonization in International Commercial Law', *Virginia Journal of International Law*, p. 743, Abstract: <http://papers.ssrn.com/sol3/papers.cfm?abstract_id=169209>.

STIGLER 1964
> Stigler, G.J., A Theory of Oligopoly, *Journal of Political Economy* 1964, pp. 44-61.

STIGLER 1972
> Stigler, G.J., Economic Competition and Political Competition, *Public Choice* 1972, pp. 91-106.

STIGLITZ 1983
> Stiglitz, J., The Theory of Local Public Goods, in: Zodrow, G.R. (ed.), *Local Provision of Public Services: The Tiebout Model After Twenty-Five Years*, New York: Academic Press 1983, pp. 17-53.

STUURMAN 1995
> Stuurman, C., *Technische normen en het recht, Beschouwingen over de interactie tussen het recht en technische normalisatie op het terrein van informatietechnologie en telecommunicatie* (thesis Vrije Universiteit Amsterdam), Deventer: Kluwer 1995.

STUYT 1999
> Stuyt, R.A.E., 'Technologiespecifieke regelgeving', *Informatierecht/AMI* 1999/2, pp. 17-21.

SUMMERS 1985
> Summers, R., Towards a Better General Theory of Legal Validity, *Rechtstheorie* 1985, p. 65 et seq.

TIEBOUT 1956
> Tiebout, C., A Pure Theory of Local Expenditures, *Journal of Political Economy* 1956, pp. 416-424.

TIMSIT 1996
> Timsit, G, Les deux corps du droit – essai sur la notion de régulation, *Rev. Française d'Admin. Publique*, 1996, p. 375 et seq.

TRACHTMAN 1993
> Trachtman, J.P., International Regulatory Competition, Externalization, and Jurisdiction, *Harvard International Law Journal* 1993, pp. 47-104.

TREBILCOCK AND HOWSE 1998
> Trebilcock, M. and Howse, R., 'Trade Liberalization and Regulatory Diversity: Reconciling Competitive Markets with Competitive Politics', *European Journal of Law and Economics* 1998, pp. 5-37.

TRUDEL 2002
>Trudel, P., L'influence d'Internet sur la production du droit, in: Chatillon, G.(ed.), *Le droit international de l'Internet*, Bruxelles: Bruylant 2002, p. 87 et seq.

D'UDEKEM-GEVERS AND POULLET 2001
>d'Udekem-Gevers, M. and Poullet, Y., Internet Content Regulation: Concerns from a User Empowerment Perspective about Internet Content Regulations, *Computer Law and Security Review* 2001, p. 371 et seq.

UKROW 1999
>Ukrow, J., *Self-regulation in the media sector and European Community law*, Saarbrücken 1999.

US FEDERAL GOVERNMENT 1993
>US Federal Government, *The National Information Infrastructure: Agenda for Action*, September 1993.

VAN DEN BERGH 1998
>Van den Bergh, R., 'Subsidiarity as an Economic Demarcation Principle and the Emergence of European Private Law', *Maastricht Journal of European and Comparative Law* 1998, pp. 129-149.

VAN DER HOF 2002
>Van der Hof, S., *Internationale on-line overeenkomsten. Internationaal privaatrechtelijke aspecten van on-line business-to-business en business-to-consumer overeenkomsten in Europa en de Verenigde Staten*, The Hague: Sdu 2002.

VAN DER HOF 2005
>Van der Hof, S., *Digital Signature Law Survey*, updated 12 February 2003, <http://rechten.uvt.nl/simone/ds-lawsu.htm>.

VAUBEL 1991
>Vaubel, R., A Public Choice View of International Organization, in: Vaubel, R. and Wilbert, Th.D. (eds.), *The Political Economy of International Organizations,* 1991.

VERHOVEN 2002
>Verhoven, J., Analyse du contenu et de la portée du principe de subsidiarité, in: Delpérée, F. (ed.), *Le principe de subsidiarité*, Bib. Faculté de Droit de l'UCL, LGDJ-Bruylant, 2002, p. 376 et seq.

VIVANT 1996
>Vivant, M., Cybermonde: droit et droit des réseaux, *Semaine juridique*, n° 3969, 1996.

WEST, DEDRICK AND KRAEMER 1997
>West, J., Dedrick, J. and Kraemer, K.L., 'Back to the Future: Japan's NII Plans', in: Kahin, B. and Wilson, E.J. (eds.), *National Information Infrastructure Initiatives. Vision and Policy Design*, 1997, Cambridge, Massachusetts: The MIT Press.

WITHERS 2003
>Withers, K., 'Reform of ICANN – Mission Impossible?', *World Internet Law Report*, No. 2, 2003, pp. 32-35.

WHITE HOUSE 1997
>Clinton, W.J. and Gore Jr., A., *A Framework for Global Electronic Commerce*, 1 July 1997, <http://www.nyls.edu/cmc/papers/whgiifra.htm>.

WHITE HOUSE 1999
>White House, *Memorandum for the Heads of Executive Departments and Agencies. Facilitating the Growth of Electronic Commerce*, November 1999.

WILSEY AND BAUER 1996
> Wilsey, M.F. and Bauer, J.M., *Toward a New Paradigm in Telecommunications. Analysis and Current Implementation of the Telecommunications Act 1996*, 1996, Report prepared for the Canadian Radio- Television and Telecommunications Commission, The Institute of Public Utilities, Michigan State University, East Lansing, Michigan.

WINSTON 1986
> Winston, B., *Misunderstanding Media*, Cambridge: Harvard University Press 1986.

WONG 1997
> Wong, P-K, Implementing the NII Vision: Singapore's Experience and Future Challenges, in: Kahin, B. and Wilson, E.J. (eds.) *National Information Infrastructure Initiatives. Vision and Policy Design*, 1997, Cambridge, Massachusetts: The MIT Press.

YUILL 2003
> Yuill, B., 'As Data Privacy Laws Evolve Globally Many Nations Consider European Model', *Electronic Commerce & Law Report*, 16 April 2003, pp. 384-386.

ZEKOS 1999
> Zekos, G.I., 'Internet or Electronic Technology: A Threat to State Sovereignty', *Journal of Information, Law and Technology (JILT)*, 1999 (3), <http://www.law.warwick.ac.uk/jilt/99-3/zekos.html>.

ABOUT THE EDITORS AND AUTHORS

PROF. DR. DAN L. BURK is Oppenheimer, Wolff & Donnelly Professor of Law at the University of Minnesota, Law School, <http://www.law.umn.edu/FacultyProfiles/BurkD.htm>.

PROF. DR. HERBERT BURKERT is professor of Public Law, Information and Communication Law and President of the Research Center for Information Law at the University of St. Gallen, Switzerland, <http://www.herbert-burkert.net/index.htm>.

DR SIMONE VAN DER HOF is a research fellow and assistant-professor in Law and ICT at the Tilburg Institute for Law, Technology, and Society, Tilburg University, the Netherlands. Her main research interests are private (international) law aspects of electronic commerce, regulation of electronic authentication and electronic identification, legal aspects of information security, the concept of 'openbaarheid' [the public nature of information] in a networked environment and access to government information

DR BERT-JAAP KOOPS is a research fellow and associate professor in Law & Technology at Tilburg University, the Netherlands. His main research interests are criminal law and technology, in particular cryptography, investigation powers and privacy, computer crime, and DNA forensics. He is also interested in other topics of ICT law, such as information security, identification, digital constitutional rights, and general principles of ICT regulation.

DR MIRIAM LIPS is working at the Center for Law, Public Administration, and Informatization (recently renamed Tilburg Institute for Law, Technology, and Society), Faculty of Law, Tilburg University as an associate professor. Since November 2003, she is also a Research Fellow at the Oxford Internet Institute, University of Oxford, UK. Her research and teaching activities focus on the following topics: digital citizenship, e-Governance, personalisation, identity management, ICTs in Public Administration and ICTs and Regulation.

DR SJAAK NOUWT is assistant professor at the Tilburg Institute for Law, Technology, and Society (TILT).

PROF. DR. YVES POULLET is professor at law and President of the Centre de Recherche Informatique et Droit of the Facultés universitaires Notre-Dame de la Paix in Namur (Belgium), <http://www.droit.fundp.ac.be/cv/ypoullet.html>.

PROF. DR. CORIEN PRINS is professor of Law and Informatization at Tilburg University. She chairs the Tilburg Institute for Law, Technology and Society (TILT). Her present research topics include (international) regulatory questions of ICT, electronic commerce, consumer protection in an ICT-society, biometric technology, e-government, privacy and anonymity, identity and personality issues.

DR MAURICE SCHELLEKENS is since 1995 active as a researcher at the Tilburg Institute for Law, Technology, and Society and its predecessor: the Center for Law, Public Administration and Informatization. He has a background in both law and computer science.

PROF. DR. KEES STUURMAN is professor of Information Technology Regulation. His research activities cover a wide range of topics varying from e-commerce law (contracting issues, the electronic signature and consumer protection), computer contracts, legal aspects of certification and standardisation, to liability issues relating to information technology and telecommunications. Currently, his work mainly focuses on the field of regulatory aspects of information technology and other 'high technologies' (e.g., biotechnology and nanotechnology) and specifically on self-regulation such as, codes of conduct, standards, certification, etc.

INDEX

INFORMATION TECHNOLOGY & LAW SERIES

1. E-Government and its Implications for Administrative Law – Regulatory Initiatives in France, Germany, Norway and the United States (The Hague: T·M·C·ASSER PRESS, 2002)
   Editor: J.E.J. Prins / ISBN 90-6704-141-6
2. Digital Anonymity and the Law – Tensions and Dimensions (The Hague: T·M·C·ASSER PRESS, 2003)
   Editors: C. Nicoll, J.E.J. Prins and M.J.M. van Dellen / ISBN 90-6704-156-4
3. Protecting the Virtual Commons – Self-Organizing Open Source and Free Software Communities and Innovative Intellectual Property Regimes (The Hague: T·M·C·ASSER PRESS, 2003)
   Authors: R. van Wendel de Joode, J.A. de Bruijn and M.J.G. van Eeten / ISBN 90-6704-159-9
4. IT Support and the Judiciary – Australia, Singapore, Venezuela, Norway, The Netherlands and Italy (The Hague: T·M·C·ASSER PRESS, 2004)
   Editors: A. Oskamp, A.R. Lodder and M. Apistola / ISBN 90-6704-168-8
5. Electronic Signatures – Authentication Technology from a Legal Perspective (The Hague: T·M·C·ASSER PRESS, 2004)
   Author: M.H.M. Schellekens / ISBN 90-6704-174-2
6. Virtual Arguments – On the Design of Argument Assistants for Lawyers and Other Arguers (The Hague: T·M·C·ASSER PRESS, 2004)
   Author: B. Verheij / ISBN 90-6704-190-4
7. Reasonable Expectations of Privacy? – Eleven Country Reports on Camera Surveillance and Workplace Privacy (The Hague: T·M·C·ASSER PRESS, 2005)
   Editors: S. Nouwt, B.R. de Vries and J.E.J. Prins / ISBN 90-6704-198-X
8. Unravelling the Myth Around Open Source Licences – An Analysis from a Dutch and European Law Perspective (The Hague: T·M·C·ASSER PRESS, 2006)
   Authors: L. Guibault and O. van Daalen / ISBN 90-6704-214-5
9. Starting Points for ICT Regulation – Deconstructing Prevalent Policy One-Liners (The Hague: T·M·C·ASSER PRESS, 2006)
   Editors: B-J. Koops, M. Lips, J.E.J. Prins and M. Schellekens / ISBN 90-6704-216-1